Harald Szeemann

Individual Methodology

François Aubart, Julija Cistiakova, Haeju Kim, Lucia Pesapane, Fabien Pinaroli, Karla Gabriela Roalandini Beyer, Yuka Tokuyama, Sadie Woods

Under the editorial direction of Florence Derieux

AF623106

Harald Szeemann
Individual Methodology

Table of Contents

Part IV: Information

Foreword

Yves Aupetitallot

The choice of Harald Szeemann, a proposal that we addressed to the various actors of the project, seems self-explanatory. His historical position, his achievements, and his notoriety are acclaimed unanimously. I also had the personal memory of some of the questions that I had formulated some ten years ago concerning the role that Szeemann had played in the socialization of the avant-gardes and, by extension, in their spectacularization.[1] The participants of the 16th Session, who carried out this project under the tutorship of Florence Derieux, were able to access Szeemann's archives, which are preserved at the Fabbrica rosa (the pink factory) in Maggia, near Locarno in Switzerland. The materials are new, and the approach is original, when, for instance, part of the study is devoted to the Agency for Intellectual Guest Labour.

François Aubart,[2] Julija Cistiakova,[3] Haeju Kim,[4] Lucia Pesapane,[5] Fabien Pinaroli,[6] Karla G. Roalandini-Beyer,[7] Yuka Tokuyama,[8] and Sadie Woods[9] have provided an additional dimension to this editorial project, ensuring that their approach is in no way an attempt at historicization. During the professional opening of the 9th Lyon Biennial, their project, entitled *Everybody Wants to Rule the World*, will gather the responses from curators, to their question: "During our ten-month curatorial program we studied the methodology of Harald Szeemann, and the tools he created for himself to develop his practice in an autonomous way. What are the specificities that make your curatorial practice unique?" The film that will be made as a result will be presented at Le Magasin in Grenoble before being diffused in various artistic institutions in France and abroad.

Initially invited to be one of the 50 curators of this biennial, the figure of Harald Szeemann guided our choice of Una Szeemann, his daughter, who presents a work carried out in collaboration with Bohdan Stehlik. They invited the artist's father, Josef Stehlik, to participate in a piece entitled *Yves Aupetitallot, curateur/Josef Stehlik, sculpteur/Una Szeemann—Bohdan Stehlik, Supersober, artistes/2007*.

We would like to thank all those who made this project possible in one way or another. The eight participants of the 16th Session, first of all, who worked on it for several months together with their tutor, Florence Derieux, who, with much determination and precision, accompanied them in their enterprise; the coordinator of the Ecole du Magasin, Alice Vergara-Bastiand, who provided the conditions to make the project possible; the pedagogical team, Catherine Queloz and Liliane Schneiter, who encouraged the project's first beginnings; Lionel Bovier and the team of JRP|Ringier, who through their advice helped with the realization of this publication.

We would also like to thank our partners: the Institut d'Art Contemporain (IAC) of Villeurbanne, which hosted the production of the film; the Ecole d'Art, Lyon, which provided material and technical assistance; the Fondation d'entreprise Ricard; Pro Helvetia; the Repubblica e Cantone Ticino—Fondo Swisslos; and the Department of Curating Contemporary Art—Royal College of Art, London, with whom we will develop, together with our publisher JRP|Ringier, a collection of "curatorial notebooks."

[1] See among others Yves Aupetitallot, "Het Banket van Trimalchio," *Vertoog en Literatuur/Cahier 5/Orthodoxie (...) Applaus*, Meulenhoff, Antwerp, 1993, p. 195–207. Discussion about the films of Jef Cornelis, with Yves Aupetitallot, Johannes Cladders, Jef Cornelis, and Stefan Germer, Kunstverein, Munich, March 12, 1992.

[2] François Aubart received his Masters in History of Art in 2004; his thesis concerned art and activism. While completing his postgraduate studies in the Administration and Conservation of Artworks, he assisted the curatorial team of the Mamco in Geneva. He then worked as a production manager at the Contemporary Art Center of Brétigny. He recently co-curated the exhibition *Imbéciles habitants* in Kermingham, in Brittany, France. He contributes to art magazines such as *Archistorm* and *Frog*.

[3] Julija Cistiakova is an artist and curator born in 1979 in Lithuania. In 2004 she obtained her Masters of Visual Arts at Vilnius Academy of Fine Arts. She participates in and curates contemporary art exhibitions and festivals, particularly in Lithuania and Russia. Her main interests lie in the interactions between art, science, and technology; the theory of the absurd and of irony; as well as contemporary society and globalization.

[4] Haeju Kim was born in 1980 in Busan, South Korea. She participated in the realization of exhibitions such as *Less Ordinary* (2002) and *Mix Max* (2004) Art Sonje Center, and *Real_Interface* (2002) at Space Ima, both in Seoul. She worked as a coordinator for the Anyang Public Art Project in 2005 and for the Busan Biennial in 2006. Even though her work experience has mostly been developed in the public sphere, her interests increasingly concern contemporary dance and performance in relation to visual arts. Making her "footsteps following not what is outside the eyes, but what is within" she is also searching for "the true mystery of the world which is the visible not the invisible."

[5] Lucia Pesapane is an art historian and design critic, born in 1981 in Milan, Italy. Specialized in contemporary art, she has developed an interest in design; her research concerns the links between these two disciplines. She worked as an assistant in exhibition spaces in Milan (Galleria Massimo De Carlo) and in London (Chisenhale). She is currently news editor for the internet magazine www.design-italia.it, and works as a journalist for the Italian magazine *tema celeste*. If she hadn't dedicated herself to contemporary art, she would have been a synchronized agonistic swimmer.

[6] Fabien Pinaroli is an artist and curator. The father of two children, he graduated in visual arts in 1992. He then worked as a graphic designer, and later as an artistic director at the MCI, Lyon. In 2003 he started working as a curator for a not-for-profit organization, the *Contemporary Art Group* in Annonay, France, where he also developed educational programs. He is interested in bypath and micro-resistance strategies used by artists, as well as in curatorial devices that allow experimentation and the experience of art where it is not expected.

[7] Karla G. Roalandini-Beyer was born in 1976 in Mexico City. An art-history graduate, she also completed theater studies in New York and Barcelona. She participated in the realization of exhibitions such as *José Chávez Morado*; *Kurt Schwitters*; *Shirin Neshat*, and *Angela Gurría* at the Museum of Modern Art in Mexico. She worked as cultural manager and editorial coordinator for the project *Arcodata capítulo México 05*. She has also curated the following exhibitions: *Naturaleza móvil*; *Recolecta*; *Poder visual, placer visual*. She currently works as a researcher in the department of exhibition coordination at the Museo del Palacio de Bellas Artes in Mexico City. She regularly contributes to art magazines, websites, and exhibition catalogues.

[8] Yuka Tokuyama is a curator and researcher on contemporary art and architecture; she has lived and worked in France since 2005. From 2000 to 2005 she worked as an assistant curator at the National Museum of Art in Osaka, Japan. She developed several projects as an independent curator at the same time: *artplan*, a research project on the alternative art scene in Japan, and *do it yourself [nation kawaï]*, a workshop and installation project in Kobe. Through her practice she focuses on the relationship between art and its environment: a trans-disciplinary expression between visual art, architecture, design, and everyday life.

[9] Sadie Woods is a Chicago-born visual artist and electronic musician. She studied photography and vocal performance at Columbia College, receiving her BA in Liberal Arts. Upon graduation, she worked in arts administration, gallery management, and program coordination at Marwen, collaborating with local non-profit organizations as a guest curator representing emerging artists of the Chicagoland area. Sadie also freelanced as curator and gallery coordinator for *Translucent Chocolates* and as an electronic music instructor for the non-profit *Rock for Kids*, while exhibiting and performing in exhibitions. She is currently working on several projects with djs in Chicago and in Grenoble.

Preface

Yves Aupetitallot and Mark Nash

For two decades, the Ecole du Magasin, which accompanies and supports the emergence of curators on the artistic scene, has avoided following any specific model in order to be able redefine itself for each new session. Today, the topic of "curating" on which it focuses—i.e. the methodology and positions of the conceptualization and the organization of exhibitions—is comfortably established in the artistic field. Now routine, it thrives on a critical apparatus that nourishes it while allowing different positions; now familiar, it has fallen into certain academic patterns.

This is therefore a favorable moment to critically reconsider the phenomenon through the examination of some of its most significant examples, in particular those who could be considered, one way or another, its founders. With this in mind, the Ecole du Magasin—Centre National d'Art Contemporain in Grenoble and the Department of Curating Contemporary Art—Royal College of Art in London joined forces with JRP|Ringier to produce a series of "curatorial notebooks"; this first publication is devoted to Harald Szeemann.

The Ecole du Magasin has chosen to devote this collective project to the critical study of Harald Szeemann's working tools and methodology, and to publish the results in this book, which has been conceived as a complement to the catalogue of his exhibitions published by Tobia Bezzola and Roman Kurzmeyer.[1] More than any other curator, Harald Szeeman has been associated with a notion of curating as an authorial artistic practice (to use Michel Foucault's term). In an interview with Natalie Heinich,[2] he proposed extending the notion of creative authorship to the curatorial field. Following his death in 2005, we are now able to begin a process of constructing a discursive historical legacy, and to begin to appreciate the epistemological shift that he instigated in curatorial theory and practice.

Our thanks go in particular to the Szeemann family—Ingeborg Lüscher, Una Szeemann and Jérôme Szeemann—for their generosity and engagement with this project.

We would also like to extend our gratitude to Tobia Bezzola for his support throughout the research. This project could not have been possible without his precious collaboration as well as that of the members of Harald Szeemann's team (Juliette Duca, Josy Kraft, Gianna Ruepp, Jérôme and Una Szeemann, Christoph Zürcher), of Balthasar Burkhard, of the authors and their publishers, of the artists, the curators, and the critics who were willing to share their experiences and knowledge; this is the expression of our profound thanks.

[1] Tobia Bezzola, Roman Kurzmeyer (eds.), *Harald Szeemann: with by through because towards despite*, Springer, Vienna/New York; Voldemeer, Zurich 2007.

[2] Nathalie Heinich, *Harald Szeemann, un cas singulier: entretien*, L'Echoppe, Paris 1995.

Introduction

Florence Derieux

It is now widely accepted that the art history of the second half of the 20th century is no longer a history of artworks, but a history of exhibitions. However, this critical history still largely remains to be written. The question becomes all the more pressing as this history coincides with the appearance of a new professional category, that of the curator. This figure, who Walter Benjamin described as being like that of a smuggler, and Felix Fénéon that of a catalyst, is now unavoidable. Today multiplied to excess, the curator constitutes an object of curatorial and critical study in order to reveal the dialectical springs, working methodologies, and tools of implementation of the practice. Harald Szeemann is often regarded as the genitor of the genre; the study of his methodology and curatorial practice thus seems to constitute a logical introduction to such a project.

Harald Szeemann realized his first exhibition exactly 50 years ago; this was *Painters-Poets/Poets-Painters,* organized in 1957 at the Kunstmuseum in St Gallen. He explained that its organization consisted of an endless flow of meetings and discussions with all the actors of the art world: "From the beginning, meeting artists and looking at important shows was my education—I was always less interested in formal art history." [1] Very early on indeed, he defended the idea that art history must focus on what he called the *intense intentions* rather than on masterpieces. In order to escape the traditional question of styles and artistic movements, he chose to concentrate his interest on the *Individual Mythologies,* while in order to provide his Agency for Intellectual Guest Labour with a direction, he invented the *Museum of Obsessions*. Thus he largely contributed to define an activity that emerged simultaneously with Conceptual art during the 1960s, thus years after he had found his medium.

The adaptation of the institutional structure to artists and their needs is one of Harald Szeemann's major contributions. His exhibition *When Attitudes Become Form* became the model of an evolution that is, a posteriori, considered indispensable. By elaborating the conditions of the exhibition adapted to new artistic practices, he considerably influenced the modalities of the production of art shows. In particular he introduced a rupture into the very concept of the exhibition by inventing the structural position of "independent worker": the curator, creator, and author of the exhibition—he preferred to call himself an "exhibition maker." By creating his Agency, he managed to organize his activity, and simultaneously to define it in relation to artistic, economic, and political fields. Whereas today the work of the curator only too often simply consists in appropriating artists' projects, it appears all the more important to study the methodology and the practice of this tutelary figure for whom the curator can and must position him/herself as a free creative agent.

In 1988 Szeemann transformed a former factory in Maggia, near Locarno in Switzerland, into a gigantic archive, a sort of think tank and creative factory established as the headquarters of his archive and his Agency (the Fabbrica rosa). The part played by this archive in the writing of a history of exhibitions seems essential. It constitutes a resource, a place for conservation, and also a potential place of the "fabrication" of this history. Szeemann's archive, the true place of his praxis, was the starting point of the research that we undertook, and which was carried out by the eight participants of the 16th Session of the International Curatorial Training Program. The research was based on an invaluable documentation thanks to an exceptional opportunity kindly offered by the Szeemann family to access the archive at the Fabbrica rosa. It was developed in three interdependent parts: a publication, an exhibition (October 7, 2007–January 6, 2008, Le Magasin, Grenoble), and a website (www.ecoledumagasin.com/session16).

The publication *Harald Szeemann: Individual Methodology* results from research carried out in the archive of the Swiss curator in Maggia. It is conceived as a tool for those interested in curatorial practices and the history of exhibitions. The research—an informative as well as critical analysis—is based on unpublished documents as well as testimonies from some of Harald Szeemann's closest collaborators. The editorial approach aims at enlightening the self-organization that he established, revisited and optimized over his entire career, and which, unlike his exhibitions, has been only slightly researched and documented so far. The editors pay tribute to Harald Szeemann through the title of the book, inspired by his personal universe (the *Individual Mythologies*). In the same way the titles of its four parts—*Situations, Concepts/Processes, Works, Information*—echo the subtitle of his most famous exhibition *When Attitudes Become Form* (1969).

Situations, the first section of the book, contextualizes the period of Harald Szeemann's activities in terms of the theoretical issues that have been discussed in the field of art. The essay *This Funeral Is for the Wrong Corpse* by Hal Foster first appeared in his book *Design and Crime (and Other Diatribes)* published in 2002. The author goes back to the funeral pronouncements of the past four decades on the end of art, of modernism, of postmodernism, and the traumatic but also potential effects on artists. Jean-Marc Poinsot delivers an original contribution with his essay untitled *Art and its Context or the Question of Culture*, which is published here for the first time. In this text, he evokes the major changes that occurred after the Second World War, and outlines a genealogy of the curators who "anticipated the role that contemporary art was to play in our societies today," and recalls the role of predecessor played by Harald Szeemann. The interview with Tobia Bezzola—curator at the Kunsthaus Zürich and Szeemann's collaborator over several years—retraces the itinerary of the *permanent independent curator* from the end of the 1950s to 2005, and analyzes the evolution of Szeemann's positions. Finally, the series of photographs by Balthasar Burkhard allows readers to discover the curator's archive and the "Fabbrica Harald Szeemann" in Maggia.

The second section—*Concepts/Processes*—is developed in two parts: the first study focuses on the creation and functioning of Harald Seemann's archive from Bern to Maggia, and the second on the establishment and organization of his Agency for Intellectual Guest Labour. This part, which is essential for the understanding of Szeemann's working methodology as an independent curator, includes numerous documents (photographs, plans, correspondence, etc.) and testimonies of his collaborators. It appears that the ideas to build his own archive and to establish his Agency arose at a crucial moment in the future development of his career, the moment of his resignation of the position as director of the Kunsthalle Bern in September 1969. Szeemann chose to become independent curator and developed a system that aimed at its own institutionalization and at leaving his mark on history.

The third section of the book—*Works*—examines two essential exhibitions: *documenta 5,* which he realized in 1972, and *L'Autre—4th Lyon Biennial* in 1997. This section enables readers to evaluate the importance and intricacy of experiments made by one of the greatest innovators in exhibition making, but also to understand Szeemann's practice and its evolution over the 25 years that separate these two exhibitions. It also sheds light on their relation to their artistic and historical contexts. If *documenta 5* constituted the sum of the experiments conducted by Szeemann since Bern, it also represented the source of his future experiments. *d5* provided him with the opportunity to rethink the institution in other forms. Later on he developed a model of "turnkey" exhibitions, which he optimized while pursuing his personal research around his *Individual Mythologies*. The 4th Lyon Biennial perfectly illustrated the final result of his method at a time when it became obvious that the art world had become an integral part of the cultural industry.

The fourth and last section of the book—*Information*—adds to the analytical material available on Harald Szeemann with a biography as well as an exhaustive chronology of his exhibitions between 1957 and 2005, which is accompanied by numerous illustrations.

Harald Szeemann affirmed that he was "interested only in the diverging conscience, because it is there only that the utopian energies exist."[2] He defined himself as "an untamed thinker who nourishes himself with the mythical and utopian nature which the human spirit and human activity take on. I am therefore anti-scientific, a speculator, an anarchist (not a terrorist); I like the obsessive because in art only a partial subjectivity can one day be considered objectively."[3] By asserting the subjectivity of the curator who, by gathering together artworks elaborates a discourse sometimes very distant from their individual significance, he redefined the curator's role. By transferring the place of the production of art within space, and the duration of the exhibition, he modified the relations between the curator and the artist. In particular, he showed that curatorial practice is a form of art in itself.[4]

Thus Harald Szeemann exerted a lasting influence on the history of exhibitions and the way in which both curatorial practice and its associated theories are conceptualized today in the field of contemporary art. Throughout his career, he was able to repeatedly rupture with the very exhibition practices he had to a large extent helped define. These ruptures manifested an extraordinary ability to ceaselessly revaluate his own methodology and curatorial practice, his artistic choices and positions, as well as the workings and issues of the art world; all this in an artistic and political, economic and cultural context that was undergoing constant change. What also made Szeemann unique was the way in which he was simultaneously able to reconcile personal desires with professional constraints.

[1] Hans Ulrich Obrist, "Mind over Matter. Interview with Harald Szeemann," in *Artforum*, November 1996.

[2] Anaïd Demir, unpublished interview with Harald Szeemann, September 1999.

[3] Harald Szeemann, *Museum der Obsessionen*, Merve Verlag, Berlin 1981, p. 20. Quoted by Jean-Marc Poinsot, "Harald Szeemann. Quand les attitudes deviennent forme et quelques problèmes du musée d'art contemporain," *Collection*, capcMusée d'art contemporain, Bordeaux 1990, p. 33.

[4] This position has generated much criticism and opposition, namely from certain artists who, like Daniel Buren, see Szeemann as a "superartist." See Buren's contribution to the catalogue *documenta 5*, C. Bertelsmann Verlag, Munich 1972. See Note [3], p. 96–97.

Part 1: Situations

This Funeral Is for the Wrong Corpse

Hal Foster

This text was initially published in Hal Foster's book untitled *Design and Crime (and Other Diatribes)*, Verso, London/ New York 2002, p. 123–143. It is reprinted here with the generous permission of the author and the publisher.

"It is self-evident that nothing concerning art is self-evident anymore," Adorno wrote in 1969, "not its inner life, not its relation to the word, not even its right to exist [...] In many ways, expansion appears as contraction." Today, 30-plus years later, might this statement circle back so as to include its own implicit assumption about "the end of art"? In other words, might "the end of art" be one more thing about art that is not "self-evident anymore"?

In the trivial sense, of course, this end never came, but then "the end of art" never meant a literal stop to paintings, sculptures, films, novels, and all the rest; what was at issue was the formal innovation and historical significance of these mediums. For many believers art had long served as the essential index to its culture, to its age, or (in its strongest Hegelian formulation) to the realization of Spirit in History. Yet for some time now art has not possessed this symbolic weightiness: today it seems divested not only of its role as a signpost to history but also of much regard for historicity—that is to say, for any necessary working-through of its own historically given, problems. One might go further: contemporary art no longer seems "contemporary," in the sense that it no longer has a privileged purchase on the present, or even "symptomatic," at least no more so than many other cultural phenomena. If the first principle of art history, as Heinrich Wölfflin once put it, is that "not all things are possible at all times," this premise appears challenged in the present, for good and for bad, with the result that, for some commentators, art history is as kaput as art is. [1]

Adorno offered his version of "the end of art" at a time when such proclamations—concerning the end of ideology and philosophy as well—came fast and furious. In 1965, for example, the Minimalist artist Donald Judd averred that "linear history has unraveled somewhat," and soon thereafter the Conceptual artist Joseph Kosuth announced that modernist painting and sculpture were finished. [2] But, Kosuth added in a "dialectical" fillip that made all the difference, these specific mediums were now sublated in the general idea of Art, and this Art with a capital A was henceforth the proper object-medium of advanced artists. Presented as the end of Hegelian art history (modernist and otherwise), this position was instead its epitome—of art transcended in philosophy, in art-as-philosophy. The philosopher Arthur Danto had a similar epiphany, which he also dated to the mid-1960s with his first encounter with the *Brillo Box* of Warhol, and in a series of books begun in the 1980s he has made this vision of transcendence his own. [3] According to this argument, Warhol perfected the Duchampian question of "what is art?" and so, intentionally or not, brought art into philosophical self-awareness. But by the same token art no longer had any philosophical work to do: its essential rationale fell away, and henceforth it could do *whatever*—to be evaluated, if at all, by the philosopher-critic according to its degree of philosophical interest (we see, then, who is privileged in this account). This "end of art" is presented as benignly liberal—art is pluralistic, its practice pragmatic, and its field multicultural—but this position is also not so benignly neo-liberal, in the sense that its relativism is what the rule of the market requires.

Two other versions of the end, further to the left, also emerged in the 1980s. The first, poststructuralist account was triumphal in tone: art is no more, "representation" is all; the history and theory of art are subsumed by the history and theory of representations, to be understood in terms of textual production and psychological reception. (Visual studies have taken over this version, with revisions that ground representation in social practices.) The second, Marxist account was more desperate: here art is not subsumed by the theoretical category of representation but overwhelmed by the practical dominance of "the image," the primary form of the commodity in a spectacle economy, from which art can no longer pretend to be distinct.[4] I don't disagree with certain aspects of either argument, but they concede too much too quickly, and I want to recover some of what they surrender. I also don't deny that our condition is largely one of aftermath—that we live in the wake not only of modernist painting and sculpture but of postmodernist deconstructions of these forms as well, in the wake not only of the prewar avant-gardes but of the postwar neo-avant-gardes as well. But there are other responses to this condition than triumphalism or desperation, or indeed melancholy (at the very least we need not pathologize it further). Here I want to ask another kind of question: what comes after these ends, or perhaps (if they did not quite occur) in lieu of them? As the Mekons sang of the death of socialism after 1989, might these funerals be for the wrong corpse?

Let me review this condition of aftermath briefly, and begin with the wake of modernism and postmodernism. [Previously,] I alluded to a "dialectic of modernism" that formalist critics like Clement Greenberg and Michael Fried extracted from advanced painting from Manet to Frank Stella. This "dialectic" was pledged to formal unity and historical continuity, and, like the history of premodernist art according to Wölfflin, it was governed by a double dynamic of a continuous "palling" in perception and problem-solving in form; at least in this account (which ignored market considerations), this is what drove the ceaseless search for stylistic variations in modernist painting. As we have seen, this Wölfflinian modernism ran into the sand in the 1960s, but it was kept in place as a foil for practices that emerged to contest it, such as Minimal and Conceptual art, Process and Body art. These practices critiqued this modernism, but in so doing they also continued it, at least as a reference. In its very decay modernism thus radiated an afterlife that we came to call postmodernism (here the term pertains only to critical art of this sort).

This doubling of modernism and postmodernism can be gleaned from a glance at a signal mapping of site-specific art. In "Sculpture in the Expanded Field" (1979) Rosalind Krauss presented a structuralist account of such art: neither modernist painting nor modernist sculpture, it emerged as the negative of these categories, and soon opened onto other categories, such as "architecture" and "landscape" and "not-architecture" and "not-landscape."[5] These terms provided the points of reference by which Krauss plotted the practices of "marked sites" (e.g., Robert Smithson), "site constructions" (e.g., Mary Miss), and "axiomatic structures" (e.g., Sol LeWitt). Implicit in this account is that postmodernist art was initially "propped" on modernist categories, with all the ambiguity of (in)dependence implied by the word, but that it soon "troped" these categories, in the sense that it treated them as so many completed practices or given terms to be manipulated as such. This map also now registers certain changes since that time: over the last three decades the "expanded field" has slowly imploded, as terms once held in productive contradiction have gradually collapsed into compounds without much tension, as in the many combinations of the pictorial and the sculptural, or of art and architecture, in installation art today—art that, for the most part, fits well enough into the pervasive design-and-display culture [I] critiqued elsewhere. This is only one indication of how postmodernist art, which emerged as a troping of modernist categories, is now trumped in turn.

As a result, the model of a formalist modernism challenged by an expansive postmodernism no longer drives or describes significant developments in art or criticism. And the same must be said of its historical double, the model of a prewar avant-garde recovered by a postwar neo-avant-garde (e.g., of Dadaist devices or Constructivist structures recovered in Fluxus or Minimalism). Here again the debate runs back to the mid-1960s when, for radical critics like Guy Debord, the avant-garde was already bankrupt. "Dadaism sought to abolish art without realizing it," Debord wrote in *The Society of the Spectacle* (1967), "and Surrealism sought to realize it without abolishing it."[6] The failures were reciprocal for Debord, and any attempt to revive such attempts, as in the various neo-Dadas of the 1950s and 1960s, were farcical: far better to have done with the entire project. This opinion, which evokes the famous charge of Marx in *The Eighteenth Brumaire of Louis Bonaparte* (1852) that history occurs twice, the first time as tragedy, the second time as farce, was upheld by Peter Bürger in his influential *Theory of the Avant-Garde* (1974). In fact, Bürger extended the critique: the repetition of the historical avant-garde in the neo-avant-garde was not only farcical; it also reversed the original project to reconnect the institution of autonomous art with the practice of everyday life—recouped it for the very institution that was to be challenged in the first place.

Benjamin Buchloh has exposed the historical lacunae in this argument, and I have posed another model of neo-avant-garde repetition that is not merely recuperative.[7] More importantly, the 1970s and 1980s saw critical elaborations of the neo-avant-garde, and the 1990s and 2000s have witnessed various attempts to recover unfinished projects of the 1960s as well—that is, to set up a further "neo" relation of recovery vis-à-vis Conceptual, Process, and Body art in particular. Yet this work has not yet demonstrated whether critiques as singular as Conceptual, Process, and Body art can be transformed into a tradition (or tradition-substitute) coherent enough to support contemporary practice. As a result, the recursive strategy of the "neo" appears as attenuated today as the oppositional logic of the "post" is tired: neither suffices as a strong paradigm for artistic or critical practice, and no other model stands in their stead. For many this is a good thing: it permits artistic diversity; "weak" theory is better than strong; and so on. But, as I have argued elsewhere in this book, our paradigm-of-no-paradigm can also abet a flat indifference, a stagnant incommensurability, a new Alexandrianism, and this post-historical default of contemporary art is no improvement on the old historicist determinism of modernist art. All of us (artists, critics, curators, historians, viewers) need some narrative to focus our present practices—situated stories, not *grands récits*. Without this guide we may remain swamped in the double wake of post/modernism and the neo/avant-garde. Rather than deny this aftermath, then, why not admit it and ask "what now, what else?"

Let me recall another riddle posed by Adorno in the mid-1960s, which is still an unsettled origin of so much art today. If his worry about the arbitrariness of art begins his *Aesthetic Theory*, his riddle about the relevance of philosophy opens his *Negative Dialectics* (1966): "Philosophy, which once seemed absolute, lives on because the moment to realize it was missed."[8] Here Adorno responds to another famous charge of Marx, this one in the "Theses on Feuerbach" (1845), that philosophers have only interpreted the world when the point is to change it.[9] In a sense, just as philosophy missed its moment of realization, so the avant-garde missed its moment; and I wonder if this parallel guided Adorno and, further, if we might substitute "art" where he writes "philosophy." In this case, might art be granted the ambiguous stay of sentence that Adorno grants philosophy—the possibility of "living on"? (Again, this is the possibility that critics like Debord and Bürger foreclose in the same moment.) If so, what might this "living on" be in the present? Not the overt repetition of avant-garde devices that characterized much neo-avant-garde art of the 1950s and 1960s (e.g., monochrome painting, collage, readymade objects), and perhaps not the attenuated working-through of such strategies that characterized much neo-avant-garde art of the 1970s and 1980s either (e.g., institution-critiques that are sometimes difficult to decipher even for initiates). Maybe this living-on is not a repeating so much as a making-new or simply a making-do with what-comes-after, a beginning again and/or elsewhere.

At this point I can only sketch a few versions of this living-on, which I will call "traumatic," "spectral," "nonsynchronous," and "incongruent." As these categories tend to cross, this taxonomy is artificial, and my disparate examples (which include fiction and film) do not pretend to be comprehensive; nonetheless, they may begin to evoke this condition of coming-after. Even as the practices I have in mind often treat given genres or mediums as somehow completed, they do not pastiche them in a post-historical manner. On the contrary, they are committed to formal transformations—as long as these transformations also speak to extrinsic concerns. In this way these practices point to a semi-autonomy of genre or medium, but in a reflexive way that opens onto social issues ("a closed world that is open to the world" is how one contemporary artist puts it); in so doing they often belie these very oppositions of intrinsic and extrinsic, inside and outside.[10] Through formal transformation that is also social engagement, then, such work helps to restore a mnemonic dimension to contemporary art, and to resist the presentist totality of design in culture today.

My first version of living-on involves *traumatic* experience. Of course, for the avant-garde to be recovered, it first had to be lost, and this breach, which began with its suppression by Nazis and Stalinists in the 1930s, was deepened with the trauma of war and Holocaust in the 1940s. More than a historical divide in art, this breach induced a cultural blockage, "a failure to mourn," that long persisted. In our own time, however, this failure (or refusal) of memory has promoted a compensatory imperative to remember in the form of new museums and trauma studies of all sorts—an imperative that sometimes seems more automatic than mnemonic. In both popular culture and academic discourse "trauma" has come to float free as a general signifier of the structuring not only of subjectivity but of history as such. Today some of the most provocative novelists and filmmakers also conceive experience in this paradoxical modality—of experience that is *not* experienced, at least not punctually, that comes too early or too late to be registered consciously, that can only be repeated compulsively or pieced together after the fact. Often for these novelists (I think of Paul Auster, Russell Banks, Dennis Cooper, Don DeLillo, Steve Erickson, Denis Johnson, Ian McEwan, Toni Morrison, Tim O'Brien, and W.G. Sebald among others, but such filmmakers as Atom Egoyan should also be cited) narrative runs in reverse or moves very erratically, and the peripeteia is an event that happened long ago or not at all, in keeping with the ambiguous nature of trauma as real or fantasmatic.

As one might expect, contemporary art that treats "the German Question" is often concerned with the traumatic, whether in terms of the ruins of the Nazi past (as evoked by Hans Haacke in his extraordinary *Germania* installation in the 1993 Venice Biennale, where he broke apart the marble floor of the Nazi-era pavilion) or the unburied persistence of this past in reconstructed Germany (as evoked by Gerhard Richter in his equally extraordinary *October 18, 1977*, a 1988 suite of paintings concerning the Baader-Meinhof gang). However, my example here is a 1989 installation by Robert Gober that evokes the trauma of American racism, and so exceeds the limits of the last century. In one room Gober hung wallpaper of penises and vaginas, anuses and navels, sketched in white line on black ground and punctuated with chest-high drains, and in another room wallpaper of schematic drawings of two men in light blue on pale yellow, one white and asleep (from a Bloomingdale's beefcake advertisement), the other black and lynched (from a 1920s Texas cartoon). If the first background presented sexual difference as the overlooked pattern of our everyday lives, the second suggested that racial antagonism is another occluded structure of our daily grinds. Each room was further split into two registers: in the center of the first was a bag of doughnuts on a pedestal; in the center of the second a wedding gown attended by bags of "Fine Fare, Cat Litter" set along the wall (all objects and images looked found but were handmade). Thus, from space to space and from images to objects, Gober put a series of oppositions in play: male and female, bachelor and bride, white and black, immaculate gown and stale food, purity and pollution, dream and reality, and, above all, sexual difference and racial difference.

Rather than map these oppositions onto one another, however, Gober intertwined the terms in an ensemble that evoked the intricacies of fear, desire, and pain deep in our political imaginary of race and sexuality. The installation prompted the viewer to tease out this old American knot in the form of a broken allegory: What is the relationship between the two men? Does the black man haunt the white man? Does the white man dream the black man? If so, does the white man conjure the black man in hatred, guilt, or desire? Is the woman implied by the wedding gown the object of their struggle? If so, is she the pretext of their violence, the relay of their longing, or both? What is the role of heterosexual fantasy in racial politics? Of racial fantasy in heterosexual politics? And how does homosexuality or homosociality come into play? Finally, how does one disarticulate all these terms—clarify them in order to question them? Traumatically mute, the installation intimated that our traumas of identity and difference are collective as well as individual, and that our racist-homophobic past lives on, nightmarishly, in the present.

The Gober installation developed certain elements of Duchamp, such as the bride from *The Bride Stripped Bare by Her Bachelors, Even* (1915–1923), his large glass divided into two registers, and the diorama of sexual difference from *Etant donnés* (1946–1966), his mannequin splayed in a landscape on view at the Philadelphia Museum of Art. The installation thus existed in the shadow not only of traumatic history but of significant art; the first helped to charge the second, the second to frame the first, and in the process both were transformed in the reciprocal way noted above. [11] Of course such "shadowing" by artistic precedents is primordial; it is the primary element that allows any art to be constituted as such, as a discipline that lives on at all. But often the shadowing in contemporary art is more literally *spectral*. It is announced as such in many titles (there are "ghosts" in Paul Auster, Jim Jarmusch, and Rachel Whiteread, to cite but one example in fiction, film, and art); it also operates formally at the level of genre or medium. The shadowing I have in mind has little of the "anxiety of influence" described by Harold Bloom in modernist poetry; yet neither is there much "ecstasy of influence" along the postmodernist lines of the high-spirited meta-fiction of university novelists like John Barth and Robert Coover, or of the homage-laden neo-genre cinema of film-school directors like Martin Scorsese and Brian de Palma. [12] The shadowing in play today is more muted, a sort of outlining and shading, in the manner that *Mrs Dalloway* (1925) outlines and shades *The Hours* (1998) by Michael Cunningham. [13]

This spectrality informs the recent work of Jim Jarmusch, in particular *Dead Man* (1995) and *Ghost Dog* (2000), both of which exist in the shadow of old genres. In the hire of a minor mobster, "Ghost Dog" is a black assassin who lives according to the ancient code of Japanese warriors; *Ghost Dog*, then, is an amalgam of Gangster and Samurai films that "comes after" these genres in a way that renders both at once archaic and exotic, strangely animated. *Dead Man* has a similar relation to the Western: the story of the westward journey of a young man from Cleveland named William Blake, it is a repository of genre themes from silent Westerns to anti-Westerns: a white man befriended by an Indian guide, an innocent man tracked by murderous bounty-hunters, the West portrayed as a field of rapacious death. If *Dead Man* treats the Western as if from its own afterlife, it is also produced out of the passing of the West; and both its protagonists are spectral as well: William Blake is mistaken by his native guide "Nobody" for a spirit from the dead—as the great Romantic visionary who must be returned to the afterworld. At several levels, then, the film is a spirit-quest of the already-dead. "After the end of history, the spirit comes by *coming back* [revenant]," Derrida writes of the "hauntology" that he deems "the dominant influence on discourse today"; "it figures *both* a dead man who comes back and a ghost whose expected return repeats itself, again and again." [14]

In contemporary art this ghostly persistence is especially strong in the work of Rachel Whiteread. In the late 1980s she began to cast everyday objects like bathtubs and mattresses, closets and rooms, in materials like rubber and resin, plaster and concrete. As the objects are used as molds, the castings are the negative spaces of these things; as a result they are at once obvious in production and ambiguous in reference. For though her sculptures are based on utilitarian objects and everyday sites, they negate function and harden space into mass, and though they appear whole and solid, they also seem fragmentary and spectral. More ambiguously still, these literal traces suggest symbolic traces, memories of childhood, family, and community: they conjure up "the cultural space of the home" as a place of beginnings overwhelmed by endings, as a place haunted by absence. [15] For this reason her work is often associated with the uncanny, that is, with the return of familiar things made strange by repression, and sometimes her death-masks of familial objects and maternal spaces do render the homey *unheimlich*. But in the end they do not evoke the return of the repressed so much as the persistence of the lost: they are less *unheimlich* than homeless in effect. Not only psychological, these castings "carry the marks of history written on the social body." [16] In this regard they too possess the double reflexivity mentioned above: they recall both Minimalist objects and Pop signs, but they render both ghostly—spirits of the social past.

This is especially true of her most celebrated work, *House* (1993), a concrete casting of a terrace house scheduled for demolition in a working-class neighborhood of East London. Her negative imprint of these vanished rooms was inscribed not only with the outlines of window sills, door frames, and utility lines, but also with the traces of past inhabitants; as such it stood in a park for a time like an unrequited ghost. Its great provocation was to connect the psychic and social in this way, to link "the lost spaces of childhood" with the lost working-class culture of East London, both threatened by rapacious development. Perhaps its opponents grasped this connection—the local council first approved the casting, then voted to demolish it—or perhaps they refused a public sculpture that did not idealize social life or monumentalize historical memory. In any case *House* is a public sculpture that is obdurate in its living-on—though it no longer exists materially.

A third strategy in the condition of coming-after is the staging of *nonsynchronous* forms; prominent practices that feature outmoded genres include the slide projections of James Coleman, "the drawings for projection" of William Kentridge, the narrative silhouettes of Kara Walker, and the filmic installations of Stan Douglas. [17] The strategy here is to make a new medium out of the remnants of old forms, and to hold together the different temporal markers in a single visual structure. Once more, in the best instances, a double reflexivity is at work: a medium is (re)constituted in a recursive way that is nonetheless open to social content—in a way, moreover, that reminds us that "form" is often nothing but "content" that has become historically sedimented. In his drawings for projection, for example, Kentridge links an old tradition of satirical drawing (William Hogarth, Honoré Daumier, George Grosz, Ben Shahn, and so on) with an archaic technique of filmic animation (devices like irises, inter-titles, and musical accompaniment). He synchronizes these nonsynchronous forms, then trains them on occluded aspects of apartheid life in his native South Africa. This artisanal kind of projected drawing thus points to lost moments in art history (e.g., before the industrialization of cinema) that serve as formal analogues to lost moments in social history—lost in the sense of suppressed, skipped over, or displaced.

"The outmoded" might be too inflected by Surrealist associations to capture this last connection between displaced forms and histories. The Surrealists, Benjamin writes in his 1928 essay on the movement, were "the first to perceive the revolutionary energies that appear in the 'outmoded' [veraltet], in the first iron constructions, the first factory buildings, the earliest photos, the objects that have begun to be extinct, grand pianos, the dresses of five years ago, fashionable restaurants when the vogue has begun to ebb from them. They bring the immense force of 'atmosphere' concealed in these things to the point of explosion."[18]

Such a weird array of things is not the stuff of a renewed medium; on the contrary, it is part of the Surrealist project to "explode" conventional categories of cultural objects. In this way it presumes a reified tabulation of artistic mediums to disrupt—which, as argued elsewhere in this book, is precisely not our problem. There is the further dilemma that "the outmoded" might now be outmoded too, recuperated as a device in the very process that it once seemed to question—the heightened obsolescence of fashion and other commodity lines. Yet one aspect of the outmoded is still valid, the one plied by most of the artists mentioned above, and Surrealism is again a touchstone. "Balzac was the first to speak of the ruins of the bourgeoisie," Benjamin writes in a later comment on the Surrealists. "But only Surrealism exposed them to view. The development of the forces of production reduced the wish symbols of the previous century to rubble even before the monuments representing them had crumbled."[19] The "wish symbols" here are the capitalist wonders of the 19th-century bourgeoisie at the height of its confidence, such as "the arcades and interiors, the exhibitions and panoramas." These structures fascinated the Surrealists nearly a century later—when further capitalist development had turned them into "residues of a dream world" or, again, "rubble even before the monuments which represented them had crumbled." According to Benjamin, for the Surrealists to haunt these outmoded spaces was to tap "the revolutionary energies" that were trapped there. But it may be more accurate (and less utopian) to say that the Surrealists registered the mnemonic signals encrypted in these structures—signals that might not otherwise have reached the present. This deployment of the nonsynchronous pressures the totalist assumptions of capitalist culture, and questions its claim to be timeless; it also challenges this culture with its own wish symbols, and asks it to recall its own forfeited dreams of liberty, equality, and fraternity. It is this mnemonic dimension of the outmoded that might still be mined today.

Of course what counts as the outmoded has changed radically. Not long ago film was the medium of the future; now it is a privileged index of the recent-past, and so a primary element in a nonsynchronous protest against the presentist totality of design culture.[20] In this regard what early arcades were for the Surrealists, early cinema is for contemporary artists like

Stan Douglas and Janet Cardiff: a repository of old sensations, private fantasies, and collective hopes—"residues of a dream world." "Both in terms of presentation and the subject matter of my work," Douglas has remarked, "I have been preoccupied with failed utopias and obsolete technologies. To a large degree, my concern is not to redeem these past events but to reconsider them: to understand why these utopian moments did not fulfill themselves, what larger forces kept a local moment a minor moment: and what was valuable there—what might still be useful today." [21] To cite only one instance in his work, *Overture* (1986) is a film installation that combines archival footage from the Edison Company from 1899 and 1901 with audio text from *Remembrance of Things Past* (1913–1922). The old film was shot from a camera mounted on a train engine as it passed along cliffs and through tunnels in British Columbia; the Proust is a meditation on the state of semi-consciousness that exists between sleeping and waking. There are six extracts from Proust and three sections of film (with tunnel passages extended by black leader), so that when the footage recurs it is matched with a different text, in a way that tests our sense of repetition and difference, memory and displacement. *Overture* is concerned not only with the transition from sleeping to waking, with the rebirth of consciousness that is also a return to mortality, but also with "the passing of narrative form from one medium, the novel, to another, film." At this juncture, a utopian possibility simultaneously opens up and shuts down. [22] It juxtaposes moments of rift—in subjective experience as well, as in cultural history—when other possibilities of self and expression are glimpsed, lost, and glimpsed again. "Obsolete forms of communication," Douglas has commented, "become an index of an understanding of the world lost to us." To recover these forms is to "address moments when history could have gone one way or another. We live in the residue of such moments, and for better or worse their potential is not yet spent." [23]

If the strategy of the nonsynchronous is to hold together markers of different times, then the strategy of the *incongruent*, the fourth and final one to be mentioned here, is to juxtapose traces of different spaces. I have in mind the hybrid objects and sited tableaux of David Hammons, Jimmie Durham, Felix Gonzalez-Torres, Rirkrit Tiravanija, and Gabriel Orozco. Often performative and provisional, this work projects a lyrical kind of criticality: it complicates found things with invented ones, reframes given spaces, and frequently leaves behind enigmatic site-specific souvenirs as it does so.

Above I suggested that the expanded field of postmodernist art has largely imploded, and that the recovered devices of neo-avant-garde art are mostly attenuated. Paradoxically enabled by historical distance and/or geopolitical difference, these artists have turned this imploded field into the departure point for an expansive practice once again, in which certain aspects of both postmodernist and neo-avant-garde art are recovered. For example, like postmodernist "sculpture in the expanded field," this postcolonial sculpture in the incongruent field is defined, at least initially, in the negative: "Not the monument, not the painting, not the picture," Durham has remarked of his unnamable objects. Rather, like neo-avant-garde artists before him, he seeks an "eccentric discourse of art" that poses "investigatory questions about what sort of thing [art] might be, but always, within a political situation of the time." [24] This formulation pertains to the others as well; and, as might be expected, the "investigatory questions" are framed with neo-avant-garde devices that are renewed through displacement and/or estrangement. For instance, Hammons has offered pathetic objects for sale on the street that exist in a parodic relation to commodity exchange (e.g., found doll shoes, snowballs in various sizes), and Tiravanija has made gift offerings in galleries that point to an alternative to the capitalist nexus of art (e.g., his own preparation of Thai dishes). Again a double reflexivity is at a premium here: "what sort of thing [art] might be ... within a political situation."

Not the monument, not the picture: Gabriel Orozco often mixes these categories with mundane life. He has played subversively with the most traditional of sculptural procedures, such as modeling and cutting.[25] In *Yielding Stone* (1992) he rolled a plasticine ball in the street in such a way as to pick up random bits of urban detritus: here the tradition of modeling was recast as an almost automatist practice, in which the everyday world, not the expressive artist, made the marks. In *La D.S.* (1993) Orozco shifted not the agency of sculpture but the object. Rather than conventional materials of wood or stone, he cut an old Citroën DS in half, excised a portion, and stuck the two parts together again: here the tradition of carving was reshaped into an almost readymade practice, in which destruction and reclamation were also combined. In this practice of incongruent objects in an imploded field, Orozco may transfer the attributes of one medium to another medium, as in *Yielding Stone* where the indexicality associated with photography becomes the property of sculpture.[26] So too a sculptural process may prepare a photographic tableau, as in *Island within an Island* (1993) where the (de)compositional strategy of installation art sets up the photograph—in this case a miming of the Lower Manhattan skyline in the background with found debris in the foreground. Folding medium onto medium, space onto space, island onto island, Orozco often wins critical pleasures from the otherwise painful ironies of dislocation and dispersal. After the events of September 11, 2001, this work of subversive mimicry has also taken on new meaning as an image of remembrance, of coming-after and living-on.[27]

[1] Heinrich Wölfflin, *Principles of Art History* (1915), New York/Dover 1950 (this remark dates from 1922). Two points of clarification: first, this is a question only of the end of art as an index to history, and here expectations were set too high to begin with. And, second, art might continue to represent contemporaneity in some quarters, but it does not define it.

[2] Donald Judd, "Specific Objects," *Complete Writings*, The Press of the Nova Scotia School of Art and Design, New York/Halifax 1974, p. 184. See Joseph Kosuth, "Art and Philosophy I and II," in *Studio International*, October–November, 1969. Also see Thierry de Duve, "The Monochrome and the Blank Canvas," *Kant after Duchamp*, MIT Press, Cambridge Massachusetts 1996; and Rosalind Krauss, *A Voyage on the North Sea*, Thames & Hudson, London 1999.

[3] See, among other texts, Arthur Danto, *Philosophical Disenfranchisement of Art*, Columbia University Press, New York 1986; and *After the End of Art*, Princeton University Press, Princeton 1997. The first title might be more accurately rendered "artistic reenfranchisement of philosophy." The breakdown of a formalist modernism prompted end-of-art theses in the 1960s and the advent of a post-historical postmodernism furthered them in the 1980s.

[4] See Victor Burgin, *The End of Art Theory: Criticism and Postmodernity*, Humanities Press International, Atlantic Highlands, New Jersey 1986; Fredric Jameson, *Postmodernism or The Cultural Logic of Late Capitalism*, Duke University Press, Durham 1991; and *The Cultural Turn*, Verso, London 1998. Jameson surveys end-of-art theses in *The Cultural Turn*, and Perry Anderson surveys end-of-history theses in *A Zone of Engagement*, Verso, London 1992.

[5] See Rosalind Krauss, "Sculpture in the Expanded Field," in Hal Foster (ed.), *The Anti-Aesthetic: Essays on Postmodern Culture*, New Press, New York 1983.

[6] Guy Debord, *The Society of the Spectacle*, Zone Press, Cambridge 1994, p. 136.

[7] See Benjamin Buchloh, *Neo-Avantgarde and Culture Industry*, MIT Press, Cambridge, Massachusetts 2000; and Hal Foster, *The Return of the Real*, MIT Press, Cambridge Massachusetts 1996.

[8] Theodor Adorno, *Negative Dialectics*, Continuum, New York 1973, p. 3.

[9] Karl Marx, "Theses on Feuerbach," in *The German Ideology*, International Publishers, New York 1978, p. 123. "Perhaps," Adorno comments, "it was an inadequate interpretation which promised that it would be put into practice" (*Negative Dialectics*, p. 3).

[10] Stan Douglas quoted in Scott Watson et al., *Stan Douglas*, Phaidon Press, London 1998, p. 28.

[11] More precisely, the formal device from past art (e.g., the use of the enigmatic image of the body-part by way of Duchamp and Surrealism) inflects contemporary politics of race and sexuality, and vice versa.

[12] See Harold Bloom, *The Anxiety of Influence: A Theory of Poetry*, Oxford University Press, New York 1973. I borrow the phrase "ecstasy of influence" from my Princeton colleague Elaine Showalter.

[13] There are many different moods of this shadowing. In *The Names* (1982) Don DeLillo has a character remark: "If I were a writer ... how I would enjoy hearing that the novel is dead. How liberating, to work in the margins, outside a central perception. You are the ghost of literature. Lovely." "I felt, at the same time," W.G. Sebald writes of a similar condition in *The Rings of Saturn* (1995), "both utterly liberated and deeply despondent" (see note 27).

[14] Jacques Derrida, *Specters of Marx*, Routledge, New York 1994, p. 10 and p. 37. Only a generation ago the master thinkers of modernity—Marx, Freud, and Nietzsche—were returned to the present to radical effects—by Althusser, Lacan, Derrida, Foucault, Deleuze, and others. Today, after the supposed end of Marxism, the attacks on Freud, and the exposés of Nietzsche, these figures live on far more spectrally, and they are often disguised in self-defeating ways (e.g., Marx rewritten as a philosopher, Freud as a literary critic). These shades don't seem to haunt much or many anymore, and intellectuals now focus on "traces" and "vestiges." In *Twilight of the Gods* Nietzsche wrote of the influence of "posthumous men"; have we become post-posthumous?

[15] Jon Bird in James Lingwood (ed.), *House*, Phaidon Press and Artangel Trust, London 1995.

[16] Ibid.

[17] The classic text on the non-synchronous is Ernst Bloch, "Non-Contemporaneity and Obligation to its Dialectic" (1932), in *Heritage of Our Times*, University of California Press, Berkeley 1991. Rosalind Krauss has elucidated the role of the outmoded in Coleman and Kentridge in "' ... And Then Turn Away?'," in *October*, n° 81, Summer 1997; "Reinventing the Medium," *Critical Inquiry*, Winter 1999; and "'The Rock': William Kentridge's Drawings for Projection," in *October*, n° 92, Spring 2000. All these practices demonstrate that new mediums are not necessarily techno-futuristic and anti-mnenomic—on the contrary.

[18] Walter Benjamin, "Surrealism: The Last Snapshot of the European Intelligentsia," in *Reflections*, Harcourt Brace Jovanovich, New York 1978, p. 181–182. I discuss this passage in *Compulsive Beauty*, MIT Press, Cambridge Massachusetts 1993.

[19] Benjamin, "Paris, Capital of the Nineteenth Century," ibid., p. 161.

[20] This position is distinct from the modernist melancholia of a Godard or a Wenders about the "death of cinema"; it seeks to mobilize this "death."

[21] Stan Douglas quoted in *Stan Douglas*, p. 116.

[22] Scott Watson, "Against the Habitual," in ibid. p. 46. Watson underscores the influence of the topos of habit not only in Proust but in Samuel Beckett on Proust (in his short 1931 text *Proust*).

[23] Douglas quoted in ibid., p. 9 and p. 29.

[24] Jimmie Durham quoted in Laura Mulvey et al., *Jimmie Durham*, Phaidon Press, London 1995. These artists suggest an artistic equivalent of the "minor literature" defined by Deleuze and Guattari in their 1975 study *Kafka: Toward a Minor Literature*, University of Minnesota Press, Minneapolis 1986: "The three characteristics of minor literature are the deterritorialization of language, the connection of the individual and the political, the collective arrangement of utterance."

[25] See Benjamin Buchloh, "The Sculpture of Everyday Life," in Alma Ruiz (ed.), *Gabriel Orozco*, Museum of Contemporary Art, Los Angeles 2000.

[26] See Molly Nesbit, "The Tempest," in ibid.

[27] One last version of aftermath to mention here is not so sanguine. W.G. Sebald has offered his own term for the structure of feeling within this condition: "vertigo" [*Schwindel*] in his 1990 novel of that name. This is the mental state of life "amidst the remains of our own civilization after its extinction," as he puts it in *The Rings of Saturn* (1995). It is a melancholia that, paradoxically, is detached from its lost object—because there are too many lost objects to track, so many that it makes one vertiginous (again: "I felt, at the same time, both utterly liberated and deeply despondent"). In a sense the vertiginous is a combination of the non-synchronous and the incongruent, of displacements or disorientations in both time and space; and Sebald's narratives at once enact this vertigo and seek to survive it. Like Gerhard Richter in his *Atlas*, a compendium of photographs, private and public, Sebald constructs his work out of archives of personal pasts vectored by public pasts. The result is an unnamable genre that is both fictional and non-fictional, that lives beyond these genres just as pre-modern texts lived before them. Of special interest here is his use of banal photographs and old traces of travels as in Surrealist novels (e.g., train tickets, hotel receipts, journal entries)—all as indexical markers to ground his excursions into history, literature, and fantasy. Yet—and this is key to the vertigo of coming-after—these indices are as "anomic" as they are "mnemonic." They enact the dialectic between the two terms that Benjamin Buchloh also finds in the Richter *Atlas*, in which the two share in each other, in which (for example) the photographic is ambiguously both. As Sebald puts it in *The Emigrants* (1992), in a paradox crucial to vertigo, "and the last remnants memory destroys." This destruction is never total, or rather memory is sometimes enabled by this destruction: "Whenever a shift in our spiritual life occurs and fragments such as these surface," he writes in *The Rings*, "we believe we can remember." But this is quickly qualified: "In reality, of course, memory fails us. Too many buildings have fallen down, too much rubble has heaped up, the moraines and deposits are insuperable."

Art and Its Context or A Question of Culture

Jean-Marc Poinsot

This text was originally written for the symposium *L'art contemporain et son exposition* (*Contemporary Art and Its Exhibition*) at the Centre Georges Pompidou, Paris, October 7–8, 2002. It has been resumed and extended by the author for this publication.

In 1991, Seth Siegelaub was commissioned to plan an event exploring the development of conceptual art between 1960 and 1990. Seth Siegelaub, a former art dealer and freelance curator with a reputation for originality, had long since stopped working in the art field when he was called on to work on the project, which was initially to consist of three parts: a written record of works by artists active in the late 1960s, a publication in which the artists discussed the period 1960–1990, and an exhibition of works by the same artists produced in the 1990s. The project, entitled *The Context of Art/The Art of Context. Artists on Art, the Art World & Life since 1969*, was published alongside the artists' responses in *Kunst & Museumjournaal* in 1996. Considered from the standpoint of Siegelaub's current occupation, publishing books on communication, traversing this long period of time was like a sort of fiction, with the micro-milieu of contemporary art "becoming progressively integrated into the dominant values, practices, and aspirations of a (capitalist) social life." Like Rip van Winkle [1] waking from a 30-year sleep, he looked back at an unknown society, trying to compare the memory of radical and anti-institutional stances with today's world, where the artist seems to have become just a cog in the cultural industry machine.

In referring to this project, my intention is not to discuss another non-exhibition by Seth Siegelaub, but simply to borrow his time machine to compare a number of exhibitions between the early postwar period and the end of the 20th century, beginning with the *11th documenta* exhibition. Okwui Enwezor opened his preface as follows: "Almost 50 years after its founding, *documenta* finds itself confronted once again with the specters of yet another turbulent time of unceasing cultural, social, and political frictions, transitions, transformations, fissures, and global institutional consolidations. If we take on board these events in all their historical significance, along with the forces that today are reshaping the values and views of our world, the prospects for contemporary art and its position in producing and explicating critical models of interpreting the features of the contemporary imagination could not be more daunting and demanding." [2]

Without wishing to discuss the author's rhetoric, it quickly becomes apparent that his point of view emphasizes the perception of the rifts overlooked by Western visitors, so much ground has history lost as a dynamic in terms of reading events, both in daily life and in art, since the emergence of postmodernism. This same feeling of a rift unquestionably drove Okwui Enwezor in his placing of works, objects, films, and so on at *documenta*. Faced with the traces and consequences accumulated or juxtaposed in these shifts and frictions, the visitor was struck by a great wave of disorientation—all the more so since, in espousing the exhibition's democratic principles, Enwezor emphasized a cultural rather than aesthetic approach and attached little importance to creating a homogeneous model integrating artworks featuring different media, viewpoints, and contexts of production. Take Igloolok Isuma Productions' films on and by Inuits, and Sanja Ivekovic's 1982 video *Personal Cuts*, for example. The former claimed an ethnic identity and rejected the anthropological gaze, while the latter was a strictly artistic montage in which images of a totalitarian system were cut with a performance symbolizing the disjointed and atomized construction of the subject. The opposition was simple, powerful, and dialectic in a critical artwork which produced the work of mourning necessary to escape the totalitarian control of individual consciences, while the series of films on the Inuits, impressive as an act of witness and for their closeness to their subject, had little or nothing to do with the contemporary art world or market. Rather than confronting visitors with an anecdotal and pseudo-anthropological cultural discontinuity evoked by various objects or images all considered eligible for artistic status, this juxtaposition placed them at the heart of the irreducible nature of cultural difference. The point was not to create a "shared exoticism" [3] but rather a concrete experience of cultural differences that globalization tends to assimilate into one overall marketplace.

documenta 10 and *documenta 11* included complementary programs drawing on global media space—TV, radio, internet, cinema—and its capacity to juxtapose simultaneously a range of products and realities that would formerly have been irreducible and non-comparable. However, where Enwezor drew on the differences in status between different types of cultural objects, Catherine David's principal focus was on productions considered part of the art market and its history, even if their approach and staging were in some cases critical. Her exhibition brought together strong personalities and in one of the catalogues she herself appears in a sophisticated photograph that shows only her hands and her eyes (an image within an image). [4] Her political vision and her open approach to the world were based on a practice internal to art—an art of named creators. Her catalogue presentation demonstrates her discreet use of segregation and dissociation: "To complement the exhibition in the city we have published a book which situates artistic productions from 1945 to today in their political, economic, and cultural context of appearance and in light of the multiple shifts and redefinitions that have now become manifest with the process of globalization." [5] To this should be added the inclusion in the program of various cultural figures such as historians, philosophers, and scientists, over the 100 days of the exhibition. [6]

Both in her analysis of events and her approach to the elements of the exhibition, Catherine David clearly dissociated art and its context, despite the shifting limits within artistic practice. She drew on these extensions and re-definitions of art as a theme, such as the obvious, and rather well handled, example of documentary photography. However, in so doing, she simply followed the general trend of critics and historians of photography, represented in her team by Jean-François Chevrier. The photographers chosen by Okwui Enwezor for his *documenta* were a long way from the heart of contemporary aesthetic values.

We have here two opposing viewpoints. Catherine David observed major changes and developments between 1945 and 1997 but considered that while art and the world have changed, they still face one another. Okwui Enwezor was more interested in the system that opposed the expression of alterities than in confronting art with a changing world, even if, as a result, the purely artistic dimension took a back seat. In fact, in this context, he deliberately sidelined the role of the curator and his team and invited a large number of collectives to participate.

Although Seth Siegelaub, Catherine David, and Okwui Enwezor agree that there have been major changes since the end of the Second World War, they do not all measure them by the same yardstick. Seth Siegelaub has noted an institutionalization of contemporary art and the erosion of its critical value. Catherine David believes that art remained a critical value in the teeth of the triumph of global capitalism and sees her role as defending this value, while Okwui Enwezor sees de-colonization as abrogating the notion of the autonomy of art: "To understand what constitutes the avant-garde today, one must begin not in the field of contemporary art but in the field of culture and politics, as well as in the economic field governing all relations that have come under the overwhelming hegemony of capital." [7]

Is it meaningful to return to the colonial era with Walter Benjamin? Yes, certainly, because in those days exhibitions shaped values just like today. In "Paris, Capital of the Nineteenth Century" (1939), Benjamin wrote, "World exhibitions glorify the exchange value of the commodity. They create a framework in which use value recedes into the background. They open a phantasmagoria which a person enters in order to be distracted." [8] He thereby denounced an operation that had always been the essence and the raison d'être of exhibitions—extracting objects, particularly works of art, from their initial position or circulation, to give them a new meaning and value by virtue of their displacement and regrouping for the gaze of a nascent audience. Becoming more commonplace has not stripped exhibitions of their principal quality. Duchamp with his readymade art was not alone in having seen this possibility, and the path he paved was not unique. The context of the exhibition makes it possible to present any object, including literary objects and work, as Paul Valéry and Julien Cain demonstrated at the 1937 Exhibition, as well as ideas—and not just those of Conceptual artists—and the immaterial, as Jean-François Lyotard showed in 1985, not forgetting video and cinema that are such a feature of today's exhibitions. Works of art earned their autonomy by showing themselves thus to the public gaze, and moreover it was this autonomy that enabled Duchamp to test it and prove that selecting non-artistic objects did not endanger its existence. Such were the beliefs about the value of the artwork and the efficiency of the exhibition that it was often forgotten that the objects selected could speak about themselves and the society that produced them, in other words about culture.

It is too often assumed that this autonomy of art came to dominate by itself or that its history predates modernity. However, this is belied by the existence of a contemporary art program at the Musée des Arts Décoratifs in Paris between 1953 and 1985—the only such program open to living artists until at least the end of the 1960s. François Mathey [9] exhibited contemporary art with particular attention to commissioning, decor, and social relevance. Thus, in conjunction with Matisse's paper cutouts or Dubuffet's paintings, he exhibited toys, films and film sets (Georges Méliès), works of contemporary design, comics, science fiction, and "bachelor machines." [10] In the cinema, Buren, Mosset, Parmentier, and Toroni displayed paintings that the audience saw without looking at them. What is interesting about this program is the way it used ambiguity and confrontation to bear witness to the fact that the autonomy of modernist art, promoted in the same period in New York and heightened by increasing numbers of museums of contemporary art in North America from the early 1960s, may not have been as exclusive and dominant a model as it appeared. One might argue that Paris was small fry in the art world at that time, but it would be wrong to ignore the fact that Dubuffet was exhibiting his collection of Art Brut and that he gave a hundred or so paintings to the museum. In the period around 1960, the Musée des Arts Décoratifs in Paris was the only museum in France in a position to question the confrontations of contemporary and past art, visual, commercial, and marginal culture, pathological and children's art, industrial or craft-produced art, and Western and non-Western culture. Although this museum was not the only one to challenge the limits of art and other forms of popular and elitist culture, it was the furthest beyond control. François Mathey was not a theorist and he did not have a political vision of culture, but he was one of the few people in Europe in the period around 1960 to question the relationship between art and culture. The ICA and the Whitechapel in London, the Stedelijk Museums in Amsterdam, and especially Eindhoven under Jan Leering, [11] developed other analyses and experiences, while a little later Harald Szeemann in Bern furthered their thinking in his own way. They all anticipated the role that contemporary art was to play in our societies today and were particularly interested in the relationships and bonds between art, culture, artists, the audience, and the public authorities. Jan Leering developed his theoretical thinking, acquisitions policy, and exhibitions in parallel. He questioned the role of the museum as a site for contemporary art in education as a place where the social functions of art were formulated and as an element of the artistic economy. He wanted to give art the vital social role it enjoyed in the Middle Ages, and developed thematic exhibitions based on socio-cultural data, such as the 1972 *The Street* exhibition, which had the explicitly stated aim of reaching a new audience. [12] His interest in artists such as El Lissitzky, Theo Van Doesburg, and Laszlo Moholy-Nagy contributed to making the collection the historical basis for the ideas he developed in his exhibitions. For his exhibitions, he recreated Tatlin's *Monument to the Third International* and Lissitzky's *Proun* room, which indicates the importance architecture had for him, while exhibitions such as *Scharoun* (1968), *Bouwen voor de industrie* (1968, featuring 200 photographs by Bernd and Hilla Becher), and *Gaudi* (1971) opened a path followed much later by Szeemann, most notably with the exhibition *Penchant for a Synthesis of the Arts* (1983), which included artists already shown at Eindhoven.

Leering was aware of the danger of drawing on the political arena for the theme of certain exhibitions, but he considered that it was a risk worth taking. However, his successor Rudi Fuchs refocused the program of exhibitions purely on contemporary artists and excluded all thematic exhibitions.

Jan Leering's role was all the more important since he contributed to the re-evaluation of the social function of art through his acquisitions, reconstitutions, exhibitions, aesthetic choices, and theories at a time when institutes of contemporary art were springing up all over Europe. He reconsidered the social commissioning of art in the early part of the 20th century, when for example his French counterpart François Mathey was behind the project to commission Le Corbusier to design the chapel at Ronchamp in 1950–1955.

Harald Szeemann was not an architectural engineer like Leering. However, his PhD dissertation in art history on the origins of modern book illustration "Die Anfänge der modernen Buchillustration: Die Buchillustration der Nabis und ihre Kontakte zu 'Revue Blanche,' 'Théâtre de l'œuvre,' Alfred Jarry, Ambroise Vollard" Bern, 1960), reflected the broad approach to modern art that he was to expand and affirm through contact with colleagues. It was no coincidence that he shared an understanding of contemporary art that was very open to many of contemporary culture's themes and productions. The museums run by his older colleagues were interested in taking up his exhibitions because they worked along similar lines. Yet the dialogue was far from straightforward. The discrepancy between Leering's project *The Street* in Eindhoven and Szeemann's project in Bern was as much a matter of form as of essence. Leering's objective was not to stage the exhibition in the display windows of a department store. What Leering had to say about *The Street* was based on an analysis that, though comparative, was nonetheless rooted in the Dutch cityscape, because he was trying to create a direct interaction with the inhabitants of Eindhoven.

Harald Szeemann also had discussions with François Mathey about the exhibition *The Bachelor Machines* (1975), designed from the outset for a long tour to cities as varied as Bern, Venice, Brussels, Düsseldorf, Paris, Malmö, Amsterdam, and Vienna. Its documentary components and the commission given to Jacques Carelman to build the machines based on descriptions and models by Alfred Jarry, Raymond Roussel, and Franz Kafka made it the perfect example of an "exhibition as means of expression" which was more than "the sum of isolated situations." It was also an exhibition in which original artworks were so much in the minority that François Mathey felt it necessary to write to Harald Szeemann that "it seems to me that it is necessary to warn the public that it is not an art exhibition, that it lies beyond good and bad taste, that it is a question not only of morals, but much more so of psychoanalysis or even metaphysics." [13]

The work on the imagination, in other words on the links woven not only between works of a different nature, such as literature, the visual arts, architecture, and so on, but also between scientific knowledge and non-scientific knowledge and practices such as those of Emma Kunz [14] with which Szeemann compared the drawings to some *Bachelor Machines*, without, however, including them in the traveling exhibition, is another form of re-centering the exhibition away from masterpieces toward culture, a methodology that Szeemann then shared with a few colleagues.

The examples they provide are clear enough proof that the question of the autonomy of art was not the object of unanimous agreement, and that Clement Greenberg's dogmatism and William Rubin's radicalization of Alfred Barr's modernism cannot be considered the sole stages prior to the rethinking prompted by the consequences of globalization, as Thomas McEvilley attempted to demonstrate in his writings on primitivism, postmodernism, and the exhibition.

In his critique of *Primitivism*, curated by William Rubin at MoMA in 1984, McEvilley laid great emphasis on the refusal to date tribal objects and the de-contextualizing effect this created. [15] In fact, the exhibition detaches and reintegrates the objects it displays and the effects its produces are the result of the authors' intentions. Today, questioning the cultural is the real change of context, as it marks the deep transformations noted by Catherine David and Okwui Enwezor in the immediate postwar period. These transformations were difficult for some thinkers to grasp, such as T.S. Eliot, who was such a rich source of inspiration for Rudi Fuchs. In his *Notes Towards the Definition of Culture* (1948), T.S. Eliot wrote "We can assert with some confidence that our own period is one of decline; that the standards of culture are lower than they were 50 years ago; and that the evidences of this decline are visible in every department of human activity." [16]

The class assumptions that underlie T.S. Eliot's point of view have been largely invalidated by the strategies of globalization that have replaced social classes with age groups and "minority groups" that are much easier to identify in terms of consumption. It is far from clear that art has been able to anticipate this development, in spite of its capacity for criticism. However, this does not mean that globalization has had no impact on the construction of the cultural models at work in artistic production and in exhibitions. In exhibitions as varied as *Présumés innocents* (Bordeaux, 2000) on the theme of teen culture; *Every day*, the theme of the 11th Sydney Biennial (1998); or *Partage d'exotismes* (*Shared Exoticisms*, Lyon, 2000), organized according to a basic anthropological plan, I have noted as much fragmentation and as many consumerist, yet global, divisions of our experience of daily life. Artists and curators alike share the responsibility for these alignments and assimilations, but the true cultural issue is elsewhere and is probably not so much a context as a demand for another existence, another type of identity.

[1] The hero of a short story by Washington Irving, 1819.
[2] Okwui Enwezor, "Preface," in *documenta 11—Platform 5*, Hatje Cantz, Ostfildern-Ruit 2002, p. 40.
[3] Translator's note: the author is refering to *Partage d'exotismes* (*Shared Exoticisms*)—*5th Lyon Biennial* (2000), curated by Jean-Hubert Martin.
[4] *documenta x Kurzführer*, Hatje Cantz, Ostfildern-Ruit 1997, p. 6.
[5] Ibid., p. 12.
[6] Ibid., p. 12.
[7] Okwui Enwezor, "The Black Box," in *documenta 11—Platform 5*, p. 45.
[8] Walter Benjamin, *The Arcades Project*, Roy Tiedemann (ed.), Harvard University Press, Cambridge-London, 1999.
[9] See François Mathey, *Ecrits*, RMN, Paris 1993.
[10] When hosting an exhibition curated by Harald Szeemann.
[11] See Carel Blotkamp, Marjon van Caspel, Frans Haks et al., *Museum in Motion, Het museum voor moderne kunst ter diskussie*, Staatsuitgeverij, 's-Gravenhage 1979.

[12] Initially planned together with other partners, in particular Harald Szeemann who produced his own version at the Loeb department store in Bern, Leering's exhibition was less artistic in content. It took place at a time when Leering was distancing himself from the model of the artist as the sole producer of masterpieces. This position, which eventually led Leering to leave his museum for a museum of natural history, doubtless influenced Harald Szeemann, who, in the early 1970s, declared that he had taken the system of solo exhibitions as far as it could go.

[13] Letter from François Mathey to Harald Szeemann, February 19, 1976, "following the brief visit of the B.M. [Bachelor Machines] to Düsseldorf," François Mathey Archive, Bibliothèque Centrale des Arts Décoratifs, Paris.

[14] In the same letter to Szeemann, Mathey wrote, "In the final analysis, what saves the B.M. for me is the mystical attitude of someone like Emma Kunz and I now regret that this spiritual aspect to the problem was not exhibited at Paris because her transcendent vision of the world is the only way to escape the obsession of the closed world of sex."

[15] See Thomas McEvilley, *Art and Otherness. Crisis in Cultural Identity*, Documentext, Kingston, New York 1992.

[16] T.S. Eliot, *Notes Towards the Definition of Culture*, Faber & Faber, London 1962, p. 19.

Interview with Tobia Bezzola [1]

François Aubart and Fabien Pinaroli

Maggia, April 14, 2007

FRANÇOIS AUBART AND FABIEN PINAROLI

Harald Szeemann's education and early activities are something we know little about. He apparently studied art and archaeology, worked in the theater and practiced journalism and graphic design. We also know that he spent some time in Paris writing a thesis on Alfred Jarry, who continued to be a key figure for him. Can you tell us about that period?

TOBIA BEZZOLA

Between 1953 and 1960 he spent a lot of time in Paris, in fact he lived partly there and partly in Bern. In the 1950s Paris was the center of the arts and cultural world, with the life of cafes, Giacometti, Sartre, the loose coterie around Jarry. He certainly met Breton and lots of other people—he wasn't at all shy. Then there were the theaters and the French *cinémathèque*—there were no such film archives elsewhere and he spent an enormous amount of time there. He had also made many contacts thanks to Arnold Rüdlinger, the director of the Kunsthalle Bern, who was working with Fernand Léger and other artists of the time based in Paris. He and Szeemann saw each other each time Szeemann came to Paris, and they would go together to visit various artists in their studios, including Joan Mitchell and Sam Francis, for example.

FRANÇOIS AUBART AND FABIEN PINAROLI

He soon gave up his acting career to create what he called "one-man theater," which he liked better than the collaboration that traditional theater involved. Do you think that might have influenced his approach to exhibition organizing and explain why he defined himself as an "exhibition maker"?

TOBIA BEZZOLA

Absolutely. The idea of a traveling group which puts on productions without having a fixed connection with any institution was definitely the model for his Agency.

FRANÇOIS AUBART AND FABIEN PINAROLI

There were other artists who had been working for some years along these lines, in the hope of controlling the means of production and reaching a degree of autonomy relative to the standard art world circuit. Do you think that in creating his Agency Szeemann was supporting this changed approach, by inventing a flexible organization close to artists?

TOBIA BEZZOLA

Perhaps, insofar as those artists were beginning to put on their own exhibitions. In the 1950s, when he began, the relationship between curators and artists was undergoing change. Museum directors like Franz Meyer and Arnold Rüdlinger still represented a hierarchical system, they still wore suits and ties. They visited artists in their studios and selected from the available stock, saying "I'll have this one, or that one ... " Nowadays, when someone mounts a major exhibition with an artist, it is the artist who often controls the project and makes the choice of which pieces to show. Artists have become their own curators. Conceptual art and site-specific art in particular have played a part in this change, and Szeemann had a profound understanding of these currents. But the organization of the Agency was really inspired by the theater.

FRANÇOIS AUBART AND FABIEN PINAROLI

Szeemann created the exhibition entitled *When Attitudes Become Form* in Bern in 1969. He let the artists install their own works without interfering too much in the operation, an approach that was very fashionable at the time. We know that subsequently he began to pay scrupulous attention to the way pieces were shown: he was capable of moving a work by a few centimeters, after the technical staff had already hung it. In your view, at what point and why did Szeemann take charge of the display of his exhibitions?

TOBIA BEZZOLA

I think that it was his experience with *Happening & Fluxus* in 1970 that led him to see that this wasn't working any more. All the Fluxus artists from Europe and America were there, but theirs was a network that had already existed for a decade or so. So as not to bend over too far in the direction of a merely historical exhibition, Szeemann decided to invite the Viennese Actionists as well. That decision seems to me to have been disastrous. There had already been quarrels and conflicts between the older Fluxus artists, and Otto Mühl and Hermann Nitsch. The resulting scandals showed Szeemann the limits of the laissez-faire approach to his artists. It was that more than anything that moved him toward taking more control and directing operations himself.

FRANÇOIS AUBART AND FABIEN PINAROLI

The period during which he was the director of the Kunsthalle Bern was marked by an enormous number of exhibitions, which followed close on one another's heels and rarely lasted more than a month. On top of that, they took very varied and avant-garde forms. How much did that experience influence his planning for *documenta 5* in Kassel in 1972?

TOBIA BEZZOLA

Every aspect of *documenta* originated in Bern—the inclusion of vernacular art, popular culture, science-fiction, "Art Brut" or outsider art, including the various activities and demonstrations which coincided with the exhibition. *Ex Voto*, which was organized in Bern 1964, already dealt with religious art. He reintroduced the experiment he had first tried out in *When Attitudes Become Form*, of working directly on site with the artists. Indeed, one can see *documenta 5* as a summing-up of his years in Bern. This was the first time he had drawn, in this way, on his previous experience, and he expanded this approach in the years that followed.

FRANÇOIS AUBART AND FABIEN PINAROLI

documenta 5 marks the end of a period in which Szeemann had criticized the institutionalization of art and sought to break up the existing frameworks. He had already mounted *Happening & Fluxus* and then *The Street* in 1970. With *documenta 5*, he clearly seems to be trying to reinvest in the museum. Yet the exhibitions he produced subsequently question the limits imposed by the museum. In your view, at what point did he manage to reconcile these opposing positions?

TOBIA BEZZOLA

This was why he asked Hans Heinz Holz, a Marxist theorist who at that time was Germany's answer to Althusser, to write the long text that introduces the catalogue. He would always say to me, "I invited Holz to write that text because I knew that then all the Marxists would shut up, and I could do whatever I liked." There is in fact a difference between the initial plan for *documenta 5*, written by Bazon Brock, and the final one. In the end, it was Szeemann who became its sole artistic director, and he enjoyed organizing a spectacular show. He couldn't care less about the sociological or critical content. He didn't want it to be a political demonstration, he wanted it to be an art show. That was a tense, eventful time: in Germany it was the beginning of the period of the Red Army Fraction's terrorism. Subsequently he directed *The Bachelor Machines* in 1975 and *Monte Verità* in 1978, neither of them designed to attract the general public. By the standards of the time they took a bizarre form, calling into question the idea of the art museum by simultaneously displaying everyday objects and works of art. But I think it was with *Penchant for a Synthesis of the Arts* in 1983 that the two positions were combined. On one hand, that show was an experimental undertaking by Szeemann's Agency, and on the other hand it was structured and organized like a classic museum exhibition. Perhaps it was at that point that he really accepted institutions as they are and began to adapt to the different conditions he encountered. Moreover, we shouldn't lose sight of the fact that he first began to criticize institutions at the beginning of the 1970s, but 15 years later they had changed significantly, partly because a new generation of directors had taken over.

FRANÇOIS AUBART AND FABIEN PINAROLI

The exhibition entitled *Grandfather: A Pioneer Like Us* had already taken place in 1974, and it too, like *The Bachelor Machines*, displayed objects on an equal level with artworks. How far are these shows representative of a particular concept of the exhibition, and of a period that you yourself have called a "period of research"?

TOBIA BEZZOLA

Those were the most experimental of his exhibitions. They went beyond normal institutional practice and were apparently inspired by what artists like Daniel Spoerri with his *Musée sentimental* [Sentimental Museum], or Marcel Broodthaers with his *Musée d'Art Moderne, Département des Aigles* [Museum of Modern Art, Department of Eagles], were trying to do in the same period.

FRANÇOIS AUBART AND FABIEN PINAROLI

The ideas of "Intense Intentions" and the "Museum of Obsessions" formulated after *documenta 5* reveal a very particular approach to art but also a conception of the exhibition as a medium, as a way for its creator to express subjective ideas. From that point on he was criticized for subordinating the works displayed to his own purposes. How did he react to this criticism?

TOBIA BEZZOLA

He cared very little about criticism of any kind.

FRANÇOIS AUBART AND FABIEN PINAROLI

Szeemann was very explicit about the difficulties inherent in his position as an independent curator. It was for pragmatic reasons that he accepted the position offered by the Kunsthaus Zürich in 1981. The status of "permanent independent curator" which he demanded and was able to negotiate with the institution was unprecedented. Can you tell us about this contract and the kind of commitment it involved?

TOBIA BEZZOLA

The Kunsthaus had a team of four or five permanent curators. In this particular contract it was agreed that he would assist the museum's management with acquiring works for the permanent collection and that he would be in charge of a number of exhibitions. He was paid an annual base salary for his acquisition work and an additional salary that varied according to the exhibitions planned. Szeemann also took charge of projects that he did not himself originate: the *Eugène Delacroix* exhibition of 1987, for example, was a project initiated by the Kunsthaus. That exhibition required a great deal of work, and he would never have done it of his own accord. He certainly took a great deal of interest in organizing it, especially the part relative to Baudelaire and French Romanticism, but it was a project that the institution had decided to undertake. In the same way, *Egon Schiele and His Time* in 1988 was a Kunsthaus project; they wanted to display the Leopold collection, assembled by the greatest collector of the "Vienna 1900" period. So Szeemann was sometimes put in charge of mounting exhibitions devised by Felix Baumann, the director of the Kunsthaus. *Alfred Jarry* in 1984 was his own project, and it was the *Bonnard* exhibition, organized by one of the permanent curators, which gave him the opportunity to mount it. His position enabled him to remain independent and thus to pursue his personal projects.

FRANÇOIS AUBART AND FABIEN PINAROLI

At that period there appeared a new style of exhibition, *Zeitlos* (*Timeless*) in 1988 being an example: for these Szeemann focused on the exhibition space and sought out locations that were not designed to display artworks, such as the Hamburger Bahnhof in Berlin, the Deichtorhallen in Hamburg, and the Chapelle de la Salpêtrière in Paris. Was this a real paradigm shift or the natural evolution of his practice as a curator?

TOBIA BEZZOLA

I would say that this question relates to some specific historical and cultural developments which go well beyond his particular work. During the 1980s, contemporary art began to attract the general public, and many cities started to look for big shows to put on. Szeemann was ready to respond to this new situation. But one can also see an element of his response in the *Grandfather* exhibition, which he mounted in his own flat. After *documenta 5*, the biggest show, he wanted to put on the smallest, but to take as much care with it as he had with the big one. That experiment was truly the start of something new, a kind of stage set. At the Kunsthalle Bern and also in Kassel, this emphasis on the three-dimensional did not yet exist. With *Grandfather*, he tried out a spatial design using objects that had belonged to his grandfather. The question he asked himself was this: "How to go about exhibiting objects, which, for the most part, are not artworks but the things my grandfather used in his hairdressing salon, yet without displaying them in the traditional way that we find in historical museums, where objects are shown with their explanatory notices, all organized in thematic or chronological order? How to imitate the artist who installs his sculptures in an exhibition space in such a way that the object conveys information beyond its historic significance"? When he spoke of the works he displayed he always said "They have to breathe." This interest in spatial breathing applied especially to sculpture. For more than a decade his chief concern was to create what he called "poems in space." He started to develop this aspect with *Grandfather* and pursued it throughout his career: it culminated at the end of the 1980s with his "auratic" exhibitions. These consisted of many monumental sculptures displayed in immense spaces, the setting conveying a kind of pathos. When this approach began to seem clichéd, toward the end of the 1990s, he realized that he could not spend the rest of his life traveling around the world looking for enormous spaces in which to install works by Richard Serra, Walter De Maria, and Bruce Nauman. I think that was when his interest in thematic exhibitions revived and he devised *Visionary Switzerland* in 1991, *Austria in a Net of Roses* in 1996, and finally *Visionary Belgium* in 2005.

FRANÇOIS AUBART AND FABIEN PINAROLI

This series of exhibitions focused on individual countries, or geographical regions such as the Balkans. *Blood & Honey: The Future is in the Balkans* in 2003, presented a very personal view of the regions in question, which some people found simplistic and caricatured. At the same time, they revive the technique of mixing artworks with objects and documents from other areas of the culture. Can we see them as an attempt to reconnect with the thematic approach of the 1970s?

TOBIA BEZZOLA

Definitely, but the difference was that this time he also incorporated what he had learned in the course of developing his exhibitions into major spectacles.

FRANÇOIS AUBART AND FABIEN PINAROLI

In the 1990s, biennials and big shows multiplied and attempt to present an objective view of the world art scene. Can you identify any particular methodology, curatorial practice, or relationship to art in Szeemann's shows?

TOBIA BEZZOLA

I don't think that is where his contribution to the theory and practice of the exhibition is to be found.

FRANÇOIS AUBART AND FABIEN PINAROLI

Was there nothing individual, no Szeemann touch, in these major events?

TOBIA BEZZOLA

I don't think so. Sometimes he managed to bring an artist to public attention, but mostly the result was rather predictable. He was always somewhat constrained in putting on these big events—by the commissioners, the collectors, the gallery owners, and of course by the costs involved—but he always insisted on including the works he himself wanted and he made very few concessions. He knew that an exhibition of this kind was also a form of publicity, that it was meant to be talked about. In Lyon or Venice he didn't have the luxury of putting on an exhibition that was completely esoteric, individual, incomprehensible, alien to the world of art, the market, and the press.

FRANÇOIS AUBART AND FABIEN PINAROLI

So there was nothing new about displaying the works of Asian artists at the Lyon Biennial in 1997, then at the Venice Biennial in 1999 and in 2001?

TOBIA BEZZOLA

It was in fact the first time that so many of these artists had been shown at once, but many of them were already well known in London, Paris, and so on. It was much the same in the case of the Balkans show.

FRANÇOIS AUBART AND FABIEN PINAROLI

You describe this period as marked by constraints inherent in the kind of activity he was involved in, but didn't any of these exhibitions give him some breathing space, even if he had to work within the system?

TOBIA BEZZOLA

No. To overcome this system he would have had to been able to exit from it for five years and carry out the kind of research he had done, for instance, for *The Bachelor Machines*. That show is the classic example of his work: it was incomprehensible to people at the time, it was a synthesis of scientific, artistic, and philosophical study. But at the same time he was flattered by these invitations, and he enjoyed directing the Venice Biennial. For his generation, that was "the" biennial. But organizing an event like that takes an enormous amount of time and energy. The whole thing had become so gigantic that he was unable to redefine the framework that he was presented with, which he had been able to do in the 1972 *documenta*. All the pavilions were directed by the various countries present, and he was in charge only of the international pavilion. He succeeded in getting the Arsenale for the international exhibition, and he was very proud of being able to use that fantastic space. He put all of his energy into choosing the artists and the works eligible for display. All the same, he was sorry to see the art scene return to such a conventional level, and he regretted the loss of the adventurous, experimental spirit of the 1960s and 1970s. But he was a pro, a journeyman, and he knew how to adapt to whatever conditions he encountered.

[1] Tobia Bezzola is a curator at Kunsthaus Zürich, where he worked as an assistant to Harald Szeemann from 1992 to 1996.

Fabbrica Harald Szeemann, 2005

Balthasar Burkhard

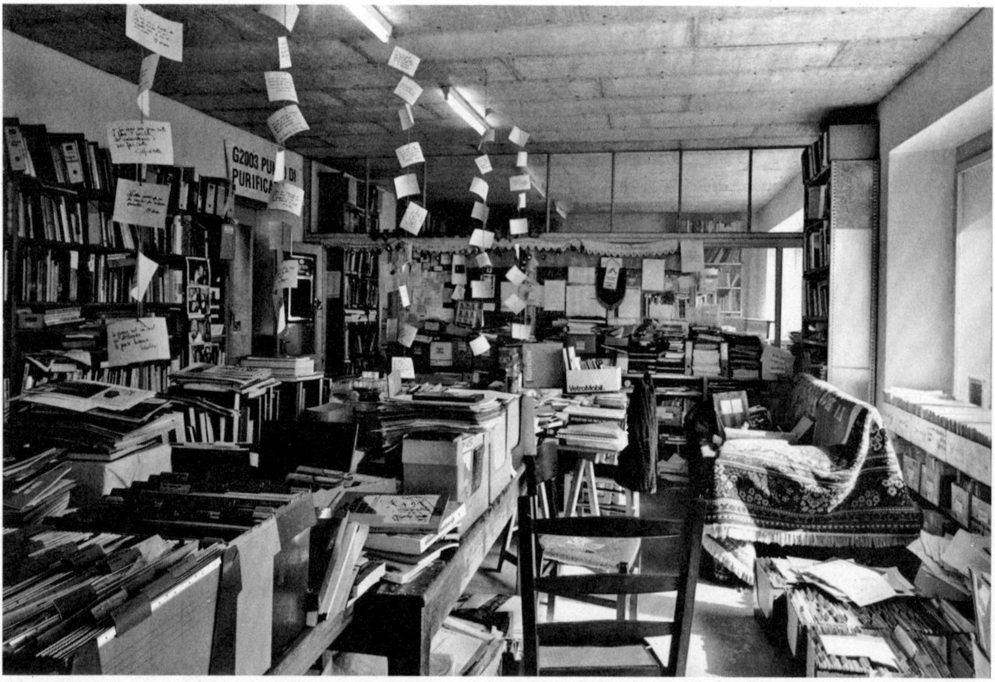

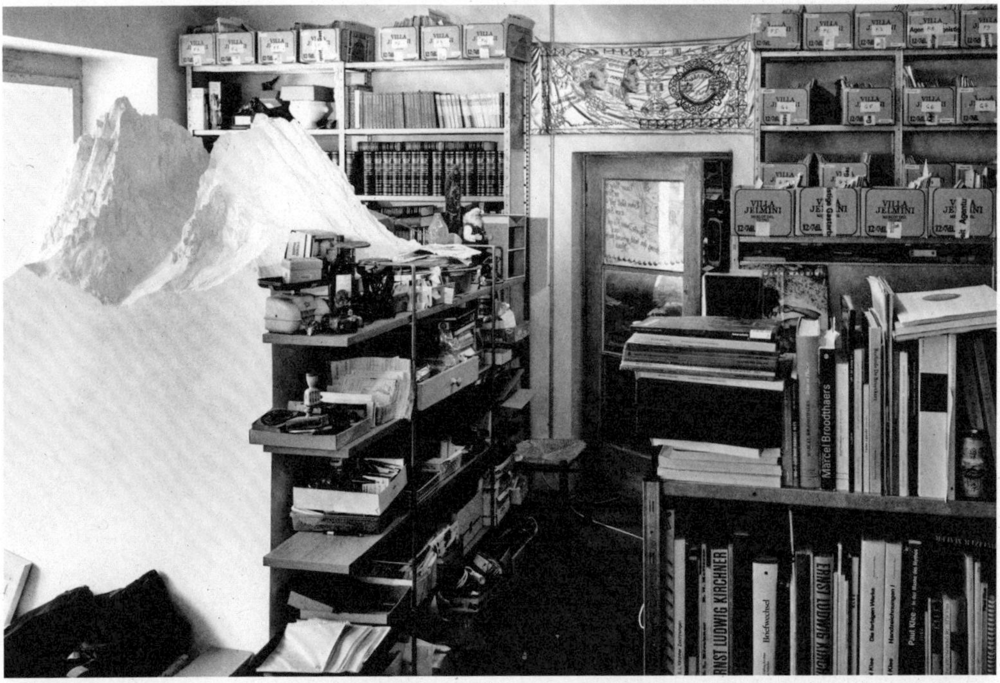
VILLA JELMINI
Marcel Broodthaers
ERNST LUDWIG KIRCHNER
ERNST LUDWIG KIRCHNER
Briefwechsel
Paul Klee

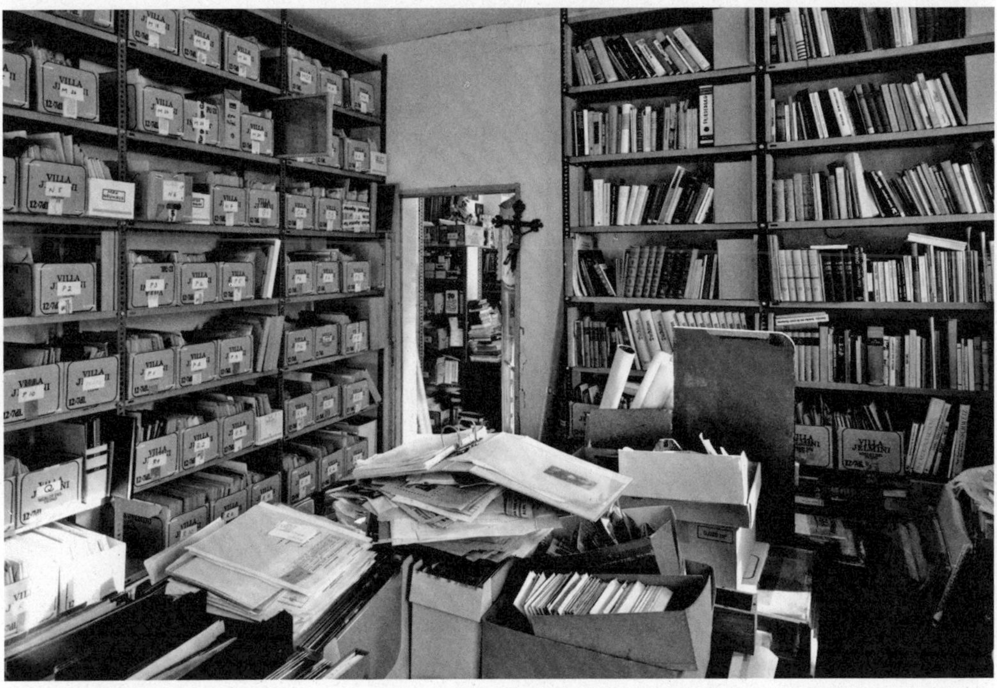
VILLA JELMINI

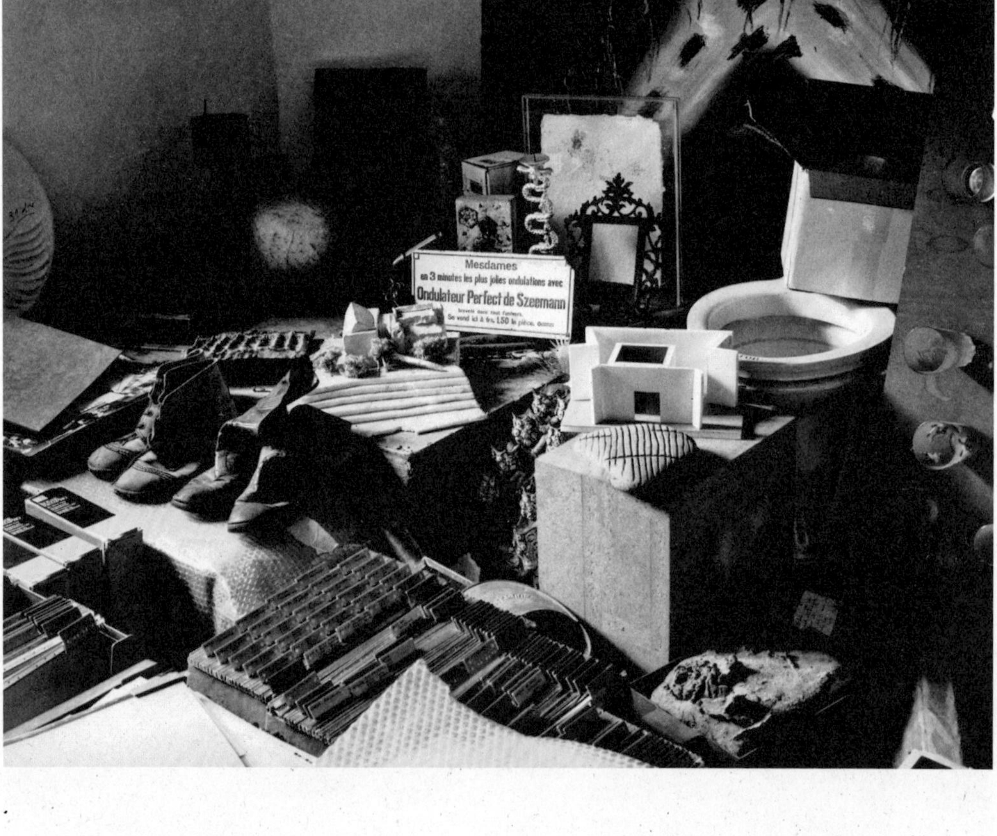
Mesdames
en 3 minutes les plus jolies ondulations avec
Ondulateur Perfect de Szeemann

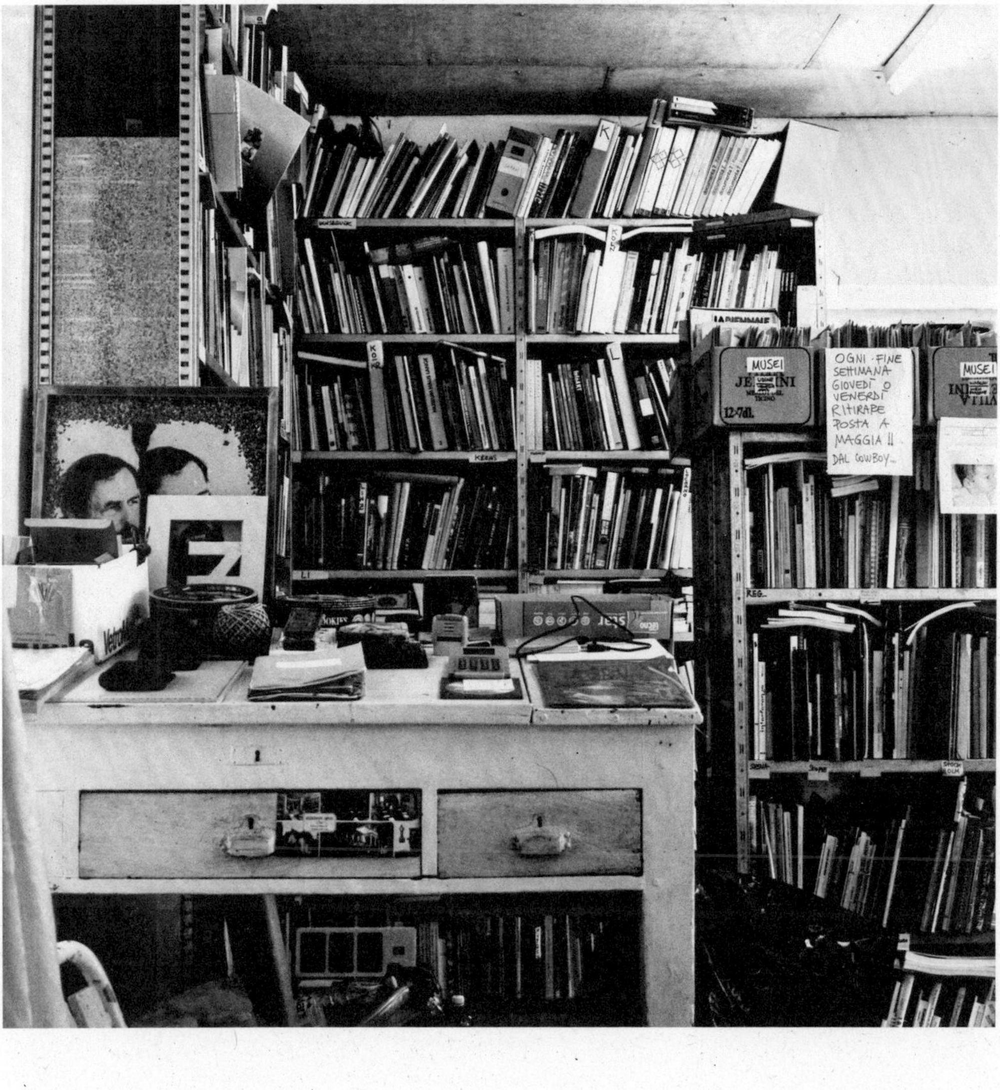
MUSEI
OGNI FINE
SETTIMANA
GIOVEDÌ O
VENERDÌ
RITIRARE
POSTA A
MAGGIA !!
DAL COWBOY...
MUSEI

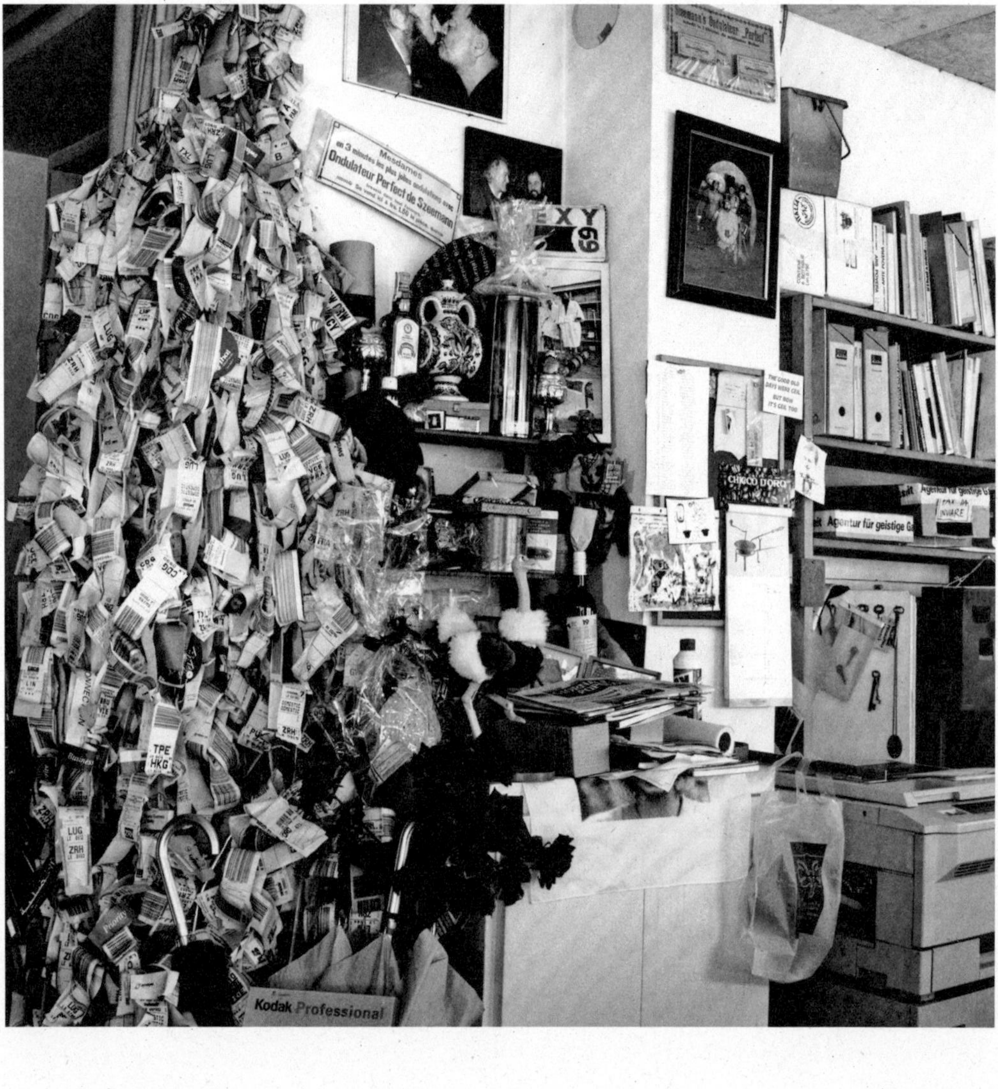
Mesdames
Ondulateur Perfect de Szeemann
Agentur für geistige
Kodak Professional

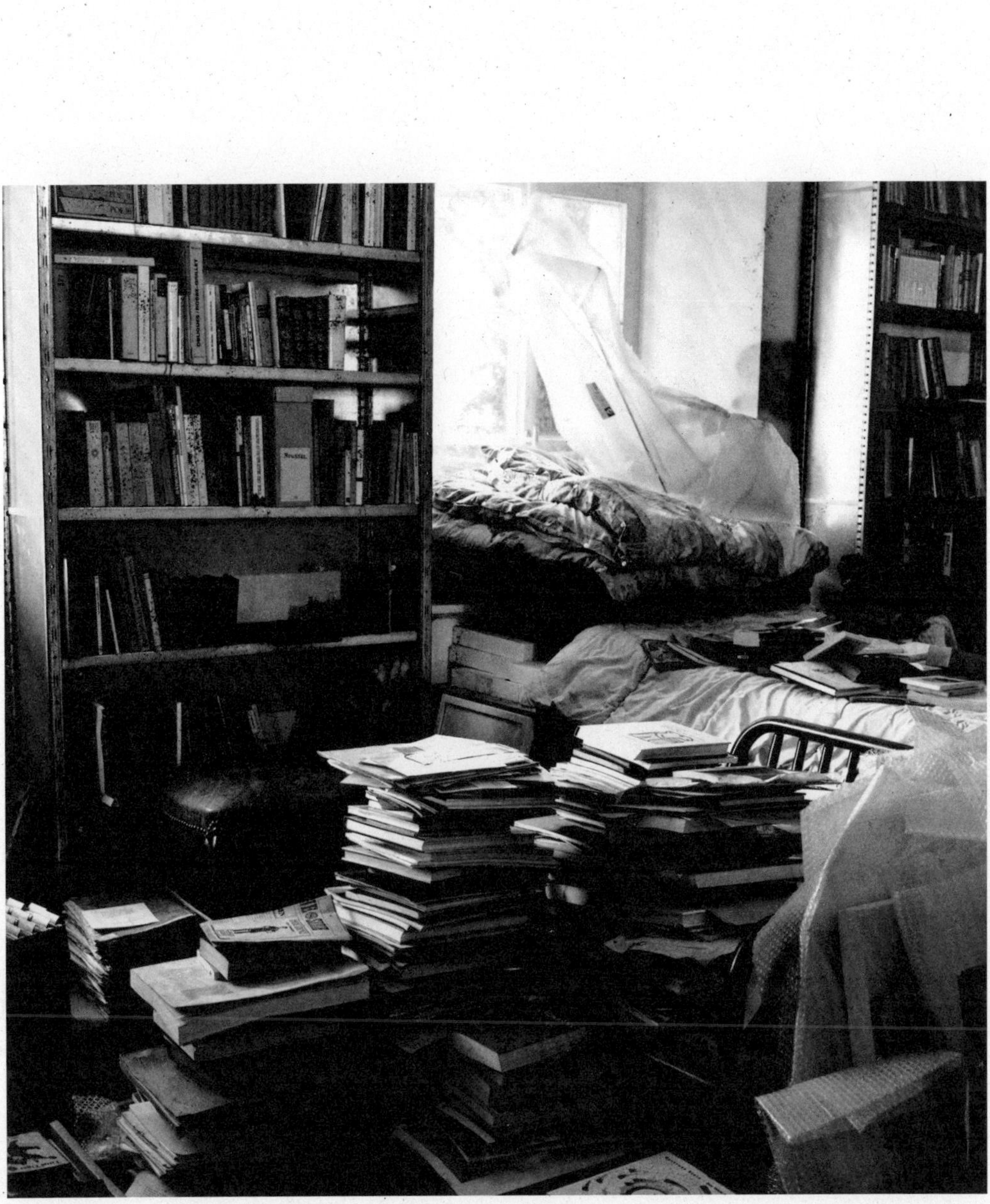

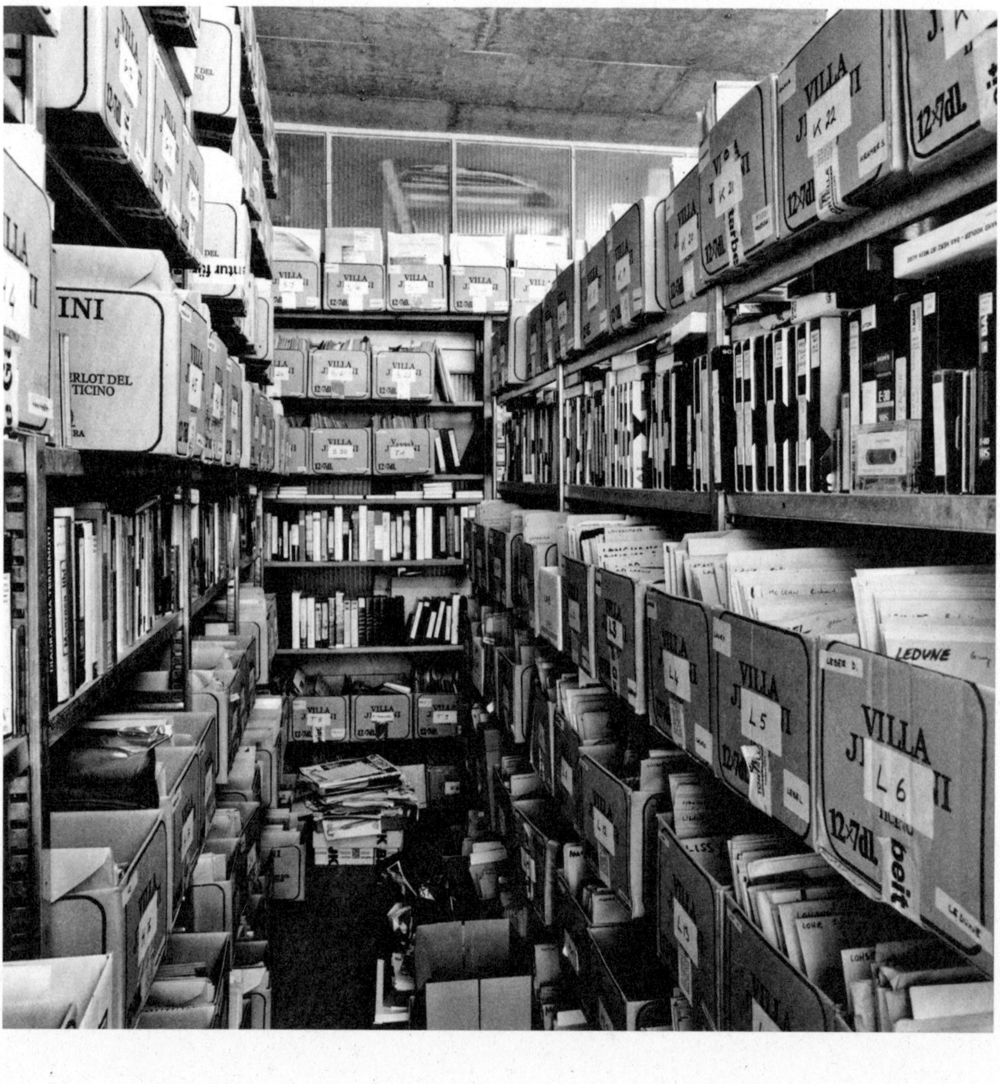
VILLA
INI
ERLOT DEL
TICINO
12×7dl.
K 22
L 4
L 5
L 6
LEDUNE
beit

Part II:
Concepts—Processes

1) *Harald Szeemann's Archive*

The Archive
François Aubart and Sadie Woods

Harald Szeemann's statement that his archive created itself seems obvious, given that it resulted from the simple fact of conserving documents.[1] It is therefore impossible to put a date on its existence. However there is an event in Szeemann's professional life that tells us a great deal about its importance to him. In 1969, after the furor over *When Attitudes Become Form* (1969), he was forced to resign as director of the Kunsthalle Bern. This prompted him to invent a new activity: that of independent curator. Having been forced to step down by the committee and public authorities, Szeemann would subsequently always be wary of institutions. Criticizing the bureaucratic, rigid, and consensual tendencies of such structures, he proposed instead a new way of doing things based on a subjective, autonomous vision, which allowed more freedom than the administrative strait-jacket of institutions. But he also kept what constitutes the core of his organization: the archive that he built up at the Kunsthalle over eight years. Most of it he now took with him. He took the documentation on exhibitions and the works, and the correspondence with the artists. These were added to the other documents he kept in his apartment on Münstergasse, Bern, where he lived from 1962 to 1971.[2]

Subsequently he lived at Gerechtichkeitgasse 23, where he organized the exhibition *Grandfather: A Pioneer Like Us* (1974) just before he moved. In 1973, Balthasar Burkhard, who had decided to live in the United States, sold him all the photographs he had taken at the Kunsthalle exhibitions. Szeemann's new flat was at Gurtengasse 4. It housed a collection of documentation that is recorded in a series of photographs that are surprising both for their subject matter and their static, staged quality [pages 43, 44, 45].

In 1972 Szeemann met Ingeborg Lüscher at *documenta 5*, and began spending more and more time with her at her home in Tegna, in the Ticino. He began keeping some of his documents there and when, in the mid-1980s, they decided to live together in Tegna, the couple asked Ingeborg's friend, architect Christoph Zürcher, to design and build a new house for them there. In addition to the usual rooms, this would also need to house Szeemann's archive, which, at the time, was scattered between Bern, where he still had a flat, his flat at Spitalackerstrasse 64 in Zurich, where he was working, and the Ticino. Disconcerted by the management of such a mass of documents, the only conservation system Zürcher could come up with was one based on a system of drawers. Szeemann rejected this, saying that he needed to be able to walk through his archive and absolutely had to have his documentation visible and within reach. Eventually, the architect heard of an old factory that was for sale in the neighboring village of Maggia. This offered an ideal solution: Ingeborg's studio would be in the basement, while the two floors above would house Szeemann's archive. From 1986, Szeemann would store an impressive number of documents in this building of some 300 square meters.

This mass of documents was the starting point of and a major resource for our research. As we see it, Szeemann's archive is a result; it is the culmination of a process of accumulation and organization set up several decades earlier. It is also a finalization, for that process has come to an end. To understand the workings and necessity of this archive, we therefore consider it necessary to go back to the late 1960s, when the process was set in motion.

At the time when Szeemann started his activity, documentation on modern and contemporary art was rare and inaccessible. The network of exhibition spaces for contemporary art was in its infancy, in Switzerland and elsewhere in Europe. All information was therefore precious and its loss a real risk. Hence the need to compile data. Consequently, this mechanical conservation of all documents would remain the *modus operandi* of the archive even after the creation of many more sources of information. From the 1950s to the 2000s, the number of documents, means of communication, and players in the art world grew exponentially, transforming a discreet milieu into a space saturated with information. But in spite of these changes in the cultural landscape, there was absolutely no change in the organization of the archive. However, its volume and its requirements grew dramatically. The solution chosen to deal with the swelling flow of data was to accelerate the processing rather than to change the system. This shows how important this archive was to Szeemann, not just as an information center, but also as a practice. For while his ambition of attaining exhaustive knowledge had become obsolete, his way of doing things remained unchanged.

Although he himself described it as a "chaos [that] may become a classic," it is likely that his archive was subjected to an extremely rationalized classification process from a very early stage.[3] In the later years of his activity this process took on a truly impressive scale. To make it function required three full-time staff: two archivists and a secretary.[4] Employed and paid by Szeemann himself, they handled correspondence, processed the mail, archived documents, and did the accounts, which the curator no longer had time to do himself. At the time he was working simultaneously on several major exhibitions. When one was opening, another was in the production process, and the one after was in conception. This frantic activity, the gigantism of what was supposed only to be a private documentary collection, and the human organization that it required, inspire a mechanical vision, conjuring up images of an exhibition factory at work in this pink building that its users nicknamed the "Fabbrica rosa," and whose original function had been replaced by that of housing the documentation and providing the exhibition maker with a work space.

The comparison does not stop with the building. The specificity of their contents also makes Szeemann's archive a tool that was specific to his activity. As an intellectual worker, he kept theoretical works, but also the administrative documentation needed to anchor his practice in a particular economic and organizational fabric. This heterogeneity of origin reflects the specificity of his activity and made his archive a place suited to the conception and production of exhibitions. The same systematic approach was adopted with working documents, right from the beginning of his career. The fact that when Szeemann left the Kunsthalle Bern he took with him documents that were supposed to stay there, can be seen as an attempt to scuttle the ship that had cast him away. Above all, however, it reflects Szeemann's need to reproduce the organization he had invented in the public domain on a private scale, in his new, emerging function. This began, logically enough, with the archive.

According to Jacques Derrida, the archive is the place of beginning—where things begin—and of command—where the social order is asserted. [5] As the place where official documents are deposited, the person who controls it controls the power of interpretation. By appropriating this power, which is supposed to remain in the public domain, Szeemann was reproducing the functioning of an administration in his set-up as an independent curator. He thus meant to keep total, absolute control over what he initiated. The principle governing this initiative never varied. During the Bern phase, too, the archive simply grew; its form of existence was never questioned. The principle of appropriating the necessary administrative documents was always respected, whatever the circumstances or partners. Even when working at the Kunsthaus Zürich, Szeemann made sure to obtain copies of almost all documents, which duly filled the Fabbrica. Institutional records were paralleled by a personal trace: the impersonal, mechanized archiving of the institution indeed became the writing of a personal narrative. But whereas an administration would discard certain information, either accidentally or because it was obsolete, Szeemann's archive was designed to conserve absolutely all the documents that entered it.

It was probably as much the place itself as this systematization that was the subject of the photographs taken in the Gurtengasse flat in the 1970s. Devoid of all human presence, these images presented the autonomous archive as a sanctuary-like place that commanded a contemplative attitude. The fact that it was recorded in this way suggests that even then the archive was conceived as an object of fascination. This relation to systems of classification is in some sense reminiscent of theaters of memory, a model that inspired Szeemann in his theorization of his practice as an exhibition maker. According to his description, "externally, [the Museum of Obsessions] resembles the Theater of Memory by the Venetian Giulio Camillo (1480–1544), a complex use of a system of memory." [6] The art of memory is a mnemonic procedure that originated in Antiquity and was used as a way of memorizing speeches. [7] The idea was to construct a mental architecture in which each space is filled by a symbolic object. When the orator needed to recall his words, he imagined himself walking through this structure, following the thread of his argument. Under the influence of hermetic thought, this principle of the spatial arrangement of symbols became a mystical formula providing access to the hidden possibilities of knowledge and to boundless knowledge about the world of meanings. Thus, Giulio Camillo built a mobile structure whose component elements, and therefore all things, could be combined and recombined at will.

This mixing of signs and symbols, allowing obscure systems to open onto new interpretations, was reused by Szeemann to imagine sequences of works. It would seem highly plausible that the same logic based on classification and connection should inform the archive, and this provides a way of thinking about the multiplication of organizational systems that it contains. Szeemann himself stressed his concern to combine different types of classification in the interview he gave about the archive. [8] Furthermore, Balthasar Burkhard recalls that Szeemann had a keen interest in the art of memory and claimed that it was possible to invent systems that would enable the user to remember a vast number of things. [9] However, since Szeemann never theorized his practice of the archive, it would be pointless to assert that his archive obeyed some signifying system. That said, at least one element from the techniques of memory was used there, namely, a surprising and fascinating visual appearance. This characteristic is prominent in Yates' account of the art of memory, and also in the description given by Patricia Falguières of the *Wunderkammer*, another place founded on systems of classification and knowledge. [10] Falguières points out that while the *Wunderkammer* was conceived essentially for the benefit of its owner, who was placed at its center and thus had an all-embracing vision, these chambers did also have a public function. As the private property of their user, they were nevertheless tools of representation. [11]

Now, Tobia Bezzola tells us that while only a few people were allowed to use his archive, Szeemann did enjoy showing people round his Fabbrica.[12] As Gianna Ruepp confirms, "People liked that. He was a fascinating talker who did it as if the Fabbrica was not his own."[13] This suggests that Szeemann's archive was more than just an intellectual and practical tool. And its use as a place of representation also sheds light on those spaces where he piled up personal objects, knickknacks, and works of art. As an organizer of exhibitions working on an independent basis, he said, "I naturally need a presentation area for my clients. It is important for me to see how they react because it's laid out rather by chance. For example, there are several periods and origins here, objects put together by chance, without any aesthetic intention. You can see my grandfather's world with the *Perfect Ondulator*, an Anarchist flag, a votive image, a pennant from James Lee Byars that he brought along one day when I met him at the station ('Harry, Harry, Hurry, Hurry'), and then a few gifts from artists such as a canvas by Immendorff, a walking stick from Virnich, a maquette of our house in Tegna, a work by Dieter Roth, a composition by Arman, a sculpture from Mexico City, a sculpture by Ingeborg [Lüscher], an elephant's tooth."[14]

Seen as a tool of representation, what this archive conserves then turns out to be its actual owner.[15] For it contains, in extremely rigorous form, all Szeemann's correspondence, all the documents he needed and all documents relating to him in one way or another. This "self-archive" leaves almost no area of his life in the dark. The limitless capitalization constructs its own history and, in its frenzy, seems to leave no room for secrecy. What we find here is as much history as consciousness of history itself. It is impossible not to assume that this traceability was deliberately planned. And planned, moreover, by a man of the theater who had always constructed and mythicized his own career and was aware from a very early age of the historic role he was about to play.[16] This mechanization of the conservation of documents, which allows a global understanding of Szeemann's activities does, however, leave its own area of the unknown, of the "unarchiveable." And, for all its apparent objectivity, the history that it allows us to construct may only be the rough draft of a pre-written autobiography.

[1] Cf. Karin Prätorius, "Interview with Harald Szeemann," p. 45.

[2] Between these two dates, Szeemann occupied two flats in this street, first at n° 16, then at n° 48.

[3] Cf. Prätorius, "Interview with Harald Szeemann," p. 45.

[4] Those who knew him said Szeemann preferred to work alone, but as of 1991 he was forced to employ (a) part-time assistant(s). There was a succession of people working for varying durations up to 1998, which is when he recruited Juliette Duca and Ivana Falconi. In 2002, Gianna Ruepp was taken on as his secretary and accountant.

[5] Jacques Derrida, *Archive Fever: A Freudian Impression*, University of Chicago Press, Chicago/London 1995.

[6] Harald Szeemann, "Le Musée des obsessions, propositions pour une *documenta* future," *Ecrire les exhibitions*, La Lettre volée, Brussels 1996, p. 68.

[7] For a history of this practice, see Frances A. Yates, *The Art of Memory*, Routledge and Kegan Paul, London 1966.

[8] Cf. Prätorius, "Interview with Harald Szeemann," p. 45–46.

[9] Telephone interview with Balthasar Burkhard, June 4, 2007.

[10] Patricia Falguières, *Les chambres des merveilles*, Bayard, Paris 2003.

[11] "Collections have a public status because they manifest the prince's public virtue, because they are an element, an emanation of his magnificence, that is to say, of his capacity to ensure a representation." Ibid., p. 93.

[12] Cf. François Aubart, "Interview with Tobia Bezzola," p. 62.

[13] Interview with Gianna Ruepp, Locarno, April 12, 2007.

[14] Hans-Joachim Müller, Gaudenz Meili, *Verzauberung Auf Zeit, Harald Szeemann*, 76 min., color, sound, 1992.

[15] Szeemann's archive was in this respect closely linked to his Agency. Both were practical tools that ultimately became means of representation for their inventor.

[16] Note that in 1969 Szeemann published a text in the *Berner Tagblatt* talking about *When Attitudes Become Form* as an event in the past. In it, he passed himself off as the director of the Kunsthalle speaking one or two decades after the exhibition, which he described as a seminal event. See Harald Szeemann, "When Attitudes Become Form (Quand les attitudes deviennent forme), Bern 1969," Bernd Klüser, Katharina Hegewisch (eds.), *L'art de l'exposition. Une documentation sur trente expositions exemplaires du XXème siècle*, Editions du Regard, Paris 1998, p. 376.

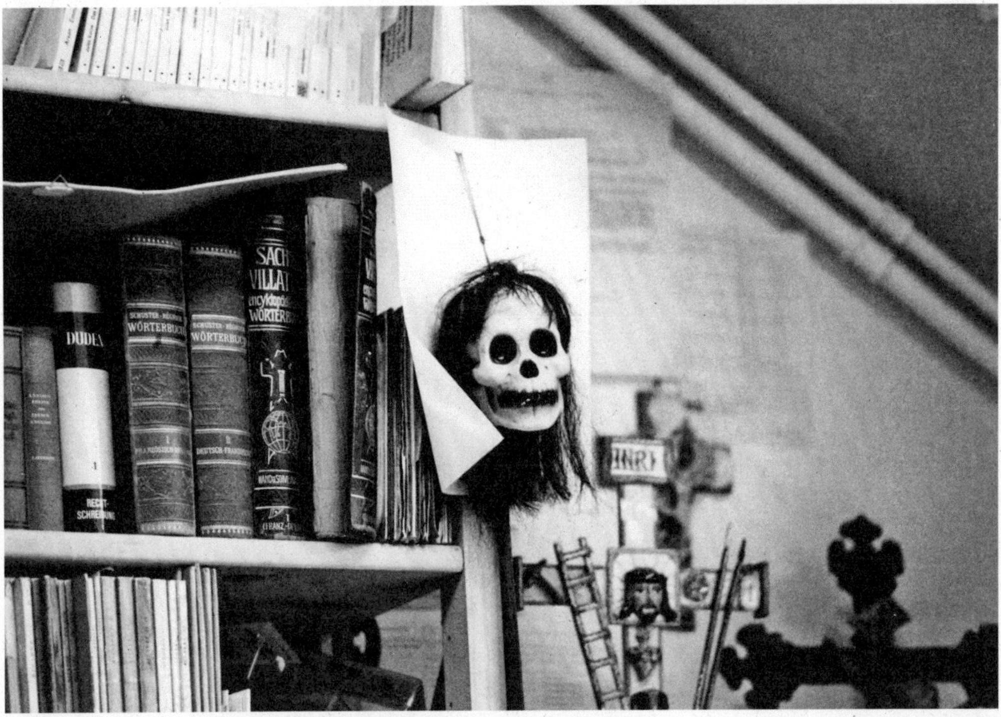

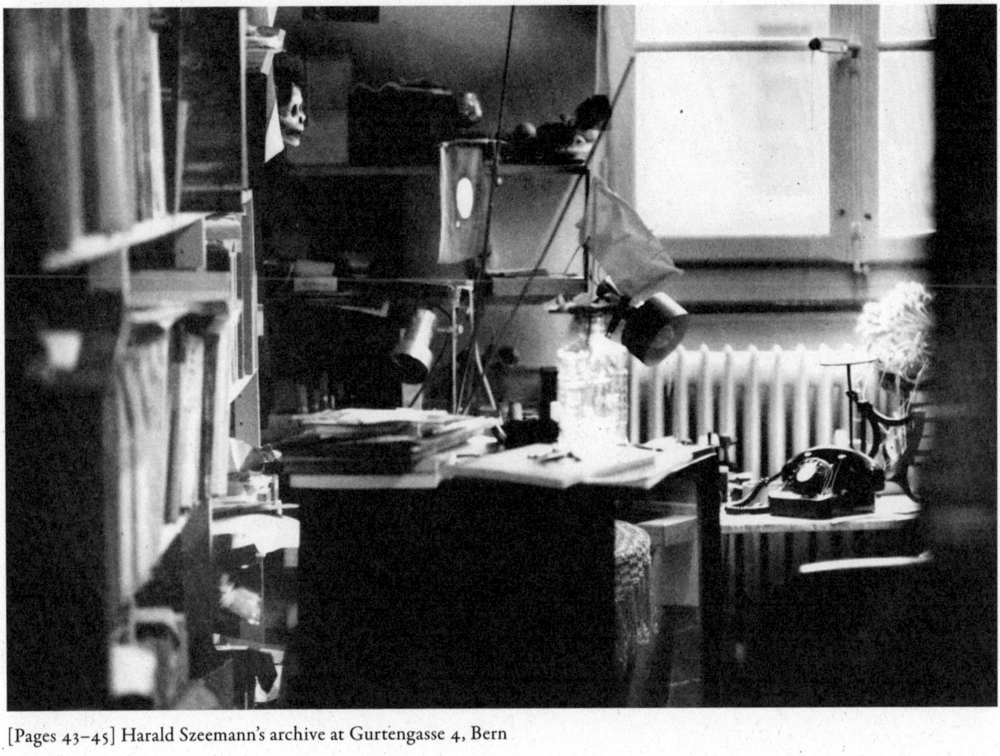

[Pages 43–45] Harald Szeemann's archive at Gurtengasse 4, Bern

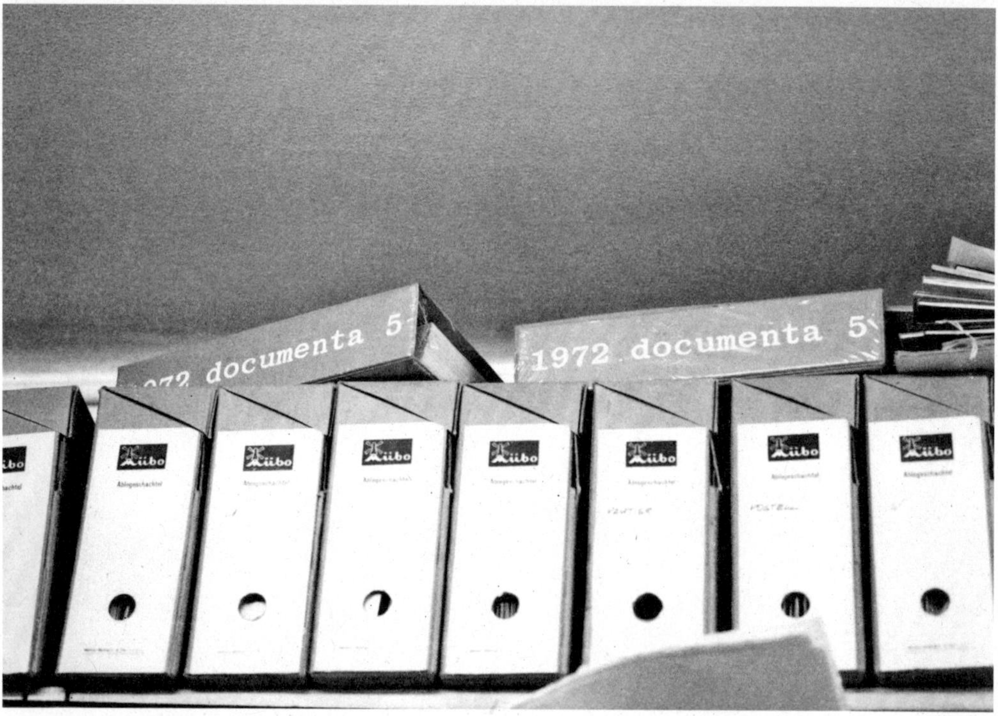
documenta 5
1972 documenta 5

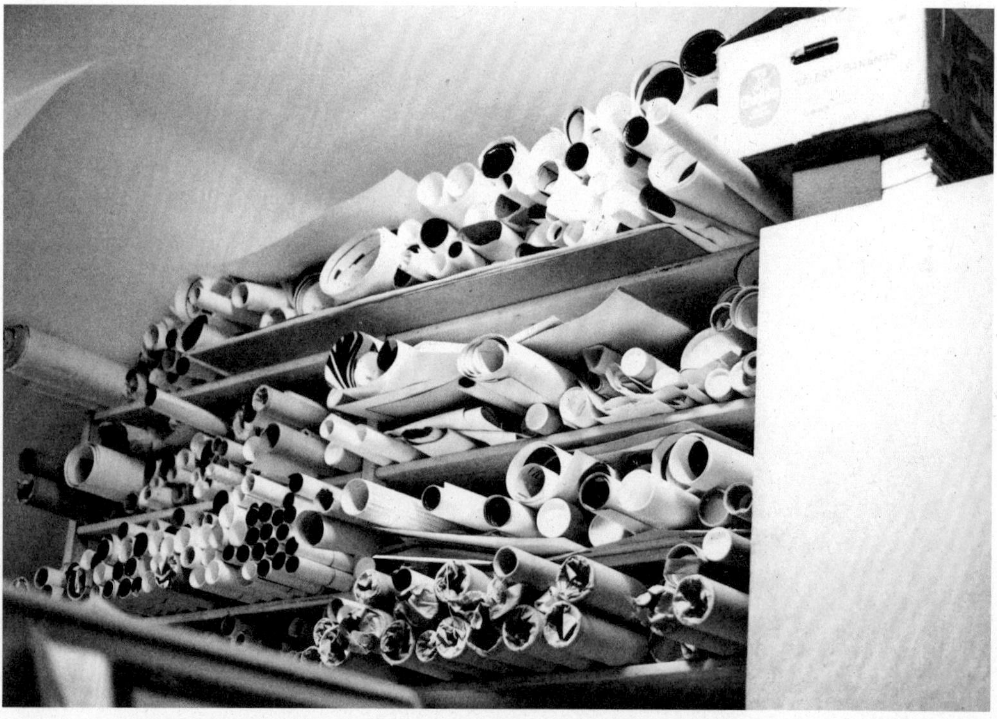

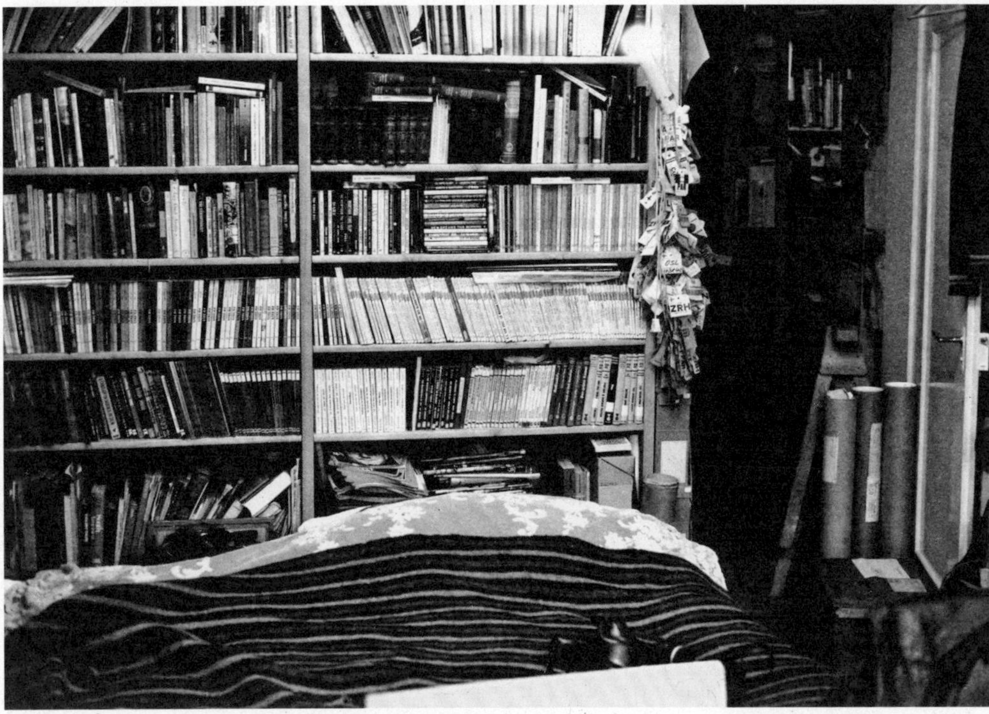

Interview with Harald Szeemann

Karin Prätorius

This interview was first published in Beatrice von Bismarck et al. (eds.), *Interarchive*, Verlag der Buchhandlung Walter König, Cologne 2002, p. 338. It is reprinted here with the generous permission of the author and the publisher.

KARIN PRÄTORIUS

If you compare your own archive to a "conventional" one, in what ways is it different?

HARALD SZEEMANN

Perhaps my chaos will also become classic.

KARIN PRÄTORIUS

What is your archive about? How did you get started?

HARALD SZEEMANN

It created itself.

KARIN PRÄTORIUS

What do you use your archive for and how?

HARALD SZEEMANN

As a diviner, and for exhibitions.

KARIN PRÄTORIUS

Do others know about your archive? If others can use your archive, how and for what purpose do they use it?

HARALD SZEEMANN

Those who are interested in what I do, and when things are difficult to find elsewhere.

KARIN PRÄTORIUS

Since when does your archive exist? Would you think of it as completed?

HARALD SZEEMANN

No date of origin. Till death do us part.

KARIN PRÄTORIUS

How do you decide what is going to be archived? What are the criteria for archiving something?

HARALD SZEEMANN

Whims and moods.

KARIN PRÄTORIUS

How do you deal with the different aspects of (dis)order? If you had the possibility of completely reorganizing your archive, what would you do?

HARALD SZEEMANN

No time for that.

KARIN PRÄTORIUS

Do you regard your archival practice as an act of self-archiving?

HARALD SZEEMANN

Why not?

KARIN PRÄTORIUS

What can archives achieve ideally?

HARALD SZEEMANN

To suggest or to trigger memory.

KARIN PRÄTORIUS

Of what importance (if at all) is the internet to your archive?

HARALD SZEEMANN

Acquiring information.

KARIN PRÄTORIUS

Would you perhaps ask completely different questions?

HARALD SZEEMANN

The rhizome question!

My archive jumps from abandoned libraries, to certain exhibitions (tending toward entire collections, Monte Verità, Art Brut), to the documentation of my own work (ordered by special aspects because of the increasing number of people interested in it or writing dissertations), to media reference libraries (film, theater, dance, literature, outside of Europe), to ordered convulsions (artists alphabetically, museum collections, and thematic group exhibitions ordered alphabetically by location, ditto for gallery exhibitions with several artists), to movements and "styles" if there is no other possibility (alphabetically), to authors and agents (alphabetically), and correspondence with them (alphabetically), to dictionaries and encyclopedias and magazines, to compulsions forming around the themes of "Pavilion of Sexuality," "Money and Anger," "La Mamma," and "Visionary Belgium," and of course to the next Biennale. Unbound, everything in Merlot cases, the more I drink, the more I organize. When I diet, my organizing slows down.

Description: How Does the Archive Function?

François Aubart and Sadie Woods

Equipment

Harald Szeemann's archive uses eight rooms in the factory in which it is housed. For the sake of clarity, we have given them names that, unless otherwise indicated, we chose ourselves.

In the *Office* is a computer, and documentation on exhibition venues.

The *Work in Progress Room* was the name used by Harald Szeemann for the space where most activity took place. It contains mainly letters and invitations. It also houses a collection of videos, a television, and a worktable over six meters long.

The *Monograph Room* is where books on artists are kept.

The *Groundwork Room* contains catalogues of collections and documentation about Monte Verità.

Art magazines are kept in the *Magazine Room*.

The *Ritter Saal* (Knight's Room) was thus named by Szeemann because of its exposed beams, which give it a medieval feel. It contains theoretical works, photographic archives, and shelves exclusively for documentation on Joseph Beuys and Marcel Duchamp. Szeemann called these accumulations the "Beuys Island" and the "Duchamp Island."

Upstairs are the *Literature Room* and the *Fax Room*. The first contains works of literature. The second has mainly documents about Szeemann's projects and, of course, the eponymous faxes.

According to accounts we have heard, when he moved to Maggia Szeemann did not anticipate the increase in the number of documents. We will describe the archive as we found it, assuming that its principle remained unchanged. The only thing that changed was the quantity.

This archive contains a variety of documents classified in different ways. It seems that, at one time or another, all these documents played a role in preparing, producing, or documenting an exhibition. Here we will describe the different kinds of documents and their classification, in accordance with how they were needed for making an exhibition. The theoretical documentation and the information about the artists are the first necessities; they are the basic materials. We find the theoretical works organized in accordance with several different themes, mainly in the *Knight's Room*, and also in the *Work in Progress Room*. Forming ensembles that reveal Szeemann's main interests, they serve as the base for the gestating intentions behind his exhibitions. It is tempting to include among these the literary works found in the *Literature Room*, the art journals kept in the *Magazine Room* and the collections of magazines such as *Der Spiegel, Paris Match*, and *Playboy*. [1]

Finally, Harald Szeemann invented a last classification of theoretical elements: these are collections of press clippings. As Juliette Duca explained to us: "He told us about the article that interested him and we cut it out and filed it away. We put it in an envelope on which the name of the article was written. The envelopes were stored alphabetically in different boxes, depending on whether the subject was an event, an individual, or a city." [2] These boxes are in the *Fax Room*.

In addition to this theoretical documentation there is the material about the artists. This is found mainly in the *Monograph Room*, where the books are kept in alphabetical order. Tobia Bezzola points out that when the bulk of the documents about a given artist became too big they were moved to individual shelves. [3] This was the origin of the "Beuys Island" and the "Duchamp Island" in the *Knight's Room*.

In addition to these ensembles of monographs, the invitations, press releases, and correspondence by mail, fax, and email were filed away alphabetically in boxes from bottles of Villa Jelmini, Szeemann's favorite wine. These boxes are found mainly in the *Work in Progress Room*. In order to organize the archiving of these documents, a precise system was set up to regulate the circulation of mail. This arrived at Szeemann's personal address in Tegna, and from there he or an assistant took it to Maggia. First of all it was displayed in so-called "pre-selection" boxes that allowed rapid consultation of the newly arrived correspondence. The person in charge of the mail kept an up-to-date list of the incoming mail. Szeemann read this list and decided what to do with the mail. Once read and processed, these documents were stored in accordance with their subject. Juliette Duca: "Invitations for exhibitions by an artist were filed in the folder on the artist in question. The ones for group shows were filed in the *Office*, alphabetically, by the town in which the exhibition took place." [4] All communications were archived using the same procedure. Faxes printed on carbon paper, and by nature erasable, were photocopied, and emails were printed out. There are thus boxes in alphabetical order dedicated to correspondents who are not artists.

It is worth noting an aspect of the procedure regarding emails, which, while it may not tell us anything about the processing of information, does tell us a great deal about the mechanical, ordered character of the work that was done. Szeemann wrote by hand, not on a keyboard. Thus, when he was traveling and an email arrived, it was printed out and faxed to his hotel. Having read it, Szeemann replied by hand and faxed the answer to his assistant, who transcribed the contents into an email to his correspondent. Gianna Ruepp adds that the same principle was applied when he was at Maggia: "He wrote everything out by hand: texts, letters, requests for loans, etc. But since it had to circulate by Internet, he gave it to me to type out." [5]

Processing

All the documentation described here was accessible and could be used to prepare an exhibition. To this end, it was consulted and assembled on the big table in the *Work in Progress Room*. Juliette Duca points out that "the size of this table made it possible to have three different work points; he simply had to change places in order to work on a different project." [6] On this table, then, he piled up all the necessary documentation. The administrative documents and written exchanges were stored there in hanging compartments containing folders. The good thing about these was that they were easy to transport. Serving as a mobile desk, these folders containing useful, already sorted documentation could be easily transported when traveling to the venue hosting the exhibition. Josy Kraft recalls: "We worked with a folder that traveled with exhibition. Thus, all the members of the team had access to the same information." [7]

Christoph Zürcher rounds out this information by indicating that, "during the exhibition, all the documents were assembled in the folder. After the montage, everything was put back in place." [8] After use, the documentation returned to its place in the archives. All that was left were the documents relating to the project in question. These were preserved together in archive boxes kept in the *Fax Room*. This room contained all the folders relating to exhibitions, conferences, and texts given by Szeemann, in chronological order. Photographs of the exhibitions were sorted in boxes with hanging files in the *Knight's Room*, by name of artist and by alphabetical order, or in accordance with certain themes. Over time, the archive was completed by two kinds of documents, those required for the elaboration of a project and those that provided a record of it. We can thus take a different approach to Szeemann's statement that the archive created itself. In effect, the documentation assembled in the prospective phase was the point of departure for projects, implying the creation of a certain number of documents that in turn furnished the archive. In sum, documention did indeed create documention and the need for documention.

[1] Since many artists contributed to *Playboy*, this collection was no doubt the starting point for a project that was never carried through.
[2] Interview with Juliette Duca, Maggia, April 13, 2007.
[3] Cf. François Aubart, "Interview with Tobia Bezzola," p. 58.
[4] Interview with Juliette Duca, Locarno, April 12, 2007.
[5] Interview with Gianna Ruepp, Locarno, April 12, 2007.
[6] Interview with Juliette Duca, Locarno, April 12, 2007.
[7] Interview with Josy Kraft, Basel, March 30, 2007.
[8] Interview with Christoph Zürcher, Maggia, April 11, 2007.

Plans

General Plan of the Archive

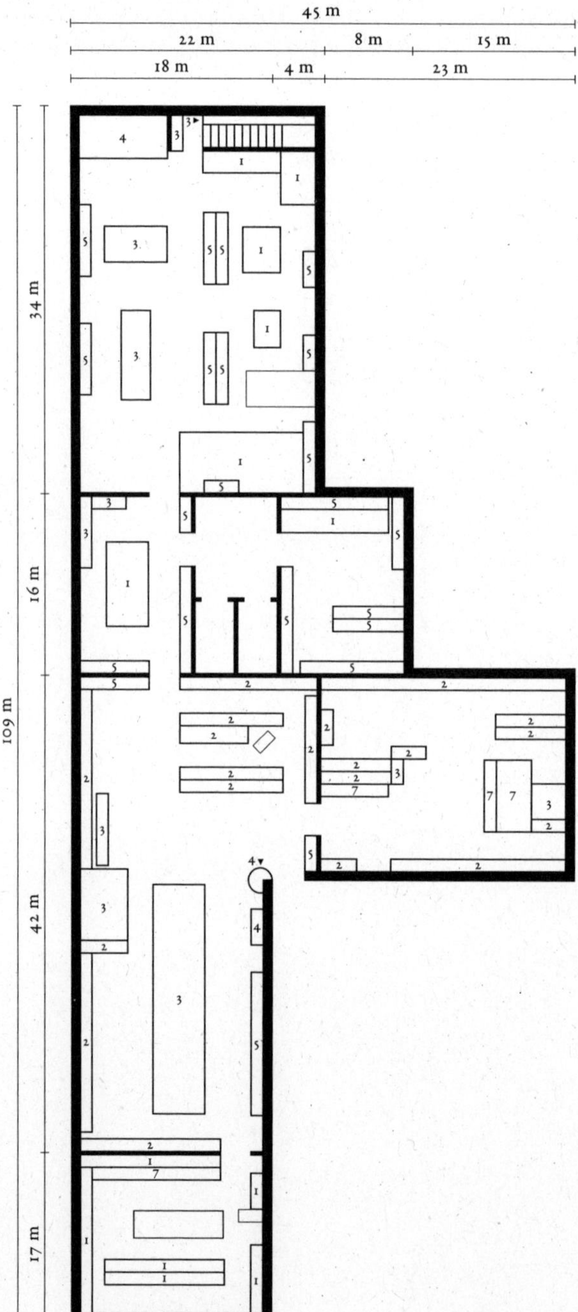

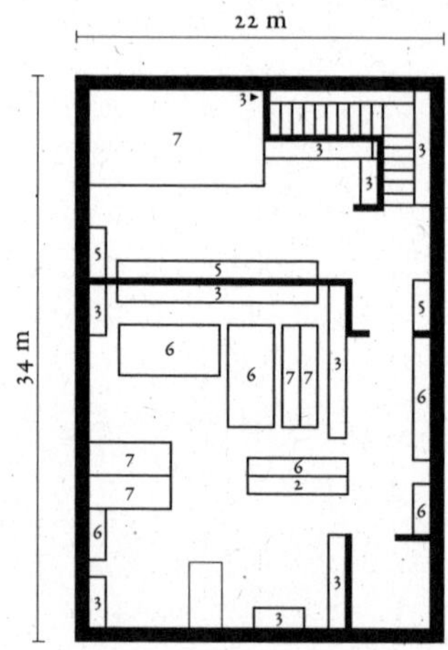

1 – Venues
[galleries, private and public institutions]

2 – Individuals
[artists, critics, curators, museum directors]

3 – Documentation
[in progress and past projects]

4 – Collection
[personal objects]

5 – Books
[dictionaries, encyclopedias, theory]

6 – Press
[clippings, journals, magazines]

7 – Documents to be filed

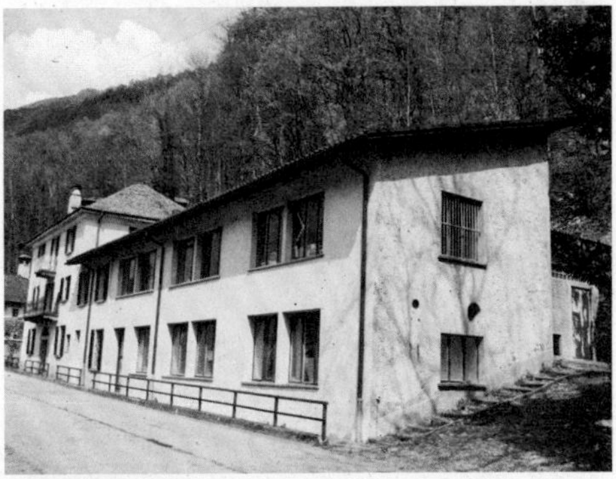

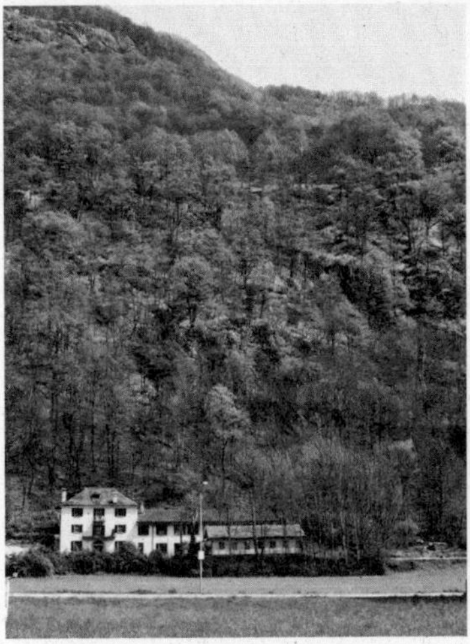

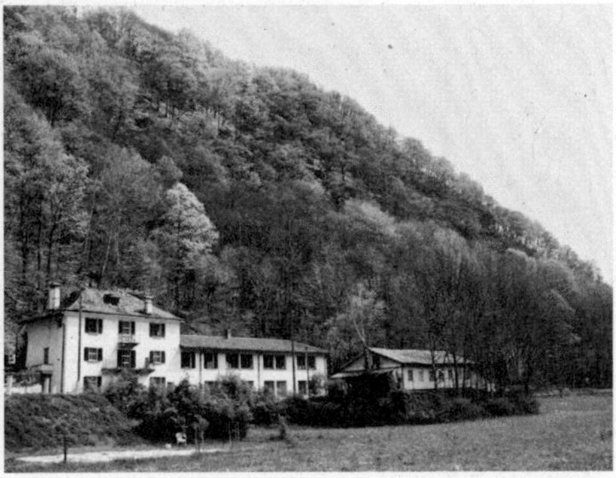

La Fabbrica rosa, Maggia

Office
Work in Progress Room
Monograph Room

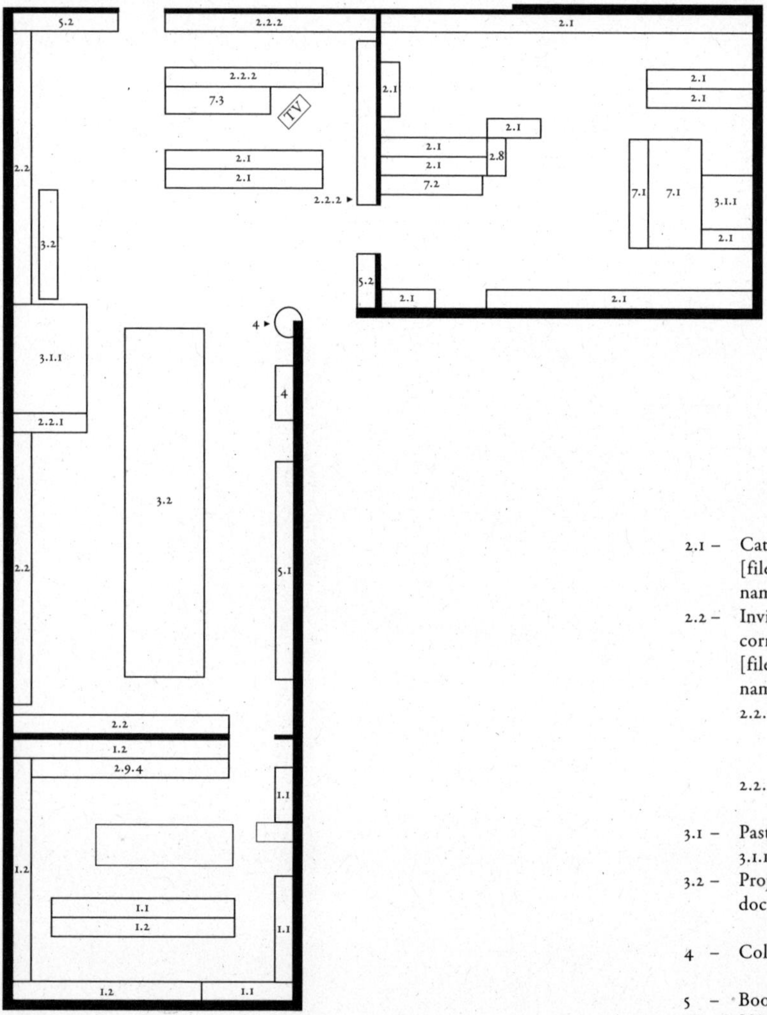

1.1 – Exhibition catalogues [filed in alphabetical order by city]

1.2 – Invitation cards and correspondence [filed in alphabetical order by city]

2.1 – Catalogues and monographs [filed in alphabetical order by name]

2.2 – Invitation cards and correspondence with artists [filed in alphabetical order by name]
- 2.2.1 – Correspondence with critics, curators, and museum directors
- 2.2.2 – Videos

3.1 – Past project documentation
- 3.1.1 – Exhibition posters

3.2 – Projects in progress documentation

4 – Collection of personal objects

5 – Books [filed by theme]
- 5.1 – Art movements: books, and exhibition catalogues
- 5.2 – Dictionaries, directories, encyclopedias, thesauruses

7 – Documents to be filed
- 7.1 – Miscellaneous documents and objects
- 7.2 – Monographs
- 7.3 – Artist's videos
- 7.4 – Mail

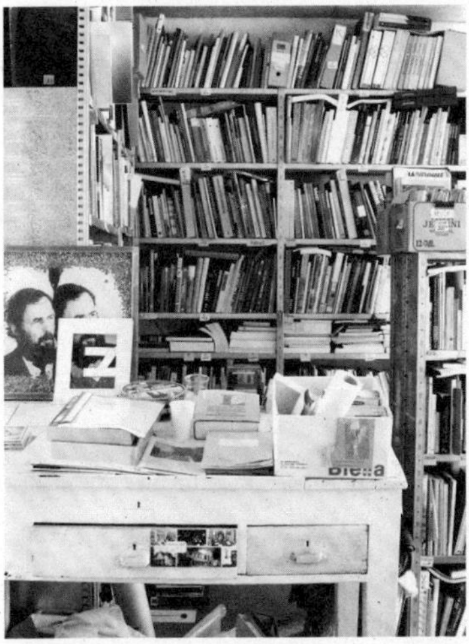

Office

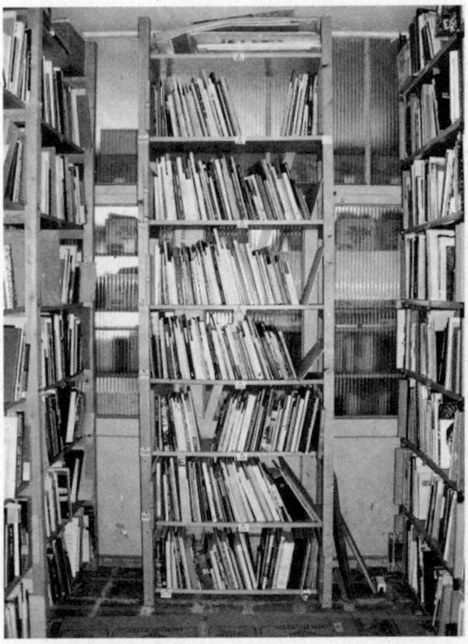

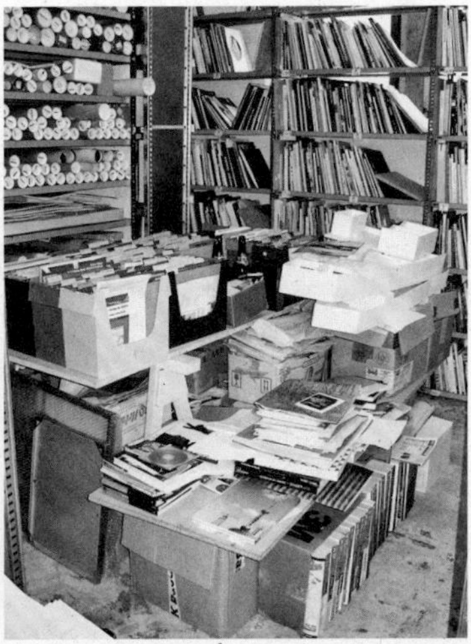

Monograph Room

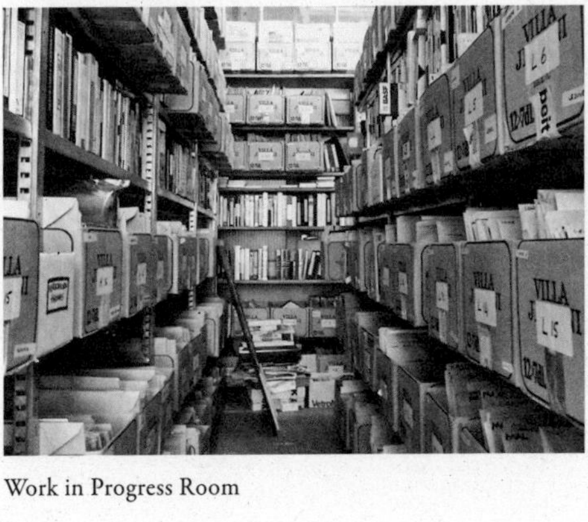

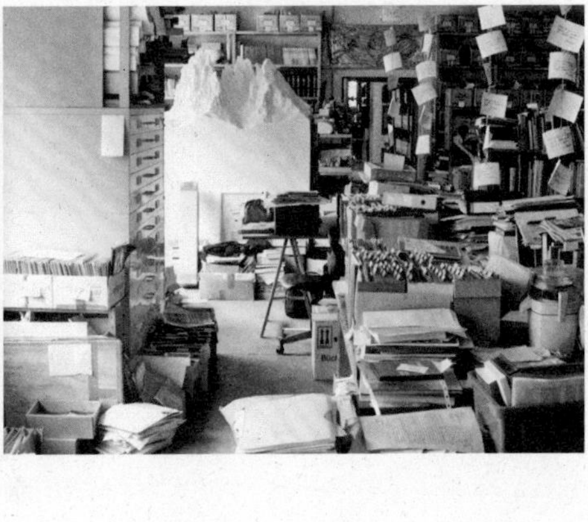

Work in Progress Room

Knight's Room (Ritter Saal*)
Groundwork Room
Magazine Room

Knight's Room

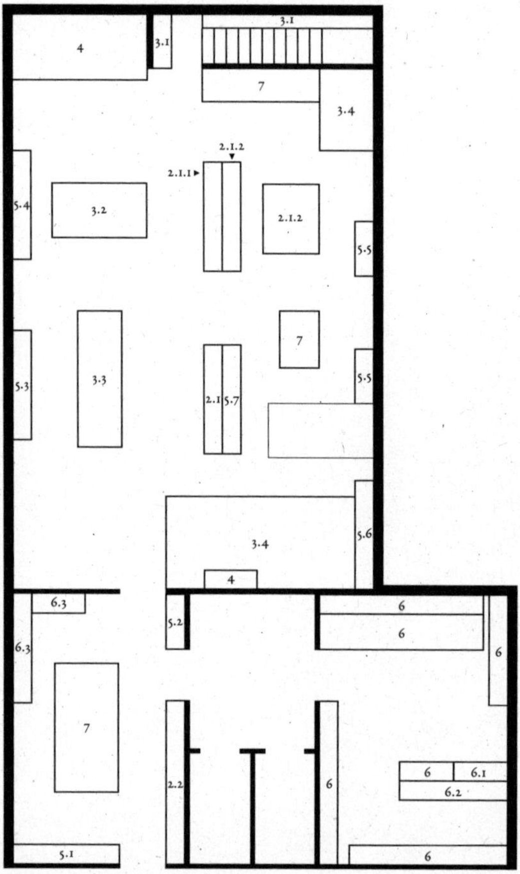

Groundwork Room

Magazine Room

2.1 – Exhibition catalogues and monographs
[filed in alphabetical order by name]
- 2.1.1 – "Duchamp Island"*
- 2.1.2 – "Beuys Island"*

2.2 – Invitation cards and correspondence with artists
[filed in alphabetical order by city]

3 – Past projects documentation
- 3.1 – Exhibition catalogues
- 3.2 – Exhibition photographs
- 3.3 – Photographs of historical figures
- 3.4 – Exhibition posters

4 – Collection of personal objects

5 – Books
[filed by theme]
- 5.1 – Anarchism
- 5.2 – Architecture, "Broodthaers Island,"* catalogues of exhibition collections
  [filed in alphabetical order]
- 5.3 – Anthropology, Philosophy, Psychology, Theosophy
  [filed in alphabetical order by author]
- 5.4 – Cinema, Comics, Photography
  [filed in alphabetical order by author]
- 5.5 – Literature
  [filed in alphabetical order by author]
- 5.6 – Erotism
  [filed in alphabetical order by author]
- 5.7 – Swiss Art
  [filed in alphabetical order by author]

6 – Press: Art Magazines
- 6.1 – *Playboy* magazine collection
- 6.2 – *Paris Match* magazine collection
- 6.3 – Cinema press clippings

7 – Documents to be filed

* Term used by Harald Szeemann

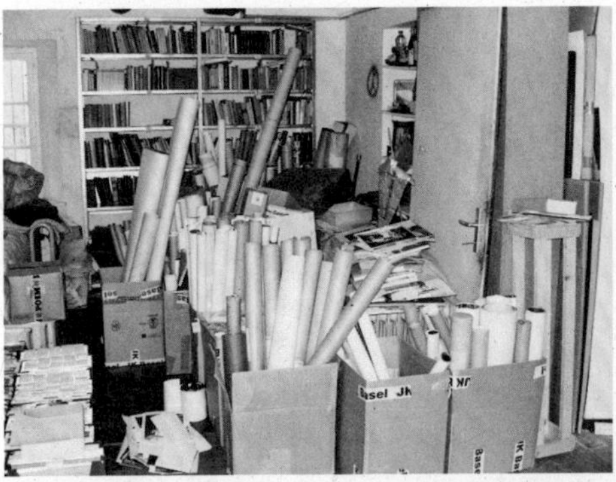

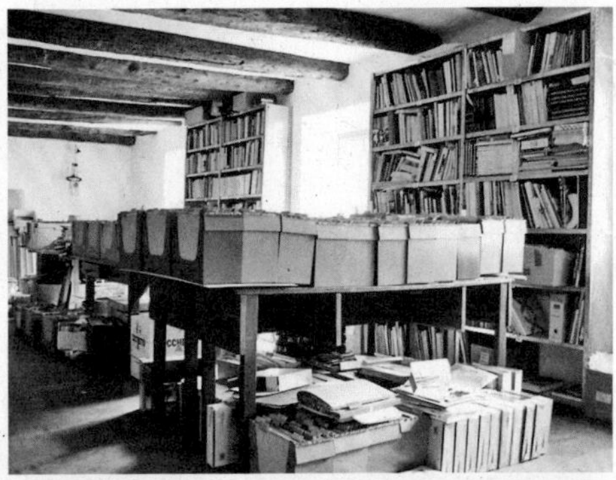

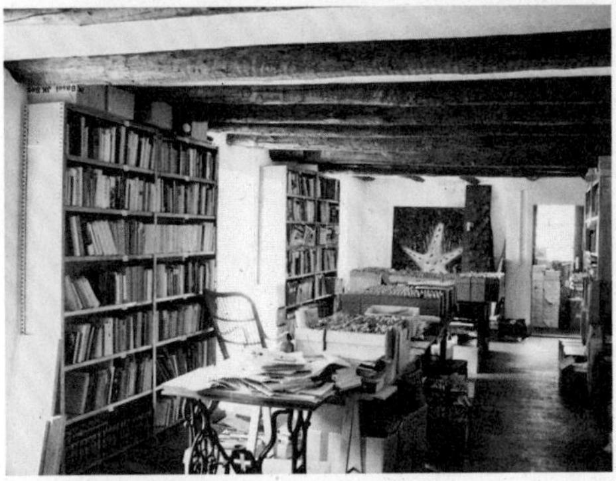

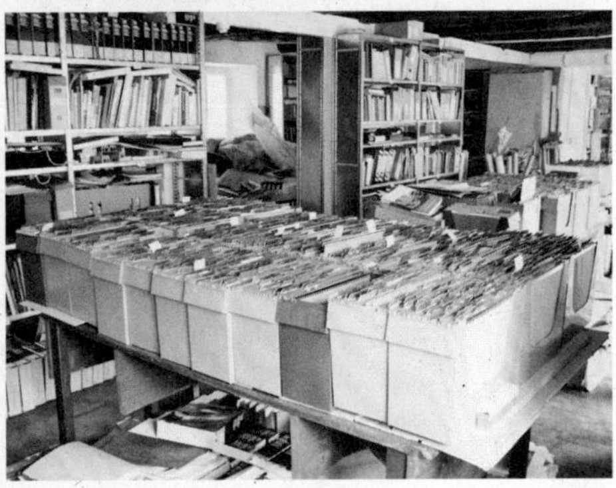

Knight's Room (Ritter Saal*)

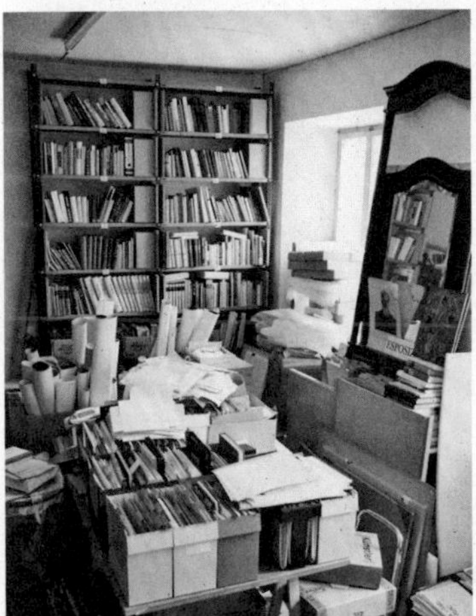

Groundwork Room

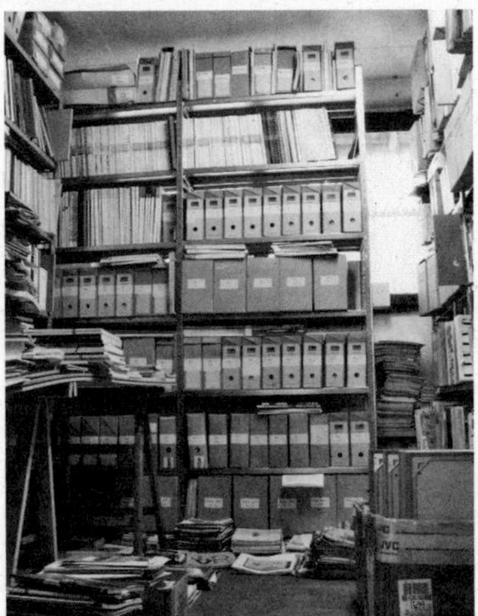

Magazine Room

Staircase
Literature Room
Fax Room

Literature Room Staircase

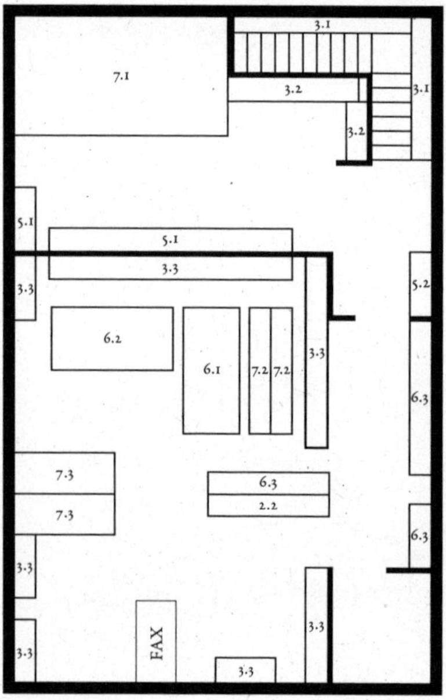

Fax Room

2.2 – Correspondence
[filed in alphabetical order by name]

3 – Past project documentation
- 3.1 – Exhibition catalogues
- 3.2 – Monte Verità documentation [filed in chronological order]
- 3.3 – Administrative paper documentation of projects [filed in chronological order]

5 – Books [filed by theme]
- 5.1 – Literature [filed in alphabetical order by author]
- 5.2 – Traditions [filed in alphabetical order by author]

6 – Press
- 6.1 – Article selections to be clipped
- 6.2 – Press clippings [filed by theme]
- 6.3 – *Der Spiegel* magazine collection [filed in chronological order]
- 6.4 – Ticino press clippings

7 – Documents to be filed
- 7.1 – Miscellaneous objects
- 7.2 – Recent project documentation
- 7.3 – Miscellaneous documents

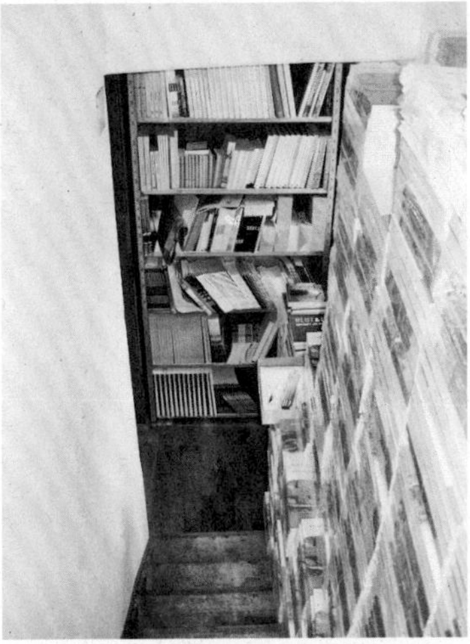

Staircase

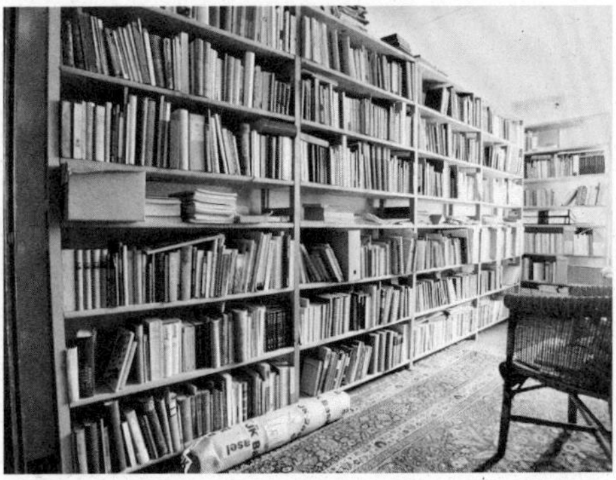

Literature Room

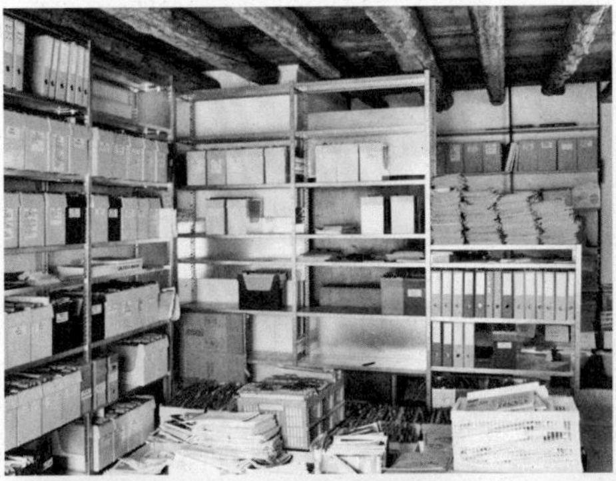

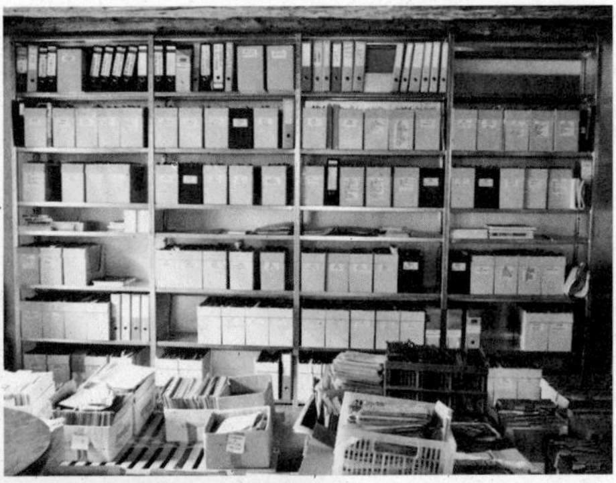

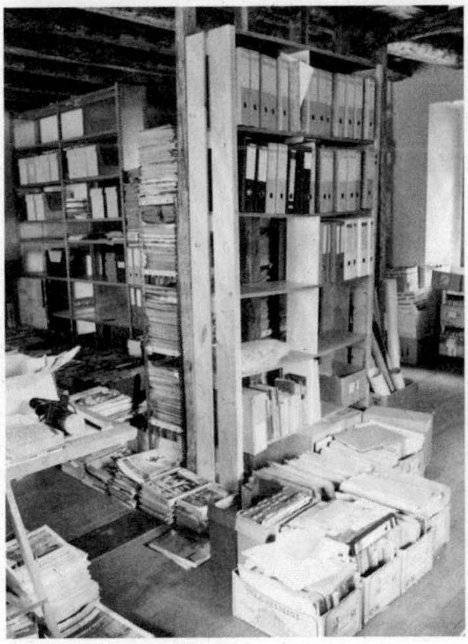

Fax Room

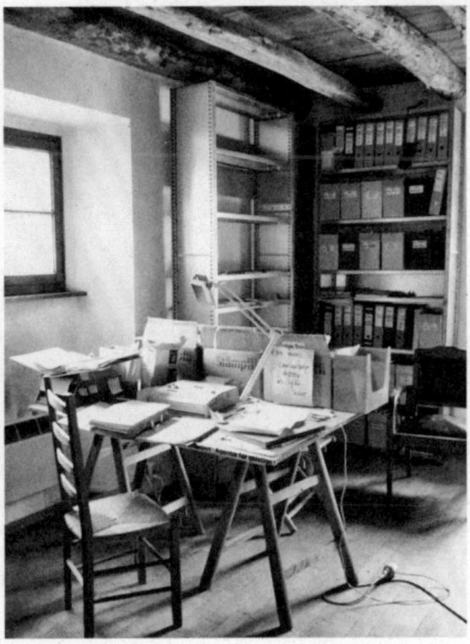

Interview with Tobia Bezzola

François Aubart

Fabbrica rosa, Maggia, April 14, 2007

We begin the interview in the Knight's Room.

FRANÇOIS AUBART

When did you work here in the archive with Harald Szeemann? Which project did you work on?

TOBIA BEZZOLA

I worked mainly on the Joseph Beuys exhibition, especially on the catalogue, bibliography, documentation, and a small glossary produced for the event. All the preparatory work for the exhibition was carried out here.

FRANÇOIS AUBART

Can you describe the successive stages of this work?

TOBIA BEZZOLA

There was of course research on the works, their current location, and at the same time substantial work on preparing Beuys' bibliography, which was the most complete at the time it was compiled. The exhibition was not designed chronologically like a retrospective; in both the exhibition and catalogue, the works were organized thematically, grouped by subject. But we still wanted to offer a chronological approach. The bibliography was conceived as an insert, a small book that included the bibliography itself, a biography, and a chronological list of exhibitions and films. That was the documentary component on Beuys. At the time, I could only find this information here, because it had not been published. Here I found all the invitations to gallery openings—for example, to all the shows at Konrad Fisher Gallery in Düsseldorf. I had to hunt through everything, because these were mostly group shows. This information was only to be found in the archive. We also procured everything that had been published on Beuys in order to do our work.

FRANÇOIS AUBART

Is the "Beuys' Island" the result of all these acquisitions, or did the collection exist before the preparatory work for the exhibition?

TOBIA BEZZOLA

Initially the works on Beuys were shelved with other artists, and there must have been less than half of what there is now. Later the quantity of works became so large that, I suppose for practical reasons, Szeemann had to shelve them in their own special area. Here, then, was where I did all the work on the bibliography. The other part of my work was done at the Kunsthaus, since that was where the technical aspect of the exhibition was handled: contracts, loan details, insurance, correspondence, and so on. Exhibitions like the Beuys show were organized by Szeemann via the Kunsthaus offices. The secretaries and assistants did all the preparatory work. There was a little office where he dropped in once or twice a week, on his way to Zurich airport. He would stay for shorter or longer periods and work his way gradually through all the paperwork.

FRANÇOIS AUBART

Did he make copies of the documents produced by the Kunsthaus to store here in his own archive?

TOBIA BEZZOLA

It was always a bit mixed up, because people would fax him things directly here in Maggia and those of course were not archived in the Kunsthaus. Let's take a look at what is in the files.

We move into the Fax Room.

"Beuys: Kunsthaus" are the catalogue texts, "Beuys: interviews, conferences, guided tours," "Beuys: critical reactions, press cuttings," "Beuys: Vienna Story"—that was the affair of a fake Beuys which Szeemann made the mistake of writing about. It caused a scandal and gave us a lot of problems, because Joseph Beuys had died only a short time before and his widow made a great fuss about it. Szeemann was used as a cover by the forgerers. "Beuys: Kunsthaus press cuttings," "Beuys: Madrid," "Beuys: Paris," "Beuys: Zurich press," "Beuys: Madrid, Paris, Vienna press." As you see, the real heart of the exhibition is not here, because it's at the Kunsthaus. All the paperwork relative to loan requests, correspondence with the lenders, and so on, is at the Kunsthaus. Here there are only the files managed directly by Szeemann. Oh no—I see some duplicates, but these are copies made by his assistants at the Kunsthaus, and the same documents are also in Zurich.

FRANÇOIS AUBART

Gianna Ruepp, one of his assistants who worked here, told me that part of her work involved copying and filing documents, so one can assume that he pursued his work in Zurich in the same way.

It seems that when he was away from the archive he would often ask the people who worked here to find documents for him, and would specify their location very precisely. Do you know if each of the rooms had its own name?

TOBIA BEZZOLA

I don't know, it's possible. He would say to me, for instance, "You'll find it in 'Monte Verità.'" But I wasn't in the same position as Gianna Ruepp, I used the archive but I didn't organize it.

FRANÇOIS AUBART

Do you know if other people have come here to use the archive to do similar research to yours, but on other topics?

TOBIA BEZZOLA

Yes, certainly: for instance, Roman Kurzmeyer spent a lot of time here preparing the 1991 exhibition called *Visionary Switzerland*. Later on there were probably fewer people, because the Biennial shows like Lyon or Venice were less thematic exhibitions, which didn't call for archival research, and also involved primarily new works. That meant going to visit the artists, seeing works, and having catalogues sent here. In any case the catalogues for the Venice Biennial were produced on site, I believe.

FRANÇOIS AUBART

One of the things that surprised us was the presence of a fax machine on this upper floor.

TOBIA BEZZOLA

That's because the fax disturbed Szeemann. It made too much noise when it was downstairs, it would be ringing and printing out faxes constantly. At the end of every day there were kilometers of faxes! That's the only reason it's here in the upstairs office.

FRANÇOIS AUBART

Did he explain his reasons for not using email?

TOBIA BEZZOLA

He couldn't type, whereas he could write out his faxes in longhand. For emails, he would handwrite a draft and Mme Ruepp would key them in for him.

Here are the documents for the 1975 *The Bachelor Machines* exhibition. I expect there is some other material here somewhere on the logistics and technical organization of that project. In most cases exhibitions were mounted by institutions and at least some of the documents remained with them, but in this case he was the sole organizer and the center of operations was here—unlike the following one, *Monte Verità* in 1978, which was already a production of the Kunsthaus in Zurich. The same was true for the subsequent exhibitions.

FABIEN PINAROLI

I've actually just come across a text in *The Bachelor Machines* files called "Comment on pourrait imaginer une collaboration entre les scientifiques et les organisateurs d'expositions" ("How to devise a collaboration between academics and exhibition organizers").

TOBIA BEZZOLA

Yes, that project dealt directly with the question of how to present academic research in the form of an exhibition. That essay is a description of the exhibition, where he already talks a little about everything that is to be shown. He collaborated with several scholars for the show—Jean-François Lyotard, Bazon Brock, Jean Clair.

FRANÇOIS AUBART

In *Ecrire les expositions* (*Writing Exhibitions*),[1] there is a piece in which he draws a parallel between the act of organizing an exhibition and the workings of a bachelor machine.

TOBIA BEZZOLA

Yes, it's possible that the text you're holding is a draft of the finished piece.

It's interesting that it was never published. But you have to be careful with these unpublished pieces, because he liked to rework his texts over and over. I think that in the two books he published with Merve, *Museum der Obsessionen* (*The Museum of Obsessions*, 1981) and *Individuelle Mythologie* (*Individual Mythology*, 1985), he selected the texts he actually wanted to make public. These are really essential texts, programmatic essays from that period. Later on he published another book with Lindinger & Schmid,[2] but it was a collection of writings of very varying quality. As you'll have noticed, he wrote an enormous amount of texts for particular occasions, on request, such as talks or little blurbs for particular artists. He produced successive layers built up out of his existing writings, a type of collage from which he would generate the new text.

Everything is in these layers. It really began with the 1957 *Painters-Poets/Poets-Painters* exhibition in St Gallen. That exhibition already included Antonin Artaud and many other figures, who continued to play a part throughout Szeemann's career. Hugo Ball too, who was at the origin of the idea of *Monte Verità*, which Szeemann started to visit back then. That was in 1959, and the *Monte Verità* exhibition was 20 years later. His work often proceeded like that. There is rarely anything new or truly different. His whole universe was formed in Bern: if you look at the entire history of programming at the Kunsthalle Bern, it's hard to find a single thing that he did afterward which was not already present in a radical but smaller and preliminary form in a show in Bern. Things simply became bigger, more important, more expensive.

The idea of *The Bachelor Machines* dates back to the *Light and Motion* exhibition of 1965. The theme started there and led to another and so on. In his later years there was an enormous amount of recycling. He knew the works and the owners who would lend them and could reuse them in different contexts. One instance is the model of Kafka's torture machine. I believe it was in the 2002 exhibition at the Victor Hugo house, *Aubes—Rêveries au bord de Victor Hugo* (*Dawn Songs and Reveries at Victor Hugo's Side*), and was also shown in 1996 in *Austria in a Net of Roses*. For the 1997 Lyon Biennial, *L'Autre* (*The Other*), he reused the model of the *Palais idéal* (*Ideal Palace*) by Facteur Cheval constructed in 1983 for *Penchant for a Synthesis of the Arts*.

His archival work took him in the same direction, a preservation of memory. He never started from zero, he always began planning an exhibition with what was already on his mind. This was true, for instance, of the 1995 exhibition marking the centenary of the cinema, *Illusion—Emotion—Reality. The Seventh Art in Search of the Six Others: One Hundred Years of Cinema*, which included many works he had already shown. What was new for him there was rather the film programming, though even that was not entirely new: in the 1960s he went regularly to the experimental film festival at Knokke-le-Zoute, the most important festival of non-commercial art film at the time. At the start of every project he would pull out some of his older acquisitions and combine them with new works. It's true that after the *Penchant for a Synthesis of the Arts* in 1983 he no longer really did any research, but this was because he had a stock of works to draw upon. He could put together half the exhibition in his head or from his archive before he had to start looking for anything new. I don't mean that he simply repeated himself: these were recontextualized works, and obviously it's not the same thing to show Kafka's torture machine at Victor Hugo's house and as part of the *The Bachelor Machines* exhibition. It was also an active process, one of the key elements of his thinking—the way an exhibition can create juxtapositions is much harder to do at a conference or in a lecture. This is why he chose the title *Ecrire les expositions* (*Writing Exhibitions*). An item like Kafka's machine functions like a paragraph which can be inserted in one or another text, or even as a footnote in a quite different context.

FRANÇOIS AUBART

Do you know if each of the rooms in this building was used for different kinds of work?

TOBIA BEZZOLA

Szeemann came to this room only to pick up faxes, in the evening. Before he had assistants—he only had any in the last five years—he worked alone. He was downstairs at the big table. That's where he had his files, work that needed to be done, incoming letters, and so on.

FRANÇOIS AUBART

Do you know if he had a specific goal in mind in archiving and filing his photographs?

TOBIA BEZZOLA

I think it was mostly not to have to throw them away. After the close of each exhibition a certain amount of photographic material would have been assembled which was impossible to return to the owners, due either to the cost or because the owner was unidentified, but it all had to be kept in case it was eventually requested. Otherwise he would use them in lectures. He gave an enormous number of lectures.

FRANÇOIS AUBART

Do you see any reason for preserving all these different documents permanently?

TOBIA BEZZOLA

Szeemann belonged to the pre-Internet generation, when there were very few resources. When he started out, in 1950, there were a few books in the university library, a few in the hands of collectors and art connoisseurs in Bern, a few more in the bookshops. He was always in the habit of buying everything he could. He hated libraries, he never borrowed anything from the library. When he was preparing his exhibition on Austria, for example, he went and visited all the small art museums, he stopped at every antiquarian bookseller and bought whatever he found interesting. He never came back from anywhere without at least 20 kilos of books.

Nowadays we say we can find everything on the Internet, but in the 1950s people believed that you had to personally own all the available information on this or that topic.

FRANÇOIS AUBART

It's surprising, though, that he was never attracted by the Internet and the massive amount of information that it offers.

TOBIA BEZZOLA

It was too late—it's a generational difference.

FRANÇOIS AUBART

Do you know if a lot of people came to see him here? Did the archive also function as a meeting place?

TOBIA BEZZOLA

No, it was strictly a workplace. People would come to do work on Szeemann, or on Monte Verità. The subject inspired a great deal of research on architecture, science, medicine, dance, the occult. It was also tied to the history of the region, and Szeemann was always happy when someone was doing research, aware that this information could not be found anywhere else. But he would not have let anyone use his own Joseph Beuys archive, for example. That was not a public archive but one of the tools of his own work.

Catalogues were sent to him on a regular basis: he wouldn't plan to buy the most recent catalogue from the Basel art fair, for instance, but having received one he never threw it away.

[1] Harald Szeemann, *Ecrire les expositions*, La Lettre volée, Brussels 1996.

[2] Harald Szeemann, *Zeitlos auf Zeit—Das Museum der Obsessionen*, Lindinger & Schmid, Regensburg 1994.

2) *Harald Szeemann's Agency*

The Agency for Intellectual Guest Labour

Fabien Pinaroli

"Szeemann is an inscrutable Chinese, oh sorry, inscrutable Swiss. Why inscrutable? Because he looks dumb but he isn't really dumb. And he has been like a Band-Aid for the whole world—art politics and art world and art trends—since 1968, when he called himself 'Gastarbeiter,' you know, the guy who belongs nowhere but is everywhere." [1]
Nam June Paik

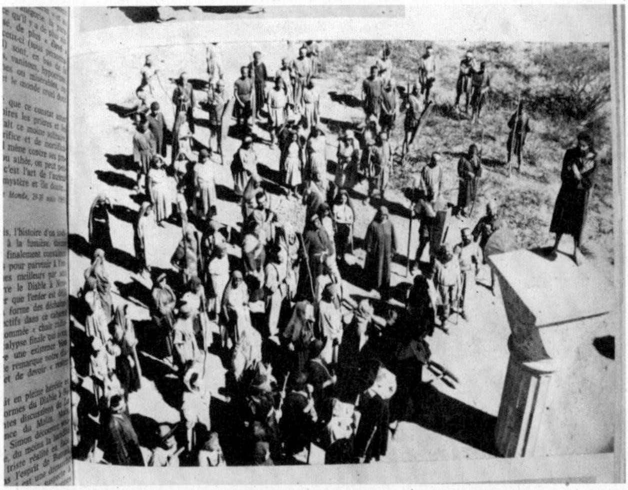

Image from Luis Buñuel's film *Simon of the Desert*, 1964. Published in the monthly review *L'avant-scène*, n° 94–95, July–September 1969.

On October 1, 1969, [2] in order to be able to propose exhibitions to art institutions and thus to practice his profession on an independent basis, Harald Szeemann founded a virtual agency, the *Agentur für geistige Gastarbeit*, translated as "Agency for Intellectual Guest Labour, which is seasonal, even mercenary, because the labor can be exported. We call it simply the Agency [...] Open as it is to every suggestion and stimulus, filtered through a single ego, the Agency combines all authorities (legislative, executive, administrative, etc.) and all specialized departments." [3]

The Agency was inspired by the model of the "one-man theater" Szeemann had invented in Bern during the 1950s, but he alludes in his writings to another model: "The character of the Agency's operations thus resembles the life of Simeon Stylites on his pillar. It was only due to his isolated existence that his life became an enterprise providing multiple services and benefits to others, who made use of his very existence as a service." [4] St Simeon Stylites was a Christian anchorite from the fifth century, who spent the last 40 years of his life standing or kneeling on top of a pillar. By creating the Agency, Szeemann left the institutional world in the same way that Simeon Stylites left the religious world. Every eye was upon him, miracles were attributed to him, and finally he was canonized.

« En 1969, mon budget global (fonctionnement, salaires, etc...) était de 200.000 francs suisses. J'en ai dépensé 500.000. Les 300.000 manquants, je les ai récupérés par les catalogues, la publicité, les affiches, les entrées — et la vente de mes expositions à l'étranger. Pendant 8 ans 1/2, j'ai vécu dans l'illégalité totale.

Si je m'étais contenté de mon budget, je n'aurais même pas pu imprimer un catalogue. Celui d' « Attitudes » m'a rapporté 40.000 francs suisses; les affiches Lichtenchtein : 14.000. Les entrées de mon exposition internationale de la photo : 15.000. Pour « Attitudes », Philip Morris nous a donné 25.000 dollars. Il fallait payer le voyage de 50 artistes, les nourrir, les loger... »

— Justement : ça ne vous gêne pas de servir en quelque sorte de public-relation pour l'industrie ? En France, beaucoup d'artistes refusent d'être les hommes-sandwichs de la production commerciale. Plus généralement, ils considèrent que le circuit des galeries et des musées n'accepte de promouvoir que « l'acceptable », le raisonnable, ce qui ne met pas en cause la culture dominante. D'où ces violentes attaques qui, par exemple, harcèlent actuellement le musée de New-York. D'où les doutes d'un animateur prestigieux comme Hulten, à Stockholm qui se demande à quoi il sert...

— Les artistes acceptent l'argent de Philip Morris, pourquoi pas moi ? Je leur ai posé la question. Et dans la mesure où c'est moi qui m'occupe de tout, je suis libre.

Des expositions politiques

— Mais seriez-vous libre d'organiser une exposition de contestation sur les affiches de mai ou sur le SPD ?

— D'une façon générale, dans mon agence, je ne traite qu'avec les villes, les conseils municipaux. Mon exposition « Happenings et Fluxus » en novembre 1970 (Cologne, Stuttgart, Londres) contiendra les dernières propositions de J.J. Lebel, qui sont exclusivement politiques.

Il y aura Kaprow, Vostell, Dine, Oldenburg, Kudo, Ben, Beuys etc... Tout cela sortira du cadre « culturel ». Pourquoi pas ? Ce que je risque, au pire, c'est qu'on ne me demande plus d'exposition. A Berne, je devais temporiser : un coup explosif, un coup modeste. Maintenant, je propose : il y a toujours une ville d'accord. Je parle d'action dans la rue, de conditionnement, de champ libre, d'agressions. Ils acceptent. A l'agence, j'ai 14 projets en cours. Je travaille tellement en Allemagne que j'ai l'impression d'être un émigré italien qui envoie son salaire au pays...

— Ils acceptent le désordre, l'agitation. Pourquoi ?

— D'abord, les municipalités allemandes n'ont pas de tradition artistique. (Ne serait-ce qu'à cause du nazisme). Elles veulent un vernis. Souvent, bien sûr, c'est un alibi : on échoue dans la pollution, on tente le coup dans la culture. Ça coûte moins cher. Ils savent aussi que l'art rapporte, ils lisent ça dans les journaux.

Ce n'est pas de l'argent perdu. Ça crée du mouvement. Pour une ville, avoir une « image » d'avant-garde, c'est toujours excellent. Vous trouvez ça excitant, vous, comme affiche : « Paris, désert culturel » ? Un budget artistique permet aussi d'assurer la subsistance d'une minorité créatrice : les artistes. Ils vont où ils peuvent manger, à Cologne, Dusseldorf, New-York. Enfin, il est vrai que dans les villes où il y a une agitation progressiste, ça canalise pas mal de choses. Aux Etats-Unis, en Allemagne qui sont des pays instables et inquiets politiquement, on a besoin de soupapes. La culture pourrait servir à ça...

Comme on me disait finement : « Au moins quand ils occupent les musées, ils sont occupés... ! » Là encore tout dépend des artistes. C'est leur bataille. Je ne suis pas là pour décider à leur place. Mais pour faire connaître leurs idées, leurs actions, où qu'elles mènent...

Extract from the magazine article "Paris désert culturel. Le diagnostic du Dr Szeemann," ("Paris Is a Cultural Desert. Dr Szeemann's Diagnosis"), in *Le Journal de Paris*, Paris, April 8, 1970, p. 31–32. This article is one of those he preserved carefully in the archives (ten copies in total).

Closely in touch as he was with the changes taking place in artistic production, Szeemann experimented at the Kunsthalle in Bern, from 1961 to 1969, with new ways of supporting artists' work. In October 1969, at the same time that he founded the Agency, he also took part in a study group with museum directors seeking to reform the institution of the museum. Their active support for contemporary art led them to prefer the type of museum whose organization was not so heavy-handed and expensive, focusing on the flow of information and experimentation rather than the typical emphasis on the collection and conservation of artworks.[5]

In founding his Agency, Szeemann expressed an intellectual affinity with the neo-avant-garde. He chose as his model some of the creative processes he had seen used, for instance, by the "happening" artists, who sought to make an impact on the public by creating interventions or situations: "I wanted to attack the spirit of ownership, which for me was tied to the notion of art as an object or an end result. I sought to recognize and participate in a kind of art that depended entirely on the moment of the experience ... This of course meant calling into question the modes of presenting, selecting, and understanding artworks, and the logical consequence of this progression was to break out of the confines of the museum." [6]

The funding of the Agency also arose from his reflections on who should "sign" an exhibition. Szeemann hesitated between the idea of the Agency, which would be an anonymous collective, with a rejection of the notion of the author, and the need to mount signed exhibitions as a way to express his own subjectivity. An interview from December 1970 indicates that these questions had still not been resolved: Szeemann repeatedly asserts a desire to work within a collective, but he recognizes from the very beginning of the interview that the public requires that the exhibitions they visit be "identifiable with the personal profile of the exhibition maker." [7] Among the documents dating from 1969 to 1972, which Szeemann preserved in his archive, this interview is one of the few to express so much hesitation. It also looks back critically at the Agency's first year of operation. [8] Szeemann realized that the initial impetus for the Agency in its first incarnation—work within a collective, the desire to abandon individual authorship, the importance of the process rather than the finished product—was a necessary but not a sufficient condition for what he was trying to implement. At the end of 1970, he describes his job as an organizer of exhibitions very precisely, and in particular the various types of interaction with artists, institutions, the public, the media, and so on. His methodology had to be honed with his own tools, and since the concept of the Agency formed part of this, it too had to evolve.

This mutation is expressed through the changes in the mottoes adopted by Szeemann. In April 1970 he had a set of rubber stamps made for the Agency. The first of these, *Besitz durch freie Aktionen ersetzen* ("Replace ownership with free actions"), summarizes his preoccupations and philosophy during the first years of his activity. Subsequently Szeemann modified the focus of the Agency, which became an instrument for working on thematic, subjective, signed exhibitions. There then appeared a second, much more pragmatic, motto, *From vision to nail.* [9] His job as "exhibition maker" was thus precisely defined and demanded a special positioning. He was to redefine it progressively over the next ten years.

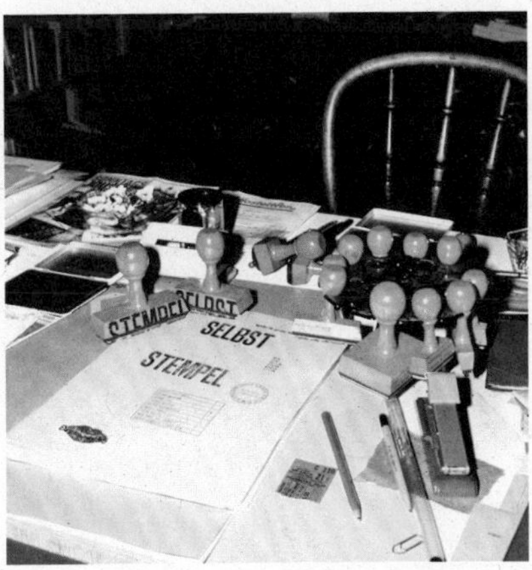

Harald Szeemann's desk was set up and photographed using Ektachrome, a film format intended for reproduction. Photographs were produced and distributed by Harald Szeemann to represent the Agency.

Drucksache

Agentur für geistige Gastarbeit

SÄLÜ / CIAO BELL...	
GUTEN MORGEN	
GUTEN TAG	
GUTEN MITTAG	
GUTEN NACHMITTAG	
GUTEN ABEND	
GUTE NACHT	
WIE GEHT ES IHNEN ?	
MEINE AGENTUR LIEBT SIE	

Monsieur Jean-Marc Poinsot

Paris 16e

FRANCE

Berne, le 13 avril 1970.

Cher Poinsot,

Merci de votre lettre. Est-ce que je peux rajouter à la liste

Kowalski
Flavin
Nauman

Pour le reste, on verra, comme vous écrivez.
Amitiés et à bientôt.

Besitz durch freie Aktionen ersetzen

Harald Szeemann
en son absence,
Mme Miescher, secrétaire

SELBST STEMPEL

mit
von
durch
wegen
gegen
trotz

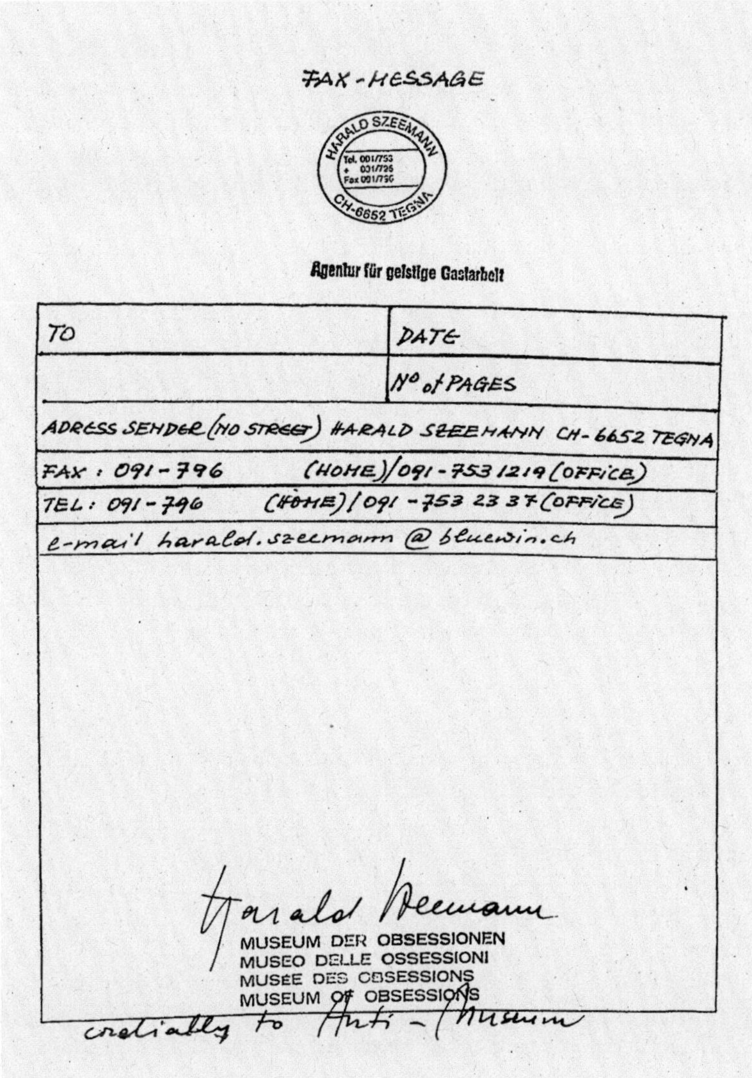

FAX-MESSAGE

HARALD SZEEMANN
Tel. 091/753
+ 091/796
Fax 091/796
CH-6652 TEGNA

Agentur für geistige Gastarbeit

TO	DATE
	No of PAGES

ADRESS SENDER (NO STREET) HARALD SZEEMANN CH-6652 TEGNA
FAX: 091-796 (HOME)/091-753 1219 (OFFICE)
TEL: 091-796 (HOME)/091-753 23 37 (OFFICE)
e-mail harald.szeemann@bluewin.ch

Harald Szeemann
MUSEUM DER OBSESSIONEN
MUSEO DELLE OSSESSIONI
MUSÉE DES OBSESSIONS
MUSEUM OF OBSESSIONS

cordially to Anti-Museum

Model of a fax cover sheet. This document was published by Harald Szeemann as a postcard.

[Page 66] Duplicate of a letter written to Jean-Marc Poinsot in 1970. It is stamped by Szeemann with the series of rubber stamps he had just created (the poster for the exhibition *8½: documentation 1961–1969*, Paris, 1970, dating from the previous month advertises the Agency but does not feature any stamps). These stamps are similar to those made in the same period by certain Fluxus artists.
From top to bottom they read:
"Drucksache": impression of a lipsticked mouth stamped "Printed Matter"
"Agentur ... ": Agency's seal, which Szeemann was to retain in the same format for 35 years
"Salü/Ciao bell ... ": list of polite expressions ("good morning, good day, good midday, good afternoon, good evening, good night, how are you? my Agency loves you ... ")
"Besitz durch ... ": Agency's motto, "Replace ownership with free actions"
"Selbst": myself
"Stempel": stamp
"mit, von, durch, wegen, gegen, trotz": with, of, by, because of, against, in spite of.

The Bachelor Machines: the only exhibition signed and financed by the Agency

In 1975, the exhibition *The Bachelor Machines*, which required two years of preparatory research, was conceived as a "turnkey" exhibition. It was taken up by eight different institutions, none of whom had initiated any of the production.[10] This was the Agency's only independent and self-financed project up to that point. It was also the last, for the difficulties inherent in organizing such a project, and its time-consuming character, drove Szeemann to look for a less radical way of operating. The next exhibition he organized, *Monte Verità*, in 1978, was, for example, produced by the Kunsthaus Zürich.

From a series of documents found in the archive we can reconstruct the last stages of the financing of *The Bachelor Machines*: they describe the concept, as well as the financial picture of the exhibition, and the production of the catalogue. Harald Szeemann had to produce the project himself by taking out a personal loan for the necessary funds.[11] In the catalogue he jokes about his solitary position at the Agency, which he describes as a bachelor machine: "I have an idea. Under the guise of an Agency, I take on the job of making the idea a reality. The Agency devises the keyword and the overall plan and assigns the development of the concept to me. In turn, I assign its execution to the Agency. The Agency informs me that I am the only one appointed. I ask the Agency what resources are available. The finance office informs me that no resources or staff can be put at my disposal at least for the moment ... until the start of the preparation stage, when one cannot do without assistance from others."[12]

Harald Szeemann's team

Assistance from others was indispensable. Over the years, Harald Szeemann therefore built up a reliable team, which participated in the realization of all his exhibitions. Three figures in particular formed the core of the group. From 1972 on, Josy Kraft was in charge of transporting the artworks. After trying to build specialized departments for transporting works of art within the large companies he worked for, he founded his own business (Kraft Els AG in Basel) and took care of transporting and installing works for Szeemann. In the same period Jérôme Szeemann helped his father to carry out the various projects he organized. For *The Bachelor Machines* in 1975, he installed the exhibition in the eight museums on the tour along with his father, and he later worked with Josy Kraft. Christoph Zürcher drew up the plans for the 1978 *Monte Verità* exhibition. He later became Szeemann's in-house architect and built the installations and constructions based on Szeemann's sketches.

From the 1980s up until 2005, this team formed part of Szeemann's "exhibition-making" system. He assembled the team, but it was not an official part of the Agency. Since he avoided burdensome administration, he asked the institutions who hired him to contract directly with the architect and the transport company (and with other collaborators as needed). Josy Kraft describes the way the team operated: "The museums of course had their own teams of technicians, but we were involved as well. For instance, at the Kunsthaus Harald worked with them to install the paintings and the easy pieces, and we came in at night or at weekends to install the more complicated pieces, such as those by Beuys. For *Zeitlos* (*Timeless*, 1988), at the Hamburger Bahnhof in Berlin, there was no infrastructure and we did the whole thing. For *Illuminate* (1989), the museum was brand new and their team was inexperienced, so we did the whole thing. In especially difficult cases many of our friends and students helped out. Everybody was paid as a freelancer: Harald negotiated with the institutions. Since he didn't officially have a company, he couldn't pay anyone ... The Agency had no accountant because the museums always have their own; he asked me to be in charge of logistics, while Christoph Zürcher was in charge of architecture. Harald would draft the different costs and send them to the institution, which managed the budget."[13]

The Kunsthaus Zürich

After he organized the *Monte Verità* exhibition produced by the Kunsthaus Zürich in 1978, Szeemann was hired by the museum in 1981. He became a "permanenter freier Mitarbeiter" (permanent independent collaborator), which he translated as "free collaborator." This was the start of a long period of collaboration with this institution, which ended in 2000 when the director, Félix Baumann, left his position. Harald Szeemann functioned as an advisor for acquisitions, and his international reputation made him into a kind of ambassador for the Kunsthaus. He also achieved financial security, as his contract established a base salary as well as additional fees for each exhibition he organized.[14]

During this period Szeemann had both rights and obligations at the Kunsthaus. He had the use of an office, assistants, secretarial staff, and the museum's infrastructure. As he said, "It's an immense advantage, and this is why I am so happy to collaborate with Zurich, because I have one of the largest exhibition spaces in Europe, not for traditional shows organized by museum conservators but for Mario Merz, Sigmar Polke, Cy Twombly, contemporary artists ... And at the same time I can do shows like Jarry, Victor Hugo, undertakings which are very expensive because of the transport and travel involved ... They require six months' work which I could not possibly finance by myself."[15] Szeemann benefited from one of the great advantages of an institution: "Only institutions can borrow; people do not lend to a private individual like me—paintings worth millions! Of course not."[16] He was one of a group of four curators at the museum with whom Félix Baumann discussed the exhibitions to be organized and divided up the responsibility: *James Ensor* (1983), *Eugène Delacroix* (1987), and *Egon Schiele and His Time* (1988) appear to have been among those that were Szeemann's responsibility.[17]

Szeemann's reputation grew and he began to mount larger and more spectacular exhibitions. He had not broken out of the confines of the museum but rather had come to lean upon it. In every case his team was involved: he worked on the display with the architect, had his expert do the framing, hung the show with the team, who also transported the works, and so on. The idea of collective work still existed, but it did not include the conception or the signature. Szeemann was the boss who had learned to delegate.

The Agency could have disappeared during Szeemann's time at the Kunsthaus. Instead it became the symbol of his independence and the uniqueness of his approach. It continues to be talked about, thanks to the stamp that he added to all his correspondence.[18] From 1981 onward he revived the Agency in his book entitled *Museum der Obsessionen*, in which it became *The Agency for Intellectual Guest Labour in the Service of a Possible Vision of the Museum of Obsessions.*[19] In this book, the Agency/Museum of Obsessions pair has the function of providing a basis for Harald Szeemann's practice in written form. However, he omits some of the ideas developed in the early years of his creative activity in the ideological context with which we are familiar. The Agency thus becomes a message sent out to the art world, but at the same time constitutes a tool for mythmaking.

The concept of the Agency invented by Szeemann as a discourse and symbol of his autonomy can easily become meaningless: "Myth is speech stolen and restored. Only, speech which is restored is no longer quite that which was stolen: when it was brought back, it was not put exactly in its place."[20] The Agency forms part of the "Szeemann myth" that it incarnates. He created it at the start of the 1970s with the aim of "breaking out of the confines of the museum"; as early as 1972 he announced in the preface to the *documenta 5* catalogue that, "An artist's relationship to museums once again goes without saying, and there are signs suggesting that as soon as we manage to free museums from their dreadful reputation as places of consecration, they will become what they once were, thanks to the artworks themselves."[21] Ten years later he became associated with the Kunsthaus, and from 1981 to 1996 the exhibitions he organized were mostly mounted in this museum.

During that period he mounted on average one independent exhibition per year. The concept of the Agency was nonetheless reinforced and used as a basis for his practice. From the start of his career, Szeemann had a strong sense of his place in history.[22] To solidify this historical construction, he invented two tools: the archive at the Fabbrica rosa and the Agency for Intellectual Guest Labour. The first was a system for processing information, the second a leitmotif which ensured that he would retain a permanent image as a creator of exhibitions and an independent professional.

It is noteworthy that these two tools have something in common: they were both developed during a period of retrenchment (geographical in the case of the Fabbrica, conceptual in the case of the Agency) and both nonetheless became remarkably powerful, due to Szeemann's position as an outsider combined with his undaunted pragmatism.

[1] Gaudenz Meili and Hans-Joachim Müller, *Verzauberung auf Zeit/Harald Szeemann*, color, sound, 76 minutes, 1992.

[2] Cf. Urs and Rös Graf, "Interview with Harald Szeemann," p. 83.

[3] Harald Szeemann, "Le Musée des obsessions," *Ecrire les expositions*, La Lettre volée, Brussels 1996, p. 57. The word *Gastarbeit* in German has a double meaning: literally the idea of "work on demand," it emphasizes the risk Szeemann took in leaving his institutional post. On the other hand, *Gastarbeiter* is the word for immigrant workers who send the money they earn back to their families in their own countries. In Switzerland at the time they were viewed with some animosity. By giving his agency this name, Szeemann announced his solidarity with these foreign workers (he himself has a foreign-sounding name), and in a reversal of their situation he traveled to foreign countries and sent his earnings back to Switzerland.

[4] Ibid. Among the models that inspired the Agency, Szeemann also mentions two independent republics: Robinson Crusoe's Island and Cuba.

[5] François Mathey, Pontus Hulten, Eduard de Wilde, Michael Kustow, Pierre Gaudibert, Georges-Henri Rivière, Jean Leymarie (interpretation by Harald Szeemann), "Echange de vues d'un groupe d'experts," in *Museum*, special issue "Problèmes du musée d'art contemporain en Occident," vol. 24, n° 1, 1972, p. 4–32.

[6] Yann Pavie, "Entretien avec H. Szeemann," in *Opus International*, n° 36, June 1972, p. 39.

[7] Cf. Graf, "Interview with Harald Szeemann," p. 83–89.

[8] For the rare documents that assess these years critically, see Yann Pavie's interview of eighteen months later, in which Szeemann offers an even more negative assessment of these early years. Pavie, "Entretien avec H. Szeemann," p. 39–44.

[9] "The agency was a one-man enterprise, a kind of institutionalization of myself, and its slogans were both ideological ('Replace Property with Free Activity') and practical ('From Vision to Nail')." Hans Ulrich Obrist, "Mind over Matter—interview with Harald Szeemann," *Artforum*, November 1996, full text online at http://www.findarticles.com/p/articles/mi_m0268/is_n3_v35/ai_18963443/pg_1). Only the first motto forms part of the series of stamps produced in 1969; the phrase *From Vision to Nail* was thus to appear later.

[10] The institutions were: Kunsthalle Bern; Venice Biennial; Palais des Beaux-Arts, Brussels; Städtische Kunsthalle, Düsseldorf; Union Centrale des Arts Décoratifs, and Musée de l'Homme et de l'Industrie, Paris; Malmö Konsthall; Stedelijk Museum Amsterdam; and Museum des 20. Jahrhunderts, Vienna.

[11] A proposal of December 1974 from the bank Armand von Ernst & Cie is included in the files of *The Bachelor Machines*. This is for a short-term loan of 120,000 CHF, due to be repaid in full by December 31, 1976. The exhibition tour is described in detail along with the payments expected from the institutions concerned. This bank is thanked on the first page of the catalogue, from which one gathers that the loan will indeed be issued. See document reproduced p. 79.

[12] Harald Szeemann, "Les Machines célibataires," *Junggesellenmaschinen/Les Machines célibataires*, Alfieri edizioni d'arte, Venice 1975, p. 11.

[13] Interview with Josy Kraft, Basel, March 30, 2007.

[14] From 1970 to 1975, the exhibition maker's independence did not automatically mean financial security. After *Happening & Fluxus* (1970) and *documenta 5* (1972), Harald Szeemann was taken to court by the institutions who demanded that he reimburse the deficit.

[15] Nathalie Heinich, *Harald Szeemann, un cas singulier: Entretien*, L'Echoppe, Paris 1995, p. 37–38.

[16] Ibid.

[17] He was also allowed to mount other side exhibitions in conjunction with those intended for the general public: he presented *Victor Hugo* in conjunction with the *Delacroix* exhibition in 1987 and *Alfred Jarry* with the *Bonnard* retrospective in 1984.

[18] For 35 years, Harald Szeemann demonstrated an unwavering consistency in using this stamp on all the messages he sent to the outside world. The design of the stamp did not change; it was not a logo that needed to be updated but a message that Szeemann regularly transmitted from the Fabbrica.

[19] In 1981, Szeemann published *Museum der Obsessionen* as a collection of his various writings. The fact that all his rubber stamps were reproduced on the inside front cover of the book indicates the importance they held for him. Two texts in particular define the Agency and the Museum of Obsessions. Written between 1974 and 1980, they had previously been published in part (and in some cases in different languages and journals): Harald Szeemann, "Agentur für geistige Gastarbeit im Dienst der Vision eines Museums der Obsessionen" and "Museum der Obsessionen," *Harald Szeemann, Museum der Obsessionen; von/über/zu/mit,* Merve Verlag, Berlin 1981, respectively p. 107–124 and p. 125–136.

[20] Roland Barthes, *Mythologies*, Hill and Wang, New York 1975, p. 125.

[21] Cf. Harald Szeemann, "Preface to the catalogue," p. 104.

[22] Three weeks before the opening of the 1969 exhibition *When Attitudes Become Form*, the majority of the American artists invited by Szeemann took part in another exhibition, *Op Losse Schroeven*, at the Stedelijk Museum in Amsterdam. Szeemann published his journal and carnet de voyage in the catalogue released a few months later, focusing on the repercussions of *When Attitudes Become Form*. This is how the Stedelijk Museum, one of the greatest European museums, provided Harald Szeemann with the conditions for making *When Attitudes Become Form* historical. See Harald Szeemann, "How does an exhibition come into being? Diary and Travelogue of the preparations and consequences, and only of these, for the exhibition *When Attitudes Become Form: works, concepts, processes, situations, information,*" Tobia Bezzola, Roman Kurzmeyer (eds.), *Harald Szeemann: with by through because towards despite*, Springer, Vienna/New York; Edition Voldemeer, Zurich 2007, p. 244–261.

Annex Documents

The following document is a translation of a letter about *The Bachelor Machines* exhibition, which was written in French by Harald Szeemann (October, 1974). Szeemann was aiming to pre-sell the exhibition, the budget of which amounted to 150,000 CHF, to different institutions.

The Bachelor Machines

The History and Reasons for the Project

During the preparation of *documenta 5*, I was faced as never before with the project of a big contemporary exhibition that does not want either to give up its character as an immediate event resulting from the historical prestige of the artwork, or to give up making visible the concern to appropriate "the exhibitions as a means of expression" by avoiding the simple addition of isolated situations. Since then I have been looking for themes that could combine the two things. The *Grandfather* show was an exhibition exercise that combined a part that was the intervention and interpretation of documents with a part that was the reconstitution of the environment. It was at the same time a reflection on the way of presenting a future museum of obsessions in which the reason for the obsession, the system of thought and behavior, all have as much value as the "precious or artistic document." The museum of obsessions which, in its purest form, is based on primary obsessions linked to four elements in the form of a proposition, perhaps in an official cultural context, placed in an internal and visual dialectics with a history of the art of intensities that does not distinguish between the finished work and the unrealized intense intention (a typical example: Leonardo). For the time being, and above all for practical reasons, I think it is impossible to make a proper museum of obsessions (lack of money and the old-fashioned structure of the system of activities of official cultural spaces), but it is possible to come close to the meaning and to the heart of this concern, based on parallel works that can take the form of autonomous exhibitions. The modern myth of bachelor machines highlighted 20 years ago by Michel Carrouges strikes me as in a way containing all the elements that could lead to a new kind of exhibition that does not deny the benefits of the past but does use them to different ends. Here is the visualization of a myth that can be read on different levels. The bachelor machine, as an associative image, has the character of a "Gesamtkunstwerk"; it is a closed circuit, the result of sublimation, with religious, erotic, or political themes. Historically, it follows the Symbolists' myth of the "femme fatale," another model of refusal, of sterility, confronting a society that was more and more caught up in its own closed circuit of production and consumption. In the museum of obsessions, the bachelor machine would be the witness to thought-through obsession; the suicide machine, the perpetuum mobile of the mad would be the examples and the fruit of primary obsession.

Visualization

The situation immediately confronts visitors with the two definitions of the BM [bachelor machine], that of Carrouges (cultural context), and that of Deleuze (sociological/anti-psychiatric), and two fairly popular attempts to accustom them to the problem: the Frankenstein myth and the automata of the 19th century (the creation of man by the machine and the refusal to provide the monster with a wife in the name of bourgeois morality, having already violated nature in the name of science, and, with the automata, of making machines charming by giving them a human face). A third aspect to introduce the theme comprises a few examples of the anthropomorphic aspect of the machine and the use of the machine to signify human activity. The iconography of the "femme fatale" (Munch) forms the introduction for the entrance of the machines into literature (Jarry, Roussel, Kafka), executed by Carelman, and Casares' novel, *The Invention of Morel*, in the film by Emilio Greco. Visitors will not be confronted with machines unforewarned, but will have to pass through conditioning corridors with small exhibitions on the creators and the iconography of better known bachelor machines such as the bicycle, the guillotine, and the computer, and reminding them of these Oriental words of wisdom, "that to renounce procreation brings about the birth of other worlds." A parenthesis is also opened by two figures that are marginal in this context (but major in the museum of obsessions): the bachelor character of parapsychology, through the admirable drawings of Emma Kunz, and the visualized life of Anton Muller in the form of a triptych, a model theater. The more recent bachelor machine lives—at least in art—from the consummated separation between nature and art and the sometimes naive, sometimes ironic faith that the machine can also produce unique things (the sex act, the work of art): the iconography of the painting machine (or machine for writing literary texts) provides the examples of Swift ("Laputa"), Souvestre, Jarry, and Roussel, all the way to the works of Tinguely and Kowalski. Irony, psychology, and physiognomy are emphasized in works by other artists who take the machine literally, such as Picabia, Lindner, and Klapheck. The aesthetic part ends with machines for making love, of which there are many in science fiction (*Barbarella*) and, above all, with the masturbation machine, the most famous example of which—Robert Muller's "runner's widow"—is at the same time the culmination of the iconography of the bicycle. A sociological part illustrates the bachelor and the bachelor machine used by today's anti-psychiatry and the bachelor social forms (the society of "singletons" and an example of the closed circuit that is typical in the current economy: the Italian post).

(A more detail presentation of the project will feature in a special issue of ARC on Duchamp, Paris November 1974, and his relations with the museum of obsessions in the first issue of METRO.)

Preparation

I proposed this exhibition a year ago to the Deutscher Ring insurance company in Hamburg who, ten days ago, on a pathetic pretext (that there was no space in Hamburg suited to showing the exhibition) withdrew the promise to pre-finance the project with 150,000 DM. A condition I had to meet to get this money was to find five institutions that would take the exhibition and pay a take-up fee of 15,000 DM, to which would be added a share of the insurance and transport and the purchase of a certain number of catalogues and posters at cost price. This circuit exists: the exhibition was going to be shown at the following venues: Hamburg, April–May 1975, Kunsthalle Bern, July–August; Kunsthalle Düsseldorf, September–October; Palais des Beaux-Arts, Brussels, December 1975–January 1976 (combined with an Emma Kunz retrospective); Musée des Arts Décoratifs, Paris, March–April 1975; and after—events allowing—Le Creuzot (Musée d'Art et d'Industrie), Musée d'Art et d'Industrie, Saint-Etienne, Malmö Konsthall. The Museum of the 20th Century in Vienna was interested in taking it up, and talks with the Stedelijk Museum, Amsterdam, and Louisiana are to be held.

The preparations for the exhibition have reached a point where contracts should be signed, above all with Carelman for the reconstruction of the machines in the style of Jarry, Roussel, and Kafka. The catalogue is not conceived as yet another mass of biographies but as a book, preferably in the style of the *Cahiers de Pataphysique*, in which the different specialists discuss the bachelor machine from their particular point of view: Carrouges (aggiornamento of the bc), Deleuze or Lyotard (philosophy), Gorsen (socio-psychology), Le Bott (sociology), Le Lionnais (science) and ? (theology). Jean Clair has agreed to edit and to integrate the information, biographies, etc. in the annotations.

So far I have been in contact with most of the people mentioned here but I have not yet asked for the loan of paintings (Picabia, Lindner, Klapheck) because for the version planned in Hamburg I wanted to integrate costly works of art in the form of slides in an audiovisual program (Deutscher Ring is the new owner of the machine for the "Audiovisual Preface" made for *documenta 5*). An initial judgment on the idea of the exhibition and a critique of the overly idealist approach to the theme can be found in a text written by Gorsen at the request of Deutscher Ring, and that I use in a text to be published in METRO under the title "The Bachelor Machines, or how to devise a collaboration between academics and exhibition organizers."

Finance

The 150,000 DM budgeted to start up the exhibition are divided up as follows:

1)	Reconstruction of the machines	60,000
2)	Transport, insurance for the first exhibition	20,000
3)	Photographs, enlargements	5,000
4)	Film program	5,000
5)	Purchase of a 16mm copy of the film by Emilio Greco	5,000
6)	Audiovisual program	8,000
7)	Catalogue, French/German	12,000
8)	Poster	5,000
9)	Installation of the machines	2,000
10)	Taking down the exhibition	5,000
11)	Fee Szeemann	10,000
12)	Travel	5,000
13)	Translations	3,000
14)	Inauguration	1,000
15)	Various	4,000
Total		150,000

Revenue

5 times the take-up fee by the 5 museums	75,000	
for each museum that takes it up		
Szeemann receives 2,000 DM	10,000	65,000
Catalogues		6,500
Posters		1,500
Film festival		2,000
Total		75,000

Deficit for Deutscher Ring with 5 institutions taking up the show: 75,000 DM ad 1) An unofficial estimate from Carelman allows 90,000 FF for two machines from Roussel, one from Jarry. I discussed the following formula with Carelman: this money makes the reconstruction possible for him, but he will remain owner of the work on the agreement that if he sells it he returns the money. He also undertakes to always make these machines available to us for exhibitions that could help recoup the costs. For Roussel's crystal glasses I have written to Saint-Gobain. The Kafka machine doesn't pose any particular difficulties.

ad 2) This sum represents the first transport and the amount to be covered by the first for the cost of taking down the exhibition. Each institution will pay for the transport from the preceding venue to itself, and the same for the taking down plus the insurance for the transport from the previous place and the duration.

ad 7) This sum is insufficient but increases with the order made by each institution for a certain number of catalogues and posters, which it will buy at cost price.
Included in this sum are the fees of the authors of the texts in the catalogue.

ad 11) To make this undertaking possible I have counted 10% of the initial budget as my fee and travel expenses. I would have recouped the money lost on this operation with the 2,000 DM that I would have received on each take-up fee. Up to the present, I have received 3,000 DM from Deutscher Ring. In addition, they have paid 950 DM for a plane ticket. My fees to date amount to 5,600 CHF, 6,300 DM, 150,000 ITL for travel, 2,500 CHF office expenses. Also, I have spent 2,100 CHF and 900 FF.

It goes without saying that if a museum takes upon itself the pre-financing or part of the exhibition, the budget based on the Deutscher Ring sum must be modified. For example, it would be preferable if an institution on its own dealt with financing the catalogue. We would also have to reconsider the construction of the machines. A lot of expenses for installation or ad hoc services (translations, technology, cinema) can be covered by museum personnel.
To retain the museum circuit thus composed and to meet the deadlines, we would immediately need the following sums:

Machines	FF	50,000
Texts	FF	5,000
Translations	FF	5,000
Szeemann	FF	20,000
for 1974	FF	80,000

This sum is covered by the contributions of the museums, which will pay in 1975.

15 October 1974
Harald Szeemann

Letter of agreement sent to Harald Szeemann by the Union Centrale des Arts Décoratifs de Paris for the purchase of *The Bachelor Machines* exhibition (November, 1974).

Union Centrale des Arts Décoratifs

Pavillon de Marsan Palais du Louvre / 107-109 rue de Rivoli PARIS / 742 22-84

N/réf : M.74/501/PM/amc

Paris, le 29 novembre 1974

Monsieur Harold Szeemann
Gurtengasse 4
CH. 3011 Bern
Suisse

Objet : projet d'exposition "Les Machines Célibataires"

Monsieur,

J'ai l'honneur de vous confirmer ci-dessous les conditions de l'engagement que nous avons envisagé avec vous-même, et M. Mathey, conservateur en chef du Musée des Arts Décoratifs, au sujet de votre projet d'exposition" Les machines célibataires" :

1 - L'Union Centrale des Arts Décoratifs (U.C.A.D.) participera aux frais de réalisation à Paris de ladite exposition, frais payables au fur et à mesure de la réalisation des travaux et en fonction des mémoires présentés par M. Szeemann et dans la limite de 28.200 francs (contre valeur de 15.000 DM au cours de 1,88 au 27 novembre 1974).

2 - L'U.C.A.D. remboursera sur le premier transport et sur le dernier sa part calculée en fonction du nombre de musées engagés à recevoir cette exposition, calcul effectué suivant la formule :

$$\frac{\text{coût du premier et du dernier transport}}{\text{nombre de musées}} = \text{contribution de chaque musée}$$

3 - L'U.C.A.D. règlera le montant du transport pour l'étape conduisant au musée des Arts Décoratifs.

4 - La participation aux assurances comprendra :
a) le transport visé au paragraphe 3 ci-dessus;
b) l'exposition proprement dite au musée des Arts Décoratifs;
c) la part d'assurance s'appliquant au premier et dernier transport et déterminée selon la formule de calcul figurant au paragraphe 2 ci-dessus;

5 - Les catalogues bilingues (français-allemand) et les affiches seront fournis à l'UCAD à prix coûtant et pour les quantités que l'UCAD précisera en temps utile;

6 - La participation de M. Szeemann à l'installation de l'exposition au Musée des Arts Décoratifs fera éventuellement l'objet d'un accord particulier.

.../...

Le présent engagement aura effet dès l'instant que six musées au moins, dont le musée des Arts Décoratifs, se seront engagés à participer à cette exposition.

Je vous prie d'agréer, Monsieur, l'assurance de ma considération distinguée.

P. MEILHAC
FFon de Secrétaire Général

Union Centrale des Arts Décoratifs
Pavillon de Marsan Palais du Louvre/107–109 rue de Rivoli PARIS/742 22 84

Ref: M.74/501/PM/amc Paris November 29, 1974

Mr Harald Szeemann
Gurtengasse 4
CH 3011 Bern
Switzerland

Re: exhibition project "The Bachelor Machines"

Dear Sir,

I am pleased to confirm as below the conditions of your engagement, which we discussed with you and M. Mathey, head curator at the Musée des Arts Décoratifs, regarding your exhibition project *The Bachelor Machines*:

1 – The Union Centrale des Arts Décoratifs (UCAD) will contribute to the costs of organizing the said exhibition in Paris, which costs are to be paid as the work is carried out and in accordance with the notes presented by M. Szeemann, up to a limit of 28,200 francs (the value corresponding to 15,000 DM at an exchange rate of 1,88 as on November 27, 1974).
2 – UCAD will reimburse on the first transport and on the last its share, as calculated in accordance with the number of museums committed to taking this exhibition, which calculation is carried out according to the formula:
cost of first and last transport ÷ number of museums = contribution of each museum
3 – UCAD will pay the cost of the transport for the stage leading to the Musée des Arts Décoratifs.
4 – The contribution to the insurance will include:
a) the transport referred to in paragraph 3, above.
b) the actual exhibition at the Musée des Arts Décoratifs.
c) the share of the insurance applied to the first and last transport, determined in keeping with the formula appearing in paragraph 2 above.
5 – The bilingual catalogues (French-German) and the posters will be supplied to UCAD at cost price and in the quantities that UCAD deems useful.
6 – The participation of M. Szeemann in installing the exhibition at the Musée des Arts Décoratifs may possibly be the subject of a specific agreement.

This undertaking will come into effect as soon as at least six museums, including the Musée des Arts Décoratifs, have committed to taking part in this exhibition.

Yours sincerely,

F. MEILHAC
pp. General Secretary

Letter from Harald Szeemann to the Venetian publisher Bruno Alfieri (March 1975). Szeemann made a proposal to Alfieri for the publication of *The Bachelor Machines* catalogues. Two kinds of collaboration are envisaged, and a budget with figures supplied: either he will do the French-German edition and Alfieri will do the English-Italian one, or else Alfieri will do both editions. This letter also confirms that a loan had been taken out, since Szeemann refers to it and to the interest charges. Alfieri then proposed a publishing contract in which he would be responsible for the two catalogues in two languages.

Tegna, 30.3.1975

Bruno Alfieri
San Marco 1991
Venezia Italia

Cher Bruno,

Merci d'être venu. Même s'il n'y avait pas de résultats tangents, au moins cela a clarifié la situation.

Le catalogue en 2 langues français/allemand a aujourd'hui les données suivantes

1 langue = 500'000 de signes (j'ai 399 000 aujourd'h. mais il me manque le texte de de Certeau et des notes de Jean Clair)
donc
2 langues = 1'000'000.
format = 27,5 × 17,5
avec 2 colonnes à 3000 signes, cela donne par page 6000 signes, ce qui nous amène à 170 pages de texte plus 54 pages d'images. en tout 224 pages.

Je viens d'écrire tout cela à Jean Clair en lui proposant de venir à Berne le weekend prochain.

Maintenant aux affaires

Il y a deux possibilités

a) je fais l'édition française/allemande à Berne et je te cède tout le reste quitte à ce que tu fasses des éditions en toutes les langues sauf ces deux, notamment italien, anglais, suédois, hollandais, flamand etc.

a) cont) Dans ce cas il faudrait que tu participe aux frais suivants

50% frais de préparations (films, fotos, correspondance, téléphone selon les factures,)
50% frais maquette — ca. FrS 10'500.–

je prendrai à ma charge les honoraires des auteurs et la première traduction FrS. 20'000.–

Sur toutes les éditions que tu sortira je toucherai les frais d'auteurs, soit de 10 à 15%

b) Je te cède toutes les éditions à faire, dans toutes les langues, à ce moment-là je voudrais tout de suite

pour les premiers 15'000 ex. comme droits d'auteur et [illegible] — FrS 30'000.–
les frais généraux selon les factures jusqu'à une somme de — FrS 10'000.–

de tous les exemplaires qui seront vendus après l'écoulement des 15'000 exemplaires je toucherai le 10%

De cette somme je paye les auteurs (FrS. 15'000.–) et je garde le copyright, ensemble avec toi.

Tu prends à ta charge les frais de traduction pour toutes les éditions. Là tu peux même essayer (mon contrat pour l'exposition le suggère) que c'est les musées qui payent la traduction quant au flamand/néerlandais et suédois

Tu prends à ta charge l'envoi des exemplaires du livre aux auteurs et aux prêteurs pour l'exposition et tu me cèdes en outre 100 copies de la première édition, plus 10 de chaque suivante.

③

b) cont) Si il y a des recettes supplémentaires (vente des droits au Japon par exemple) ou de reprise des textes dans des revues on les partage.

Une fois les 15'000 exemplaires écoulés on commence à faire les comptes tous les 6 mois.

Les deux solutions me permettent de récupérer les intérêts de la banque. La solution b) a pour moi l'avantage de ne plus m'occuper de la distribution ni de la vente et je n'aurai pas le risque pendant 18 mois.
La solution a) a l'avantage que je peux inclure dans le prix du catalogue vendu au musée tous les frais et les intérêts du crédit bancaire.

Il est clair que pour toi la solution b) est plus avantageuse. Au prix de 12 FrS au musée tu peux encaisser jusqu'à 4.34 FrS par exemplaire, si tu comptes

impression	60'000.– (1.000 lit l'exemplaire)
Szeemann	30'000.–
Frais généraux	10'000.–
Traduction	15'000.–
	115'000.– : 15000 = 7.66

Si moi je fais l'édition des premiers 10'000 à Berne, il faut compter

impression	80'000.– (je fais faire un nouveau devis)
auteurs	15'000.–
traduction	5'000.–
Frais généraux	10'000.–
Frais en relation avec l'expo	10'000.–
intérêts 8% pour 18 mois	12'000.–
	132'000 : 10'000 = 13.20

④

Je te joins la photocopie de la Konsthall de Malmö. C'est à cause de cette lettre que j'ai recalculé le tout et que je vois l'avantage de faire tout chez toi. Mais à ce moment-là il faut m'honorer convenablement tout l'effort depuis 2 ans.

je répète FrS 30'000.– (dont je verse la moitié aux auteurs)
+ ca FrS 10'000.– de frais généraux
FrS 40'000.–

E basta per gli affari

L'enfant n'est toujours pas arrivé, mais il faut qu'il vienne maintenant avant le début de mes périples. Ingeborg est toujours en forme, mais elle montre des signes d'impatience.

Amitiés de nous deux

Szeemann

Tegna, 30.3.1975

Bruno Alfieri
San Marco 1991
Venezia Italia

Dear Bruno,

Thanks for coming. Even if there weren't any tangible results, it did at least clarify the situation.

The catalogue, in 2 languages, French/German, is now shaping up as follows
1 language = 500,000 characters (I currently have 399,000 but I don't yet have the text by de Certeau and the notes by Jean Clair)
so
2 languages = 1,000,000
size = 27.5 x 17.5
with 2 columns of 3,000 signs, that will mean 6,000 signs per page, which brings us up to 170 pages of text plus 54 pages of images: in all, 224 pages.

I have just written all this to Jean Clair, suggesting that he come to Bern next weekend.

Now, to business.

There are two possibilities

a) I do the French/German edition in Bern and I leave all the rest to you, even if that means you doing editions in all the languages except these two, notably Italian, English, Swedish, Dutch, Flemish, etc.

a) cost) In that case, you would need to contribute the following:

50% preparation costs
films, photos,
correspondence, telephone
according to the bills

50% layout costs ca. 10,500 CHF

I will cover the fees of the authors and the first translations
20,000 CHF

On all publications that you bring out I will receive authorial fees,
about 10 to 15%.

b) I cede to you all the editions to do in all the languages, as of now I would like immediately

for the first 15,000 copies 30,000 CHF
as royalties and payment for starting up the whole event
and all the work done so far to get the 15,000 copies

the general expenses according to the bills, up to 10,000 CHF

on all the copies that are sold after the sale of the 15,000 copies, I will take 10%

From that sum, I will pay the authors (15,000 CHF) and I will keep the copyright, together with you.

You will pay the translation costs for all the editions, and here you can even try (my contract for the exhibition suggests this) to get the museums to pay for the translations on the Flemish/Dutch and Swedish.

You pay for the shipping of the copies of the book to the authors and to the lenders to the exhibition, and you give me 100 copies of the first edition, plus 10 of each subsequent one.

b) cost) If there are extra revenues (sale of rights to Japan, for example) or reprinting of texts in journals, we share it.

Once the 15,000 copies have been sold we start doing the accounts every 6 months.

These two solutions enable me to recover the bank interest.
For me, solution b) has the advantage that I don't deal with the distribution or the sale and I won't have to deal with the risk for 18 months.
Solution a) has the advantage that I can include in the price of the catalogue sold to the museum all the costs and the interest on the bank loan.

It is clear that for you solution b) is more advantageous. At the price of 12 CHF at the museum you can make up to 4.34 CHF per copy, if you count

printing	60,000	/ 1,000 lire per copy
Szeemann	30,000	
overheads	10,000	
translation	15,000	
	115,000	÷ 15,000 = 7.66

If I publish the first 10,000 in Bern, we have to allow for

printing	80,000	(am getting a new estimate done)
authors	15,000	
translation	5,000	
overheads	10,000	
costs related to the show	10,000	
interest 8% over 18 months	12,000	

132,000 ÷ 10,000 = 13.20

I enclose the photocopy from the Malmö Konsthall. It is because of this letter that I have recalculated everything and see it as advantageous to have everything done by you. But that means giving me fair recompense for all my efforts over these two years.

I repeat 30,000 CHF (of which I pay half to the authors)

+ approx. 10,000 CHF in overheads

40,000 CHF

E basta per gli affari

The child hasn't arrived yet but he needs to come now, before the beginning of my travels. Ingeborg is still on form, but she is showing signs of impatience.

All our best,

Szeemann

[Page 82] First page of *The Bachelor Machines* exhibition catalogue (July 1975). The Agency for Intellectual Guest Labour is given as the producer of the exhibition. This is the only reference to the Agency as the producer of an exhibition by Szeemann. In terms of financing, the exhibition is considered to be an alternative enterprise, since it received no official funding. Yet the bank Armand von Ernst & Cie as well as the insurance company Deutscher Ring are thanked.

L'exposition « Les Machines célibataires » est, en ce qui regarde son financement, une entreprise alternative dont le modèle pourrait être la production cinématographique. Son préfinancement n'a bénéficié d'aucune subvention officielle. Il a été assuré par la *Banque Armand von Ernst & Cie*, Bundesgasse 30, 3001 Berne. Une partie de la somme destinée à sa réalisation a été couverte par le *Deutscher Ring*, Compagnie d'Assurances, S.A., Hambourg.

Die Ausstellung « Junggesellenmaschinen » ist in dem Sinne ein alternatives Unternehmen, als keine öffentlichen Subventionen für die Vorfinazierung zur Verfügung standen. Die Vorfinanzierung wurde ermöglicht durch das *Bankhaus Armand von Ernst & Cie*, Bundesgasse 30, 3001 Bern, und durch einen Beitrag des *Deutschen Ring*, Lebensversicherungs-AG, Hamburg.

L'exposition sera présentée dans les institutions et musées suivants / Die Ausstellung wird in folgenden Institutionen und Museen gezeigt:

Kunsthalle Bern

Biennale di Venezia

Société des Expositions du Palais des Beaux-Arts, Bruxelles

Städtische Kunsthalle, Düsseldorf

Union Centrale des Arts Décoratifs, Paris

Musée de l'Homme et de l'Industrie, Le Creusot

Konsthall Malmö

Stedelijk Museum, Amsterdam

Museum des 20. Jahrhunderts, Wien.

Exposition / Ausstellung

Agentur für geistige Gastarbeit, Harald Szeemann, Civitanova Marche.

© Catalogue / Katalog

Alfieri, edizioni d'arte®, Industrie Grafiche Editoriali S.p.A., Venezia et / und Harald Szeemann, Civitanova Marche.

Les © pour certaines illustrations et citations sont marqués directement, dans les crédits photographiques et dans les remerciements / Die © für gewisse Abbildungen und Textzitate sind direkt angebracht, oder im Fotonachweis, oder im Dank.

Rédaction / Redaktion

Jean Clair, Paris, et / und Harald Szeemann, Civitanova Marche.

Documentation et maquette / Documentation und Gestaltung

Jean Clair, Paris, et / und Harald Szeemann, Civitanova Marche.

© Affiche/Plakat haut/oben: Loredana Urso, Couverture/Umschlag PRENATAL, S.I.A.D., spa, Milano
bas/unten: Verlag Sans Souci, Zürich
4e page/4.Seite: Markus Raetz

Impression / Druck

Fantonigrafica®, Venezia-Martellago. Juillet / Juli 1975.

Printed in Italy.

The Agency for Intellectual Guest Labour
Interview with Harald Szeemann
December 28, 1970 (first version)
Urs and Rös Graf

This document is the first version of an unpublished interview in which Harald Szeemann answered questions in the context of an investigation, "Art and the Public—the Case of Bern." A very brief extract from this interview was published under the title "Agentur für geistige Gastarbeit, Dr Harald Szeemann, Münstergasse 48," in the magazine *werk, bauen + wohnen*, Zurich, n° 4, 1971, p. 261.

URS AND RÖS GRAF

What led you to create this sort of agency? It was quite a novel idea, and rather peculiar from the point of view of the uninitiated.

HARALD SZEEMANN

After I resigned from my position at the Kunsthalle Bern in 1969, I needed to find some other kind of activity. As time went by, my initiatives at the Kunsthalle had become completely solitary, since there was no competitive spirit in the development of exhibition programming in Bern. So I opened the Agency for Intellectual Guest Labour on October 1, 1969. From around 1950, "exhibition maker" had become a profession, so I tried to pursue it without having a permanent job in a fine art museum or any sort of fixed connection with that kind of institution. In other words, I simply wanted to follow this profession in the purest way possible, without having to be concerned with all the exhibitions included in any museum's annual programming plans.

URS AND RÖS GRAF

What was the idea behind the Agency?

HARALD SZEEMANN

My first idea was to build a team, perhaps formally constituted as a company, but it very soon turned out that as far as mounting exhibitions was concerned nobody was interested in the work of an anonymous collective. On the contrary, as with art itself, what was wanted were "signed" exhibitions, in other words exhibitions which could be identified with the individual profile of the exhibition maker. [1] So the Agency has remained a one-man undertaking until this day, and that is the only form in which it has operated.

URS AND RÖS GRAF

What exhibitions have been mounted thus far on the initiative of the Agency or as a result of its work?

HARALD SZEEMANN

Since I opened the Agency I've made three exhibitions. The first of them, entitled *Agence*, took place in Paris. [2] That show's purpose was simply to launch the idea of the Agency. This bold undertaking met with a very positive response: in France, Holland, and England, where the exhibition gave rise to a lot of comment, the idea was taken up with a great deal of interest. The second time the idea was introduced was at the 1970 exhibition *The Thing as Object* at the Kunstverein in Nuremberg, where the assignment basically amounted to helping out the overburdened Kunsthalle: originally the Agency was supposed to be involved purely on paper, but we ended up going ourselves to lenders to find the works to exhibit. But while the extent of my involvement had been specified quite clearly, I ended up doing almost the entire exhibition (collaboration on the concept, organization, the loan of works), though this was absolutely not what I intended the Agency to be about—which was to make the creation of exhibitions more anonymous. However, it also turned out that this idea of anonymity created major financial problems, because nowadays most museums that put on exhibitions do not have the resources to pay a whole team. Moreover, you have to bear in mind all the sensitive problems that come up in trying to put together a team of the kind the Agency envisaged. This issue came to the fore especially at the third exhibition, *Happening & Fluxus*, which the Kunstverein in Cologne had assigned to my Agency in autumn 1970. In this assignment the entire creation of the exhibition fell to me, from the initial idea up to the actual mounting. In Cologne, I tried for the first time to carry out the entire task allotted to me in collaboration with an artist (Wolf Vostell) and a collector (H. Sohm). It subsequently turned out to be extremely hard to put together a reliable team, capable of functioning properly in a realm where the balance was always precarious, as the creation of an exhibition can often be. As far as the future is concerned, I have a new exhibition project entitled *The Street* (1971), planned in collaboration with a museum. This time the technical organization will go off without a hitch. However, this project is not a purely artistic one: the theme deals with the phenomenon of the street viewed typologically, and the critiques relating to it, and also embraces proposals for new types of street. Of course it will include a section on the street as the subject of artistic and political demonstrations. All in all, what is to be constructed is almost a simulation of a street scene. There too, we will have to overcome the difficulties of working with the four people who are collaborating on the project, in line with their co-ordination within the team. Here again, what has to be avoided is turning the project into the work of one individual.

URS AND RÖS GRAF

What have been your most important learning experiences during your activity in connection with the Agency?

HARALD SZEEMANN

As these first experiences show, each time that I have offered my services at a subordinate level for an exhibition, I have ended up instead taking on the overall organization, which is the exact opposite of the true concept behind the Agency. Moreover, as I mentioned, the experience of the Cologne exhibition brought out the enormous difficulties that emerged when I tried to pull together an effective team—difficulties that were affected equally by organizational and personal factors. But I have learned one key lesson from these experiences: in line with the upcoming *documenta* in Kassel, whose preparation is going to occupy me for some time to come, the entire problem of the conception of the exhibition has to be rethought from the beginning. Since I opened the Agency, I have learned something else: when I assess the type and amount of this independent activity, I see that in fact hardly anything is different from the work I did previously as the director of the Kunsthalle—all the more so as I have begun to invest in some of the Agency's projects so as to be able to plan some personal productions of my own. My initial *motto*, "Replace ownership with free actions," is somewhat compromised. Now that I have my own printing

[Pages 85–86] These two letters propose a revival of the exhibition *Happening & Fluxus* (1971) to six institutions. The corrections added to them show a change of formula: Szeemann moves from the first to the third person and no longer signs himself "Harald Szeemann," but "Kunstverein Köln."

An Palais des Beaux-Arts, Brüssel
" Musée d'Art Moderne de la Ville de Paris

FRANZOESISCH

Monsieur,

(Hr. Harald Szeemann)

Le Kunstverein de Cologne m'a chargé d'organiser une exposition sur le thème "Happening et Fluxus" pour novembre/Decembre 1971.
Cette exposition contient 4 parties :

(bitte ausschreiben)

Il est clair que seules les parties 1, 2 et 3 puissent être reprises par d'autres musées. Quant aux parties 1 et 4 elles dépendent avant tout des finances des musées ou cette manifestation pourrait avoir lieu. A peu près 50 artistes vont être présentés ou se présenter dans le cadre de cette exposition et de manière différente (voir liste ci-jointe).
Je me permets de vous demander aujourd'hui si la reprise de cette exposition vous intéresse. Après la clôture à Cologne l'exposition sera montrée (janvier/février) en 1971 à Stuttgart. Après cette date elle sera libre.
Quant au catalogue c'est M. Sohm ~~est~~ qui est chargé de rassembler la documentation pour un volume d'à peu près 300 pages. Il est très difficile de vous donner déjà aujourd'hui des chiffres exacts quant à la reprise. Nous avons calculé qu'avec 4 participants elle coûterait dans les DM 25'000.-- à quoi se rajouteraient les frais d'installation et de transport du musée précédent au vôtre. Il se peut que pour cette somme de reprise nous pourrons également vous livrer un certain nombre (entre 1000 et 2000) de catalogues. Sie vous êtes intéressé pour cette exposition, je vous prie de me le faire savoir ~~signaler~~ aussi rapidement que possible.
Dans l'attente je vous prie d'agréer, Monsieur, l'expression de mes sentiments les meilleurs.

~~Harald Szeemann~~

Kunstverein Köln

An I.C.A. London
" Moderna Museet Stockholm
" Louisiana
" Museum of Contemporary Art, Chicago

ENGLISCH

Dear Sirs,

~~I have been charged by~~ The Kunstverein Cologne charged Herrn Harald Szeemann to organize an exhibition about the theme "Happening and Fluxus" for November/December 1970. This exhibition will consist of 4 parts. These parts are : --------

(bitte ausschreiben)

It is evident that only part 1, 2 and ~~part~~ 3 can be taken over by other museums with regard to part ~~1 and~~ 4 ~~they~~ it depends on the financies of the respective museum where this manifestation could be organized.

~~As~~ About 50 artists are going to be presented or to present themselves during this exhibition in different ways (please find the list of the participating artists enclosed).

I would like to know whether you are interested in taking over this exhibition. After its closing in Cologne it will be shown in 1971 at Stuttgart. After this the exhibition will be available.

Mr. Sohm is charged to collect the documentation for the catalogue which willbe a book of about 300 pages. It is very difficult to give you already now the exact XXXXXXXXXX overtaking-conditions. We have calculated that with 4 participants the costs would be about XX DM 25'000.-- to which would be added the installation costs and the transport cost from the preceding museum ~~the museum taking she XXXXXX shall before~~ to yours museum. It is possible that for the indicated overtaking cost we might deliver you a certain number of catalogues (between 1000 and 3000)

Please let us know as quickly as possible whether you are interested in taking over this exhibition.

With many thanks

yours sincerely,

~~Harald Szeemann~~

Kunstverein Köln

and photocopying equipment, and a voluminous collection of documents, ownership has come to take on disturbingly large dimensions. Fundamentally, I still find myself in the situation of a director with complete control over his institution, the only difference being that I don't have to account to anyone for my financial arrangements.

URS AND RÖS GRAF

Can you tell us more specifically why it is that the concept of the exhibition has to be comprehensively rethought, and where the problems lie?

HARALD SZEEMANN

Today an exhibition director has a number of tasks to fulfill:

1 – To consult all the specialized literature on the subject;
2 – To negotiate with the artists, which is an ever more difficult task;
3 – To give accurate concrete form to the artist's ideas, without the artist being present, with only the help of manual workers;
4 – To take on the planning and writing of catalogues;
5 – To manage the publicity;
6 – To deal with the press, which is more and more interested in contemporary art news.

Now the problematic situation of the exhibition director at the present time derives from the fact that he cannot successfully carry out all these tasks by himself, which means purely and simply that he is obliged to rethink and restructure the entire phenomenon of the exhibition. I believe that during the 1970s (which will not turn out to have been all that important as a period of artistic innovation, in contrast to the preceding decade), people began to feel the need for a restructuring of the phenomenon of the exhibition, and to recognize that the most worthwhile approach was the team effort, that is, the joint work of a team which had to be assembled for the purpose. If the specialized literature now includes more and more grandiose titles like "The crisis of the museum as an institution," "The crisis of art," and so on, it's very often because fundamentally the artist realizes that as a single individual he has a harder time placing his output if he fails to obey the law of originality. The same is true for the exhibition maker, the only difference being that in his case he presents entire configurations of artworks, not single items, in other words a subjective grouping which takes on an apparently objective form. The fundamental problem of the exhibition at present can be expressed by asking the question: "How can the magic of the object, which is no longer enough for the majority of the public, be replaced?" The explanatory notice attached to an object scarcely reflects ten percent of its real nature. When you wave an object in front of the viewing public, only a remnant of its original energy survives. If you construct your own setting for it, the artist is frustrated, and rightly so. The first problem that exhibitions of the future will run into is that of establishing a connection with the public. Museum directors typically more and more want to work for the public, not for the artists. Now, it is extremely hard to work for the public. Given the number of new museums that opened during the 1960s, the percentage of visitors can only grow in the future. But in spite of everything, it remains difficult to create exhibitions with content, which truly bring the public together. One could of course imagine an exhibition on the theme of something like "Swiss Neutrality," but it wouldn't have much to do with the fine arts. And if one takes art as one's starting-point, or what is understood by art, that is to say the work of an individual who takes his own risks in creating that work, I see no other possible approach except to take that individual's body of work as the starting-point. If that work is powerful enough from a formal point of view, it is recognized as such, and requires almost nothing by way of supplementary explanation.

There are other possibilities, which involve starting from concepts foreign to art and introducing artworks to illustrate them, or else opening up new worlds of images to be shown side by side with artworks—a possibility that museums will probably move toward more and more. Another variation seems especially attractive to me—the attempt by P.F. Althaus to install *The Open Museum as a Source of Information* at the Kunsthalle Basel. In any case, this variation has already been partly implemented in France. It's odd that it only works really well in one place, the Maison de la Culture in Amiens; this is because there is a team that works very well together there, rather than a single superstar.

URS AND RÖS GRAF

You said that in the future museum directors will seek more and more to work for the public. Are there reasons for this?

HARALD SZEEMANN

Museum directors mean to introduce changes, they do actually want change. These changes can only take place on the local level, hence the idea of making exhibitions for the public. But if the content of the exhibitions is so constricted that in some sense the element of shock is eliminated, no change can occur. Aesthetic boundaries won't be pushed any further. Perhaps it's in these terms that we can characterize part of the dilemma the exhibition maker is struggling with today. If we create exhibitions with social-political themes, of course we can't confine ourselves to displaying objects chosen purely on grounds of personal taste, which would reflect an obviously elitist way of thinking. During the 1960s this dilemma was less pressing than it is now, since exhibition-makers then could count on extraordinarily intense productivity in art.

URS AND RÖS GRAF

What conditions do you have to take into account today when your Agency offers to mount a thematic exhibition?

HARALD SZEEMANN

When the Agency offers to mount an exhibition—and as everybody knows the supply of exhibitions internationally is enormous—the proposal absolutely has to present something novel. Moreover, the Agency simply cannot propose exhibitions of work by individual artists, for the very good reason that the costs involved in that kind of show can be covered by the art institutions themselves. So it goes without saying that we propose thematic exhibitions. All in all, my plan is to follow the same principles with regard to the Agency's exhibitions that I used to follow at the Kunsthalle Bern.

URS AND RÖS GRAF

Many of the critics who covered your Cologne exhibition, *Happening & Fluxus*, have raised the question of how it would play into your preparations for the upcoming *documenta* in Kassel. How far has your experience in Cologne influenced the conception of the 1972 *documenta*?

HARALD SZEEMANN

In Cologne, the idea was to present *Happening & Fluxus* in isolation as a "third force" relative both to traditional art, which continued on its usual way, and objectal art, which had expanded enormously during the 1960s. Also, no institution in Cologne really supported the artists' desire to participate in exhibitions—a crucial element which the artists of *Happening & Fluxus* continued to demand. Of course I first wanted to see how the representation of this famous "third force" would work out, but I was determined at the same time to prove that another component was becoming more important, that is to say documentation. It seemed to me essential to demonstrate how, through the introduction of documentation, the major moments represented in *Happening & Fluxus* were able to make the less intense periods meaningful. This was how we were able to establish that the movement had expanded after 1965, but that at the same time its energy had declined, from which one could conclude that *Happening & Fluxus* developed almost in parallel with Pop art and Minimalism. Moreover, from the viewpoint of the upcoming *documenta*, I also wanted to examine the operation of the triple rhythm of "documentation/personal presentation/action." Here is what I would say overall of the Cologne experience: above all, it demonstrated clearly that precarious actions highly dependent on individualities, as in *Happening & Fluxus*, or the simple organization of workshops as incorporated to the process of developing *When Attitudes Become Form* [1969], seriously threatened the reliable running of the show, and hence involved too great a risk of total fiasco to justify, in the context of *documenta*, planning it as a retrospective based solely on actions of this kind. In the light of these experiences, our team ended up returning to the concept of a thematic exhibition, along the lines originally proposed at the start of our preparatory work. To that extent the Cologne experience has had a direct influence on the conception of the upcoming *documenta*, and it is quite obviously wrong to claim, as has sometimes been done by the media, that it is impossible to evaluate *Happening & Fluxus* until one has seen *documenta 5*. There is no doubt whatsoever that *Happening & Fluxus* is a totally independent phenomenon.

URS AND RÖS GRAF

What is most likely to be the future of the Agency for Intellectual Guest Labour?

HARALD SZEEMANN

As far as the next two years are concerned, all the Agency projects have been postponed, because I'm completely taken up by the preparations for the upcoming *documenta* in Kassel, where I have been appointed General Secretary in charge of the team preparing the show. Right now I am in a phase where basically I work abroad, because the only people who can thrive in Switzerland (and I'm not speaking only of myself) are those who fulfill some useful function, such as museum or library director, and in Europe only West Germany can employ people like that. As a result, I hardly fit into the environment in Bern in the context of these deeper investigations. Foreigners are surprised to see how totally the younger generation in Switzerland rejects their country's institutions—a phenomenon which, however, has had very little effect on public life. I am in roughly the same situation with respect to Bern.

[1] Harald Szeemann himself used the English term "exhibition maker," which he especially liked as a translation of the German term "Ausstellungsmacher."

[2] This was the exhibition called *8½: documentation 1961–1969*, February 5–March 9, 1970, Galerie Claude Givaudan, Paris.

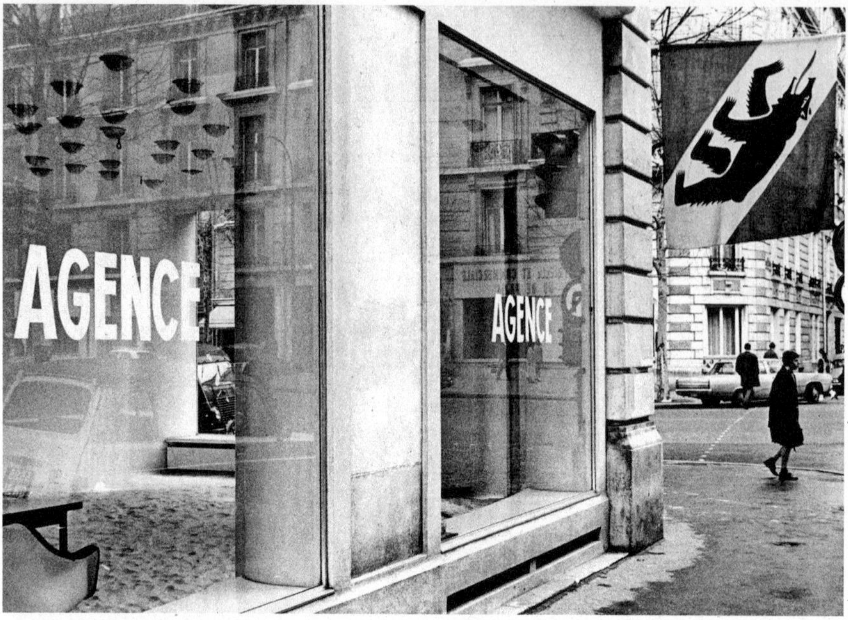

In March 1970, for the exhibition *8½: documentation 1961–1969* at the Galerie Claude Givaudan, Harald Szeemann raised the flag of the city of Bern in Paris. This show gave him the opportunity to display documents relating to his activities during the eight and a half years he had spent in Bern, and especially to publicize and promote the Agency.

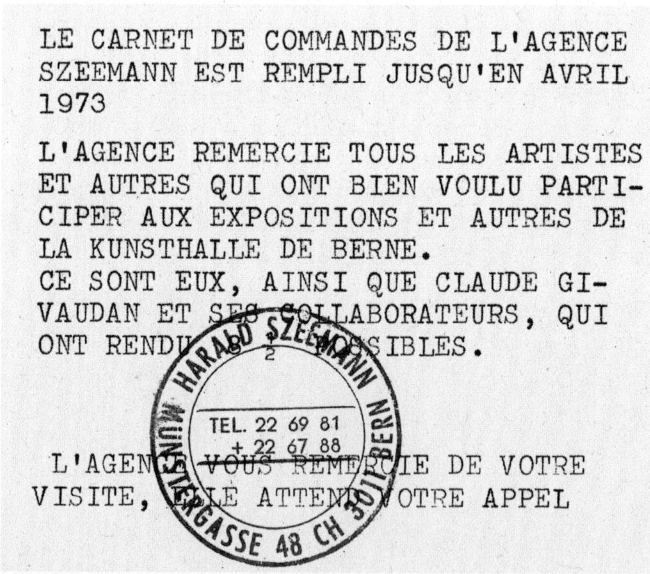

LE CARNET DE COMMANDES DE L'AGENCE SZEEMANN EST REMPLI JUSQU'EN AVRIL 1973

L'AGENCE REMERCIE TOUS LES ARTISTES ET AUTRES QUI ONT BIEN VOULU PARTICIPER AUX EXPOSITIONS ET AUTRES DE LA KUNSTHALLE DE BERNE.
CE SONT EUX, AINSI QUE CLAUDE GIVAUDAN ET SES COLLABORATEURS, QUI ONT RENDU 8 ½ POSSIBLES.

L'AGENCE VOUS REMERCIE DE VOTRE VISITE, ELLE ATTEND VOTRE APPEL

A stamp applied to the back of the poster produced for the exhibition *8½: documentation 1961–1969* (Galerie Claude Givaudan, Paris, 1970). This part of the poster displays the list of exhibitions and events organized by Szeemann in Bern.

Part III:

Works

1) *documenta 5: Questioning Reality—Image Worlds Today*, 1972

Introduction

Lucia Pesapane

"See better through *documenta 5*" [1]

documenta 5 could be viewed as the most significant and most conceptually complex exhibition of the first 15 years of Harald Szeemann's career. It was the product of three years of work following his appointment in 1969 after the controversial success of *When Attitudes Become Form* and his subsequent resignation as the director of the Kunsthalle in Bern. When *d5* opened in June 1972, it represented a synthesis of all Szeemann's interests and research up to that point: the initial idea of conceiving the show as a 100-day-long event and as an "action-art" happening under a tent in Karlsaue Park stemmed, in fact, from the workshop-cum-exhibition already tested in *When Attitudes Become Form* and the audience-participation concept adopted for *Happening & Fluxus* in 1970. But Szeemann himself admitted that "precarious actions highly dependent on individualities, as in *Happening & Fluxus*, or the simple organization of workshops as incorporated to the process of developing *When Attitudes Become Form*, seriously threatened the reliable running of the show, and hence involved too great a risk of total fiasco to justify, in the context of *documenta*, planning it as a retrospective based solely on actions of this kind. In the light of these experiences, our team ended up returning to the concept of a thematic exhibition, along the lines originally proposed at the start of our preparatory work." [2]

On the basis of these considerations, the theme was modified to *Questioning Reality—Image Worlds Today*. *d5* was conceived as a vast collection of things from our visual world, "a concentrated version of life in the form of an exhibition" to be held in the Neue Galerie and the Museum Fridericianum. This revised option, heavily influenced by theorist Bazon Brock, favored a thematic approach to the various sections and sought to answer the question, "how does art interpret the world?" Only an answer as complex as the one suggested by Szeemann would do: adopting an encyclopedic approach, he decided to show objects that did not belong to the realm of art, creating a mixture of ordinary objects and fetish items that belonged to popular, political, or kitsch culture, as well as to religious art and outsider art. *d5* could thus be perceived as a vast "cabinet of curiosities." The show was in all respects a reflection of recent artistic explorations, marked by the presence of Conceptual art (Hans Haacke, Lawrence Weiner), Body art (Viennese Actionists), Performance art (Vito Acconci, Gilbert & George,

Ben Vautier), Hyper-Realism, Joseph Beuys' "Information Office" for visitors, and recent experiments in urban development (Archigram/Peter Cook, Yona Friedman). The changes that Szeemann brought to the 1972 show were not just artistic but also administrative—after *documenta 4*, Arnold Bode (who devised the first versions of *documenta*) and the 26-member board of directors abandoned their earlier roles. Szeemann was the first outsider to be named sole General Secretary, and who therefore didn't have to share responsibilities with the board. The autonomy he gained allowed him to avoid bureaucratic delays, to maintain total freedom, to express his own vision, and to work with his own team while delegating roles. Juries and boards of directors were dropped in favor of a single art directorate and a team of trusted colleagues that included Arnold Bode once again, and also Jean-Christophe Ammann, Bazon Brock, Peter Iden, Karlheinz Braun, and Alexander Kluge. Alongside his advisors, who defined the overall context in conjunction with him, Szeemann called upon a series of outside participants to whom he entrusted the various thematic sections of *d5*, such as the architect and critic François Burkhardt (head of *Utopia and Planning*), and Marxist philosopher Hans Heinz Holz (who wrote the introduction to the catalogue).

Yet *documenta 5* was even more than that, it was an exhibition closely related to the political and social fabric of the 1970s. In the context of post-68 changes and institutional critiques, Szeemann's reaction was, somewhat paradoxically, to reinforce the role of the museum as opposed to the utopian idea of getting art into the streets—he advocated "art for art's sake." He asked artists to create their own museums for the section called *Artists' Museums*, which included contributions from Ben Vautier, Marcel Broodthaers, Herbert Distel, Claes Oldenburg, and Daniel Spoerri. At the same time, discordant voices could be heard: a petition signed and published by Carl Andre, Hans Haacke, Donald Judd, Barry Le Va, Sol LeWitt, Richard Serra, and Robert Smithson referred to the "cultural imprisonment" of works in a museum and of "aesthetic convalescence" when the curator announced his restrictions. Robert Morris had sent Szeemann a letter denying authorization to show his work, and Daniel Buren's text, *Exposition d'une exposition* (*Exhibition of an Exhibition*) described *d5* as an artwork by Harald Szeemann, the artists' own work being like brushstrokes of color used by the curator. [3] Accounts by Jean-Christophe Ammann and Johannes Cladders confirm the idea that Szeemann was an artist among artists.

Soon the German and foreign press was raising sharp questions that fuelled debate. Harald Szeemann was harshly criticized for his decision to present individual positions simultaneously rather than feature a dominant style, to display examples of popular and kitsch culture, to defend the value of an artwork and yet at the same time juxtapose it with ordinary objects, and to proclaim art's autonomy during a period of great political and social upheaval.

[1] The slogan of *documenta 5*.

[2] Cf. Urs and Rös Graf, "Interview with Harald Szeemann," p. 89.

[3] "More and more, the subject of an exhibition tends not be the display of artworks, but the exhibition of the exhibition as a work of art. Here, the *documenta* team, headed by Harald Szeemann, exhibits (artworks) and exposes itself (to critiques). The works presented are carefully chosen touches of color in the tableau that composes each section (room) as a whole. There is even an order to these colors, these being defined and arranged according to the drawn design of the section (selection) in which they are spread out/presented. These sections (castrations), themselves carefully chosen "touches of color" in the tableau that makes up the exhibition as a whole and in its very principle, only appear by placing themselves under the wing of the organizer, who reunifies art by rendering it equivalent everywhere in the case/screen that he prepares for it. The organizer assumes the contradictions; it is he who safeguards them. It is true, then, that the exhibition establishes itself as its own subject, and its own subject as a work of art. The exhibition is the 'valorizing receptacle' in which art is played out and founders, because even if the artwork was formerly revealed thanks to the museum, it now serves as nothing more

than a decorative gimmick for the survival of the museum as tableau, a tableau whose author is none other than the exhibition organizer.

"And the artist throws her—or himself and her or his work into this trap, because the artist and her or his work, which are powerless from the force of habit of art, have no choice but to allow another to be exhibited: the organizer. Hence, the exhibition as a tableau of art, as the limit of the exhibition of art. Thus, the limits art has created for itself, as shelter, turn against it by imitating it, and the refuge that the limits of art had constituted are revealed as its justification, reality, and tomb." in Daniel Buren, "Exhibitions of an Exhibition," *documenta 5*, Kassel 1972, p. 29.

First Exhibition Concepts

Harald Szeemann

The following texts document the two successive concepts for *documenta 5* proposed in 1970 and 1971.

Initial concept for *documenta 5*

Published in *Informationen*, May–June 1970.

During its meeting of April 22, 1970, the board of directors of Documenta GmbH, chaired by First Alderman Karl Brunner, asked Harald Szeemann, General Secretary of *documenta 5*, to present the concept behind the show in a text written for the general public. A meeting was held in Frankfurt on April 28 with Harald Szeemann, Karl Oskar Blase, Arnold Bode, Bazon Brock, Werner Hofmann, and Peter Iden. They drafted the following statement:

Introduction and goals:

The concept of *documenta 5* is based on two fundamental considerations. The first concerns criticism of *documenta 4*, while the second attempts to free the realm of art from the constraints of local artistic culture and occasional events. *documenta* should be a place of programmed events, an interactive space, and an accessible program structure with staggered centers of action. What local art institutions only offer in a random chronology of countless exhibitions should occur at Kassel according to an established program. The slogan of the past two *documentas*, "The 100-Day Museum," is to be replaced by "The 100-Day Event." The terms "museum" and "art" imply the idea of viewing objects and material property, then of confirming, transporting, and insuring the goods. In contrast, for *documenta 5* we can expect that all the events will be prepared and staged at Kassel, and that the organization will focus on projecting events rather than the judging and transporting of objects. *documenta 5* is not, in the first instance, a place for a static accumulation of objects, but a process of events that refer to one another. This concept is essentially didactic.

Execution of *documenta 5*:

1 – Documentation

The documentation includes thematic presentations on:

a) the problematic of certain developing trends in the visual arts ("gesture," "time," "space," "trace," "prototypical thought");

b) the problematic of material artistic production (new media and new technologies);
c) the problematic of the artist's social role (creator, part of a collective or team, solitary, individualistic);
d) the problematic of the space of social activity outside the usual circuit of studio/gallery/museum/collection (public-relations work, information output, environmental control, communication management);
e) the problematic of transmitting art (artistic education and pedagogy).

2 – Program structure

f) the material program structure is composed of specially arranged spaces designed to respond to the needs of artists, scholars, social assistants, designers, filmmakers, decision makers, planners, and players in the development of these spaces;
g) five departments are planned in the context of programmed events: the five senses, today's Modulor (seasons, growth, elements), today's framework (peace, happiness, knowledge);
h) an example of a complex thematic production is "the street," two kilometers in Auepark. Aspects include typology, criticism and new models, sociological and artistic relationships (the street as site of encounters, as space of action and demonstration, as an aesthetic situation).

Organized events will also included new artistic forms in the realm of theater. The German Academy of Visual Arts will present *Experimenta 5* at Kassel in the context of *documenta*.

3 – *documenta 5* will take place in city section of Kassel between Königstrasse and Auepark, the National Theater and the University.

4 – Documentation of *documenta*

For the first time, *documenta 5* will act not only as the producer of the exhibition and events, but also as publisher and librarian (a "kinetic" catalogue to be walked through, conventional catalogue, films, objects, educational books and activities).

In charge of execution are: Archigram, London (material program structure); Karl Oskar Blase, Kassel (information centers); Arnold Bode, Kassel (coordination); Bazon Brock, Hamburg and Frankfurt (organized events); Werner Hofmann, Hamburg (thematic shows); Peter Iden and Karlheinz Braun (*Experimenta*); Karl Ruhrberg, Düsseldorf (information); Harald Szeemann, Bern and Kassel (General Secretary of *documenta 5*, head of planning and execution). Members of the executive team are appointed by the board of directors of documenta GmbH at the proposal of the State of Hesse (Mr von Friedeburg, Minister of Culture) and the city of Kassel (Mr Branner, First Alderman).

Second concept for *documenta 5*

Published in *Informationen*, March 1971.
Text written by Jean-Christophe Ammann, Bazon Brock, and Harald Szeemann.

Introduction:

The most current formal principles governing the choice of exhibition material are:
one-man exhibition—works of one artist of immediate contemporary interest are shown.
Group exhibition—contemporary work by several artists, who are contemporaries and/or work under the same conditions, are shown.
Retrospective exhibition—the entire work of one artist is presented as an entity or a contribution toward a definite judgment.
Accrochage—non-structured ensemble of the works of separate artists, for instance at the end of an exhibition season.
Stock exhibition—the stock of the museum—generally not accessible to the public—is on exhibition during a short interval.
Private collection exhibition—collections acquired by a single collector are made available to the public.
Exhibition for representative purposes—in connection with a certain public event an exhibition is added as a further attraction.

For some time already exhibition directors generally have been tending to replace formal principles that have been adhered to up to now by those of content. The *thematic exhibition* is a result of these reflections. The whole of the material shown in an exhibition is determined by a thematic context, which
a) is derived from existing work, or
b) is formulated independently of already existing material.

In the case a) the works in the exhibition express the theme by their mutual correlation (the material on show dominates).
In the case b) the exhibition transfers the theme to the field of visual perception (the theme and the visualized thematic suggestions dominate).

d5 is a thematic exhibition with the special advantage that its theme is developed both from the existing work of individual artists or groups and from the present state of thought about general social problems. Whether the work done on *d5* is justified and effective may be judged largely from the degree to which the theme developed from existing work can be equated with the initial theme partly independent of the existing work.

We have to begin with the differentiation of the starting-points out of which the theme is developed, because on the one hand, of the artist's historic claim to autonomous unfolding of his imaginations and ideas, which can only be justified in the framework of his work; on the other hand society, too, demands that art should take on certain functions, i.e., that it should contribute to the knowledge of human conditions and their mutation in the direction of given goals which are not of predominantly artistic interest but above all of general social importance.

If a unity of theme developed out of autonomous artistic and heteronomous social ideas can be achieved, it will be possible to show how far artistic production is already comprehensible under the general and inescapable conditions of social life and how far artists are already working even on the subjective level of conditions generally obtained in social life. Meanwhile there will be no more doubt as to whether the same objective considerations condition all aspects of life in society. The question still remaining however is to what degree such objective conditions are recognizable in concrete results in each particular domain. It is a major aim of *d5* to promote the clarification of this question and especially of the problem of the significance of art in connection with the attempt to resolve these social problems.

1 – The Theme

Thematic scope regarding content derived largely from contemporary work:

Artistic production historically aims at least at the creation of autonomous reality, it produces "another world," a "world of beautiful illusions," a "dream-world," a "between-world."

Artists try to realize these aims by reflecting permanently how they can detach themselves from the given domains of social and natural reality, or at least make the difference between the two clear in their work. This is why in contemporary art so many elements of non-artistic reality are quoted and used.

Systematically and at the same time historically there are relations between:
1 – the representation of reality;
2 – the transformation of reality by transformation, of its representation;
3 – the creation of a new autonomous reality.

Here "representation" is only given as an example for one essential form of artistic work.

Against the background of the phenomena of social life in its various practical domains the theme of *d5* crystallizes as follows: it is becoming more and more urgent to be clear about what reality consists of, since reality defined as objectively determined nature has been widely replaced by the results of social life. It has become nature of a second order. Such second nature confronts man with greater demands than those of primary nature, but there is no way of finding out what differentiated, other content of reality belongs to this nature of a second order. The question regarding the content and the demands of second nature is raised even as far as in the behavior of individuals, who are constrained to adapt to reality. This second nature consists largely of credos, ideas, fantasies, utopias, of rituals, orders, commands, of feelings, perceptions, reactions, which ore accepted as realities in quite another way than for instance trees, mountains, oceans.
Historically and at the same time systematically we can speak of relations between:
1 – the cognition of reality;
2 – the transformation of reality through the transformation of the instruments of cognition;
3 – the creation of new reality.

"Cognition" is mentioned here merely as one essential form of social work.

An attempt to formulate the theme of *d5* can be derived thus from the phenomena of contemporary social life and contemporary art:
Questioning Reality—Image Worlds Today

2 – Structure

Starting from the above-mentioned considerations we can derive the structure of the theme for *d5*:

1 – the reality of the image;
2 – the reality of "what is portrayed";
3 – the identity or non identity of the image and of "what is portrayed."

or

1 – the system of images, objects, signs as a reality;
2 – the "portrayed," the signified, the objectivated as a reality;
3 – the unity or difference between the content of reality which characterizes the image or "what is portrayed."

or

1 – the autonomous, free world of images, imaginations, and projects which have no or very little relation to any other reality than their own
2 – visual representations, which are essentially instruments and procedures in one's dealing with a given reality
3 – congruents of the image and "what is portrayed," because
 a) the faculty of distinguishing between these varying levels of reality is either not yet developed or has been lost through illness

 or

 b) because it is the only way to resolve certain historical problems. Conversely, a series of cognitive processes are determined by the necessity of establishing the irremovable difference between the image and "what is portrayed."

3 – Exhibition material

What is given, is the artistic and non artistic imagery. The exhibited and quoted imagery is attributed to the three structural categories, divided into primary and secondary complexes of material. The structural category *Reality of the Image* includes
primarily:

a) Social Realism
b) Imagery of publicity
c) Kitsch
d) Art photography

secondarily:

– Comics
– Science fiction

- Political propaganda
- Mass media (magazines, newspapers, films, etc.)
- Social iconography (bank notes, flags, stamps, etc.)
- Monuments (statues, gravestones, etc.)

Reality of "What is Portrayed"
primarily:
a) Contemporary realistic painting (West-Coast realism)
b) Action photography
c) Actionism (street art & theater, May 1968)
d) Pornography
e) Design
f) Pop art

secondarily:
- Psychedelic art
- Individual mythologies
- Self-portrayal
- Traffic signs
- Formalized languages
- Caricature
- Portraiture

Identity/or Non-Identity of the Image and of "What is Portrayed"
primarily:
I – Forced identity
a) Children's painting
b) Psychotic art
c) Concretism
II – Intended identity
a) Process art
b) Real-time film
c) Real-time theater
d) Sports
e) Games
III – Non-identity
a) Conceptual art
b) Oldenburg's method (visual art)
c) Magritte's method (visual art)
d) Teaching and learning as representational arts

secondarily:
- Naive painting
- Surrealism
- Art as attitude
- The "communes"
- "Art = Life"

4 – Forms of presentation

a) derived from exhibition material:
- isolated objects/images
- confronted objects/images
- optimizing selection
- aesthetic hanging
- staging of exhibition architecture
- theatrical set
- projection of films
- action
- panorama
- environment
- light show

b) derived from the thematic aspect:
- graphic presentation
- verbal explanation
- programmed instruction (PI)
- didactic hanging
- models
- reproductions and copies
- reconstructions
- lectures
- publications
- instructions for use
- experimental audio-visual installations

5 – Domains of realization

documenta in accordance with its character as an art exhibition is especially concerned with those forms of work and experience, which are related to non-verbal languages that is to the languages of image, of object, of the body, and of signs.

Such languages are spoken today in almost all domains of social work and life. They are also used in all fields of artistic production.

It is therefore intended to conduct the inquiry not only in the field of visual art but also in that of theater, film, and mixed media, and of communication, theory, and application of artistic ideas. But of course the section of visual art will be unmistakably the center of *d5*.

The principle of the integrated exhibition will decide the placing of the different examples. Unfortunately this integration can be realized only according to the theme and not according to space. This is because of the financial, spatial, and staff conditions of *d5*.

The following sections are envisaged:

a) Visual art and social imagery
b) Art in scientific teaching and mediation of artistic ideas, theories and applications
c) Theater
d) Film

5a) This section is to be considered as the focal point of *d5*. This exhibition has to meet the highest standards of perception and of general receptivity yet developed in the visual arts, i.e., it has to satisfy the public's idolatry of objects, therefore it has to offer the authentic pictures and objects. It must be optically impressive to stimulate people's capacity for experiencing—since it has been found that the majority of exhibition visitors do not even begin to be receptive to statements, unless the event-character of the exhibition he demands is there. In order to give even greater emphasis to this release-function of the material, a great number of forms of presentation are being developed for the central exhibition of *documenta*. Each room of the exhibition will offer another procedure for stimulating the reception.

5b) Since the stimulating of the reception of the event and experience-character can only be one—if important—precondition for proper reception of the theme, there is an absolute need for a smaller second exhibition in addition to the central exhibition, where the accent lies unequivocally on categories other than those of event and experience. In this second exhibition the public should above all be offered the cognitive, psychomotor, and socio-emotional conditions for adequate reception of the theme. This exhibition within the exhibition is *The Visitors' School* of *documenta 5*.

The Visitors' School will systematically highlight the theme by means of single examples and series of examples. This necessitates forms of representation, which at first sight are incomprehensible because they are not submitted to visual laws.

This work has to be done above all by means of reproductions, plans, and models, and verbal expressions, which do not enjoy excessive popularity among regular art exhibition visitors.

But whereas conditions of production and reception of artistic creation are not just without complications and problems, there cognition and adoption cannot happen in an easy way or without effort.

Obviously *The Visitors' School* will try to do justice to the propositions of art didactics elaborated up to now. But this is by no means the same as representing the work in *The Visitors' School* as an effortless and casual game.

In detail *The Visitors' School* will prepare the working conditions for the following problems formulated in the theme of *documenta* and for its realization in the central part:

1 – Conditions for psychology of reception of reality (programmed instruction—PI and directives for experiments of public in *d5*).

2 – Conditions for theory of perception of reality (PI and models for the use of visitors).
3 – Linguistic conditions for perception of reality (differentiation of language systems above all in the field of nonverbal languages with PI and prepared working material, by means of which visitors learn to express themselves in nonverbal languages).
4 – Conditions for artistic constitution of reality (PI, experimental installations). The Zones of transition between the exhibition and *The Visitors' School* should bring the material strictly according to the aspect of the theme, which in the exhibition—because of its event character—cannot be wholly subjected in detail to the theme, for example:

If in the exhibition a real tire, a tire—photographed for publicity purposes—a tire painted by Lichtenstein from the same advertisement, and a Lichtenstein-tire used again for publicity, is shown to the public according to the main structure ("reality of the image," reality of "what is portrayed," and "identity of both"), this mutual and continuous mediation of different levels of reality will be shown as a continuum in the transitional zone.

The PI-films of *The Visitors' School* will be produced as a result of the interdisciplinary cooperation of several scientists, which should guarantee the necessary degree of control.

5c) Since the preparation of an experiment in the domain of theater has been given to *Experimenta*, an independent institution, we include here part of an exposé by Peter Iden and Karlheinz Braun, meant as a firm proposition.

Draft program for Experimenta 5 within the overall-concept of documenta 5

A – Introduction

The management of *documenta 5* planned for 1972 in Kassel has decided to ask the German Academy for Dramatic Arts and the members hitherto responsible for *Experimenta* to the Academy, Dr Karlheinz Braun and Peter Iden, to realize *Experimenta 5* as part of *documenta 5* in Kassel. Negotiations took place already in 1968, for *documenta 4*, between the *documenta* council and the directors of *Experimenta* in order to enlarge the program of *documenta* by some examples of experimental theater. The negotiations then failed for organizational reasons. Now they have been resumed and it was decided that it would be opportune to organize *Experimenta* in the year of *documenta*. This decision is based first on the fact that there is an evident relationship between recent forms of expression in visual art and contemporary form of theater, and on the other hand on cultural political reflections which call for optimal exploitation of the money government has given for cultural purposes by a concentrated effort of two institutions.

B – Structural principle

In connection with *documenta 5*, *Experimenta 5* will repeat its structural principle. Consequently it, too, will undertake to examine the various notions of reality in the context of dramatic forms. But we have to point out here that because of the greater expenses incurred by theater, the categories developed in the section of visual art can be demonstrated through theater in only a few examples. Nevertheless a crucial point of the theater program will consist in the material's classification according to didactic considerations in the some way as in the main part of the exhibition.

C – Restrictions to the structural principle necessary in the domain of theater

The necessary restrictions of the structure developed for the main part of *d5* in the theater section result from the fact that under certain circumstances it is more diffi cult here to provide the single sections with exact and striking examples, as is intended in the section of visual art. In other words: one piece may illustrate several categories of the whole concept. Besides, we cannot give precise indication in advance which pieces can be produced for Kassel or which groups can be invited. A concrete enumeration can be made only in autumn 1971. Then it will be possible to see what productions are available on the international scene or which theaters will be able to dovetail work in Kassel into their plans.

D – The three categories

It will also be important for Experimenta to examine the reception of reality as it can be observed in the different forms of theater. Consequently we will have the same three categories:

a) reality of the image
b) reality of "what is portrayed"
c) identity/non identity of the image and of "what is portrayed"

Since, as was said above, it is at the moment impossible to illustrate these three categories with relevant examples, which can then be seen in Kassel, we must be content with some historical indications.

a) "the reality of the image" is reminiscent above all of the political didactic piece (for instance Hochhuth's Guerrillas), of the operetta and the musical, of the piece suggesting Surrealism and a logical reality, and also boulevard plays.
b) the reality of "what is portrayed," the material suitable would be of, for example, Heinrich Henkel's *Eisenwichser*, and in general plays which reproduce on stage a very limited and narrow field of reality on the scale of 1:1. In addition, there will be examples of the programmed happening, too, and likewise metaphorical and parable plays.
c) Identity/non-identity between the image and of "what is portrayed" can be demonstrated by works of the Polish author Grotowski and his group or by the Laboratory in Holstebro, Denmark. This section contains works that are the result of the limited self-concerned comprehension of their makers.

It must be emphasized again that these examples are given only to explain the principle. In Kassel new material will be presented; as a rule the program should only consist of first performances. In contrast to the main part of *d5* the theatrical contributions will afford a survey about the contemporary dramatic art of Eastern and Western origin.

E – Principles of selection

Two procedures are recommended
a) the possibility of commissioned plays
b) the invitation of already existing productions
The didactic purpose of *d5* will be best realized by method a), one thing we thought of was to make a collage, for instance, out of parts of well-known theater texts, in such a way that the new composition will illustrate certain evolutions in the drama of the last ten years. Of course such concepts can only be realized in intimate cooperation with German-speaking theater groups.

Procedure b) makes it possible to bring to Kassel examples of new dramatic forms from foreign countries. The directors of *Experimenta 5* have international contacts as a result of their previous work. In spite of the competition of the Olympic Games at Munich in the same year a program of international interest can be guaranteed. We further thought to organize, as well as the dramatic events, a discussion forum for the younger theater people.

F – Places for events

The performances are planned for: Small house of the Kasseler Staatstheater; stages in the Aue gardens, in the streets, and in town squares. These three possibilities correspond to the open and closed forms of which presumably the offer will consist.

G – Time

There will be no possibility to prepare a program for the duration of hundred days. This leads us to recommend concentrating Experimenta 5 in the ten first days of *documenta 5*. There will always be the possibility to invite two or three groups at the end of *documenta 5*.

5d) Film

The film section follows the same structural system as the exhibition, *The Visitors' School* and the theater section. The Filmhistorische Gesellschaft at Berlin is now engaged in an analysis of all the material available (availability of the Russian Archives, legal questions).

Preface to the Catalogue

Harald Szeemann

documenta 5, C. Bertelsmann Verlag, Munich, 1972.

When we began planning *d5*, the art world was enjoying a triumphant period driven by the speculatory fever of art dealers with their leading stars, yet also by increasingly sharp doubts about the art market. During the two years of preparation, two radically different programs were sketched out. One was orientated toward artists, the other toward visitors. But neither was totally applicable in its pure form. An event-orientated *documenta* would, at worst, have abandoned the institution to the street and arbitrariness, whereas a seminar-type approach would have turned its back on the original(ity of the) event. Hence the *documenta* presented here is, as so often, halfway between the two, which has meant, as with the realization of all ideas, "getting our hands dirty." This *d5* has the fertile, active character of an art show yet also offers signposts to new ways of seeing in a form that, postulated as the conceptual interrogation of reality, can be perceived in current examples of art and non-art. The presentation of works is autonomous, as formally decided by the artist. The role of beholder or visitor therefore resides in differentiating the levels of reality in the work, something with which the artist is not concerned. His knowledge and analysis or discussion of the work may, on their own, have an impact that transforms the defined structures of realities, the determination or definition of various levels of reality with the work. This deliberate, desired incorporation of event-driven interpretation can only be effectuated by beholders on condition that they take *d5* and the works on show as representing all the images in the world. The misconception which assumes that this idea represents a way of valorizing non-artistry should be dismissed. The idea represents a differentiated "way of seeing," whose goal is the elimination of simple "yes" or "no" judgments.

This way of "seeing" does not go without saying, but is driven by current artistic output. Much of the contemporary painting phenomenon is willfully banal and inexpressive, presented as the abbreviation of a process—the suggestion, impulse, or first link in an iconological chain. In *Meaning in the Visual Arts* (1955), Erwin Panofsky started with the example of an encounter with an acquaintance who politely lifts his hat, then successively teased out the various signifying levels of this event and simultaneously underscored, thanks to numerous examples, each of the various levels of reality within a conventional act ranging from mere habit to fully significant gesture.

Given the nature of a *documenta* that broadly presents the first information concerning artistic trends of the past three years, it would be absolutely mistaken to once again encumber "seeing" with a value judgment as, for example, Sedlmayer did in his structural analysis of Brueghel's *Blind Leading the Blind*, when he claimed that with progressive signifying levels the beauty and value of the painting can only be enhanced.

It is true that the art of the 1970s will move toward greater significance. The innovative boom years, during which new pictorial ideas and materials were placed on an equal footing and were promoted as new adventures, seem to be over. That is why this *documenta* was able to reject the phoney freedom of a "museum in the street" and to restrict the exhibition to two buildings, the Neue Galerie and the Museum Fridericianum. (Artists of the 1970s have practically abandoned the competitive debate with extra-artistic buildings. Traces are left in nature only where nature is virgin, and then only as a counter-proof stemming from output.) But this limitation to indoor space is no longer to be understood as a protective aid to works on the assumption that, as Hofmann put it two years ago "art, to be seen as such, needs a museum context."

An artist's relationship to museums once again goes without saying, and there are signs suggesting that as soon as we manage to free museums from their dreadful reputation as places of consecration, they will become what they once were, thanks to the artworks themselves.

As a panoramic exhibition, *d5* brings together the three magisterial forms of exhibition activity: criticism, information, documentation. Parallel pictorial methods—how they emerged and how they work—provide access to the problematic of the creation, evolution, and differentiation of levels of reality; conceptual art and Hyper-Realism to provide access to trends based on a formal perspective; individual mythologies provide access to the subjective creation of myths, sustaining a claim of overall validity via pictorial formulation. This term was used in 1963 in relation to the "internal" plans through which Etienne-Martin explained and defined the large sculptures of his empirical universe as "personal mythologies." *d5* simultaneously offers information about art, paths toward art and, we hope, the prospect of a post-art-market dawn.

I would like here to thank all of you who have participated in the completion and success of *d5*: artists, volunteers, colleagues, lenders, secretarial staff, technical team, catalogue crew, the authorities, security staff, and administrators. I hope that the principle of asking a single person to take charge of *documenta*—even though he knows it can't be done alone—has been shown to work, and that this principle will be further explored on other, local occasions, especially in situations where the task is to convey the combination of production-reception that *d5* has sought to stimulate and activate.

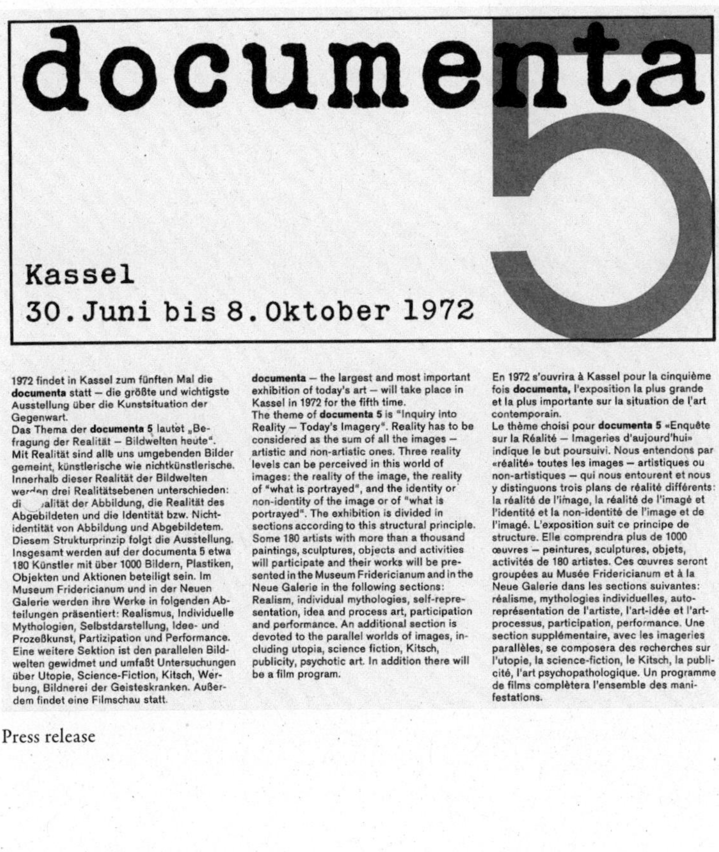

documenta 5

Kassel
30. Juni bis 8. Oktober 1972

1972 findet in Kassel zum fünften Mal die **documenta** statt – die größte und wichtigste Ausstellung über die Kunstsituation der Gegenwart.
Das Thema der **documenta 5** lautet „Befragung der Realität – Bildwelten heute". Mit Realität sind alle uns umgebenden Bilder gemeint, künstlerische wie nichtkünstlerische. Innerhalb dieser Realität der Bildwelten werden drei Realitätsebenen unterschieden: di[illegible]alität der Abbildung, die Realität des Abgebildeten und die Identität bzw. Nichtidentität von Abbildung und Abgebildetem. Diesem Strukturprinzip folgt die Ausstellung. Insgesamt werden auf der documenta 5 etwa 180 Künstler mit über 1000 Bildern, Plastiken, Objekten und Aktionen beteiligt sein. Im Museum Fridericianum und in der Neuen Galerie werden ihre Werke in folgenden Abteilungen präsentiert: Realismus, Individuelle Mythologien, Selbstdarstellung, Idee- und Prozeßkunst, Partizipation und Performance. Eine weitere Sektion ist den parallelen Bildwelten gewidmet und umfaßt Untersuchungen über Utopie, Science-Fiction, Kitsch, Werbung, Bildnerei der Geisteskranken. Außerdem findet eine Filmschau statt.

documenta – the largest and most important exhibition of today's art – will take place in Kassel in 1972 for the fifth time.
The theme of **documenta 5** is "Inquiry into Reality – Today's Imagery". Reality has to be considered as the sum of all the images – artistic and non-artistic ones. Three reality levels can be perceived in this world of images: the reality of the image, the reality of "what is portrayed", and the identity or non-identity of the image or of "what is portrayed". The exhibition is divided in sections according to this structural principle. Some 180 artists with more than a thousand paintings, sculptures, objects and activities will participate and their works will be presented in the Museum Fridericianum and in the Neue Galerie in the following sections: Realism, individual mythologies, self-representation, idea and process art, participation and performance. An additional section is devoted to the parallel worlds of images, including utopia, science fiction, Kitsch, publicity, psychotic art. In addition there will be a film program.

En 1972 s'ouvrira à Kassel pour la cinquième fois **documenta,** l'exposition la plus grande et la plus importante sur la situation de l'art contemporain.
Le thème choisi pour **documenta 5** «Enquête sur la Réalité – Imageries d'aujourd'hui» indique le but poursuivi. Nous entendons par «réalité» toutes les images – artistiques ou non-artistiques – qui nous entourent et nous y distinguons trois plans de réalité différents: la réalité de l'image, la réalité de l'imagé et l'identité et la non-identité de l'image et de l'imagé. L'exposition suit ce principe de structure. Elle comprendra plus de 1000 œuvres – peintures, sculptures, objets, activités de 180 artistes. Ces œuvres seront groupées au Musée Fridericianum et à la Neue Galerie dans les sections suivantes: réalisme, mythologies individuelles, autoreprésentation de l'artiste, l'art-idée et l'art-processus, participation, performance. Une section supplémentaire, avec les imageries parallèles, se composera des recherches sur l'utopie, la science-fiction, le Kitsch, la publicité, l'art psychopathologique. Un programme de films complètera l'ensemble des manifestations.

Press release

List of Sections, Co-Curators, and Artists

Plans of the Exhibition

The plans and the information that are gathered here are primarily taken from the two volumes of the exhibition catalogue. After having examined them, a certain number of uncertainties remain concerning the location of certain sections (absence of numbered cross-reference on the map), of certain artists in the sections (name of artist in brackets), of certain works in the exhibition spaces (absence of numbered cross-reference on the map), of certain artists in the sections and in the exhibition spaces (p. 122).

Neue Galerie

Basement

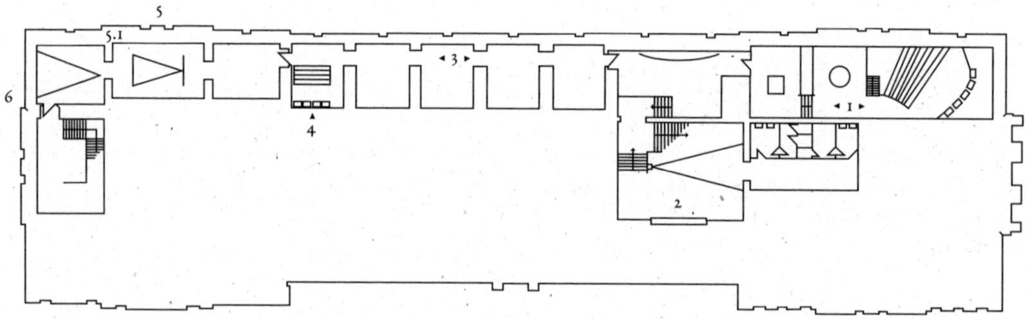

SECTIONS		CURATORS		ARTISTS	
1	Utopia and Planning	–	François Burkhardt/ Lucius Burckhardt/ Burghart Schmidt/ Mattias Eberle	– – – –	Haus-Rucker-Co Aldo Loris Rossi/ Donatella Mazzoleni Archigram/Peter Cook Paolo Portoghesi/ Vittorio Gigliotti
2	Advertising	–	Charles Paul Wilp	–	Mixed media
3	Science fiction	–	Pierre Versins	–	Mixed media
4	Play and Reality	–	Linde Burkhardt/ Ursula Barthelmess/ Hans-Henning Borgelt/ Wolfgang Hoebig	–	Audiovisual program
5	Social Iconography	–	Walter Busse	5.1	40 covers of *Der Spiegel* magazine (1960–1972)
		–	Willy Rotzler	–	New Swiss banknotes [E. & U. Hiestand, R. & E. Pfund]
6	Political Propaganda	– –	Reiner Diederich Richard Grübling	– –	Klaus Staeck Mixed media

Neue Galerie
Ground floor

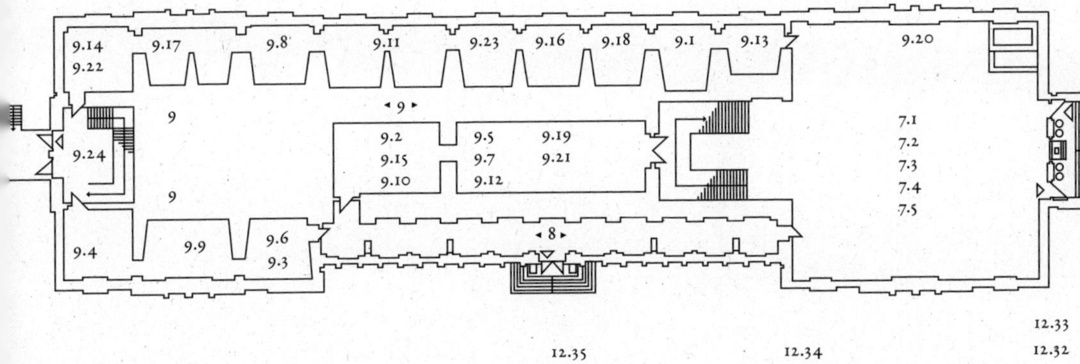

SECTIONS			CURATORS		ARTISTS
7	Artists' Museums	–	Harald Szeemann	7.1	Marcel Broodthaers: *Département des Aigles* [Department of Eagles]
				7.2	Herbert Distel: *Museum of Drawers*
				7.3	Marcel Duchamp: *Boîte-en-valise* [Box in a Suitcase]
			Director: Kasper König	7.4	Claes Oldenburg: *Maus Museum* [Mouse Museum]
				7.5	Ben Vautier: *L'Armoire* [The Cupboard]
8	Trivial Realism, Trivial Emblematism	–	Eberhard Roters/ Janni Müller-Hauck	–	Mixed media
9	Realism	–	Jean-Christophe Ammann	9.1	Richard Artschwager
				9.2	Robert Bechtle
				9.3	Claudio Bravo
				9.4	Chuck Close
				9.5	Robert Cottingham
				9.6	John De Andrea
				9.7	Don Eddy
				9.8	Richard Estes
				9.9	Franz Gertsch
				9.10	Ralph Goings
				9.11	Duane Hanson
				9.12	Jean-Olivier Hucleux
				9.13	Jasper Johns
				9.14	Howard Kanovitz
				9.15	Richard McLean
				9.16	Malcom Morley
				9.17	Stephen Posen
				9.18	Gerhard Richter
				9.19	John Salt
				9.20	Paul Sarkisian
				–	Ben Schonzeit
				9.21	Paul Staiger
				9.22	Jorge Stever
				9.23	Wayne Thiebaud
				9.24	John Wesley

Neue Galerie
First floor

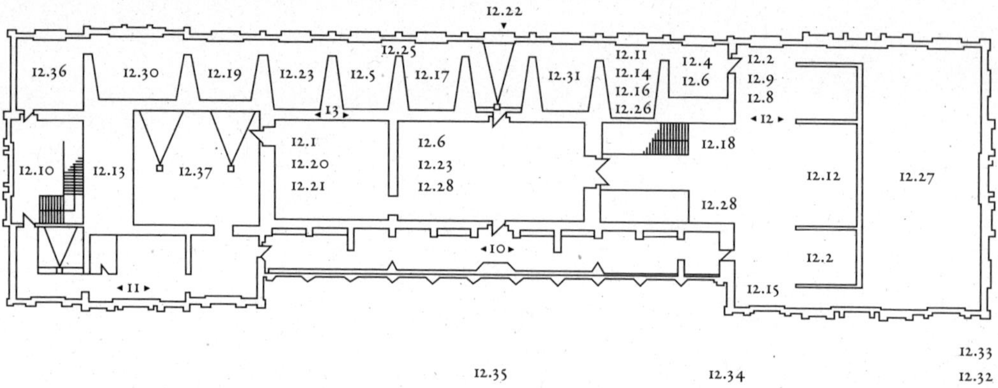

SECTIONS		CURATORS		ARTISTS	
10	Imagination and Piety	–	Ingolf Bauer	–	Mixed media
11	Imagery of the Mentally Ill	–	Theodor Spoerri	–	Adolf Wölfli
				–	Mixed media
12	Individual Mythologies 1	–	Harald Szeemann	12.1	Georg Baselitz
				12.2	Alighiero Boetti
				12.3	Christian Boltanski
				12.4	George Brecht
				12.5	Günter Brus
				12.6	Joseph Cornell
				12.7	Etienne-Martin
				12.8	John C. Fernie
				12.9	Nancy Graves
				12.10	Guy Harloff
				12.11	Auguste Herbin
				12.12	Will Insley
				12.13	Neil Jenney
				12.14	Alfred Jensen
				12.15	Jean Le Gac
				–	Ingeborg Lüscher
				12.16	Fernando Melani
				12.17	Hermann Nitsch
				12.18	Robin Page
				12.19	Giulio Paolini
				12.20	A.R. Penck
				12.21	Sigmar Polke
				12.22	Arnulf Rainer
				12.23	Edward Ruscha
				12.24	Lucas Samaras
				12.25	Rudolf Schwarzkogler
				12.26	Robert Strübin
				12.27	Paul Thek
				12.28	Robert Watts
				12.29	H.C. Westermann
				12.30	William T. Wiley
				12.31	Peter Young

SECTIONS	CURATORS	ARTISTS
		12.32 William Copley
		12.33 Luciano Fabro
		12.34 Gustav Metzger
		12.35 Edward Kienholz
	– Johannes Cladders	– Joseph Beuys
		12.36 Marcel Broodthaers
		– Daniel Buren
		12.37 Robert Filliou

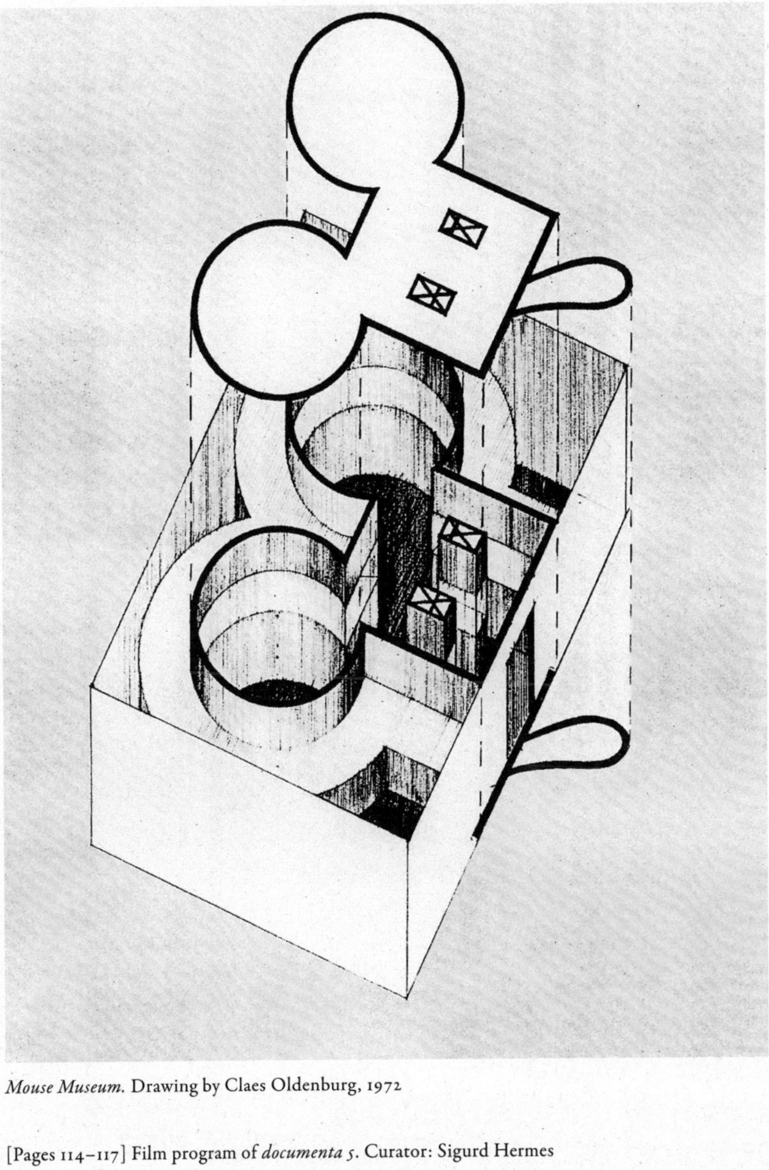

Mouse Museum. Drawing by Claes Oldenburg, 1972

[Pages 114–117] Film program of *documenta 5*. Curator: Sigurd Hermes

documenta filmschau

vom 1. 7. bis 5. 7. '72 im Kino Royal Obere Königsstraße

Je Vorstellung 3 Mark Unkostenbeitrag

Programmänderungen vorbehalten
Verantwortlich: Sigurd Hermes, Freier Mitarbeiter der d5
Die Programme des New American Cinema wurden von Klaus Feddermann in den USA zusammengestellt.

	S
13 Uhr	**New** Barry Ge Larry Got Andrew N
15 Uhr	**New** Filme vor Nekes un
18 Uhr	**Russ**
20 Uhr	**New** Paul Shar
22 Uhr	**Eroti** Filme von und

stag, 1. 7.	Sonntag, 2. 7.
can Cinema I Trilogie/Generations Portrait of Andrew Noren Fog Line and Barn Rushes The Wind Variationen	**New American Cinema III** Joyce Wieland Sailboat 1933 La Raison avant La Passion
ean Cinema I Gurtrug Nr. I SPACECUT Kaldalon	**New American Cinema IV** Stan Brackhage Scenes from under the Childhood (section II–IV)
Retrospektive I **Lorna** (dt. Fassung)	**Russ Mayer Retrospektive II** Im Garten der Lust
an Cinema II N:O:T:H:I:N:G T,O,U,C,H,I,N,G S:TREAM:S:S:ECTION: S:S:ECTIONED INFERENTIAL CURRENT	**Sozialistischer Realismus I** Mit taktischem Geschick den Tigerberg erobern Pekingoper VR China
ma voskin d Sommer	**Anderes Kino I** Werner Schroeter Der Tod der Maria Malibran

	Montag, 3. 7.		Diens
13 Uhr	**New European Cinema II** Klaus Wyborny	**A Crowd in the Face** **Percy McPhee** **Dalles Texas –** **After the Goldrush** **Chimney Piece** **Das abenteuerliche aber glücklose Leben des William Parmagino**	**Reflektionsfi** Ottomar Domnick
15 Uhr	**New European Cinema III** B & W Hein	**Work in Progress** **Documentation** **Doppelprojektion I** **Doppelprojektion II**	**Dokumentat**
18 Uhr	**Russ Mayer Retrospektive III**	**Blumen ohne Duft**	**Russ Mayer I**
20 Uhr	**Anderes Kino II** Rosa v. Praunheim	**Nicht der Homosexuelle ist pervers**	**Sozialistisch**
22 Uhr	**New American Cinema V** Michael Snow David Rimmer	**Back and Force** **Square Inch Field** **Variations on a Cellophane Wrapper** **Surfacing on the Thames** **Ratlife and Diet in North America** **Seashore**	**Politische Fi**

4. 7.	Mittwoch, 5. 7.	
	Portrait Bernd Upnmoor	
blicke		Das Schiff im Eis Der Lustmörder Das Sonnenbad Unsere Ferienreise Die Anzeige/Marek/ Rosa Lilies Für meine Freundin Boa Vergewaltigte Jungfrauen
	New American Cinema VI	
sraum I denhunde	George Landow	Institutional Quality Remedial Reading Comprehention
	Ken Jacobs	Tom, Tom, The Pipers Son
pektive IV	**Russ Mayer Retrospektive V**	
sycho		Satansweiber von Tittfield
lismus II	**New American Cinema VII**	
te Frauenbataillon	Tony Conrad	The Flicker Straight and Narrow
oper VR China	Hollis Frampton	Nortalgia Critical Noss
eit	**Bildwelt der Trivialpornographie**	
racts Canale m: ulation des Kapitals	Filme aus Frankreich, Kuba, Deutschland aus den Jahren 1918–1936	

Fridericianum Museum
Ground floor

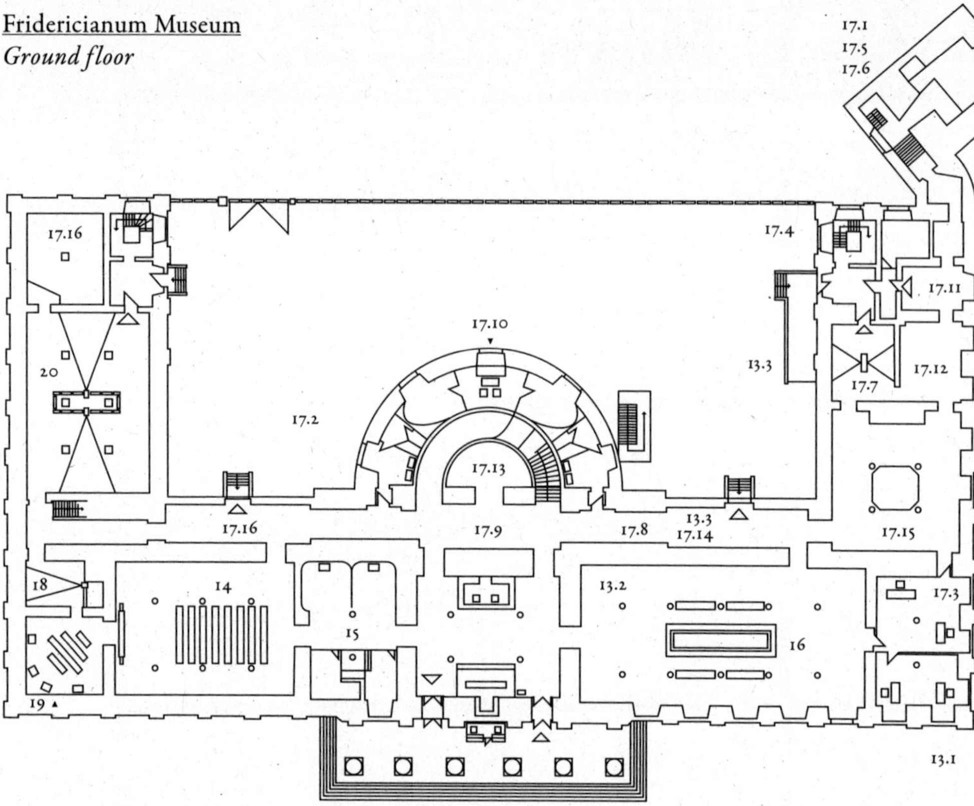

SECTIONS	CURATORS	ARTISTS
– Information		13.1 K.P. Brehmer 13.2 Christo – Hans Haacke 13.3 H.A. Schult
	– Bazon Brock/ Karl Heinz Krings	14 Audiovisual preface: audiovisual program
	– Conceptor-Film director: Karl Oskar Blase	15 Video Library: audiovisual program (interviews with institution directors, gallerists, art critics, artists, visitors)
	– Walther König	16 Book Library
– Individual Mythologies: performances—activities— changes—self performances	– Harald Szeemann	17.1 Vito Acconci 17.2 Arbeitszeit [Anatol Herzfeld/ Bertram Weigel] 17.3 Joseph Beuys – James Lee Byars – Gino De Dominicis 17.4 John Dugger/David Medalla 17.5 Terry Fox

SECTIONS		CURATORS	ARTISTS	
			17.6	Howard Fried
			17.7	Dan Graham
			–	Gilbert & George/Art for All
			17.8	Rebecca Horn
			17.9	Jörg Immendorf
			–	Joan Jonas
			–	Jannis Kounellis
			17.10	Yoko Ono
			17.11	Giuseppe Penone
			17.12	Vettor Pisani
			–	Klaus Rinke
			17.13	Günther Sarée
			17.14	Fritz Schwegler
			–	Keith Sonnier
			–	Trans-Parent Teacher's Ink [Paul Cotton/Eugenia Butler]
			17.15	Ben Vautier
			17.16	Franz Erhard Walther
18	Slides		–	Jim Melchert
19	Videos		–	Vito Acconci
			–	John Baldessari
			–	Joseph Beuys
			–	Alighiero Boetti
			–	Stanley Brouwn
			–	Günter Brus
			–	Daniel Buren
			–	Jan Dibbets
			–	Gino De Dominicis
			–	Terry Fox
			–	Howard Fried
			–	Gilbert & George/Art for All
			–	Wolf [Imi] Knoebel
			–	Barry Le Va
			–	Mario Merz
			–	Bruce Nauman
			–	Dennis Oppenheim
			–	Ulrich Rückriem
			–	Reiner Ruthenbeck
			–	Gerry Schum
			–	Richard Serra
			–	Keith Sonnier
			–	Ben Vautier
			–	Lawrence Weiner
20	Films		–	Vito Acconci
			–	Christian Boltanski
			–	Ger van Elk
			–	Rebecca Horn
			–	Christof Kohlhöfer
			–	David Lamelas
			–	Alfred Leslie
			–	Yoko Ono
			–	Lucas Samaras
			–	Richard Serra
			–	Katharina Sieverding
			–	(Holly Solomon/ Bert Spielvogel)

Fridericianum Museum

First floor

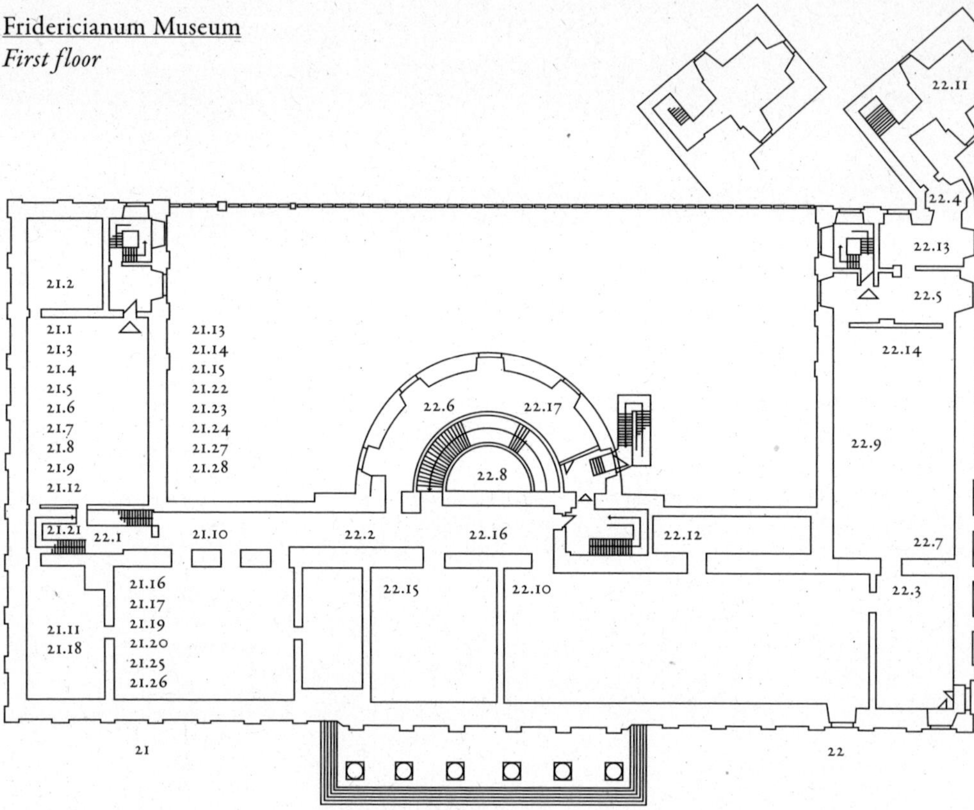

SECTIONS

21	Idea and Idea/Light

CURATORS

–	Konrad Fisher/ Klaus Honnef

ARTISTS

21.1	Vincenzo Agnetti
21.2	Art & Language Institute
21.3	John Baldessari
21.4	Robert Barry
21.5	Bernhard & Hilla Becher
21.6	Mel Bochner
21.7	Stanley Brouwn
21.8	Daniel Buren
21.9	Victor Burgin
21.10	Hanne Darboven
21.11	Jan Dibbets
21.12	Hamish Fulton
–	Dan Graham
21.13	Michael Harvey
21.14	Douglas Huebler
21.15	Wolf [Imi] Knoebel
–	David Lamelas
21.16	Sol LeWitt
21.18	Richard Long
21.17	Robert Mangold
21.19	Brice Marden
21.20	Agnes Martin
21.21	Blinky Palermo
21.22	Peter Roehr

SECTIONS		CURATORS		ARTISTS	
				21.23	Allen Ruppersberg
				21.24	Edward Ruscha
				21.25	Robert Ryman
				–	Robert Smithson
				–	David Tremlett
				21.26	Richard Tuttle
				21.27	William Wegman
				21.28	Lawrence Weiner
22	Individual Mythologies: Process	–	Harald Szeemann	22.1	Giovanni Anselmo
				22.2	Charles Arnoldi
				22.3	Pier Paolo Calzolari
				22.4	(Jud Fine)
				22.5	Hans Haacke
				22.6	Eva Hesse
				22.7	Barry Le Va
				22.8	Mario Merz
				22.9	Bruce Nauman
				22.10	Panamarenko
				22.11	Klaus Rinke
				22.12	Dorothea Rockburne
				22.13	Ulrich Rückriem
				22.14	Reiner Ruthenbeck
				22.15	Richard Serra
				22.16	(Alan Shields)
				22.17	Gilberto Zorio

Fridericianum Museum
Second floor

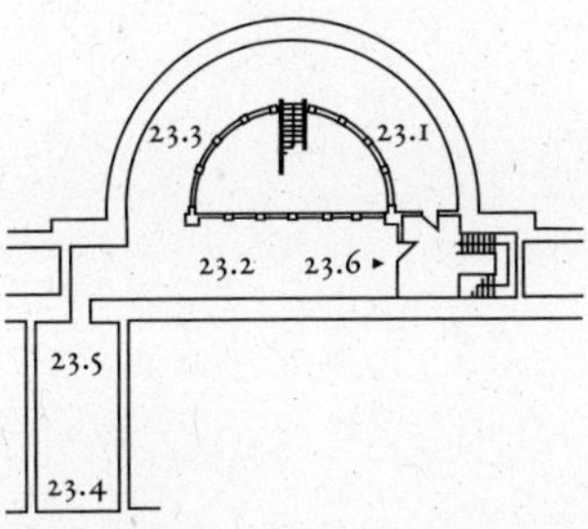

SECTIONS		CURATORS		ARTISTS	
–	Idea/Light	–	Konrad Fisher/ Klaus Honnef	23.1	Peter Alexander
				23.2	Michael Asher
				23.3	Ron Cooper
				23.4	David Deutsch
				23.5	Ed Moses
				23.6	Thomas Wudl

Fridericianum Museum
Top floor

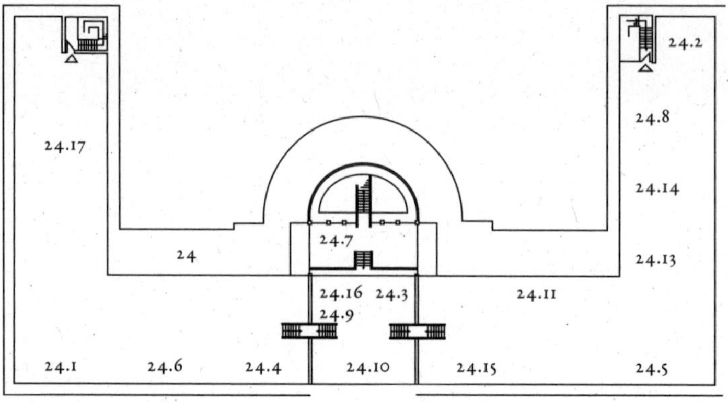

SECTIONS		CURATORS	
24	Individual Mythologies II	–	Harald Szeemann

ARTISTS

24.1 Lothar Baumgarten
24.2 Michael Buthe
24.3 Luciano Castelli
24.4 Paul Cotton
24.5 Franz Eggenschwiler
24.6 Joel Fisher
24.7 Hubertus Gojowczyk
24.8 Rolf Iseli
24.9 Thomas Kovachevich
24.10 Piotr Kowalski
24.11 Inge Mahn
24.12 Bernd Minnich
24.13 Markus Raetz
24.14 Jean-Frédéric Schnyder
24.15 André Thomkins
24.16 Rolf Winnewisser
24.17 La Monte Young/ Marian Zazeela

ARTISTS
whose artworks could not be localized:

– Siah Armajani
– Monika Baumgartl
– Gottfried Bechtold
– Marinus Boezem
– Walter De Maria
– Hermann Degkwitz
– Barry Flanagan
– Salvo [Salvatore Mangioni]
– Bernd Upnmoor
– Roger Welch

Technical Information

documenta 5: Questioning Reality—Image Worlds Today

Dates: June 30–October 8, 1972
Location: Kassel, Germany
Venues: Fridericianum Museum, Neue Galerie

Number of artists: 217
Number of visitors: 229 000

Organization chart:

General Secretary:
Harald Szeemann

Chief Executive Officer:
Karl Fritz Heise, Walter Olbrich

Curatorial Team:
Jean-Christophe Ammann, Arnold Bode, Harald Szeemann

Technical Team:
Lorenz Dombois, Jacques Caumont

Graphic design:
Prof. Karl Oskar Blasé

Poster and catalogue cover:
Ed Ruscha

Budget:

Total: 3 000 000 Deutsche Mark (DM)—initial budget

Catalogue:

Language: German
Number of pages: 757
Publisher: C. Bertelsmann Verlag, Munich

James Lee Byars, *As a SIGHT*, 1972

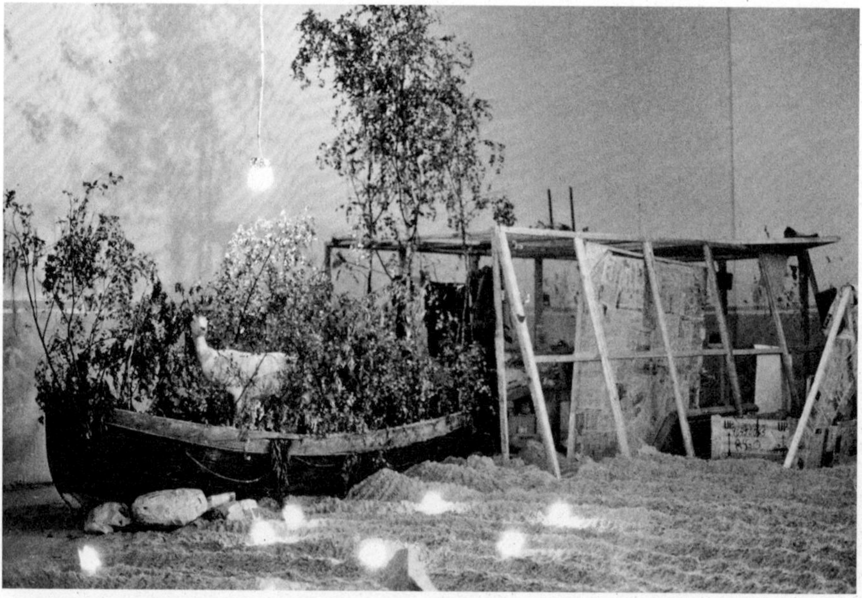

Paul Thek, *Ark Pyramid*, 1972

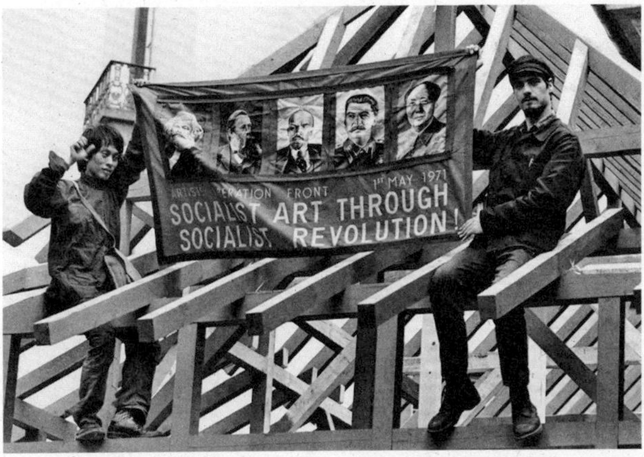

David Medalla & John Dugger, *People's Participation Pavilion*, 1972

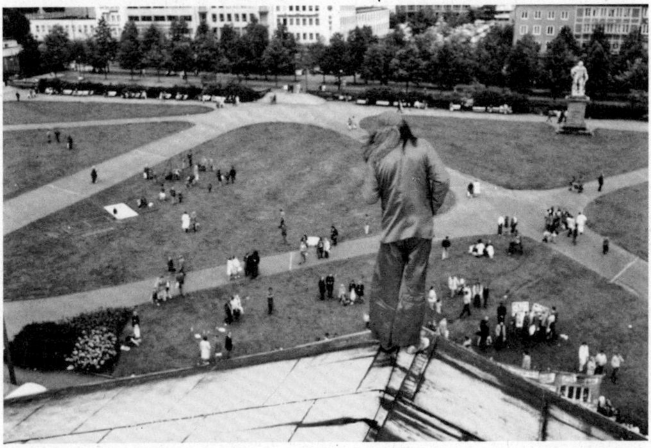

James Lee Byars, *Calling German Names*, 1972

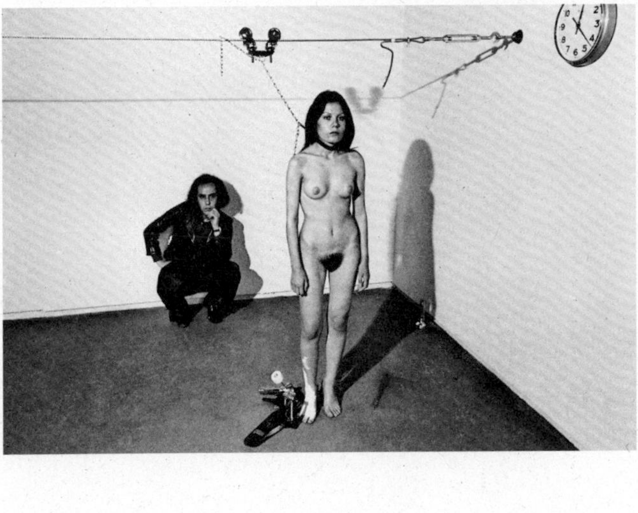

Vettor Pisani, *L'Eroe da Camera*, 1972

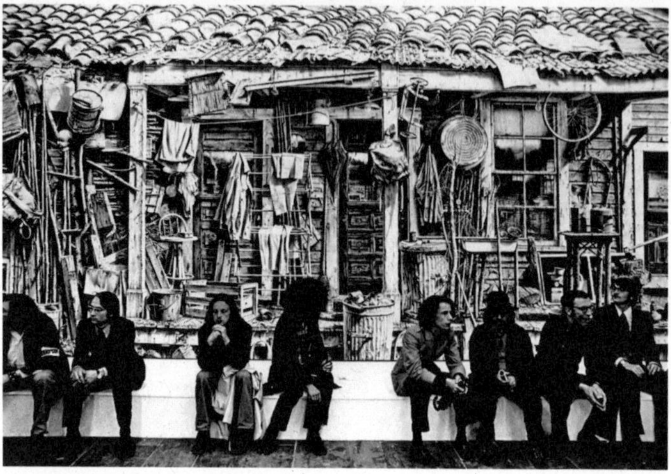

Paul Sarkisian, *Untitled (Mapleton)*, 1971–1972

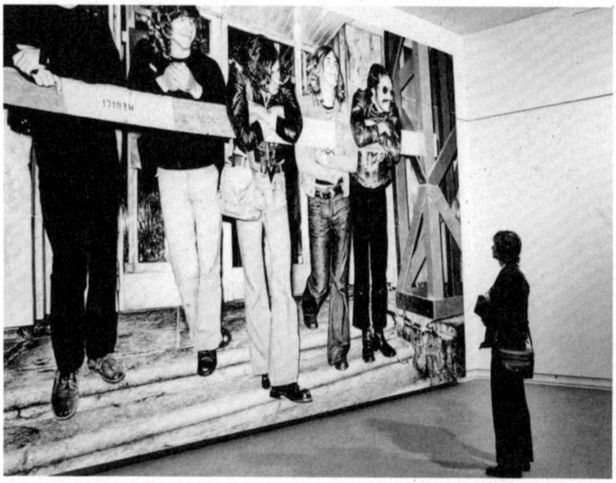

Franz Gertsch, *Medici*, 1971

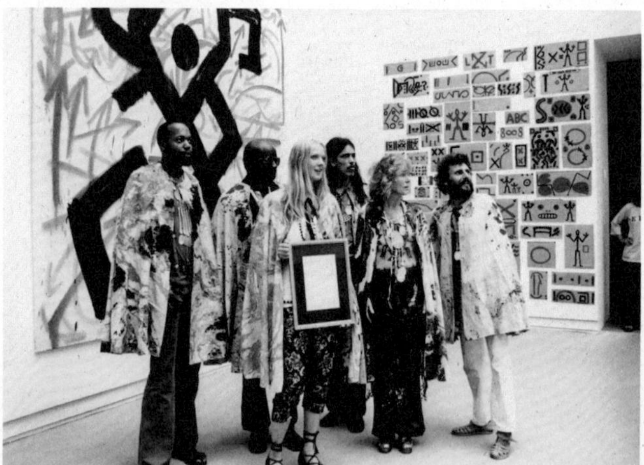

A.R. Penck

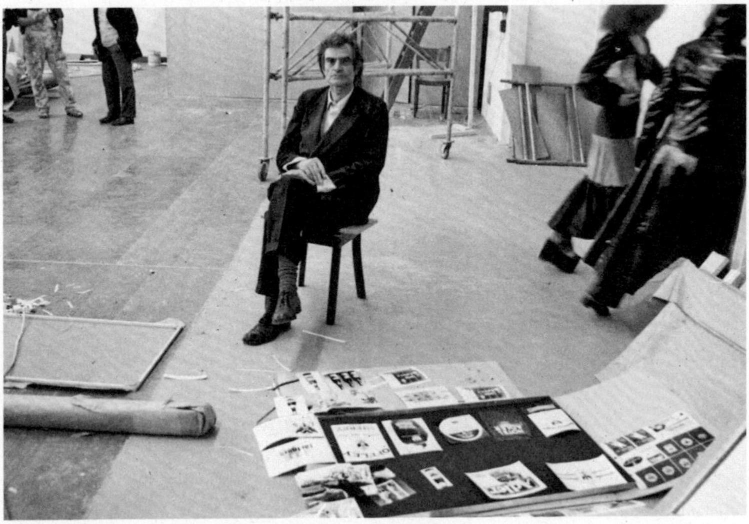

Marcel Broodthaers during the installation of *documenta 5*

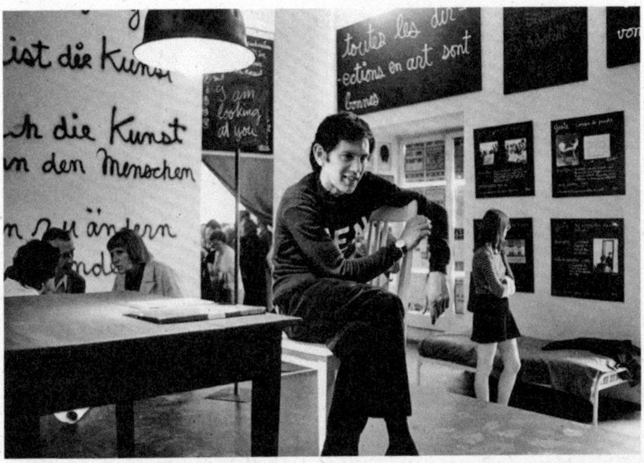

Ben Vautier, *L'Armoire*, 1972

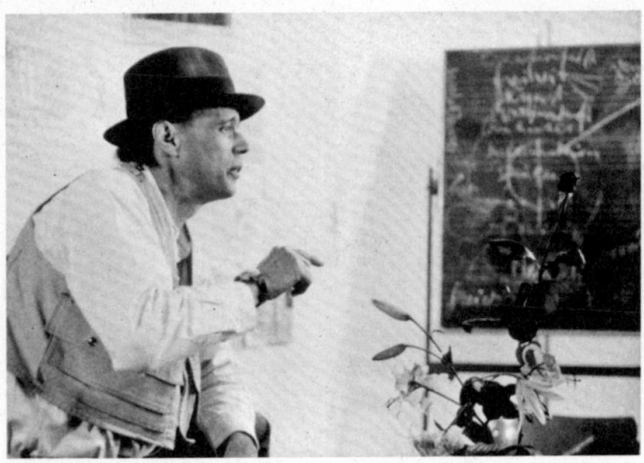

Joseph Beuys, *Office for Direct Democracy*, 1972

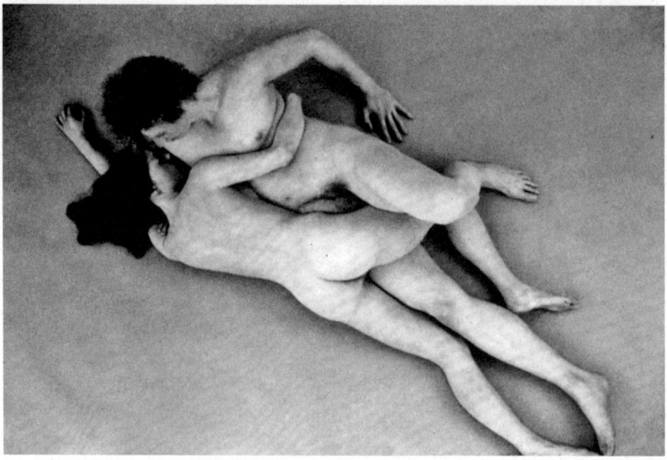

John De Andrea, *A. Anderson & N. Murphy*, 1972

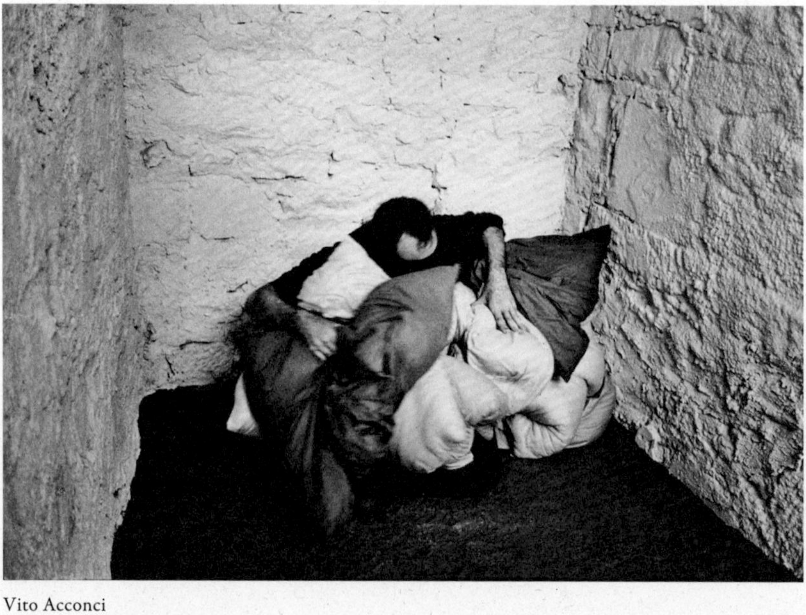

Vito Acconci

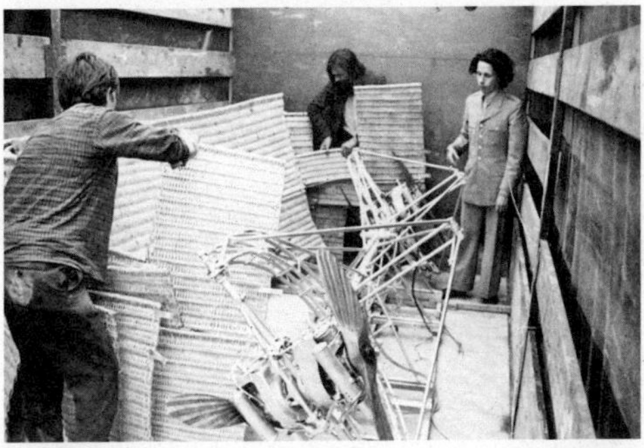

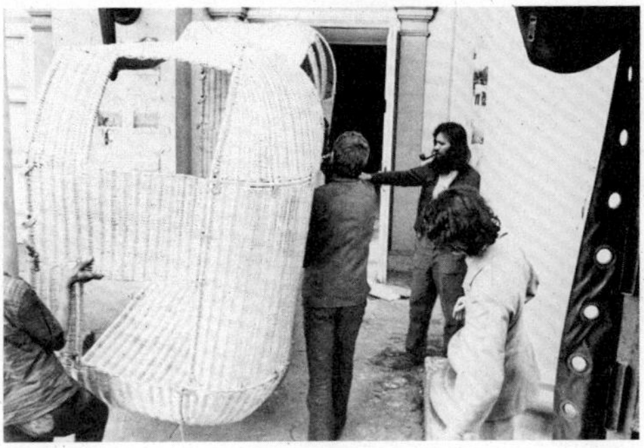

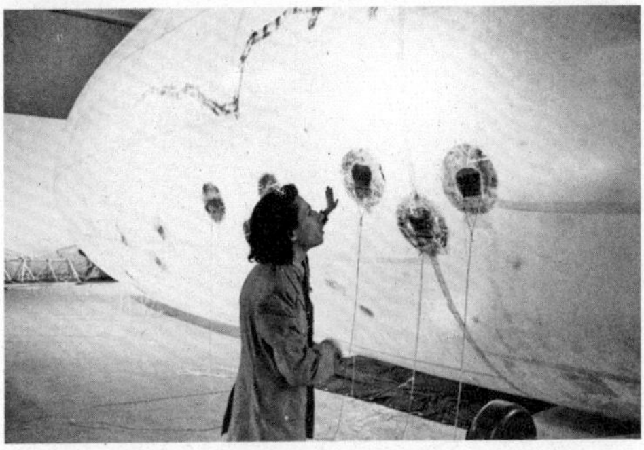

Panamarenko, *Aeromodeller*, 1969–1971

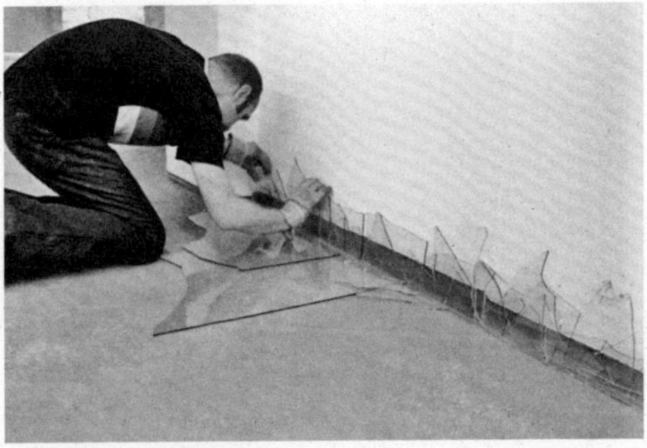

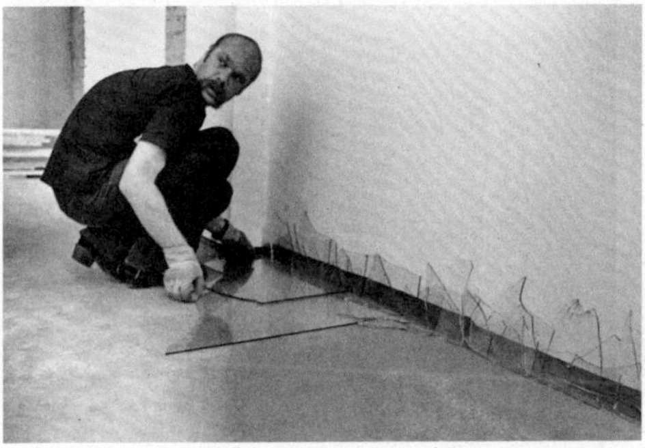

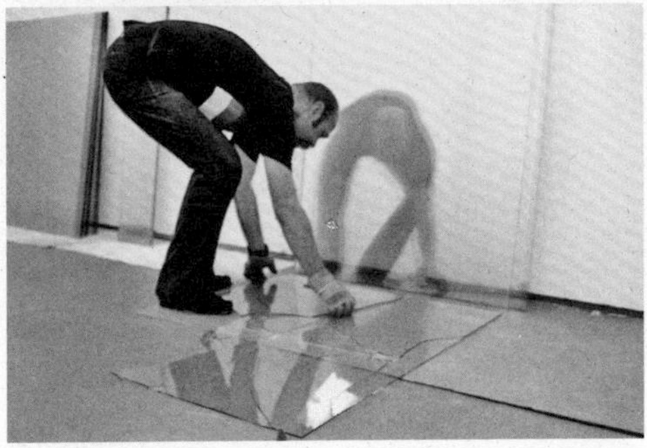

Fred Sandback

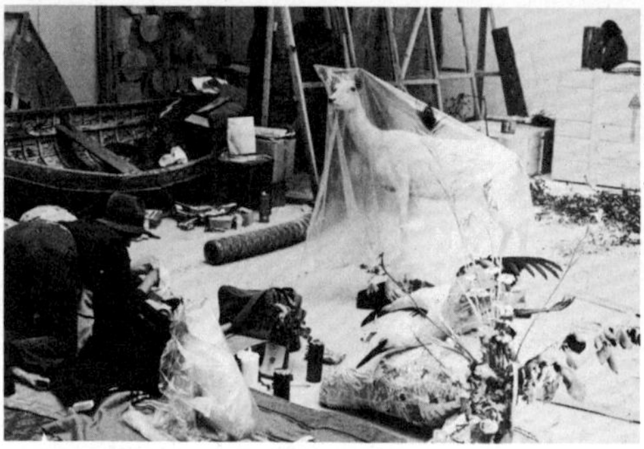

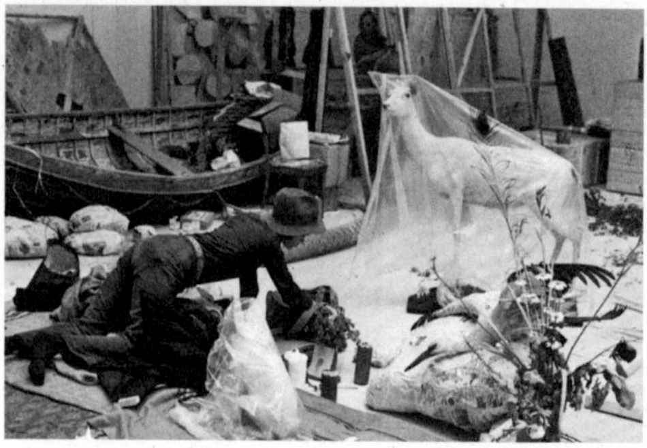

Paul Thek

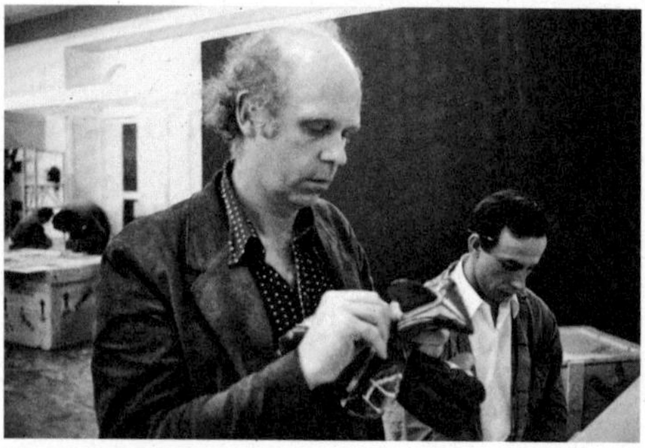

Claes Oldenburg

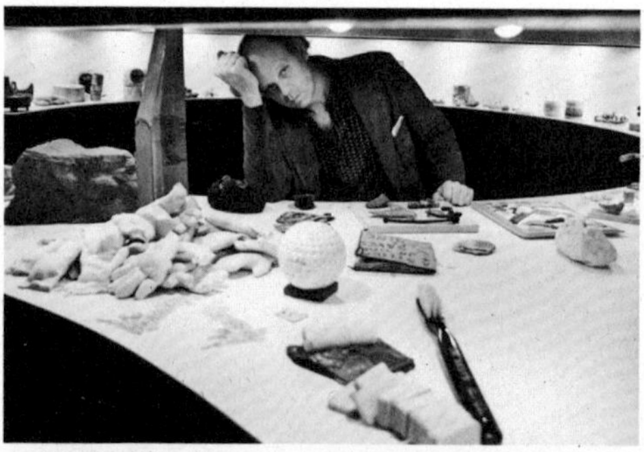

Claes Oldenburg inside his *Mouse Museum*

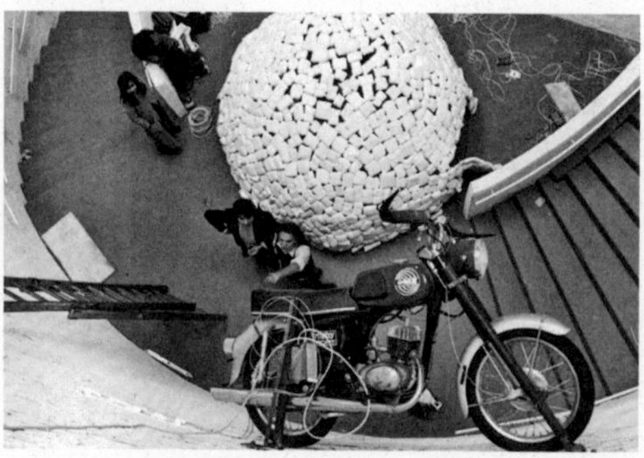

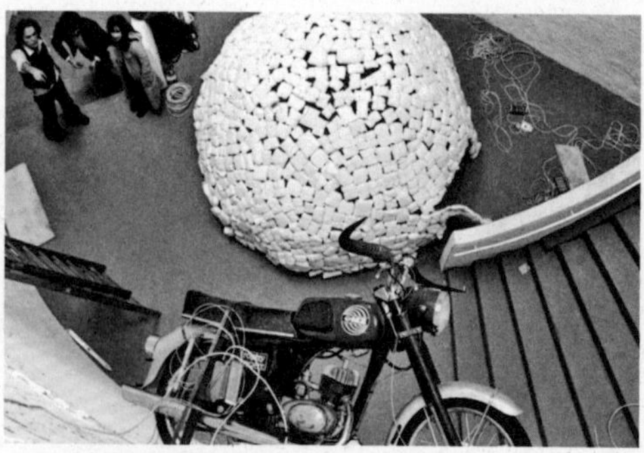

Mario Merz, *Accelerazione = sogno, numeri Fibonacci al neon e motocicletta fantasma*, 1972

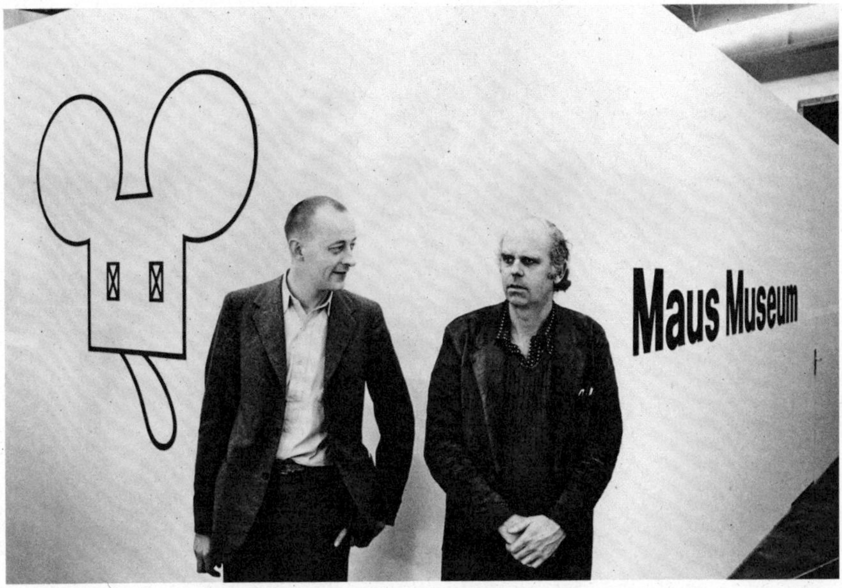

Kasper König and Claes Oldenburg in front of the *Mouse Museum*

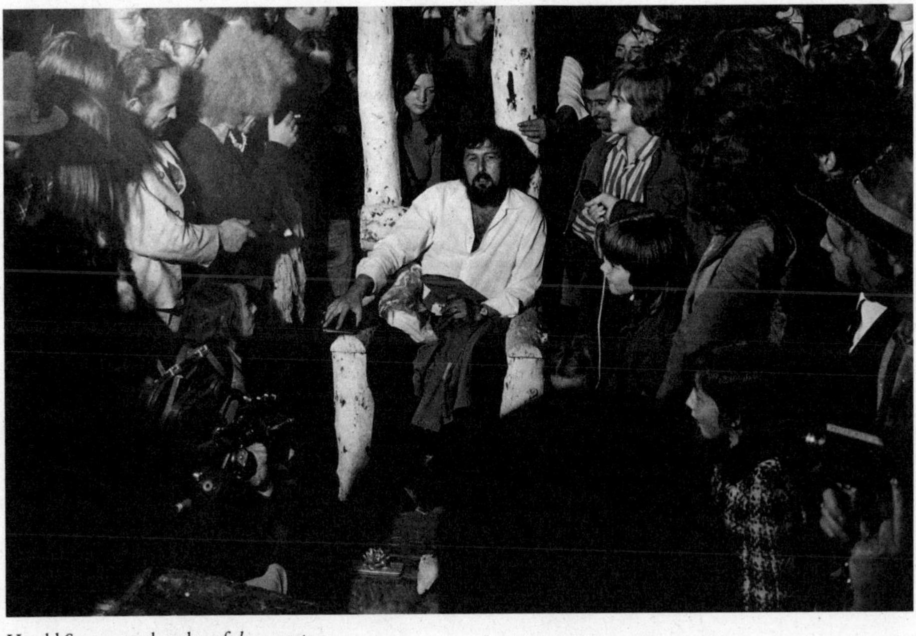

Harald Szeemann, last day of *documenta 5*

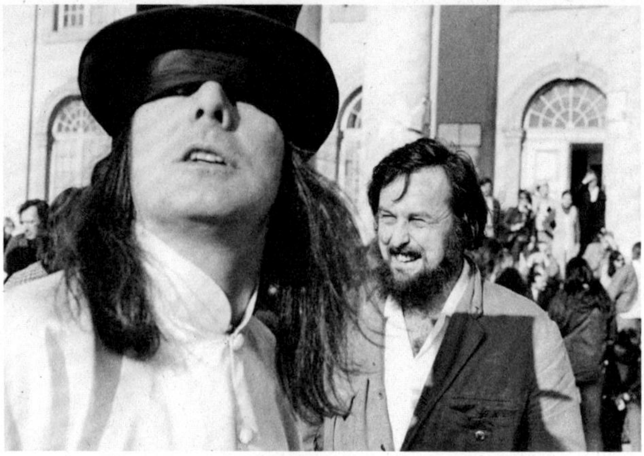

James Lee Byars, Harald Szeemann

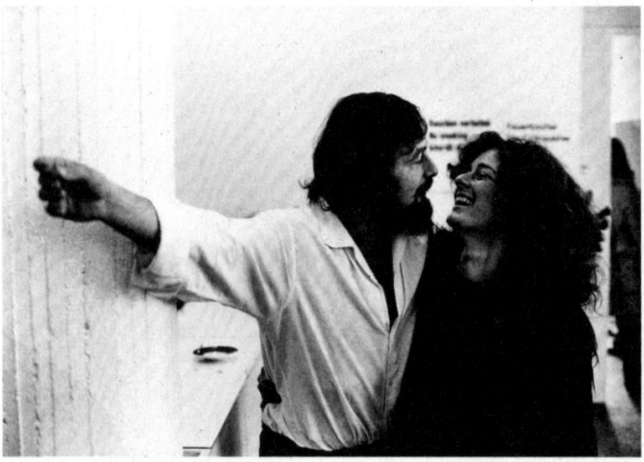

Harald Szeemann, Ingeborg Lüscher

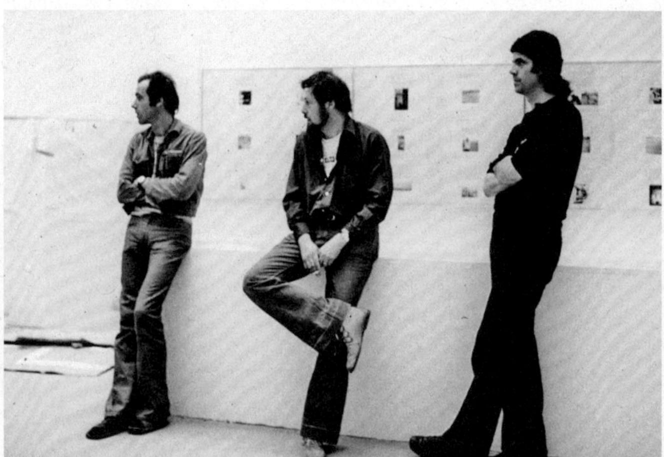

Jean-Christophe Ammann, Harald Szeemann, and an unidentified person

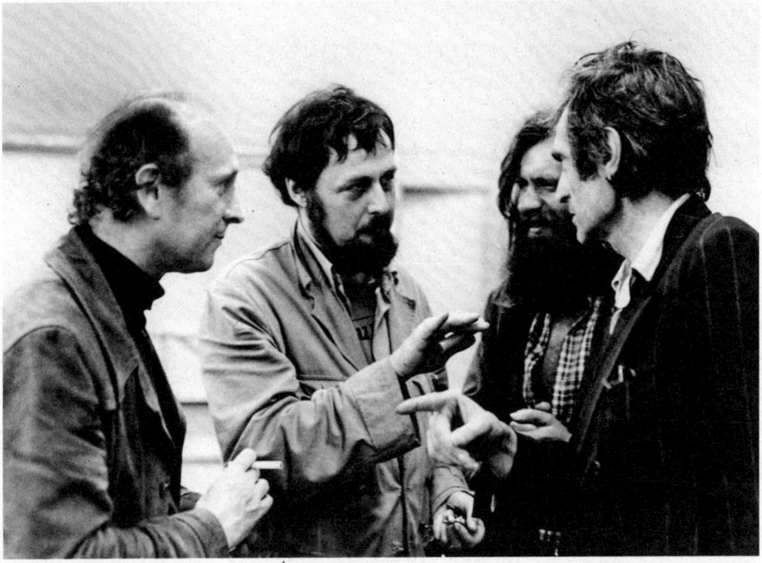

Johannes Cladders, Harald Szeemann, Jacques Caumont, Marcel Broodthaers

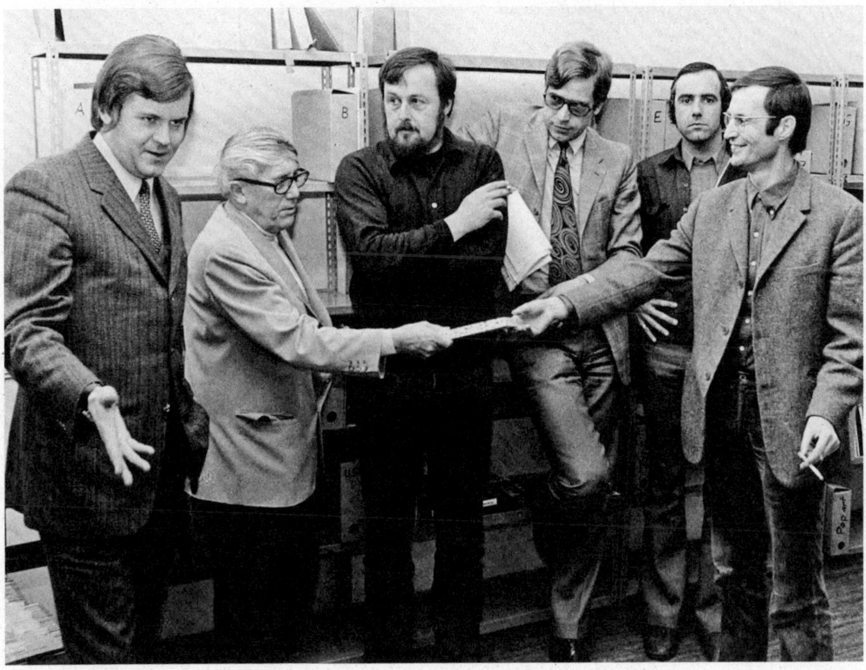

Peter Iden, Arnold Bode, Harald Szeemann, Bazon Brock, Jean-Christophe Ammann, and an unidentified person

Interviews with Harald Szeemann

Irmeline Lebeer and John Anthony Thwaites

The first interview was conducted by Irmeline Lebeer for the magazine *Chroniques de l'Art Vivant*, n° 25, November 1971. It appears here in a shortened version authorized by the author. John Anthony Thwaites conducted the second interview after the opening of *documenta 5*. It is printed here in a shortened version. All our efforts to contact the author of the interview met with no success.

First interview:

IRMELINE LEBEER

When Kassel asked you in 1969 to head the upcoming *documenta 5*, you suggested organizing a *documenta* based on "action art." When and why was this project abandoned?

HARALD SZEEMANN

The decision was motivated above all for financial reasons, but it was also due to our negative experiences at the *Happening & Fluxus* retrospective in Cologne last year.

In an event that lacks the more traditional framework of an exhibition, internal rivalries become too weighty and invasive. We feared that, on the scale of *documenta 5*, things would become completely inextricable. This doesn't mean that we are completely renouncing happenings and events, but they will only be included at the end, once the stable exhibition is already in place.

To replace the *documenta*-action, we elaborated a new concept at the end of last year, namely a thematic show divided into three major sections corresponding to the three aspects of our theme, which concerns the relationship between image and imagery as reflected in current artistic output.

IRMELINE LEBEER

What are your financial resources?

HARALD SZEEMANN

Three million deutschmarks (DM). To produce *The Visitors' School*, the theater section, and the cinema section, we would have needed 5.6 million DM. Right up to the last minute we hoped a foundation would come to our aid, but it didn't happen.

The three million deutschmarks are apportioned as follows: 2.1 million DM for the exhibition itself, including 800,000 for transport, 600,000 for insurance, 200,000 for invigilation, and 100,000 for outside contractors; then 700,000 for administrative expenses (offices, travel, etc.), 300,000 for the cost of printing the catalogue, and 200,000 for refurbishing the buildings.

IRMELINE LEBEER

How would *The Visitors' School* have worked?

HARALD SZEEMANN

Bazon Brock had planned for educational rooms where the public could try all kinds of experiments on vision and related phenomena, as well as three audiovisual machines for group learning. A prototype had already been built in Hamburg by two technicians working for Brock.

Each machine drove three screens. Viewers sat in the middle of these screens, each one with their own control panel. First they watched some basic information on screen number 1. At the end of it, they were asked whether they understood, didn't understand, or half-understood. The ones who understood received some more in-depth information on the same screen, while the people who half-understood were asked to look at screen 2, where an abbreviated version of the same information appeared, followed by some indepth material. People who didn't understand at all saw the same thing again, but with a different commentary, on screen 3. Everyone reached the end of their cycle at the same time, when they would all turn back to screen number 1 for a new piece of information.

IRMELINE LEBEER

Didn't you envisage a less costly back-up alternative to *The Visitors' School*?

HARALD SZEEMANN

Brock felt that unless we had 2 million DM, it wasn't even worth getting started. That was his viewpoint.

IRMELINE LEBEER

Will eliminating *The Visitors' School* modify the appearance of the show? Are you now going to add educational features to the thematic exhibition, properly speaking?

HARALD SZEEMANN

No, we're not going to add explanatory panels, and so on. Visitors can find all the explanation they want in the catalogue. There'll be an article on each theme and Hans Heinz Holz will write a general introduction that will provide a perspective on the whole thing.

That said, dropping *The Visitors' School* has forced us to make the exhibition more spectacular by including expensive original artworks, etc. In the section on portraits, a few silkscreens would have sufficed, because we could have relied on *The Visitors' School*, where they could be shown repeatedly. But now we're forced to go back to large, glamorous canvases that are, to a certain extent, autonomous. In that way, *documenta 5* will be more of a traditional art exhibition.

Real innovation has fallen through. I think *The Visitors' School* would have been very important to museums in the 1970s, because we can't rely eternally on moving originals around, and at a time when output is down, museums need to make a bigger effort for their visitors. Many museums feel the need, in fact, to develop their educational role.

IRMELINE LEBEER

Which artists have you invited as part of the self-representation idea?

HARALD SZEEMANN

For the moment, there are four: Beuys, with his information office; Ben Vautier (when he's not there, we'll take down his little written tablets, because we realized in Cologne that they are only interesting when he's present); Gilbert & George; and, finally, Acconci (Body art). We may extend it a little, but not to many others. The others will be represented by films and videotapes.

IRMELINE LEBEER

What's striking is the relatively modest role allocated to viewer's participation in *documenta 5*.

HARALD SZEEMANN

We worked throughout the 1960s to make viewer's participation a reality. But I think we had too many illusions, and if we offer viewers the possibility of reacting positively or negatively then we must present them with fully articulated works and not potential projects that depend on the beholder's good will. If you make a ball out of paper and stand behind that ball waiting for visitors to come play with you, and if 99 other artists do the same thing, not much will happen. That's the way it's been going lately. That's why we decided to give a real structure to *documenta 5*, which will nevertheless culminate, under the tent, with a section devoted to games and participation.

Second Interview:

JOHN ANTHONY THWAITES

In March 1971, Dr Ammann and Bazon Brock published your first draft for *documenta 5*. Since then you've had a lot of financial trouble and the exhibition has had to be reduced. Have you still been able to keep to your original conception?

HARALD SZEEMANN

Yes, I think so. The form has been reduced but the concept is unchanged.

JOHN ANTHONY THWAITES

Why has *documenta 5* been so much attacked beforehand? What is the meaning of this attempt to talk it down?

HARALD SZEEMANN

I don't think it has been more attacked than all the others were. Think of *documenta 4*—there was talk of boycotting that altogether. When I hear that the art dealers have rented a whole house in Kassel for the duration of *documenta*, I'm not worried. What people really resent is that there is someone in authority. In this case, me.

JOHN ANTHONY THWAITES

Then you don't see any fundamental difference between this and the other *documentas*?

HARALD SZEEMANN

Of course there is a fundamental difference. The title of my exhibition *When Attitudes Become Form* expresses it. From 1970-on the old aesthetic is more or less eliminated. The whole standpoint is new.

JOHN ANTHONY THWAITES

Then the exhibition is an exploration of Reality. But that as a plural term. There are a great many realities. And surely one of the most important for us is that of natural science and technology. Why are they passed over here? Especially when science fiction, their imaginary side, or perhaps their vulgarization, is included?

HARALD SZEEMANN

No, That's quite impossible. The work of art is autonomous. But it can be experienced in various ways: as information, for connections.

JOHN ANTHONY THWAITES

What is the basis of perception here? Surely it is a victory of rational over associative thinking and of thought over perception?

HARALD SZEEMANN

I think it is a question of sensibility. When one has been confronted with these things for a long time, one develops a certain feeling for them. What has disappeared is the old system of yes/no, good/bad. We are concerned now with the connections, the relationships, the situations of the work. I should say that the basis of perception—and so of selection—was a combination of empathy and theory.

JOHN ANTHONY THWAITES

Not a victory of the intellectual over the artist?

HARALD SZEEMANN

No, that's quite impossible. The work of art is autonomous. But it can be experienced in various ways: as information, for its connections, or as the way to a more concentrated statement. There are three realities.

JOHN ANTHONY THWAITES

That's what I wanted to ask next. At least three of the sections: political propaganda, socialist realism, and advertising, are unfree expressions. Their purpose is to pull a veil over reality. Then how can you use them to question or examine reality?

HARALD SZEEMANN

Unfree if you like. I should rather say applied. And that kind of work is much better for bringing out the various aspects of the Real. It's more difficult if you start out from the experience of the work of art. Here the vocabulary is much smaller. We've made a lot of progress in iconology through figures such as Panofsky; and the more one knows the more reality changes.

The point of showing "unfree" works, as you call them, is to establish a contrast. To get away from the exclusive circle. Otherwise art is going to be pulled down to the level of simple communication. You know how in student discussions it is equated with information. It is all a question of parallels. The art of the mentally ill, for example. That used to be devalued. But just there you have a sort of direct intensity.

That can all be shown in the hanging. The visitor can work his way from the illogical advertisement to the logical work of art. If he wants to—I always repeat that: if he wants to.

JOHN ANTHONY THWAITES

And is the artist valued here as a creator, or simply as a phenomenon with a particular direction?

HARALD SZEEMANN

If you compare it with the *documenta* of 1968, where a small central group formed a direction and this direction then determined the success of the exhibition—well, I think you'll see that this *documenta* is practically the opposite. There are far more artists represented. The focus is not on movements but rather on the opposite. It is true that conceptual art and New Realism do emerge, but only in relation to the rest, because all if it is seen from the thematic point of view. On the other hand not many emerge as autonomous creators—though of course the *Individual Mythologies* section is made up of personal statements. The problem is to combine the claim to personal expression with the theme of the whole.

JOHN ANTHONY THWAITES

A last question. In your original draft for *documenta 5* you and your colleagues referred to the social obligations of art. Art has functions, you wrote, which are not primarily artistic but related to society as a whole. Is that conception realized in the exhibition?

HARALD SZEEMANN

The draft was written in 1970, in the atmosphere of the 1960s. But the exhibition is taking place now. The constellation is different. Now it is accepted that social changes cannot be made by art acting on its own. But if the public accepts our way of seeing, accepts it with discrimination, then *documenta 5* is a social act.

Interview with Co-Curators: Jean-Christophe Ammann, Bazon Brock, François Burkhardt, and Johannes Cladders

Lucia Pesapane

These interviews were conducted by phone, e-mail, and postal correspondence between March and June 2007. Some of Harald Szeemann's collaborators kindly answered our questions concerning their respective contributions and experiences, namely Jean-Christophe Ammann (*Realism* section), Bazon Brock (*Audiovisual Preface* section), François Burkhardt (*Utopia and Planning* section), and Johannes Cladders (*Individual Mythologies* section).

LUCIA PESAPANE

documenta 5 was not only an artistic event, but also a political debate in terms of both its content and the way Harald Szeemann changed the rules about the way it was run. Szeemann himself was appointed General Secretary, which underscored the notion of independent curator. Did you have the feeling you were part of a team? How was the selection done? Did you choose the artists in your section, or was it done with Szeemann?

JEAN-CHRISTOPHE AMMANN

I was co-organizer and curator. I selected the works for the section *Individual Mythologies* with Harald Szeemann and alone for *Realism*. I was involved very little in the team. I worked only with Szeemann, intensely on the organizational level and, of course, on the communication.

JOHANNES CLADDERS

Harald asked me to curate a department dealing with his idea *Individual Mythologies*. I did not agree because I believed that each work of art is an *Individual Mythology*. Harald accepted my position and he gave me absolute freedom to realize my own thinking. As part of this concept, I decided to curate the contributions of Joseph Beuys, Marcel Broodthaers, Daniel Buren, and Robert Filliou. For the catalogue, I wrote a text about them titled *Die Realität von Kunst als Thema der Kunst* (*The Reality of Art as the Subject of Art*). But I also felt responsible for a lot of the other artists in the section *Individual Mythologies*. The whole organization was a little bit chaotic and produced a lot of problems. Therefore my department was referred to internally as "difficult artists."

FRANÇOIS BURKHARDT

Harald was surrounded by a group of advisers whom he'd appointed and who defined the theme of *d5* with him (Jean-Christophe Ammann, Arnold Bode, Karlheinz Braun, Bazon Brock, Peter Iden, and Alexander Kluge). Then he called on certain authors for certain specific themes. In my case the subjection of the *Utopia and Planning* section was chosen by Szeemann and he specifically asked me to elaborate it as an architect and architectural theorist. In turn, I headed a team of my own choosing, composed of Lucius Burckhardt, Mattias Eberle, and Burghart Schmidt. Harald asked us to work on the theme of architectural utopias in relation to Pierre Versins' *Science Fiction* section, and we were urged to make a distinction between science fiction perceived as "today viewed from tomorrow" and utopia conceived as "tomorrow viewed from today." Based on those given subjects, we were able to develop our section in total freedom, proposing the projects that seemed most interesting from the social and urban-planning standpoint, notably those that concerned alternative types of town development for cities in the future. We decided to devote this section to the Marxist philosopher Ernst Bloch, who wrote a great deal about social utopias, so he provided the basis for our research.

BAZON BROCK

In 1972 I was responsible for defining sub-sections of *d5* by devoting them to themes such as "The war of images," "The claim of reality within images," and "The relation between arts and images." Beyond this, I developed a version of *The Visitors' School* as an "action teaching" with mixed media (technically realized by my assistant Jeannot). I started by offering *The Visitors' School* for exhibition events like *documenta* in 1968 (*d4*) and I continued with special versions of visitor schools within *documenta* in 1977, 1982, 1992.

All the participating artists were named by the different curators, but chosen by collective decisions and of course Harry Szeemann was the moderator-in-chief. The choice of a general secretary had become necessary as a matter of public relations; the journalists, politicians, and heads of visitor organizations wanted a single person in charge and on whom they could depend to answer their questions. Beyond this pragmatic aspect, the *zeitgeist* [spirit of the time] had changed and the interference of politicians as godfathers of *documenta* was no longer possible. The spirit of the time proclaimed that everybody had to shift from arguing in terms of structuralism into patterns of individualism. Being the chosen general secretary of *documenta* gave Harry Szeemann absolute autonomy with the only condition that he wasn't allowed to spend money above and beyond the official budget.

LUCIA PESAPANE

You were, from the beginning, part of the conception of the first project for *documenta 5*, which was designed as a "100-day event" instead of "an exhibition of 100 days" because for you *documenta* was not a static collection of objects, but a "process of mutually interrelated events." This first proposal was more radical and more similar to the *Happening & Fluxus* exhibition in 1970: why was it finally changed? By whom? How was the second project (*Questioning Reality—Image Worlds Today*) conceived?

JEAN-CHRISTOPHE AMMANN

I was involved in the second project right from the beginning when we were thinking about the 100-day event, but it was mainly a strategic idea, too expensive and too difficult to realize. What was wanted was the presence of the artists on the site, what was striven for was a space of interaction, a walk-through event structure with shifting centers of activity, a vast communal studio for the invited artists. Then the project switched into a thematically oriented exhibition.

BAZON BROCK

The change of concept was inevitable, because of the necessity to insure objects. The insurance agency was not prepared to differentiate between objects and environments as instruments for the visitors and those which should not be touched, or between areas as space for the audience and spaces for the artworks themselves. The simple answer is that no insurance company would accept a non-artistic installation of art objects, instruments, scientific demonstrations, performances, happenings, action teachings, and working classes for the audiences. Therefore we had to look for a completely new structure. For us, historical examples came into play such as "Kunst und Wunderkammer," Christmas markets, pilgrim hostels, world exhibitions, warehouses, and especially guided tours known as the "Grand Tour" in the 18th century. Mediating between the visitors and the exhibition meant rediscovering the historical character of psychopompo,[1] excavation guides, and itinerant preachers. Therefore I developed a concept of itineraries, which were to be chosen one after the other by every visitor. The visitor was asked first to choose the character of a tourist, then a connoisseur, and then a pilgrim. It was a way to educate by passing through different situations and stages.

LUCIA PESAPANE

Even while remaining free, Szeemann didn't object to the institution of museums, which he exploited. According to him, *documenta 5* could afford to abandon the illusory freedom of a "museum in the street," and in fact he housed the show in the Fridericianum and the Neue Galerie. Why?

FRANÇOIS BURKHARDT

Szeemann was right, we needed to get the best out of institutions by changing them in line with his fundamental concept of innovation. His message always involved using art in a forward-looking way. In pursuing that goal, the theme of utopia could rightly be considered a model for study when transforming the present.

Harry—like us, for that matter—didn't view museums as a site of reproduction, but as a lab or workshop, a place for research in various fields which explored major social questions, the goal of which was to try to answer those questions through art. He was one of the most inspired curators ever, not only because he had a clear vision of want he wanted to do with art, but also because each time he approached a new project, he added new arguments that art should address. He knew how to grasp those major issues in contemporary society where art could intervene in a critical, positive way.

LUCIA PESAPANE

Harald Szeemann's approach to the history of art is much more similar to ethnographic and anthropological studies, rather than the approach of an art historian. Some sections can be thought of as "Wunderkammer," as a cabinet of curiosity, such as his archive. How do you consider this kind of approach to the world of art? Did you share his viewpoint? What were Szeemann's selection criteria?

JEAN-CHRISTOPHE AMMANN

Harald Szeemann and myself were exhibition makers. We did not work primarily as art historians. We were both connected to the intensity of the work of art and the authenticity of feelings, we had strongly similar ideas. Harald considered himself more as an artist. He had a vision: the *Museum of Obsessions*.

JOHANNES CLADDERS

Harald Szeemann was not an art historian, nor a curator in the traditional sense, he was an artist. Daniel Buren said: "*documenta 5* is the art work of Harald Szeemann, and we, the artists, give him the materials to make it."

FRANÇOIS BURKHARDT

Szeemann's approach to the art world was always guided by a strong position vis-à-vis social reality, thanks to his acutely critical eye. He had a sociologist's or anthropologist's ability to examine contemporary phenomena, and in addition he was able to suggest new, alternative models—his own. That led to the complexity and multiplicity of *d5*: the difference between the themes was one consequence of the complex relationship between art and society. His inquiries were related to the possibility of changing things, what he thought would be possible via the reference models that included art. He had great confidence in art's ability to point society down new paths—something that doesn't happen any more.

BAZON BROCK

One of the sections of *d5* was *Individual Mythologies*, a personal term and one of Harry Szeemann's concepts: it expressed the subjective cosmos of every artist, more than giving an objective insight toward reality. With this notion he wanted to show different attitudes, more than one style. By this it became evident that we had to include in *d5* such distinct forms of non-artistic imaging making as: images from journalism, scientific images, images as therapy, as advertisements, as fashion, as military technology.

LUCIA PESAPANE

In this multiplicity of points of view, Szeemann declared it was a democratic idea, leaving the spectator free to find his own answers. Different development phases were a way to force the visitor into a dialectic-didactic approach: to train viewers to sharpen their judgment through contradictions. Do you think this is the role of the curator: to actualize, to re-think, to re-link different aspects of reality and then to leave the spectator the possibility to share his view or to rebuild one by himself?

JEAN-CHRISTOPHE AMMANN

Yes! We built very well-organized spaces, sometimes as a whole, sometimes as little worlds with their own dynamics, but always involved in a larger dynamic of similarities and differences. It was up to the spectator to find his answer and his conclusions.

FRANÇOIS BURKHARDT

Szeemann didn't want to propose a didactic concept in the strict sense, he preferred to leave people free to find out for themselves. What enriched this show was the group of co-workers itself, where everyone was free to make a creative contribution, one that was often transversal to the theme initially chosen by Szeemann. All these relationships, taken together, yielded a variety of presentations, visions, and interpretations that constituted a great school for visitors. They could come to their own conclusions. We ourselves were enriched by the experience; Szeemann didn't impose his own knowledge, so *documenta 5* was a collective process that included him, us, and the artists, via debates and discussions. Our efforts focused, in fact, on how to get Harald's message across to visitors. He was very clear in his mind about his basic ideas, and he knew how to ensure they were respected, but at the same time he was open to our suggestions. He incarnated the idea of a legendary figure, almost a great guru.

BAZON BROCK

This multiplicity of points of view enabled the spectator not to find an answer, but to find problems. And thus to become an expert: that means developing the ability to make problems and to criticize. All the curators for *d5* were experts in that sense. In the future, educated men and women won't rely on language, religious beliefs, cultural heritage, ethnic or racial identities that they share to find their social glue; the future glue for social bindings will be extracted out of the common interest in unsolved problems with which mankind is confronted. Artists, since the development of art in the 13th century, have always been problem makers and experts in "problematizing" all the important questions that arise from human beings.

Curators therefore should be able to demonstrate how fruitful the turning toward unsolvable problems could be to open new possibilities. They should give an example of how someone could be able to "earn the fruits of their deeds."

LUCIA PESAPANE

Can you tell me of other professional experiences you shared with Harald Szeemann?

JEAN-CHRISTOPHE AMMANN

We met in 1961. I was writing about his shows in magazines, and then I started working as an assistant at the Kunsthalle Bern with him until 1968, when I became director of the Kunstmuseum in Lucerne. But we continued to work together.

FRANÇOIS BURKHARDT

I met Harald in the mid 1960s and worked with him and Brock and the Kunsthaus in Hamburg on the concept of the usefulness of art. Szeemann particularly liked this critical approach, not that of an art historian.

BAZON BROCK

Szeemann found in me an authority for his different projects and that meant that he asked me to collaborate as an author on five of his major exhibitions. He was interested in people as representatives of ideas and not of social or economic power. He was able even to fruitfully collaborate with individuals who did not agree with his ideas, attitudes, and aims. He honored adversaries as troublemakers or problem generators and we cooperated on this level extremely successfully.

LUCIA PESAPANE

Which aspects of his personality and his accomplishments did you particularly admire?

FRANÇOIS BURKHARDT

The show that most moved me was *Blood & Honey—The Future is in the Balkans*, due to Szeemann's ability to present vital issues—war, peace, ethnic problems. He had a great freedom of expression, which art constantly needs if it is to truly play its role, which, these days, is overly channeled.

BAZON BROCK

There is no chance for curators, pedagogues, mediators to rely on didactic recipes. Pedagogues never use formalized standards of teaching. Teachers and all the other characters of mediation give examples for operating or handling problems without the ordinary hope of getting rid of problems by solving them. Problems can only be solved by developing new problems. Within the visitor school, the audio-visual preface indicated thematic tours through the exhibition areas and it described the purpose of art as a strategy to turn everything into problems, even self-evident ones. Szeemann, like every scientist, artist, curator, mediator, critic, follows the humanistic program of attitudes become form, if one develops authority by authorship. All the characters mentioned have in common that they are able to argue all by themselves on proposals they make without the help of friends, popes, patriarchs, markets, or other social authorities. In all of his roles as curator, artist, cultural historian, or as one's contemporary, he aimed to develop authorship and he became a modern type of authority.

[1] Psychopompo, literally meaning the "guide of souls." A psychopompo is a mediator between the unconscious and conscious realms. In some cultures, acting as a psychopompo was also one of the functions of a shaman. This could include not only accompanying the soul of the dead, but also vice versa: to help at birth, to introduce the newborn's soul to the world.

Interview with Artists: Claes Oldenburg and Lawrence Weiner

Haeju Kim

The following interviews were conducted via e-mail and postal correspondence during the month of May 2007.

Interview with Claes Oldenburg:

HAEJU KIM

How were you first contacted by Harald Szeemann and invited to participate in *documenta 5*? Do you remember your first meeting with him? Could you please describe the situation?

CLAES OLDENBURG

I can't remember the circumstances of my invitation to *documenta 5*, but I believe the inclusion of the *Maus Museum* (*Mouse Museum*) was Kasper König's initiative. He knew the work, and was given the title of Director of the *Mouse Museum*. As I recall, Szeemann decided as a result to make a section in *documenta 5* on artists' museums. The *Mouse Museum*, however, had a separate catalogue, edited by Kasper.

HAEJU KIM

Could you tell us how the *Mouse Museum* was realized? If possible, could you please describe your collaboration with Harald Szeemann and Kasper König?

CLAES OLDENBURG

In *documenta 5*, the *Mouse Museum* consisted of a room in the shape of the Geometric Mouse in a box-like space entered by a door, in front of which there was a carpet in the shape of the "nose," on which to wipe your feet. The structure was built on the premises.

HAEJU KIM

Inside, you displayed objects that you had gathered since 1960 as well, so can the *Mouse Museum* be considered as a continuous project? Had the *Mouse Museum* already been realized elsewhere before *documenta 5*, or was it produced especially for it?

CLAES OLDENBURG

The *Mouse Museum* collection continued up to 1977, when it became fixed in a separate building specifically made for the collection by the Museum of Contemporary Art in Chicago. At the suggestion of my partner, Coosje van Bruggen, the outside of this building as well as the inside was made in the shape of the *Geometric Mouse*. A separate wing was added in the shape of a gun to hold the collected Ray Guns and a revised catalogue was made of the final collection. *documenta 5* provided the first opportunity to pull together and publicly present the *Mouse Museum*. It was the beginning of a development of the subject which was first presented in Europe in its completed form at the Rijksmuseum Kröller-Müller in Otterlo in 1979 and subsequently acquired by the Ludwig collection for the Museum Moderner Kunst, Stiftung Ludwig, Vienna. Coosje van Bruggen wrote the accompanying catalogue, to which you can refer for further information.

Interview with Lawrence Weiner:

HAEJU KIM

How were you first contacted by Harald Szeemann and invited to participate in *documenta 5*? Do you remember your first meeting with him? Could you please describe the situation?

LAWRENCE WEINER

First meeting was at the book launch for the *Xerox* book at Jack & Nell Wendler's house in NYC. He then invited me to be in *When Attitudes Become Form*. The invitation for *documenta 5* was jointly made by Klaus Honnef, Konrad Fischer, and Szeemann.

HAEJU KIM

You have been a participant in both important exhibitions *When Attitudes Become Form* (1969) and *documenta 5* (1972) organized by Harald Szeemann. Could you tell us about your participation in these two exhibitions?

LAWRENCE WEINER

The wall removal was requested by Harald and I exhibited it in Bern. For *documenta 5* I published the book *A Primar* and it was distributed at the exhibition.

HAEJU KIM

documenta 5 presented different types of images including trivial objects, publicity, socialist propaganda, and also showed diverse artworks categorized as Hyper-Real, Conceptual, Fluxus, and so on. Do you think *documenta 5* could reflect a social and artistic movement of that time? Do you think this didactic idea of showing all kind of images functioned for the public? For the artists, did *documenta 5* function as a platform to exchange ideas with others?

LAWRENCE WEINER

In fact, it functioned very well for various groupings of artists. To not only interact on an exhibition level; it put many artists in contact with artists functioning outside of their sphere.

HAEJU KIM

There was a big debate around the curatorial model presented in *documenta 5*. Robert Morris sent a letter to forbid the presentation of his work, and some of the artists signed a statement against *documenta* just before the opening. Could you tell me how this debate occurred between artists? And today, how do you see this debate and Szeemann's position in this?

LAWRENCE WEINER

The model allowed Fischer and Honnef [the collaborators who were in charge of the section Idea/Light] to build their own enclave at the Fridericianum.

HAEJU KIM

In the interview for *documenta*, Jef Cornelis asked you to define your work and you answered that it's just contemporary art, you are just a man involved in making art. Compared to the position you had 30 years ago, how would you define your work today?

LAWRENCE WEINER

Just contemporary art.

HAEJU KIM

In 1969 Harald Szeemann created his Agency for Intellectual Guest Labour. At that time, some artists created their own agency (for example Iain Baxter and NeThing & Co, and John Latham and the APG, etc.) as a way of questioning certain modalities of artworks. Can we imagine a link between Szeemann's and these artists' initiatives?

LAWRENCE WEINER

In hindsight the desire to turn cottage industries into pseudo corporate structures is the revenge of the middle class.

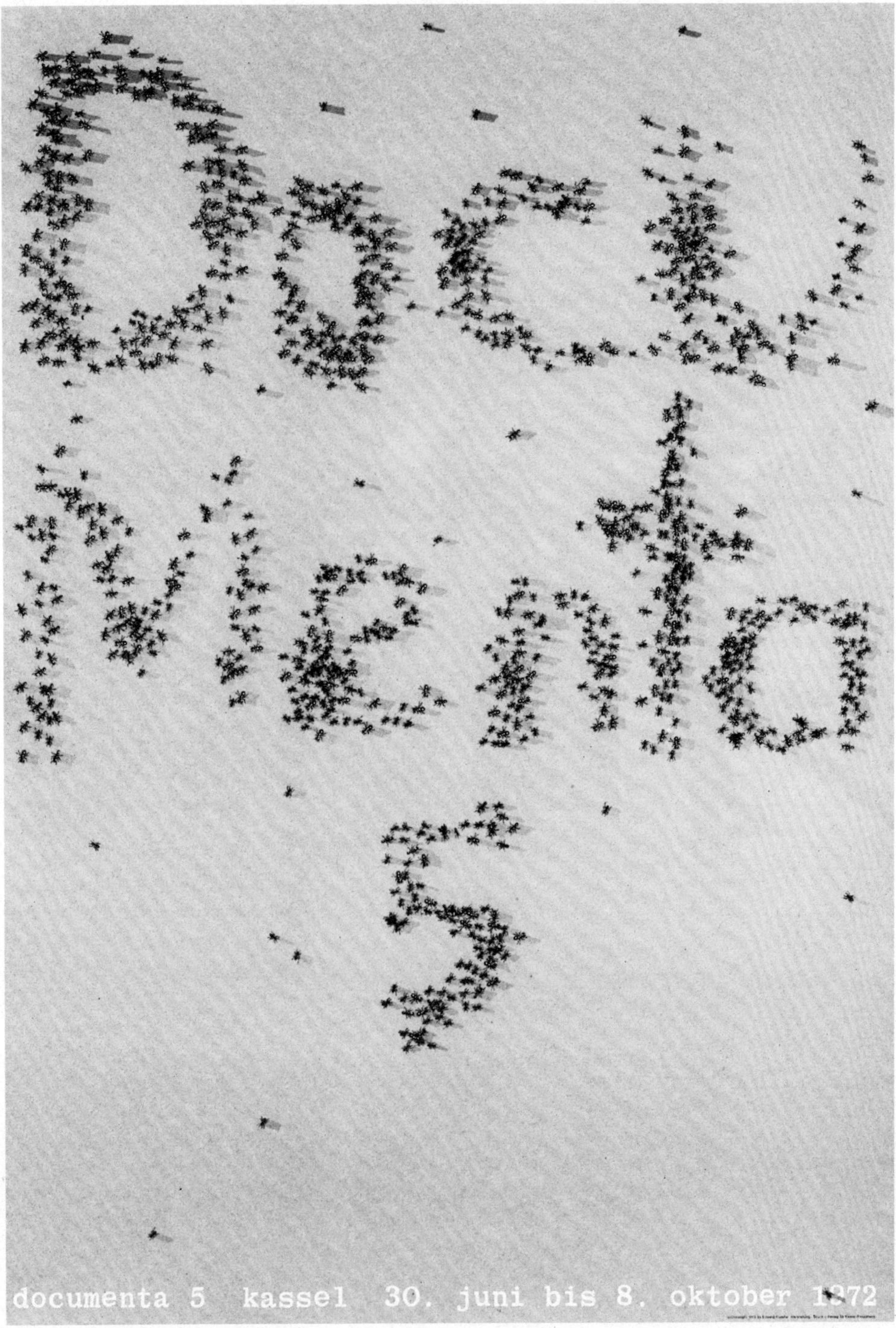

Poster and catalogue cover by Ed Ruscha

[Pages 142–143] Telegram of the petition signed by Carl Andre, Hans Haacke, Donald Judd, Berry Le Va, Sol LeWitt, Robert Morris, Dorothea Rockburne, Fred Sandback, Richard Serra, Robert Smithson

40

Telegramm **Deutsche Bundespost**

Datum	Uhrzeit	TSt 35 Kassel	Leitvermerk	Verzögerungsvermerke Datum	Uhrzeit
9411Z KASSEL D	4111TO FFM D =		16295	Gesendet Platz	Namenszeichen

ZCZC 0060 GMA484 LCD336 WU CD DPFX HL UWNX 147 NEWYORK NY 147

aus

LT

HARALD SZEEMANN — documenta GmbH — TF 16295 jederzeit zusprechen — 1/50/2 330P

DOCUMENTA 5

SCHONE AUSSICHT NO2 — 35 Kassel Schöne Aussicht 2 — 247

35 KASSELL

~~Auftrunsch~~ zustellen

Dienstliche Rückfragen

THE UNDERSIGNED AFFIRM THE FOLLOWING POINTS PROMPTED PRIMARILY IN
RESPONSE TO DOCUMENTA T BUT PERTAINING TO ALL EXHIBITIONS CONDITIONS
1 IT IS THE RIGHT OF AN ARTIST TO DETERMINE WHETHER HIS ART WILL BE
EXHIBITED IR IS THE RIGHT OF

COL LT 5 35 NO2 1

41

Telegramm **Deutsche Bundespost**

Datum	Uhrzeit	TSt 35 Kassel	Leitvermerk	Verzögerungsvermerke Datum	Uhrzeit
Empfangen Platz	Namenszeichen	Empfangen von		Gesendet Platz	Namenszeichen

2/50

aus

Dienstliche Rückfragen

AN ARTIST TO DETERMINE WHAT AND WHERE HE EXHIBITS 2 A WORK OF ART
SHOULD NOT BE EXHIBITED IN A CLASSIFICATION WITHOUT THE ARTIST CONSEN
AN ARTIST MUST HAVE THE RIGHT TO DOO WHAT HE WANTS WITHOUT CENSORSHIP
IN THE SPACE ALLOTTED IN THE CATALOGUE 4 A COMPLETE ITEMIZED

COL 2 1 3 4 A

Telegramm **Deutsche Bundespost**

Verzögerungsvermerke

Datum	Uhrzeit	TSt 35 Kassel	Leitvermerk	Datum	Uhrzeit
Empfangen		Empfangen von		Gesendet	
Platz	Namenszeichen			Platz	Namenszeichen

3/47

aus

Dienstliche Rückfragen

BUDGER OF ALL INSTITUTIONAL EXHIBITIONS INCLUDING ALLOCATIONS TO
PARTICIPANTS TRANSPORTATION CURATORIALFEE ETC SHOULD BE MADE PUBLIC
IMMEDIATELY AFTER THE EXHIBITION THIS STATEMENT RELEASED TO PRESS
CARL ANDRE HANS HA ACKE ON TUDD SOL LEWITT BARRY LE VA
ROBERT MORRIS DOROTHEA ROCKBURNE FRED SANDBACK RICHARD
SERRA ROBERT SMITHSON

~~COL~~ OK

May 6, 1972

Harald Szeemann
Documenta V
35 Kassel
Schone Aussicht 2

Dear Harald Szeemann:

I wish all work of mine withdrawn from the forthcoming Documenta V. You may post the following statement.

I do not wish to have my work used to illustrate misguided sociological principles or outmoded art historical categories. I do not wish to participate in international exhibitions which do not consult with me as to what work I might want to show but instead dictate to me what will be shown. I do not wish to be associated with an exhibition which refuses to communicate with me after I have indicated my desire to present work other than that which has been designated. Finally, I condemn the showing of any work of mine which has been borrowed from collectors without my having been advised.

Robert Morris

Robert Morris' letter to Harald Szeemann

Press coverage

Extracts selected from the abundant German and international press.

Jan Van Der Mark, "Venice & Kassel: the old and the new politics," in *Art in America*, n° 130.

"The status quo, carefully maintained at Venice where all the serene conventions of the international exhibition operated to the full, was rudely tilted at *documenta*, where a polemical and historical event, assembled under provocative categories, redefined for the 1970s the nature of the official show."

"Complaint dept," in *The Feminist Art Journal*, May 1972.

"Dear Harald Szeemann,

Europeans tend to say that we, American women, are liberated and free, but you and your staff, by your persistence in excluding women from an international survey of this caliber, have cut into their income and prestige [...]"

"Dear Friends,

It was my first intention to come back to New York and visit all the women artists on the list prepared by Lucy Lippard[1] and Brenda Miller, but I had to stay here to make *documenta* financially speaking [...] and I don't exhibit things which I know only from photographs."

Hilton Kramer, "Exhibition is a melange that assumes culture is an outworn fiction," in *The New York Times*, March 1972.

"At times resembling a carnival, at times a political convention or an academic seminar, the show includes enormous tableaux, live performances, films, lectures, soap-box orators; the 'non-artistic'—and the nastier the better—must be included as well [...] The atmosphere of the exhibition is thus heavily ideological and, despite the carnival antics and even a certain quantity of serious art, rather sinister. It shuttles between two extremes, one a rather heartless mode of theorizing and the other a mode of realism that favors the banal, the vulgar and the pornographic, especially in its more violent and sadistic forms [...]"

Arnold Kohler, "Is Art superfluous?" in *La Tribune de Genève*, Tuesday July 25, 1972.

"Here we have an entirely revolutionary exhibition. Unlike the four previous *documentas*, this is not a show of fine arts. A large banner over one of the halls bears the inscription, 'Art is superfluous,' the assertion of our fellow citizen, Ben. But that's a whole agenda, and a statement on an issue of civilization [...]"

John Russell, "Expand your notions," in *Sunday Times*, July 16, 1972.

"*documenta 5* has come to be the most talked about of all exhibitions of modern art. A new policy was evolved—one which would place the emphasis on a disinterested enquiry into why people made art, what were art's boundaries and what would happen when artists got sick of the system and would no longer go along with it. Harald Szeemann had at that time a great name as a man with a nose for the new and it was decided to give him a free hand [...] For the people under 30, who make up some 90 per cent of its audience, it has completed the demystification of art [...]"

Caroline Tisdall, "Document of a dead end," in *Arts Guardian*, July 10, 1972.

"Germany's four-yearly *documenta* exhibition is the biggest show for avant-garde art. This year the theme is reality, but our art critic reports a dead end, a weary sop to fashion. What has gone wrong?"

Lothar Orzechowski, " *documenta*, and now?" in *Argus*, October 12, 1972.

"Start from scratch or learn a lesson? The threat of a suit still hangs over 40-year-old Harald Szeemann, given an estimated deficit of 800,000 marks. Walter Olbrich has complained that part of the expenditure, especially on construction, was done without his knowledge. 'I can't imagine that Olbrich didn't know,' claims Szeemann. 'Plans always had to be submitted to the right authorities. The respective authorizations were then sent to the company management.' The basic problem lies in the fact that work and services related to the preparation of an art show are outside bureaucratic norms and are practically impossible to assess retrospectively. Szeemann willingly used the term 'irrational organization,' which can obviously lead to confusion."

Claude Bouyeure, "*documenta 5* or The Man," in *Le Monde*, 1972.

"*documenta 5*: a synthesis, summing up, review of contemporary art—this exhibition is of major significance. What's being questioned is not yesterday, today, or tomorrow—it's us. The human species, our civilization, simultaneously influenced by the heritage of the 19th century and the discoveries of the 20th in the realms of industry, sociology, psychopathology, and psychoanalysis [...] It is this latter point that appears clearest in most of the works on show. Fear, violence, mutilation, castration, and sex constantly crop up as leitmotifs [...]"

Jacques Michel, "Art seeking reality," in *Le Monde*, July 5, 1972.

"The organizers feel that artistic output arises from a sensibility that reacts to non-artistic realities—political, economic, and cultural. A quest for these realities is what is behind this post-68 event, that pivotal year for 'committed' artists [...] This *documenta* will also be marked by the institutionalization of another novelty, namely the German-Viennese Actionists, who basically perform a 'theater of the horrible' to simulate rituals of death and bodily mutilation."

François Pluchart, "documentally well done!" in *arTitudes*, n° 8/9, July–August–September 1972.

"Whatever people who are prisoners of their narrow chauvinism or any other form of ostracism—and who therefore didn't understand this show—may think, *documenta 5* is the most important international show of recent years [...] Far from being a heterogeneous collection, as might be expected prior to visiting the show, *d5* is a coherent, personal, and personalized work. This major work by Harald Szeemann sheds brilliant light on the fact that artistic practice is first of all a working out of ideas [...] Szeemann has shown that the making of both art and images is a political stance, and reminds us that all art is political, which is the only level today at which it is both justifiable and dangerous [...]"

Harald Szeemann's correspondence with François Pluchart, Bern, January 23, 1973.

"Dear François Pluchart,

Thank you for your article on *d5*. On several occasions I've stressed that the French press was the one that most contributed to an understanding of the reality of the exhibition [...] But I would like to add some information: we produced *d5* knowing that we were short a million Deutsche Mark and at that point cancelled several costly works and a participatory section involving inflatable structures [...] My disappointment resulted from the fact that three days after the opening I was declared responsible for the deficit by the finance department, and that even today I am threatened with having to repay significant sums. I agreed to do *d5* in a city largely hostile to *d5*, although recognized as necessary to its prestige. I acted in full awareness of all that, but I note only that the German press adopted this denigrating tone at the start of the show, whereas the French press did not [...]"

William P. Engel, "The organizers didn't forget the kitsch," in *Argus*, June 30, 1972.

"While we could initially expect that the social role of art would be reconsidered at Kassel, Szeemann has recently proclaimed the return of art for its own sake. He in fact feels that the political debate over art has become absurd."

Nigel Gosling, "Crystal balls in Kassel," in *Arts Guardian*, September 10, 1972.

"The fifth *documenta* triumphantly upholds its reputation for controversial and lively originality, and what the new art jargon might call on-the-ballhood [...] Unlike the Venice Biennale, which feels like an alms-house for decayed art-movements, this show is alert, militant, intelligent, arcane, erotic, and wonderfully sensitive to the agitated gusts of change which are blowing across the art scene. It is a wonderfully intriguing collection with something of the air of an old cabinet of curiosity [...] The new director had gone along with the theory that traditional art is as dead as mutton [...] It is best to visit it with an unprepared mind and your thinking cap pulled well down over your eyes."

[1] Lucy Lippard's letter to Harald Szeemann is published in Tobia Bezzola, Roman Kurzmeyer (eds.), *Harald Szeemann: with by through because towards despite*, Springer, Vienna/New York; Edition Voldemeer, Zurich 2007, p. 365–366.

Conclusion

Haeju Kim

The most significant change that *documenta 5* brought to the genealogy of *documentas* was the recasting of its structure. Up through *documenta 4*, the show was run by a committee, but with *d5* a single person took charge for the first time. Bazon Brock gave two reasons for this single delegation: the pragmatic advantages of consolidating communication and public relations, and the evolution in thinking that went from structuralism to individualism.[1] But if being named General Secretary makes us think of "the UN or the Communist Party,"[2] Szeemann could also, on his own, invite colleagues to help formulate the concept and head up the various sections of the show. This model of sole management was retained for future *documentas*, the title simply changing to Artistic Director. The concept and style of each Artistic Director became a key element that characterized each *documenta*, "a decisive prelude to the international revaluation of the curator."[3]

When Szeemann was approached, the days of Arnold Bode (who mainly did the exhibition design) and Werner Hartmann (theoretical contribution) were coming to an end—the new generation of artists and the arrival of Photo-Realism and Pop art on the art scene clashed with the abstract art that *documenta* had defended in its previous versions. In order to fulfill one of the briefs of *documenta*—an experimental, forward-looking event—the mayor of Kassel turned to Szeemann, who had just closed *When Attitudes Become Form* (1969), perceived at the time as a fringe show. Once appointed, Szeemann decided to present artists from *When Attitudes Become Form*,[4] namely the new generation—American conceptualists and Italian Arte Povera—who had been absent from the previous *documenta* in 1968. These artists became very visible on the art scene after *d5*. In fact, the following *documenta* would include 67 of them.

Another phenomenon launched by *d5* was the veritable popularization of large exhibitions. The local and international press covered the event extensively, and the surrounding polemics caught the attention of the general public. Although there was no significant increase in attendance compared to *documenta 4*.[5] the show began to welcome visitors from the general public rather than just art specialists (who had been the main audience for this event). *documenta 5* demonstrated that contemporary art was entering the era of spectacle—the next *documenta* would increase the list of artists and the exhibition area (three times greater than its predecessor), and include major projects in public places, such as Walter De Maria's *Vertical Earth Kilometer*, among others.

When it came to exhibition design for *d5*, Roland Nachtigäller reported that Szeemann put up a small number of strategically placed partition walls; the lighting was functional, employing a lot of fluorescent lamps. This offered artists and their work wide-open conditions. "Of all shows, *documenta 5* was the least designed. It had a raw and unpolished air, and many viewers' senses were initially overtaxed by its flood of high and low culture images."[6] This flood of varied works can be explained by the *Individual Mythologies* theme that Szeemann had given to one of the *d5* sections. Bazon Brock explained that the *Individual Mythologies* concept and term came from Szeemann himself, attempting to evoke the subjective cosmos of each artist rather than an objective vision of reality. Szeemann was thereby trying to show differing attitudes and a multiplicity of styles, at which point it became clear that *d5* should incorporate non-artistic forms of image production, whether stemming from journalism, science, advertising, medicine, fashion, or military technology.[7] Furthermore, Szeemann said that, "The advantage of *Individual Mythologies* is that it is a completely open-ended designation, so why not turn the tables and look among the conceptual artists, the structuralists and the realists for *Individual Mythologies*."[8]

Within the very theme of *Questioning Reality—Image Worlds Today*, Szeemann allocated a major role to the layers of his own artistic language, his personal method, and the affirmation of his own subjectivity, which are summed up in the notion of *Individual Mythologies*. They are expressed through his choices of venues, exhibition design, and hanging. He said, "I wanted to manufacture my own myth, therefore something negatively objective in relation to the role of an intermediary. I am no longer disposed to simply fill a given frame, but am increasingly inclined to project my own ideas."[9] Two years after Kassel, when planning the 1974 *Grandfather, A Pioneer Like Us* show in his apartment in Bern, he began to define the work of the agency as being "at the service of a potential visualizing of a *Museum of Obsessions*." This *Museum of Obsessions* was part of his own imaginary museum, composed of all the exhibitions he had ever organized. The relationship to this museum would give him the energy for future projects and point him in new directions.[10]

Whereas *documenta 5* asked society as a whole to confront broad issues (image, reality, art), Szeemann's next show, *Grandfather: A Pioneer Like Us*, was centered on the personal, subjective dimension. And yet both shared the idea of individual mythology. As Szeemann explained, "For me, the show *Grandfather* represented a logical development from a series of shows starting with *When Attitudes Become Form* (to go no further back), and on through *Happening & Fluxus* to arrive at *documenta 5*. In fact, *Grandfather* was a response to *d5*. We were trying to distinguish various levels of reality and draw it back into the event. The context, the museum, and the demanding framework of visitors, created constant hurdles. And yet the shifting identifications in the *Individual Mythologies* section, which only became clear in the overall framework of *documenta 5*, spontaneously worked in *Grandfather*, even if it only emerged after fully reflecting on the *how*."[11] To which he added, "From *Individual Mythologies* to *Obsessions* was just a small step. Because one can't exist without the other."[12]

[1] "The choice of a general secretary had become necessary as a matter of public relations; the journalists, politicians, and heads of visitor organizations wanted a single person in charge and on whom they could depend in define to answer their questions. Beyond this pragmatic aspect, the *zeitgeist* (spirit of the time) had changed and the interference of politicians as godfathers of *documenta* was no longer possible. The spirit of the time proclaimed that everybody had to shift from arguing in terms of structuralism into patterns of individualism." Cf. Lucia Pesapane, "Interview with Co-Curators," p. 135.

[2] "I thought it was pretty good—like at the UN or the Communist Party!" in Nathalie Heinich, *Harald Szeemann, un cas singulier: entretien*, L'Echoppe, Paris 1995, p. 21. Szeemann also said that, "It was no coincidence that my title for *d5* was that of General Secretary. I was looking for ways and means to include the East, the realism from the Soviet Union and China. Both failed, but as the letter shows: there is no resignation." in Tobia Bezzola, Roman Kurzmeyer (eds.), *Harald Szeemann: with by through because towards despite*, Springer, Vienna/New York; Edition Voldemeer, Zurich 2007, p. 322.

[3] Walter Grasskamp, "For example, *documenta*, or, How is art history produced?" Reesa Greenberg, Bruce Ferguson, Sandy Nairne (eds.), *Thinking about Exhibitions*, Routledge, London 1996, p. 75.

[4] Bezzola, Kurzmeyer (eds.), *Harald Szeemann*, p. 314.

[5] *documenta 4* was attended by 221,000 visitors, *documenta 5* by 229,000 visitors, and *documenta 6* by 343,000 visitors. This information is drawn from *Archive in Motion, 50 Years of documenta 1955–2005*, Steidl, Göttingen 2005, p. 231, p. 251, p. 271.

[6] Roland Nachtigäller, "Performing the Zeitgeist, a Roundup of Fifty Years of Staged Art," *Archive in Motion, 50 Years of documenta 1955–2005*, Steidl, Göttingen 2005, p. 231, p. 30.

[7] Cf. Pesapane "Interview with Co-Curators," p. 136–137.

[8] Bezzola, Kurzmeyer (eds.), *Harald Szeemann*, p. 318.

[9] Harald Szeemann, "Le Musée des obsessions," *Ecrire les expositions*, La Lettre volée, Brussels 1996, p. 48.

[10] Ibid., p. 58. "Whereas *Individual Mythologies* were still a language of signs, at least in the context of *d5*, Obsessions are henceforth energies that arise, grow, and close behind these languages."

[11] Ibid., p. 37.

[12] Ibid., p. 50.

2) *L'Autre—4th Lyon Biennial,* 1997

Introduction

Julija Cistiakova and Yuka Tokuyama

The history of the Lyon Biennial fits within the context of French arts policy. The Culture Ministry had been disappointed in the Paris Biennial, which it had supported from 1959 to 1985 and, rather than continue to fund it, began thinking of an event in the provinces. The Lyon Biennial was launched in 1991 under the directorship of Thierry Prat and Thierry Raspail, to coincide with the contemporary art fair created in the city in 1980. The idea was to have a big exhibition every two years that asserted the French artistic presence on the international scene. In 1997 the event in Lyon was just a young French biennial responding to the dynamism of the European art scene of the 1990s, and its existence was uncertain. However, the fact that its opening that summer would coincide with those of the Venice Biennial, *documenta* in Kassel, and the Skulptur Projekte in Münster gave its organizers an opportunity to establish the Lyon Biennial as one of the major international art events.[1] The organization of this fourth edition was thus entrusted to the Swiss curator Harald Szeemann, although its title and theme—*L'Autre* (*The Other*)—had been proposed by the artistic directors.

The socio-political situation at the time offered a number of justifications for such a theme: the collapse of the Soviet bloc and the opening up of China, for example, had brought forward the concept of globalization. The notion of alterity was also at the center of heated debates in France, where immigration was becoming a hot political issue. The French curator of the 46th Venice Biennial, Jean Clair, had himself provoked violent reactions in artistic circles with his exhibition *Identity and Alterity*.

Raspail and Prat were counting on Harald Szeemann to approach the theme of *L'Autre* in an original way: "We wanted to have a new perspective, a foreigner's perspective [...] the foreigner, the symbol of the *other*, is Harald Szeemann."[2] They entrusted him with the task of setting up a two-directional artistic enterprise: getting foreign artists to come to Lyon, and presenting French artists on the international scene.[3] By virtue of his original curatorial practice, his taste for non-historical presentations, and his encyclopedic resources in art, literature, and the sciences, for them Szeemann was the embodiment of alterity and foreignness.

Szeemann had never worked with a given theme, but right from his very first visit to Lyon he was charmed and even fascinated by the Halle Tony Garnier, the imposing 17,000 square-meter space destined to house the biennial. The beauty of this huge building, which had never held an exhibition before, persuaded him to accept the invitation. From now on he would strive to conceive "a different kind of event for a place that is different." In this splendid hall, which he said he responded to as *L'Autre*, he produced an exhibition that he described as a "love story between that grandiose building and myself."[4]

In order to convey the process whereby this exhibition was put together, we have gathered documents from both the archive of the Lyon Biennial and the Szeemann archive in Maggia.

Access to these resources has enabled us to reconstitute the different phases of conception, organization, and production of the manifestation.

The manuscript describing the artistic concept was found in Szeemann's archive. Published in parallel to the press releases, it takes us through the curator's developing ideas regarding both the concept and the selection of artists. As was his wont, Szeemann broke with norms and traditions. Thus, for *L'Autre* he presented works by artists who had never been considered as such and who, all their life, had been considered "other": Elisàr von Kupffer, the Facteur [postman] Cheval, the farmer Emery Blagdon, the writer Franz Kafka. At the same time, the exhibition plans show how he apprehended and constructed the exhibition space.

Also published here are excerpts from two interviews with Harald Szeemann. In the first, with Thierry Raspail and Thierry Prat, he discusses his participation and describes his position, the development of his main concepts, such as the *Museum of Obsessions* and *Individual Mythologies*. More generally, in this exhibition Szeemann dealt with the question of the "universality of art": "Maybe it's today's version of a Universal Exhibition. Which allows me to combine the 'considered obsessions' of *professional* artists with the 'primal obsessions' of *brut* artists."[5] He achieved this universality by conceiving of mixed assemblages of works "recycled" from his memory and archive and works discovered during his latest research. "[He] would pull out some of his older acquisitions and combine them with new works," explains Tobia Bezzola.[6] Thus, *The Torture Machine in Franz Kafka's "In the Penal Colony"* had been in *The Bachelor Machines* exhibition in 1975, and the model of the *Palais Idéal* (*Ideal Palace*) by Facteur Cheval had already been presented in the exhibition *Penchant for a Synthesis of the Arts*, in 1983. However, lack of funds meant that only a very small number of works could be produced especially for this exhibition. In a second interview, published in the journal *Ninety*, Szeemann expressed more freely his criticisms of the organization of the *Lyon Biennial*.

In order to fully grasp his methodology and curatorial practice, we have spoken to certain artists who took part in *L'Autre*, and to one of the co-directors of the event. We have also carried out numerous interviews with his close collaborators. At the time, Szeemann effectively worked with his own team, which could in many respects be considered a kind of family firm. Josy Kraft and Jérôme Szeemann were in charge of transport and the production of the exhibition, Christoph Zürcher handled the architecture and display, while Una Szeemann produced the wall texts, among other things. In another text published in this study, Josy Kraft describes the workings of this "Szeemann team."

[1] The 47th Venice Biennial was curated by Germano Celant, *documenta x* in Kassel by Catherine David, and the 3rd Skulptur Projekte in Münster by Kasper König. Cf. 16th Session, "Interview with Thierry Raspail," p. 180–183.

[2] Rachel Sukman, "Conversation with Thierry Prat," in *Terminal 5*, n° 5, October 1997, p. 11.

[3] According to Szeemann, this was a moment of crisis for the *Lyon Biennial*: "When the two Thierrys put my name forward for the *Lyon Biennial*, they also wanted me to save that institution, they wanted it to carry on and to survive." Cf. *Ninety*, "Interview with Harald Szeemann," p. 183–184.

[4] Ibid., p. 184.

[5] Cf. Jean-François Chougnet, Thierry Prat, Thierry Raspail, "Interview with Harald Szeemann," p. 177.

[6] Cf. François Aubart, Fabien Pinaroli, "Interview with Tobia Bezzola," p. 26–31.

[Pages 151–157] First Exhibition Concept for *L'Autre—4th Lyon Biennial* handwritten by Harald Szeemann

"L'autre"

" C'est un autre en moi qui n'était jamais d'accord, qui n'a jamais répondu aux questions qui lui étaient imposées." "Ne devrait-on pas dire „une autre" en toi?" „Non, un autre. Je ne mélange pas. Si je dis l'autre il faut me croire... Je crains qu'en fin de compte c'est ma patience qui est responsable et coupable de ton impatience" (Ingeborg Bachmann, Malina).

D'autres „autres"

„ Mettez-moi de l'autre côté, sur celle-ci je suis déjà grillé" (Saint-Laurent)

" Ce que tu ne veux pas qu'on te le fasse ne le fais non plus à l'autre" (Tobie 4, 16)

" Un autre homme se réjouit d'autres oeuvres" (Homère, Ulysse, 14, 228)

" Tu ne dois pas avoir d'autres dieux à côté de toi" (Moïse II, 20,3)

„ Merci, mon Dieu, que je ne suis pas comme les autres" (Luc, 18, 11)

„ Un comme l'autre" (Corinthien, 3, 8)

„ Faire l'un mais ne pas délaisser l'autre" (Matthieu 23,23)

„ Une chose me suggère la volupté, l'autre le bon sens. Ce qui est meilleur, j'en fais l'éloge, ce qui n'est pas bien est suivi par le coeur" (Ovide, Métamorphoses 7, 19/21)

„ La récompense pour toi sera dans une autre vie" (Schiller)

„ Je suis devenu un autre homme, donc aussi les objets me paraissent autres" (Goethe)

„ D'autres villes, d'autres filles" (Goethe)

„ Non seulement on s'aime dans les autres, mais on se haït aussi dans les autres" (Lichtenberg)

„ Changer de lieu ne signifie que l'échange d'une misère contre l'autre"

„ Avant d'aller à table on l'a compris autrement" (Schiller)

"L'art autre" (Tapié de Céyleran)

„la pensée autre"

„le cinéma autre"

„l'Amérique etc, etc autre

„le Temps autre"

„L'autre sexe"

„le tout est autre, l'autre est tout" etc, etc.

„le poète se fait voyant par un long, immense et raisonné dérèglement de tous les sens ..... Je est un autre" (Rimbaud)

C'est moi l'autre, l'autre c'est l'ennemi, c'est ce qui est différent, séparé, même hostile, tout ce joue entre ces deux pôles – implosion-explosion.

Cette relativation/globalisation et intériorisation de l'autre a eu des conséquences: chaque individu avec sa propre anomalité magnétique, sa chimie des sens perçoit l'autre d'une manière différente, d'un autre œil. le scénario et les oeuvres d'une exposition sont autres pour l'un familiers pour l'autre et beaucoup ce qui était autre autrefois devient très vite partie intégrée d'une mémoire collective qui elle pour une grande partie du monde est individuelle — la mythologie individuelle est un droit de l'homme – donc toujours autre pour l'autre.

Montrer „l'autre" dans un espace grandiose comme c'est la halle Tony Garnier est une mise en scène, un choix opéré entre ce qui est encore autre pour le responsable et ce dont il pense que c'est encore – peut-être on espérons-le – encore autre pour les visiteurs, donc les autres. Bref, que l'autre soit différence, écart ou égalité/similitude ou un avant, présent, futur ou un ailleurs ou une menace/danger ~~[illegible]~~ l'exposition en tant que moyen d'expression implique une douche écossaise entre le familier et la rupture.

Exemples

[l'autre dans la région]

1. le facteur Cheval
2. Etienne-Martin
   1. Modèle du Palais idéal et dessins
   2. Documents sur la falaise sculptée et le Manteau"

[le temps autre]

3. Richard Serra
   "The Hours of the Day"
4. Salvador Dali
   "la vraie image de l'île des morts d'après Boecklin"
5. Jean Tinguely
   "Méta-matic"
6. Tatsu Myashjima

[L'autre historique]

7. Goya, les disastres
8. Jacques Callot, les horreurs
9. Kubin, "L'autre côté"
10. Füssli, le cauchemar
11. Arts africains, océanien etc.
12. Art brut (Ashby)

[la nature autre]

13 Katharina Fritsch, le roi des rats
14 le Bul, les species
15 les monstres au cinéma (Freaks)

[L'autre sexe]

16 Jason Rhoades, Uno momento

[L'autre modulor]

17 Franz West, les bancs

[L'autre identification]

18 le Teddy-ours (films, collection, oeuvres Lavier, Mike Kelley

[L'autre corps]

19 Schiele, Nu jaune
20 Friederike Pezold, Alphabet
21 Molinier
22 Maplethorpe

23 Nan Goldin

24 Inez van Lamsweerde

25 Pipilotti Rist

26 Wilhelm Reich, Organon [L'autre rite, comportement]

27 Antonin Artaud, exécration père-mère / corps sans organes

28 Michaux, dessins mescaline

29 Arnulf Rainer, " "

30 Nitsch, théâtre des orgies et mystères

31 Vito Acconci, premières actions

32 Paul McCarthy, Pinocchio

33 Douglas Gordon, pièce catatonique

34 Elisar von Kupffer, le monde des béats [L'autre Narcisse]

35 Jeff Koons „I'm the greatest"

36 Messerschmidt, Têtes caractères [L'autre physionomie L'autre portrait]

37 Rainer, Dessins Messerschmidt

38 Francis Bacon

39 Lucian Freud

40 Picasso

41 Klossowski

42 Franz Gertsch

43 Marisa Merz

44 Arcimboldo

45 Documents: prostitution [la morale autre]
enfants, abus sexuels,
Bosnie/Serbie, rites africains
le phallus coupé, clitoris coupée

[L'histoire autre]

46 Hanne Darboven

[la communication autre]

47 Bruce Nauman
47a Rainer Ganahl, Interface/Internet
48 Kabakov, chapelle "soviétique [L'idéologie autre]
48a Hengbo Peng
[le mythe autre]
49 Bill Viola, Passage
[les prophéties autres]
50 Documents: sectes
Beuys: fin du XXe siècle
[la guérision autre]
51 Emma Kunz, dessins
et médicaments

52 Emery Blagden, Healing Machines

[l'architecture autre]

53 Kuwayama
53a Rachel Whiteread
54 Immendorff
[la perspective autre]
55 Escher
56 David Deutsch
57 Turrell
[le son autre]
58 Max Neuhaus
[L'objet autre]
59 Orozco
60 Douglas Gordon

61 John Armleder
61a Hains [L'humour noir autre]
62 Jon Kessler

63 Kippenberger

64 Herold

65 Serge Spitzer, Tennis sans stars [le jeu autre]
[la mort autre]
66 Cryonic movement
(documents)

67 la chambre de Lene Reckenfelder [la collection autre]

68 Toroni [la fenêtre autre]

69 James Coleman [le théâtre autre]

ce qui n'exclut pas Boltanski (la mémoire autre) Baselitz (la sculpture brute), Polke (le médiumnisme), et d'autres bons artistes mais qui ont été toujours montrés ces dernières années. Mais je pense aussi à une confrontation de la vidéo avec l'assassin coupé en tranche et la vache de Damien Hearst et puis il y a quelques jeunes anglais intéressants qu'il faut encore visiter, et j'ai vu des vidéos d'un jeune chinois très intéressant aussi (Mengbo Feng) etc, etc.

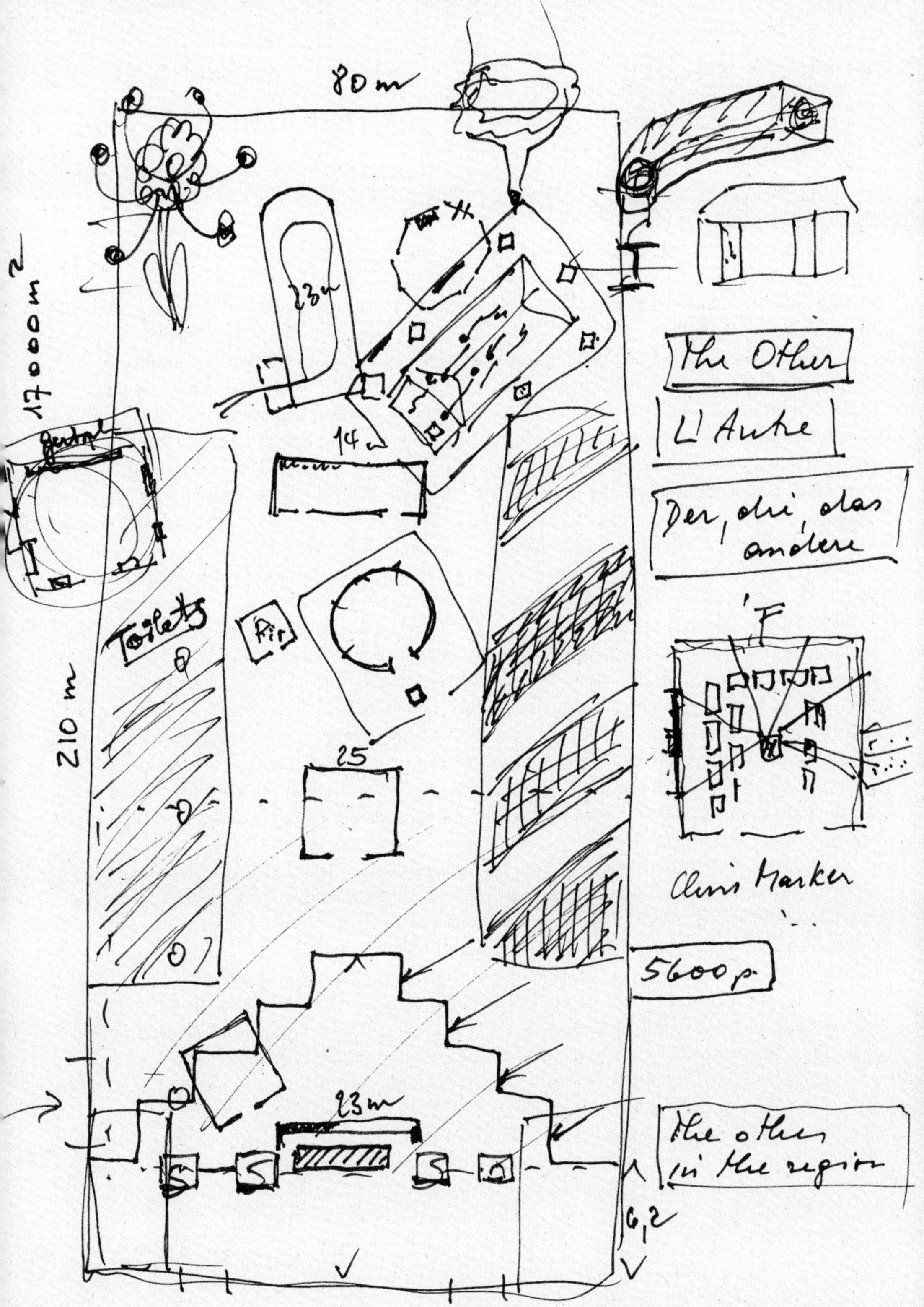

80 m
17000 m²
210 m
23m
14 m
25
23m
Toilets
The Other
L'Autre
Der, die, das andere
Chris Marker
5600 p.
The others in the region
6,2

First Press Release

Harald Szeemann

The Other

Everything is always other. In former eras, we had to wait for a long time to become capable of assembling feelings, sensations, and desires together into one entity, so that our "I" could stop feeling estranged from itself, and could overcome the permanent condition of alterity in order to feel at home with itself.

Unless, like the rebel Rimbaud, one was to proclaim, "I is another" and constantly seek to break with one's habitual behavior. The "I," whether broken into pieces or in harmony with itself, accompanied by a short-circuited "that" or moving along at a comfortable pace, is and has always been the stable or precarious platform on which the conditioned meeting with the other, fast-paced or slow-moving, takes place.

Long before television there were already the zappers and the persevering, those who sought the depths of solitude though close to the other, those who sought to thrive within the other, and those who transformed the other into an object of analysis.

There are states of fusion with others—love, puberty—and states of violence toward them. There are all the intermediate states—the exotic, the monstrous. Some people even manage to take holidays in the relational chaos. *L'Autre* (*The Other*) is limitless, never entirely tangible, a reflection of those ideal societies dreamed of by the utopians, which always failed because of the other, which in its relation to the "I" is often simply hell.

For me, at this moment, the other who must be satisfied in the coming months is the Halle Tony Garnier, the site of the upcoming *Lyon Biennial*. The theme announced is *L'Autre*—a being of undeniable and unfathomable grandeur, for without it there is no art, culture, or society. Art is always alterity, the artist always the creator of an other: another volume, another vision of the world, another physical entity, another metamorphosis, another fragmentation, composition, information.

The previous biennials have made up for lost time and fulfilled the needs of this century's art; they have displayed works that make use of the electronic media of the animated image. After *L'Amour de l'art*, a sort of event-driven organization of the spirit seems to me/us to be the most adequate form with which to build a bridge connecting the last revolution in art, in which utopia took shape, with the post-human, so as to end up at the soft-modern.

As far as the choice of artists is concerned, it can scarcely be implemented except through a dialectical, even polarized, process: not in order to identify and tie down the "other," but to make it visible within the exhibition. We will therefore avoid applying the term "other" to every artist and every work. The fast-food philosophers and the constant assault of meaningless words have made every designation obsolete.

This year the Lyon Biennial takes place at the same time as the Venice Biennial, *documenta* in Kassel, and the Münster Skulptur Projekte. It is therefore essential that we steadfastly inspire this marvelous Halle Tony Garnier to make it "other."

Second Press Release

Harald Szeemann

The Lyon Biennial is getting close ... In the magnificent Halle Tony Garnier, it promises to be one of the events of the summer. Its theme is *L'Autre* (*The Other*). But far from illustrating an eternally-changing alterity, the way the exhibition puts itself forward is to place itself at the service of artists who are always "the others" for the spectators, who are themselves the other "others." Thus, there is no illustration and no commentary, only rather hard-hitting works. Against the unfortunate consequences of the proclamation that the end of utopia is at hand, we want to set up the positive utopias of the artists, their revolutions of the visual, their sense of humor, poetry, and optimism in a period that is most strongly marked by grayness. Thanks to their works, we want to enchant, to astonish, sometimes to shock. We seek the impossible: this is what will decide the future.

The exhibition starts with *The Other* in the region itself: the *Palais Idéal* (*Ideal Palace*), constructed by Facteur [postman] Cheval, documents concerning *La Vierge au sable*, and *La maison natale* of Etienne-Martin, one of the great French sculptors, and a set of works by Ughetto, an artist from Lyon.

Four representatives of the visuals-arts revolution that took place at the end of the open the trajectory of the 1960s: Joseph Beuys, with his social sculpture; Richard Serra, with his mastery of weight and of unstable equilibrium; Bruce Nauman, who places sculpture directly in front of our eyes; and Hanne Darboven, with a work on the atom bomb, presented here for the first time.

Starting from here, there are spaces that contain surprises: Francis Bacon and his twisted male figures stand in opposition to Franz Gertsch's beautiful female faces and Jean-Olivier Hucleux's *Jumelles*.

In Pipilotti Rist's room, one can zap through this charming young artist's video programs. Stan Douglas shows us landscapes that move in and out of existence, and Douglas Gordon gives us an epic on hands. Gary Hill confronts us with the resignation and repressed revolt of foreign workers and jobless people.

Katharina Fritsch shows us a rare phenomenon of nature: *The Rat King*. In a gigantic installation, Jason Rhoades confronts us with the life, the agitations, the adventure of his genitals. And the Chinese artists? They narrate the great epic of the cultural revolution, and the newer, more down-to-earth philosophy according to which, in Deng's view, it is glorious to be rich (Pu Jie); they narrate the everyday activity of scratching oneself (Zhang Peili), and show us how meaningless the *Little Red Book* has become for the younger generation (Xu Yihui).

To be cured in a different way is the theme of a major installation made up of 500 healing sculptures by Emery Blagdon, and Emma Kunz's drawings of the polarization of flowers.

Viennese Actionism presents us its art, which breaches taboos (Brus, Mühl, Nitsch, Schwarzkogler). Rainer energizes Messerschmidt's faces and, regarding *The Torture Machine in Franz Kafka's "In the Penal Colony,"* Friederike Pezold puts forward an alphabet of the body, her new Mayo. Peter Hutchinson makes the letters of the alphabet disappear, and Raymond Hains pulls together the threads of events and places in an unsuspected way.

Who still remembers the pneumatic postal service? Serge Spitzer puts together, in a chaos of tubes, a closed circuit of pushing and pulling. The purity of pollen, this element of the most intense yellow, this place of meditation: it is Wolfgang Laib who creates it for us.

But already the fascination of narcissism takes us over: the wide-eyed world of Elisàr von Kupffer, Eugene von Bruenchenhein's *Portraits of Marie*, Marie-Ange Guilleminot's restrained emotions; and the "other" painting by Jessica Stockholder and Polly Apfelbaum. Yukinori Yanagi's drawing follows an ant. And the cinema, too, is other. The 40 benches are a work by Franz West, and the program is highly diverse: a young French soldier describes his life in Bosnia in Chris Marker's *Casque bleu*, in *Fashions* Charles Ray shows us anti-fashion, as Valie Export, in *Remote ... Remote ...* shows us her painful "displacement." Matthew Barney exhibits his world, which vacillates between Busby Berkeley and Leni Riefenstahl; the Greenberg Studios set out all the virtualities in *Seven*, the seven deadly sins.

And the life of objects: Gabriel Orozco presents his single-seater *D.S.*, and Chris Burden his steamroller, which he forces to fly. Such a large "non-aeroplane" mass has never taken to the air before. And there is the psychic suffering that generates a work. Louise Bourgeois shows us *Red Room (My Parents)*, Hans Danuser *Frozen Embryos*. What can be said about the glorious splendor of fish adorned like courtesans? And Elmar Trenkwalder's exotic garden in ceramic, or Nahum Tevet's weird architecture? And who has ever seen an artist exhibit himself, like Christian Jankowski, pigeon-fashion?

All of this can be seen in Lyon between July 9 and September 24, in the great Halle Tony Garnier, where the bell will sound and pleasure will abound.

List of Artists

Plans of the Exhibition

1 – Martine Aballéa (France)
2 – Polly Apfelbaum (USA)
3 – Francis Bacon (Ireland), (1909–1992)
4 – Gilles Barbier (France)
5 – Matthew Barney (USA)
6 – Joseph Beuys (Germany), (1921–1986)
7 – Emery Blagdon (USA), (1907–1986)
8 – Louise Bourgeois (USA)
9 – Rebecca Bournigault (France)
10 – Eugène Von Bruenchenhein (USA), (1910–1983)
11 – Gunter Brus (Austria)
12 – Chris Burden (USA)
13 – Ferdinand Cheval (France), (1836–1924)
14 – James Coleman (Ireland)
15 – Serge Comte (France)
16 – Kyle Cooper (USA)
17 – Vincent Corpet (France)
18 – Hans Danuser (Switzerland)
19 – Hanne Darboven (Germany)
20 – Stan Douglas (Canada)
21 – Nathalie Elemento (France)
22 – Etienne-Martin (France), (1913–1995)
23 – Valie Export (Austria)
24 – Katharina Fritsch (Germany)
25 – Franz Gertsch (Switzerland)
26 – Douglas Gordon (Great-Britain)
27 – Marie-Ange Guilleminot (France)
28 – Raymond Hains (France), (1926–2005)
29 – Nicolas Herubel (France)
30 – Gary Hill (USA)
31 – Richard Hoeck (Austria)
32 – An Hong (China)
33 – Jean-Olivier Hucleux (France)
34 – Peter Hutchinson (Great-Britain)
35 – Fabrice Hybert (France)
36 – Richard Jackson (USA)
37 – Christian Jankowski (Germany)
38 – Pu Jie (China)
39 – Jeff Koons (USA)
40 – Igor & Svetlana Kopystiansky (Russia)
41 – Guillermo Kuitca (Argentina)
42 – Emma Kunz (Switzerland), (1892–1963)
43 – Elisàr von Kupffer (Switzerland), (1872–1942)
44 – Wolfgang Laib (Germany)
45 – Abigail Lane (Great-Britain)
46 – Lee Bul (Corea)
47 – Ingeborg Lüscher (Switzerland)
48 – Paul McCarthy (USA)

49 – Franz Kafka (Czech Republic), (1883–1924)
50 – Chris Marker (France)
51 – Feng Mengbo (China)
52 – Franz-Xaver Messerschmidt (Austria), (1732–1784)
53 – Yan Pei-Ming (China)
54 – John Monteith (USA)
55 – Mariko Mori (Japan)
56 – Otto Mühl (Austria)
57 – Juan Muñoz (Spain), (1953–2001)
58 – Bruce Nauman (USA)
59 – Hermann Nitsch (Austria)
60 – Gabriel Orozco (Mexico)
61 – Philippe Parreno and Pierre Joseph (France)
62 – Zhang Peili (China)
63 – Manfred Pernice (Germany)
64 – Friederike Pezold (Austria)
65 – Arnulf Rainer (Austria)
66 – Charles Ray (USA)
67 – Lene Reckenfelder (Germany), (1941–1992)
68 – Jason Rhoades (USA), (1965–2006)
69 – Pipilotti Rist (Switzerland)
70 – Allen Ruppersberg (USA)
71 – Ute Schröder (Austria)
72 – Rudolf Schwarzkogler (Austria), (1940–1969)
73 – Richard Serra (USA)
74 – Pierrick Sorin (France)
75 – Serge Spitzer (USA)
76 – Jessica Stockholder (USA)
77 – Nahum Tevet (Israel)
78 – Elmar Trenkwalder (Austria)
79 – Luc Tuymans (Belgium)
80 – Henry Ughetto (France)
81 – Franz West (Austria)
82 – Wang Xingwei (China)
83 – Yukinori Yanagi (Japan)
84 – Xu Yihui (China)
85 – John Waters (USA)
86 – Chen Zhen (China), (1955–2000)

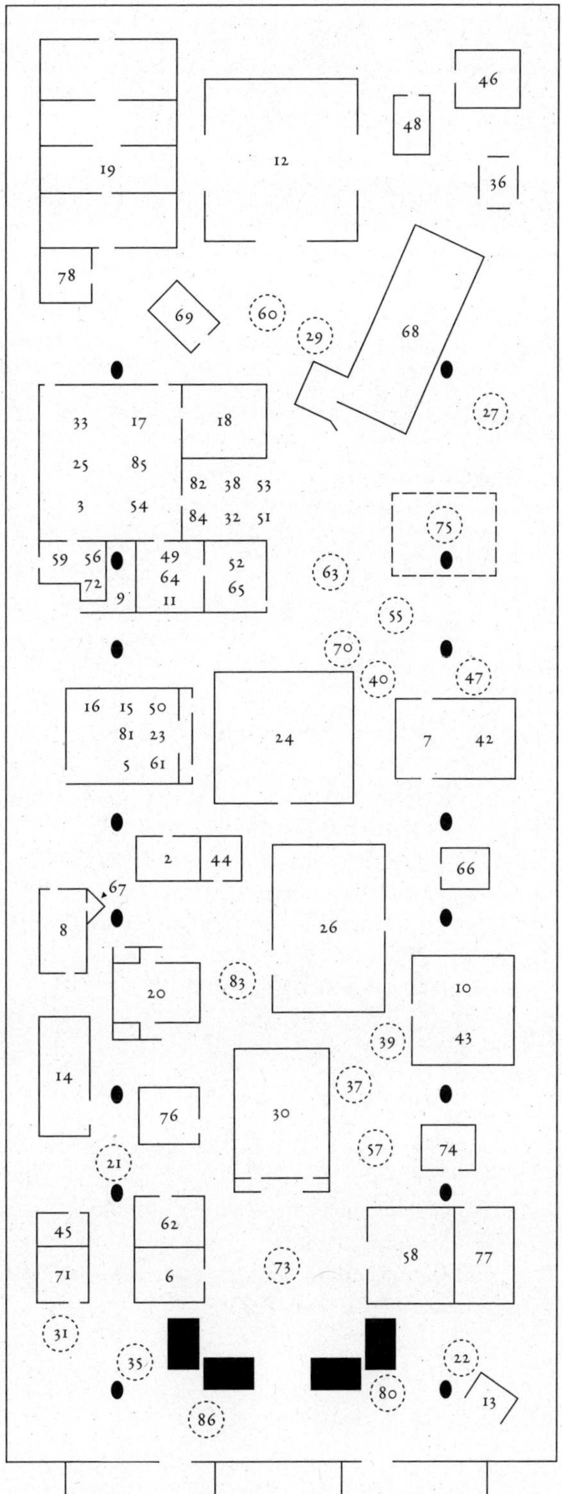

Technical Information

L'Autre—4th Lyon Biennial

Dates: July 9–September 24, 1997
Location: Lyon, France
Venue: Halle Tony Garnier, (17 000 m^2)

Number of artists: 86
Number of visitors: 78 029

Organization chart:

Guest Curator:
Harald Szeemann

Artistic Directors:
Thierry Prat, Thierry Raspail

Budget:

Total: 18 000 000 French Francs (FRF)

Direct subsidies:
City of Lyon: 7 000 000 FRF
Ministry of Culture: 5 000 000 FRF
Région Rhône-Alpes: 1 000 000 FRF
Musée d'Art contemporain de Lyon: information not communicated

Internal fundings:
Partners: 3 000 000 FRF
Ticket sales: 2 000 000 FRF

Catalogue:

Edition: 5 000
Language: French
Number of pages: 221
Publisher: Réunion des Musées Nationaux, Paris
Distributor: Le Seuil, Paris

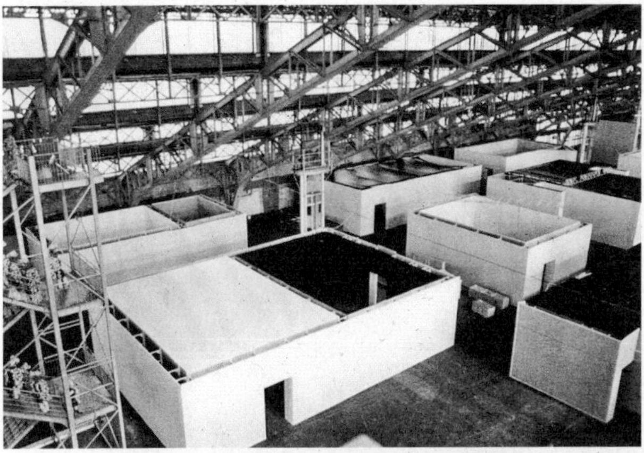

Halle Tony Garnier:
views of the exhibition spaces
under construction

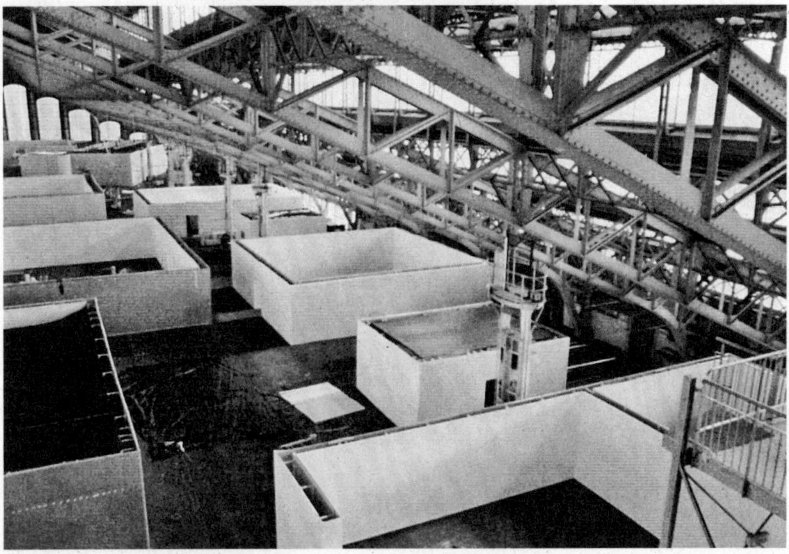

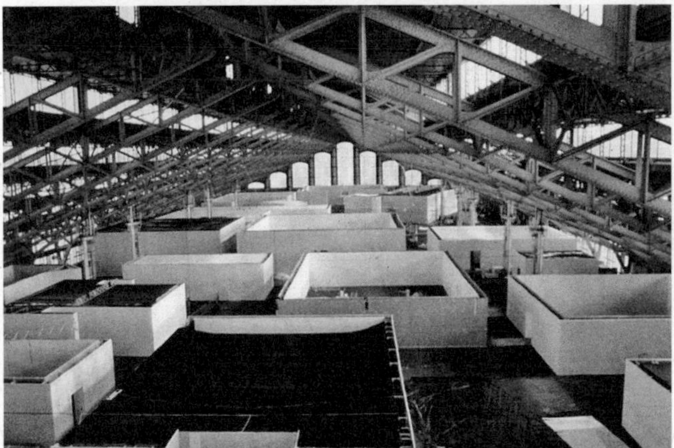

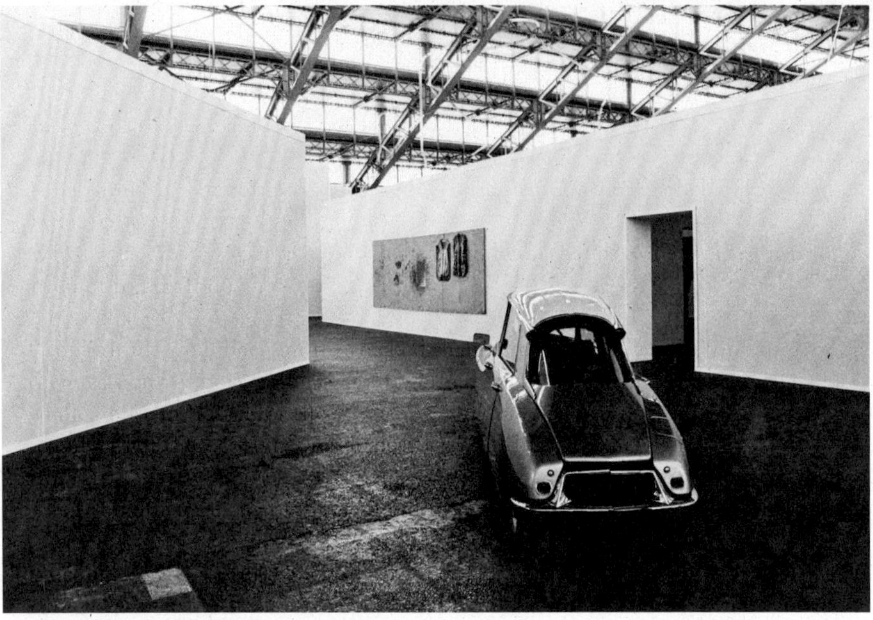

Gabriel Orozco, *La D.S.*, 1993

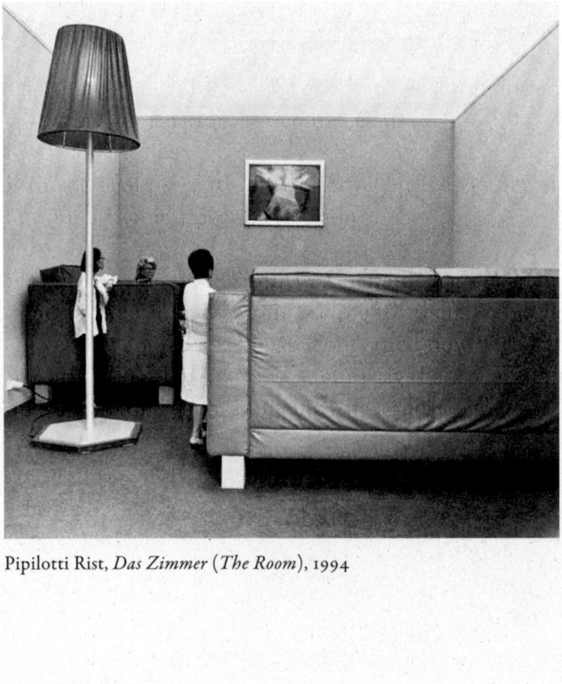

Pipilotti Rist, *Das Zimmer* (*The Room*), 1994

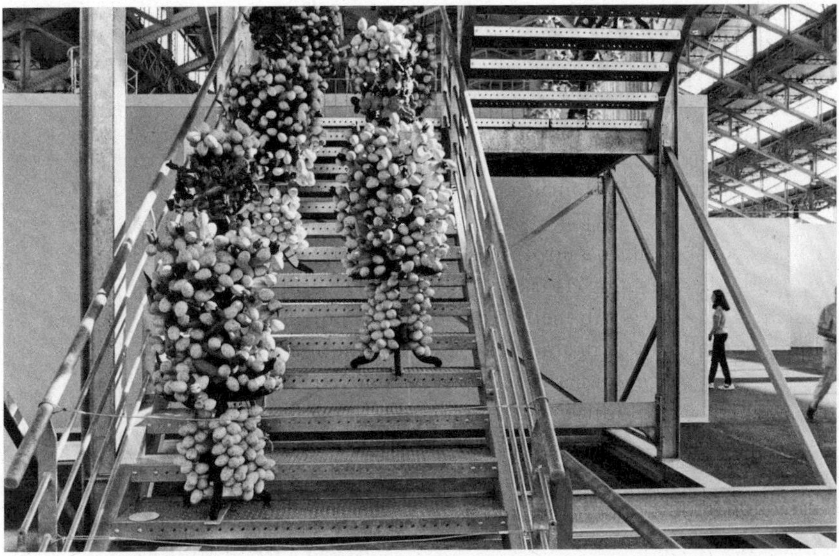

Henry Ughetto, *Tête funéraire* (*Funerary Head*), 1992

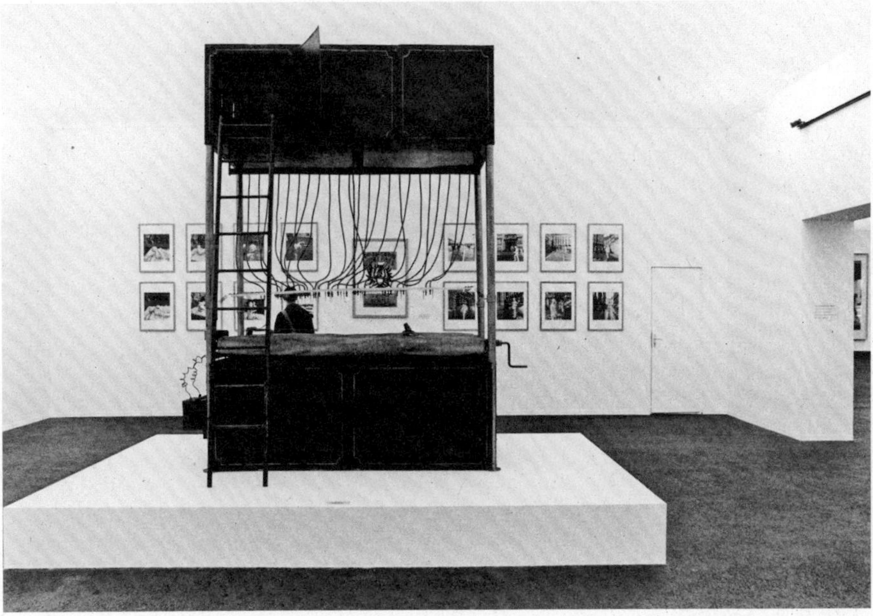

The Torture Machine in Franz Kafka's "In the Penal Colony," 1975

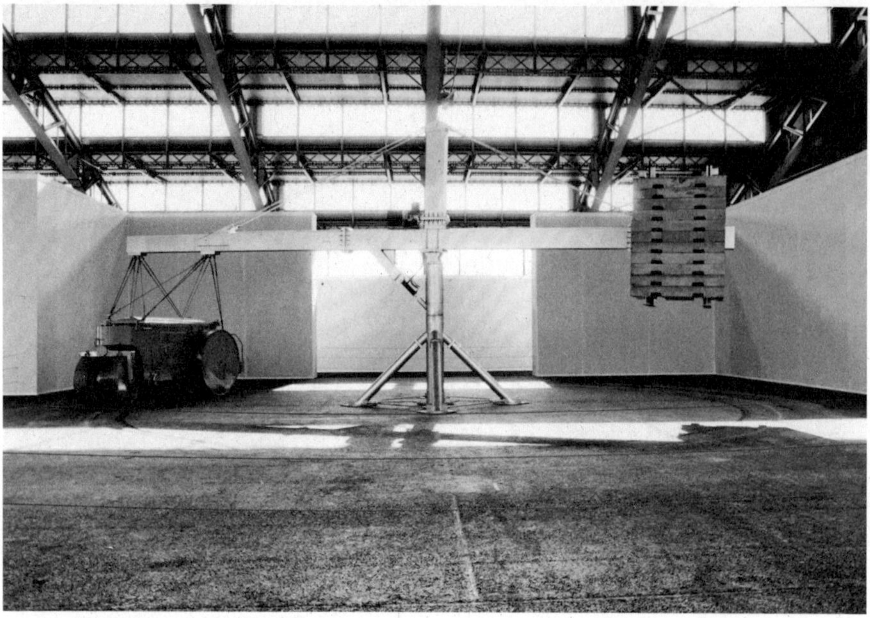

Chris Burden, *The Flying Steamroller*, 1991–1996

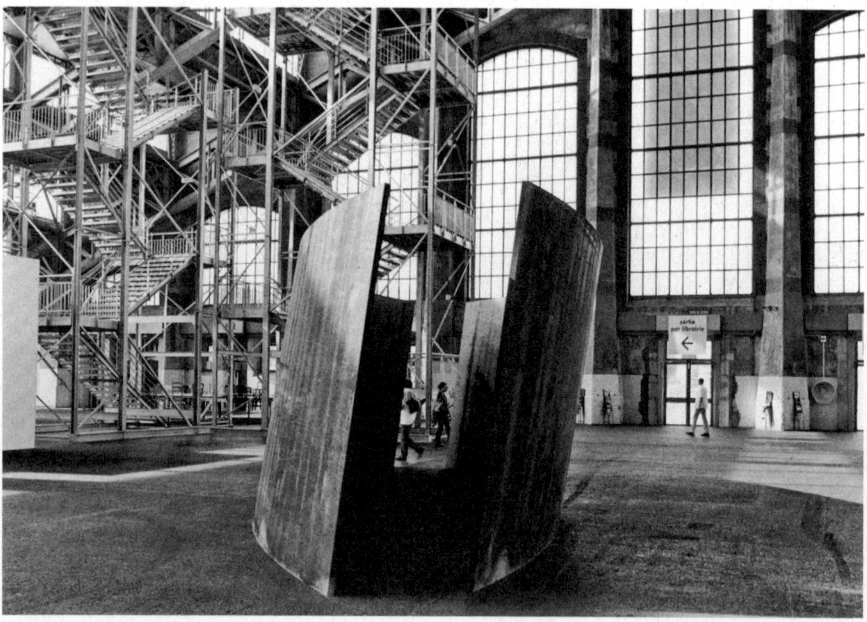

Richard Serra, *Olson*, 1985–86

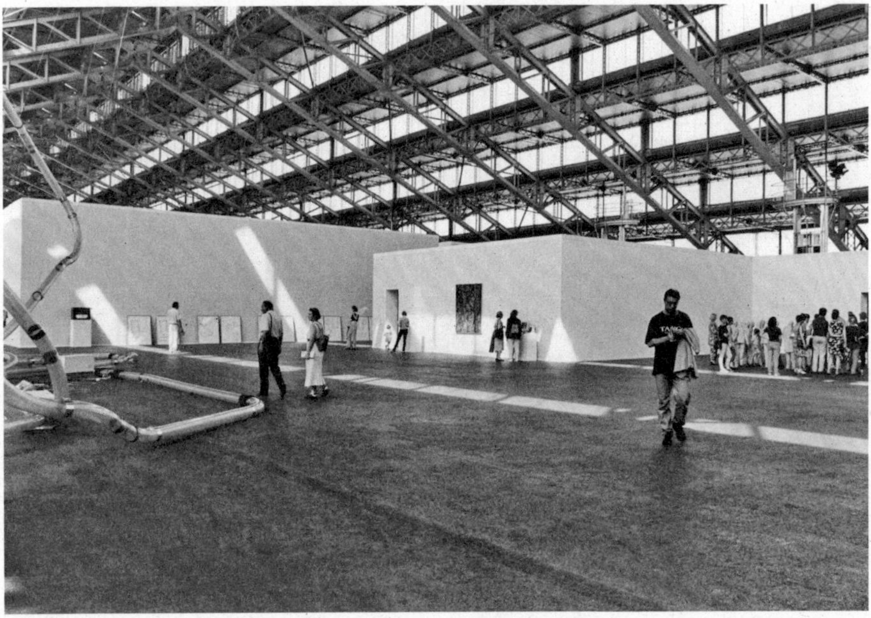

Exhibition view

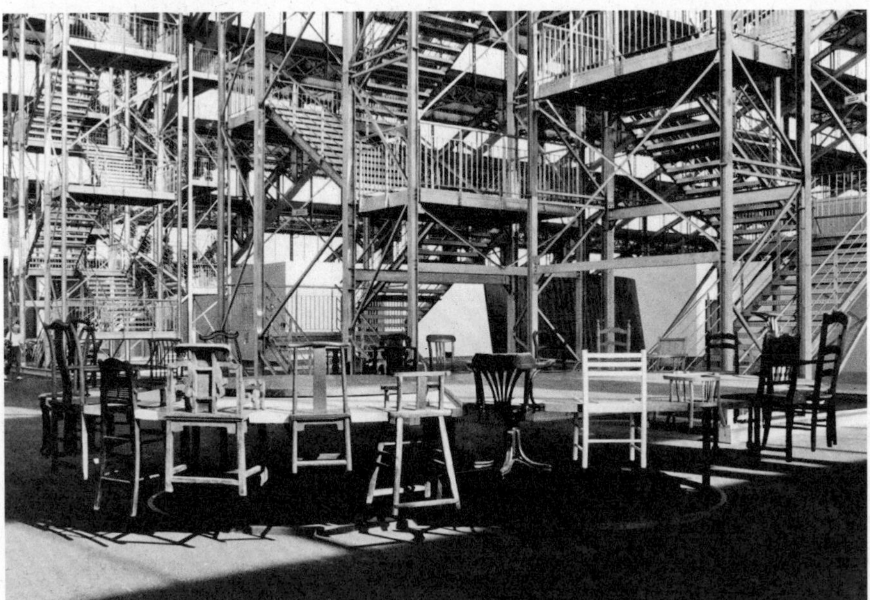

Chen Zhen, *Table Ronde—Côte à côte* (*Round Table—Side by Side*), 1997

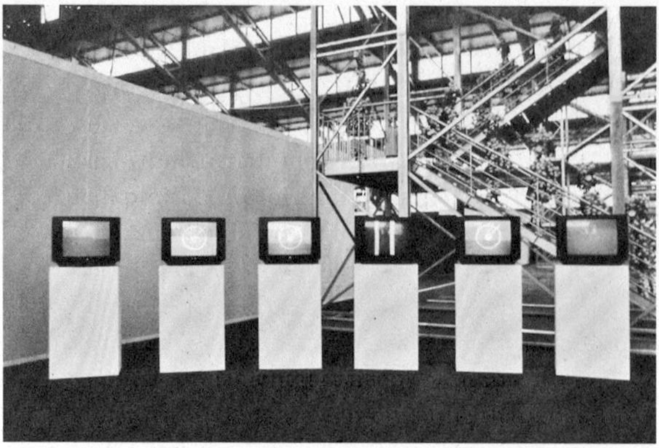

Fabrice Hybert, *Vous êtes ici* (*You Are Here*), 1997

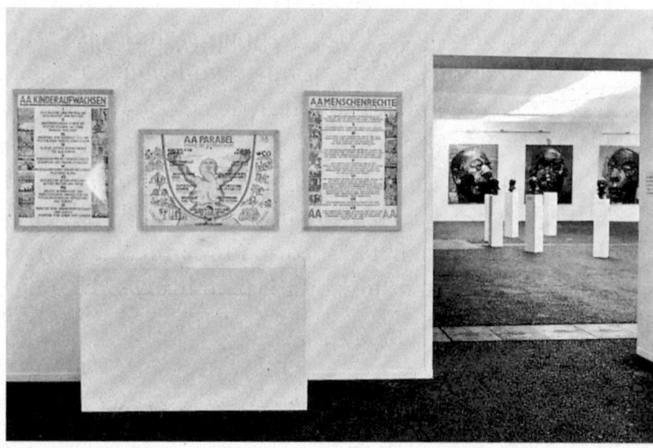

Exhibition view: Otto Mühl, Franz-Xaver Messerschmidt, Yan Pei-Ming

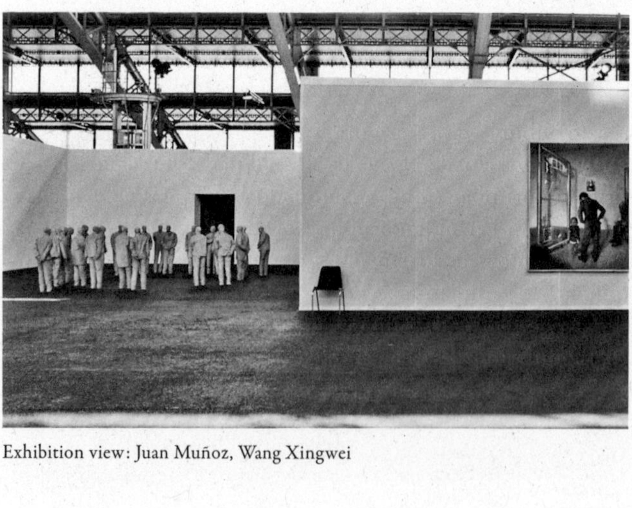

Exhibition view: Juan Muñoz, Wang Xingwei

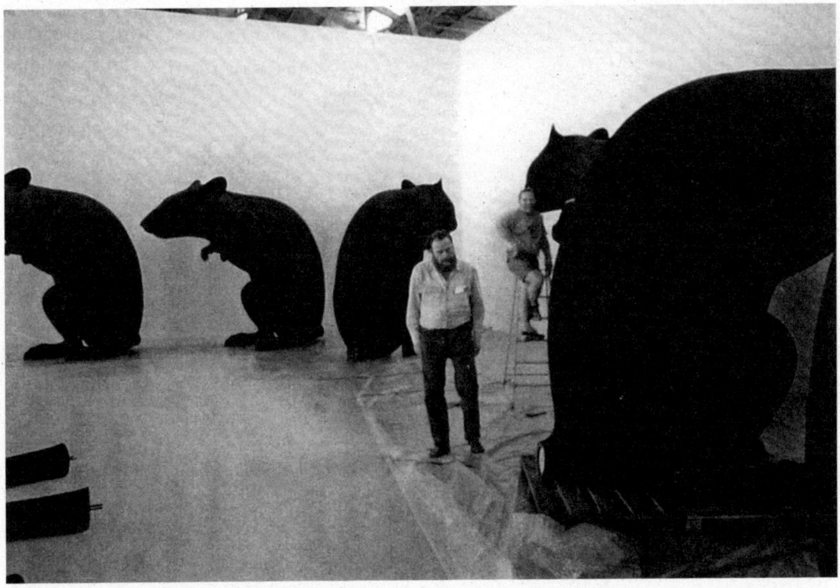

Katharina Fritsch, *Rattenkönig (The Rat King)*, 1992–1993

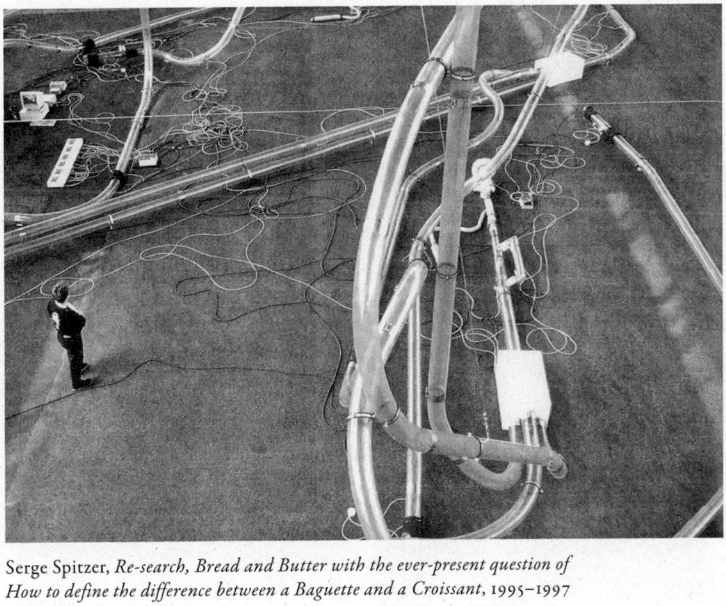

Serge Spitzer, *Re-search, Bread and Butter with the ever-present question of How to define the difference between a Baguette and a Croissant*, 1995–1997

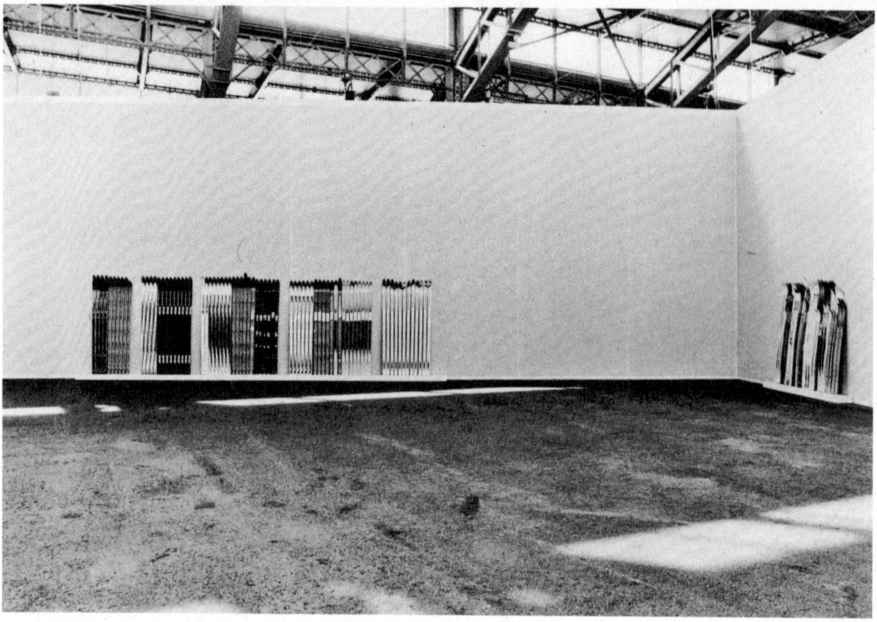

Raymond Hains, *Palissade de skis* (*Fence of Skis*), 1997

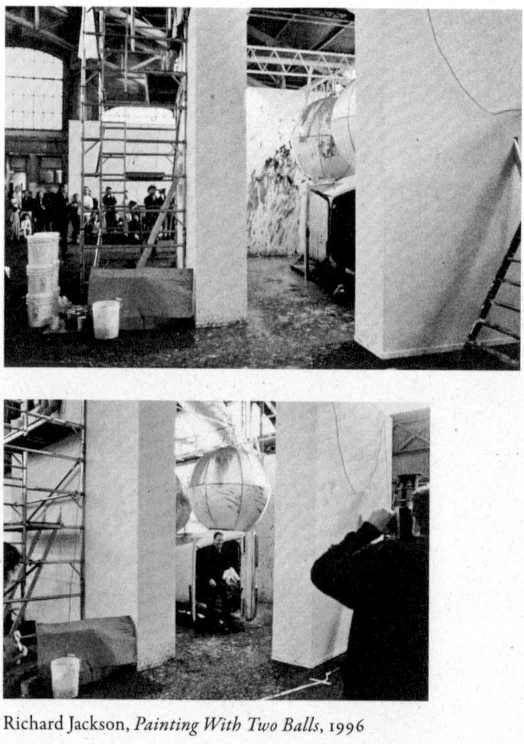

Richard Jackson, *Painting With Two Balls*, 1996

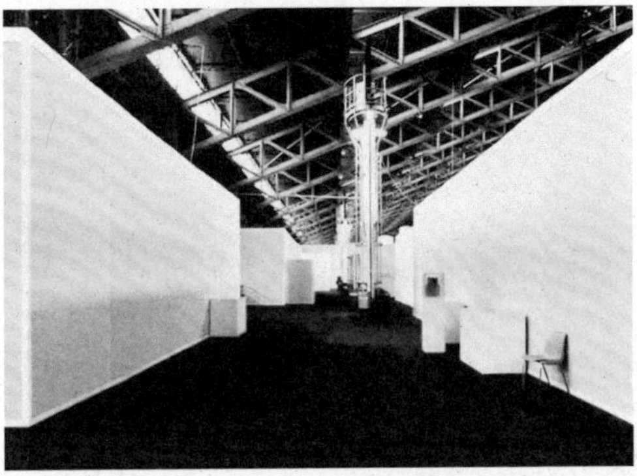

Exhibition view

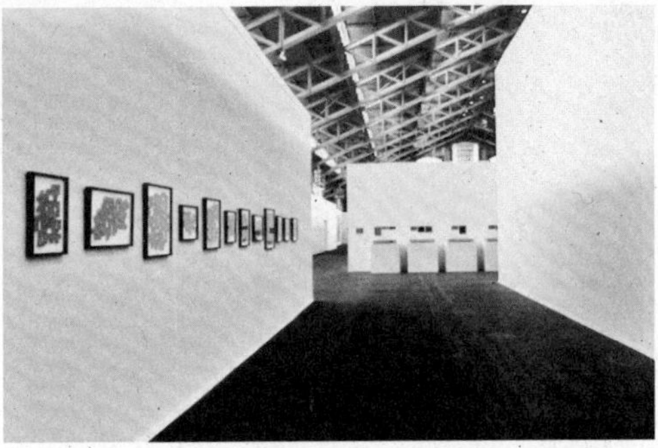

Exhibition view: John Monteith

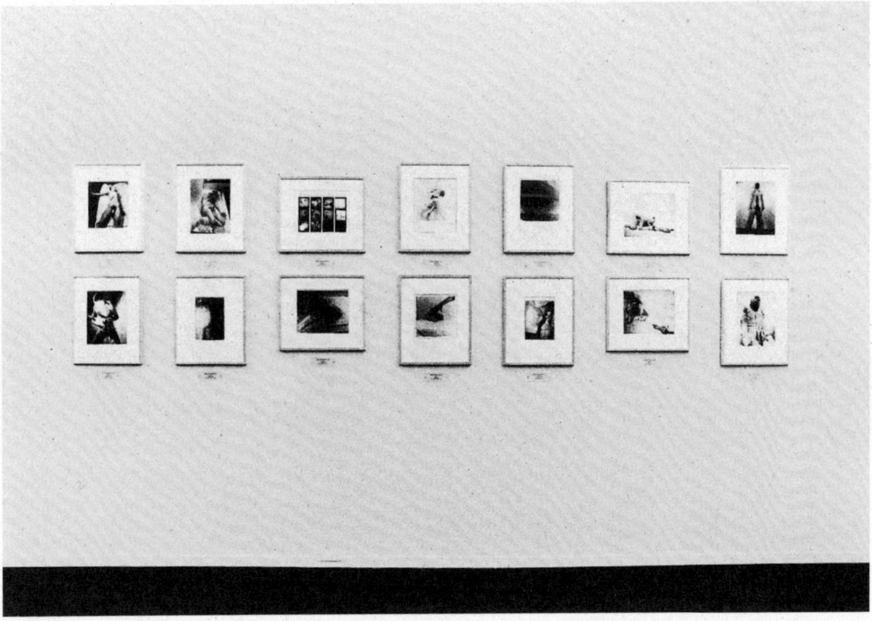

Rudolf Schwarzkogler, *16 photos of performances*, 1965–1966

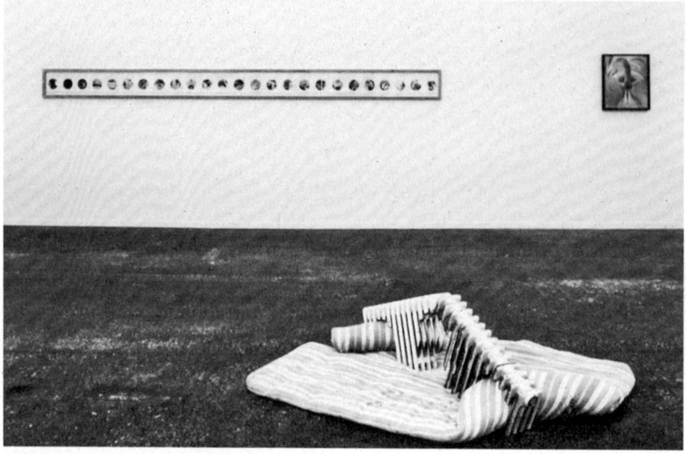

Exhibition view: Vincent Corpet, Nicolas Herubel

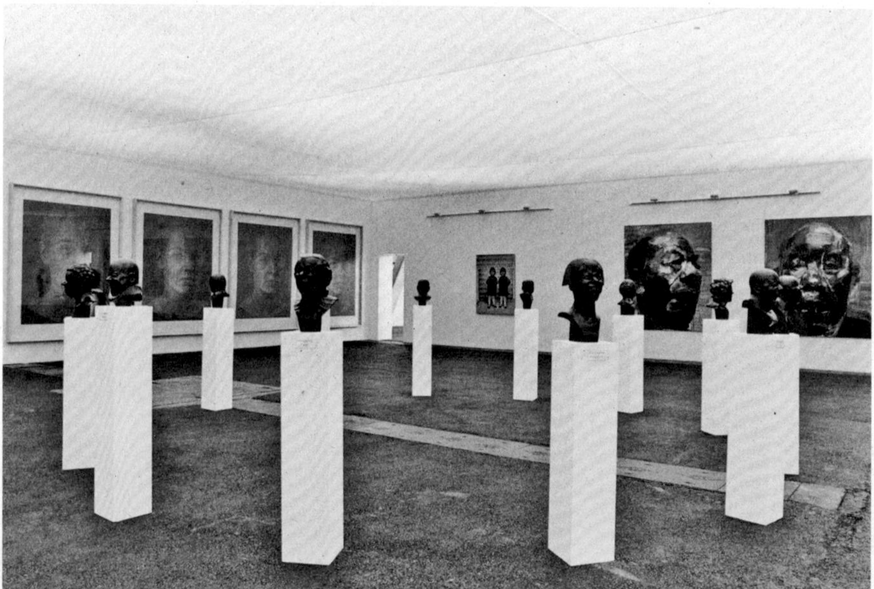

Exhibition view: Franz-Xaver Messerschmidt, Franz Gertsch, Jean-Olivier Hucleux, Yan Pei-Ming

Interview with Harald Szeemann

Jean-François Chougnet, Thierry Prat, and Thierry Raspail

The text below is a collage of excerpts from an interview with Harald Szeemann by Jean-François Chougnet, Thierry Prat, and Thierry Raspail. It was published in French as *A propos de la Biennale d'art contemporain de Lyon, 1997. Entretien avec Harald Szeemann*, La conscience du vilebrequin, Lyon 1997. It is reprinted here with the generous permission of the authors.

JEAN-FRANÇOIS CHOUGNET, THIERRY PRAT, THIERRY RASPAIL

Why is the 1997 Lyon Biennial of Contemporary Art titled *L'Autre* (*The Other*) rather than simply *Museum of Obsessions, Lyon 1997 version*?

HARALD SZEEMANN

When I was asked to work on the theme of *L'Autre*, chosen by the two Thierrys, I wondered what there was *without* "the other." Without the other, you're really stuck, at every level. It was so vast that it left me free. At the same time, I also wondered—which influenced me a little—what "the other" was for others? Artists are *always* "the others." I had no desire to write an essay on otherness, because a lot had already been done on that subject. Once the human body had been completely measured, I could show it in its entirety again. Moreover, there was a public who must not be disappointed in such a big show. Which meant, for example, you couldn't exclude a few feats of artistic prowess, things that can't be done in a museum. So I didn't arrive with a specific structure in mind. I drew up an initial list and collected a lot of proverbs that seemed related to one other. Then, when I thought about the exhibition, I pragmatically adopted these considerations.

JEAN-FRANÇOIS CHOUGNET, THIERRY PRAT, THIERRY RASPAIL

You say that to make an exhibition you have to identify with the project. That's how you work, at any rate. And yet in the name of the autonomy of artworks, you try never to "illustrate" an argument. Your project concerning *L'Autre* is unlike any other, and is most certainly not a philosophical demonstration. Though you relate to the theme ...

HARALD SZEEMANN

I try to incorporate artistic autonomy into the project without descending into illustration. I constantly ask myself if the work fits the project, relates to it. If a work stands up as such, I feel it becomes stronger as an expression of *L'Autre*. This kind of non-verbal, non-illustrative alchemy is what's guiding me until the biennial opens.

JEAN-FRANÇOIS CHOUGNET, THIERRY PRAT, THIERRY RASPAIL

But when you take a theme like *Austria im Rosennetz* (*Austria in a Net of Roses*), for example, there's something that already exists and forces you to think and move in a specific direction. With *L'Autre* it's so general ...

HARALD SZEEMANN

That's why the selection of works is not really historical. I'm trying to create a landscape, or a small town, in which each home or cabin is one aspect of "the other." It was different with *Austria im Rosennetz*. Historically, the Habsburg Empire was immense, and I had to introduce a kind of spirituality through the organization of space, the documents, and the works chosen to create an atmosphere during the visit. The Austrians felt it was the finest tribute that could be paid to their spirituality. In Bordeaux, the historical building was given from the start [*GAS*, capcMusée d'art contemporain, 1993]. Compartmentalizing that space would have been a mistake—there was a direct confrontation because the space was already structured by its nine vaults and immense columns. Which automatically created a series of virtual squares, whereas in Lyon everything has to be done from scratch. It's completely different. The architecture of the exhibition hall has influenced my selection a lot. The question is simple: what can you do in such a grandiose hall as that? Is there an artwork with the same monumentality? It's really a question of a promenade that affords a different way of seeing. For example the prophecy of Bruce Nauman's *Model for Trench and Four Buried Passages* has taken on a new form, as has Joseph Beuys's *Olivestone*.

JEAN-FRANÇOIS CHOUGNET, THIERRY PRAT, THIERRY RASPAIL

A normal art historian—or rather not normal, but French—would have tried to pin down a kind of initial "other" that might represent a breakthrough. Yve-Alain Bois, in his catalogue on *L'Informe*, spoke of Manet's *Olympia* as the trigger for a radical rupture. He argued that it was the first work that really made the public laugh. But what was important to Bois was that, with Manet, expectations crumble. You never get what you're expecting from one of his paintings, which is already an initial type of rupture. With Manet on the one hand, the Duchamp/Malevich/Schwitters trilogy on the other, and finally Fluxus and Happenings, we have a new opening, a new paradigm. Do these three historical moments correspond to three categories of "other?"

HARALD SZEEMANN

They're what I called initiating gestures. In 1964 I organized a show called *Malevich, Duchamp, Kandinsky*—without Schwitters. This trilogy seems much more correct to me, because the Schwitters of those days wasn't yet Schwitters. I also organized *Happening & Fluxus* in 1970. Back in 1964, everyone swore by—and exhibited—the Bauhaus, and only that. I claimed that the three initiating gestures prior to World War One had nothing to do with the Bauhaus, and that things had started differently. Recently when I saw a painting by Wang Xingwei, *Poor Old Richard*, in which a little Chinaman breaks *The Large Glass*—I have to honestly say that I was thoroughly delighted. Because *The Large Glass* and the whole commentary surrounding it were beginning to bore me.

When it comes to Malevich, it should be said that his new icon was a wonderful creation, because it was speculative, even though after the show in Amsterdam we can no longer really call him a good painter. But this century has only just begun to come under review. And I myself now feel that Antonin Artaud was ultimately the most fascinating figure.

My reading of history acquired an inner intensity with the organization of *When Attitudes Become Form* in 1969. But my reading isn't, strictly speaking, historical. For me, Goya is much more important than Manet, even though Manet is wonderful and his painting is extraordinary. Because Goya, at the same time, was inventing artistic journalism with his *Horrors of War*, and his vision was much more powerful and ultimately much more modern. Everyone can create his or her own "magnetic field"—with *When Attitudes Become Form* I was trying to visualize this process, make it visible.

Every year you read in the paper about cults that destroy themselves. And here [in Lyon] we have Elisàr von Kupffer, who created and illustrated his own philosophy, conceiving life as a purely spiritual state. If humanity wants to reach a higher level, it has to find an Immaculate Conception. This context is relevant to the 1997 biennial because autonomy no longer counts—the context has somehow linked everything to everything. But since you can't reconstruct your entire life, you just give a representation of it. Von Kupffer imagined heaven as a multiplication of oneself in a verdant landscape of which he was the center—always the same narcissism. That's why I would have liked to include him and to decorate the entrance to the biennial with the portrait of Jeff Koons looking like a pop star—once again turned to the exterior. Unfortunately, they won't lend us Koons's *Self-Portrait*, which I would have placed to left of the portrait of Elisàr von Kupffer at the entrance to his rotunda.

JEAN-FRANÇOIS CHOUGNET, THIERRY PRAT, THIERRY RASPAIL

What do you mean when you refer to the "autonomy" of art?

HARALD SZEEMANN

We live in a society that levels things. The decision to be an artist is still, in itself, respectable. What happens next, whether the artist becomes a saint or a whore, is his own business.

So what do you need when you get all worked up over something, which may someday really change things? Your work—your product, your creation—needs its own, almost absolute, law. Historically, once the major commissioning institutions began withering away—monarchy and church—every artist became a God who created his own world, as Wagner put it. In order to distinguish itself from external life, this world reveals its own autonomy. Intuitively, you sense that in a space like Halle Tony Garnier, attention can only be given to each work if it has a space that underscores its autonomy. And even if I don't do any interior architecture as I did in Bordeaux and Berlin [*Zeitlos* (*Timeless*), 1988], where I imposed great distances between the works to give each one room to breathe, I know that monumentality crushes autonomy. In this case, something else has to be set up, favoring isolation, the creation of neutral space. Despite all the polemics over new museums designed by celebrity architects, the determining format is that of a neutral envelope.

During certain periods, artists seek disorder in order to come up with alternatives. That's what's currently happening in England with the founding of all these autonomous venues, and it's what happened with the Nabis in the late 19th century. It started with a small group of friends. Then Bonnard became better than Vuillard and Sérusier, and the group broke up. There are times when artists don't want autonomy, especially when they form a group of friends, but later they seek it, because it's the only way to be distinctive.

JEAN-FRANÇOIS CHOUGNET, THIERRY PRAT, THIERRY RASPAIL

We're dealing simultaneously with the autonomy of art and a very close relationship to social issues. Doesn't the theme of *L'Autre* involve showing how values get reversed at one point or another? Isn't that the question?

HARALD SZEEMANN

No, I don't think so ... Maybe that's why the artist is always the "other." What was Otto Mühl trying to do in his artists' community? When the community was falling apart I would go there fairly often and I noticed that many of its members weren't artists. It became a very rich community supported by property companies, insurance companies, etc., which fed the two hundred mothers who were constantly hatching kids for future society. Almost no one accepted the initial system, so different classes henceforth existed. Yet everyone told me that Mühl had helped them to get their lives together.

There were two aspects. The bigger and richer the community became, the more it had to protect itself from the outside. First there was syphilis, then AIDS. And since there were now different classes, what had been a classless sexual revolution became a class issue once again. The lower classes no longer had the right to lay an upper-class woman. It had become an authoritarian society.

Almost all utopias end badly when put into effect (when they don't just remain in the mind or vague imagination). One individual will always impose his will on another. At that moment, it's no longer art or a utopian spirit, it becomes dictatorship.

JEAN-FRANÇOIS CHOUGNET, THIERRY PRAT, THIERRY RASPAIL

Utopia is good as long as it remains in the mind?

HARALD SZEEMANN

That's right. I feel it's the same thing in art and utopias. It's what Wagner also meant when he said that the artwork of the future would be a union of all the arts. He claimed our society had not managed to produce that, so a new society had to be conceived. In that respect he's said to be a forerunner of Hitler, but Hitler was first of all a bad artist, and if he'd been accepted by the Academy of Fine Arts in Vienna he wouldn't have done what he did.

But in the end it's the incarnation of a utopian idea. It's like the Soviet Union, when all these anarchists imagined Russia was finally liberated and everyone could live there—peasants as a positive life force, workers in the cities, intellectuals, and so on. Lenin let Kropotkin live because he was venerated, just like Mussolini let Malatesta live without harassing him. But even if those two got away, the power structure has always perverted everything—and still does.

Utopia is a little like art, because there are no statistics on the way it is "beheld." Although I might be able to say how many people visited an exhibition, I can't say what really struck them, even when visitors' books are on hand for comments.

JEAN-FRANÇOIS CHOUGNET, THIERRY PRAT, THIERRY RASPAIL

In the statement of intent that you wrote for the biennial, you say, "We want to counteract the nefarious consequences of the proclamation of the end of utopias with the positive utopias of artists." There seems to be a political dimension to this statement.

HARALD SZEEMANN

It relates to something I did when I organized the show called *Penchant for a Synthesis of the Arts* [1983]. The total artwork—"Gesamtkunstwerk"—doesn't exist. It may exist as an imagined concept in the head of an artist, especially when it includes the dream or desire for a new society that will be automatically reflected in this synthesis. Everyone is now predicting the end of utopias because communism is crumbling and capitalism is heading straight for a social divide. A certain sense of security and well-being no longer exists. At the same time, there's always this prophetic side to artists, even if they don't want to admit it, and the cynicism of a certain generation of artists is now present throughout society.

JEAN-FRANÇOIS CHOUGNET, THIERRY PRAT, THIERRY RASPAIL

Does that mean they were, or are, precursors?

HARALD SZEEMANN

No, they just sense and experience a certain state before society reaches it. Today, I feel, there are now very positive and optimistic artists, who may predict something about society. An exhibition is also designed to show artists who, through their current attitude, reject the general despair and promote optimism and a new "philosophy." I hope that in ten years' time people will say that the Lyon Biennial first showed these artists who are finally venerated precisely because they were always positive and optimistic, and we relied on their strength to hold out against despair.

JEAN-FRANÇOIS CHOUGNET, THIERRY PRAT, THIERRY RASPAIL

Is that the "regional roots" part?

HARALD SZEEMANN

Yes, but at the same time the work of Facteur [postman] Cheval had universal scope, he even drew inspiration from Universal Exhibitions when building his palace. I've been influenced by Etienne-Martin ever since his first big show in Bern [1963]. For example, by inventing the term *Individual Mythology*, he underscored my desire to shatter styles at *documenta*. Previously, there had always been a pair of unequal twins—Abstract Expressionism and geometric abstraction, or Minimalism and Pop art. For *documenta 5* [1972], it might have been Photo-Realism and Conceptual art. But I said to myself that we had to climb out of the polarization that marked the century—Surrealism versus Constructivism. We had to find something in which the artist's intensity of intention would dictate the nature of the medium to be used. So if Serra used lead, that was because lead liquefies easily and then solidifies just as easily. It marked another way of making sculpture. I've always found that Serra was a revolutionary sculptor, precisely because he didn't draw inspiration from art, but from engineering—how boats and bridges are made, structurally speaking. Bruce Nauman, meanwhile, once again raised sculpture to eye-level, which immediate produces a shock in the beholder even as it creates a feeling an enormous fragility. I selected Nauman's *Model for Trench and Four Buried Passages* for that very reason. In contrast, the decision to show Hanne Darboven's *Rutherford/Nils Bohr* was due to the fact that her work describes the birth of the atomic bomb. And it provided an opportunity to pay a negative tribute to President Chirac's nuclear test policy.

JEAN-FRANÇOIS CHOUGNET, THIERRY PRAT, THIERRY RASPAIL

In your earlier texts it seems you used the term "first-person narrative." How will such narratives be juxtaposed? What will the visitors get from these 86 tales?

HARALD SZEEMANN

You can never tell what immediate effect an exhibition has, nor how it is understood at first. I've always thought of a first-person narrative that is fueled by a multitude of artists' narratives that obviously need to be structured, situated in space, placed in a circuit. I've always said that *documenta 5* was an initiatory trail that went from numerous, "deceptive" advertising images to the single sound played by La Monte Young just below the ceiling of the Museum Fridericianum for 100 days. This sound was in fact something that completely filled you. Here [in Lyon] the space is very big, but you can also feel that tension. There are very spectacular things that grab your attention immediately, and more private works that have to be discovered slowly. I really like exhibitions as a means of expression because they offer everyone the possibility of entering and deciding how long to stay, the number of levels of meaning to explore, and so on.

JEAN-FRANÇOIS CHOUGNET, THIERRY PRAT, THIERRY RASPAIL

You say that an exhibition is usually a poem in space. You speak a good deal about confrontation and association. If the public associates Jason Rhoades with Facteur Cheval in some way, what would you say?

HARALD SZEEMANN

[...] It's great if a visitor sees Facteur Cheval at the start and then goes on to Jason Rhoades, with his different use of everyday objects, or Chris Burden, who is older and engages other problematics—he's really of the generation that's interested in weight as the source of new sculptural qualities.

An exhibition should be full of associations, reminders, formal echoes. It's a poem in space with plenty of room for free association. Maybe it's today's version of a Universal Exhibition, which allows me to combine the "considered obsessions" of *professional* artists with the "primal obsessions" of *brut* artists.

JEAN-FRANÇOIS CHOUGNET, THIERRY PRAT, THIERRY RASPAIL

What do you think of Beuys when he says, "Art can be made by everyone?"

HARALD SZEEMANN

That everybody's an artist? That's what we called the notion of expanded art, but Beuys corrected himself and asserted that he didn't mean every person armed with a brush or knife is an artist, but that everyone should be as creative as possible in his own field of activity. In that sense, it's great.

Duchamp already had the same idea—to isolate an object and put it in a museum as an artistic gesture. To transcend that, Beuys rightly said, "If Duchamp had been aware of the notion of everydayness that makes everyone creative—and that's our capital—he would have mentioned all the workers who made his urinal." With that proviso, Beuys allegedly gave a new dimension to art; but the act of returning art to the museum has been happening since Greek and Roman days. Social plasticity was a dilemma also faced by Beuys, who used found objects and readymades. To provide an "other" dimension, he was obliged to combine them. So it was more a question of assemblage. Duchamp made the initial gesture, which remained a utopia like Art and Life and so on.

JEAN-FRANÇOIS CHOUGNET, THIERRY PRAT, THIERRY RASPAIL

Visualizing what hasn't been visualized seems to be the stakes, and maybe the principle, behind all the shows you organize. Does that mean every artist or every work individually visualizes something fragmentary, and that to visualize what hasn't yet been visualized these fragments must be linked in some way or another? Are all your exhibitions based on a principle of associating works?

HARALD SZEEMANN

No, I think it's something different. I've always worked "visually," which is why artists like the retrospectives I organize—my influence isn't verbal. When I hang, when I engage in a dialogue with a painting, it leads to another way of selecting, hanging, giving room. The interplay of affinities operates in both directions—I can be demanding but then drop those demands if I fall under the sway of a work or building. One of the great advantages of the Kunsthaus in Zurich, where I work as a permanent independent collaborator, is the ability to recreate the building for every show.

I feel I've learned a lot from my own times, which are not felicitous ones, as you state in the press release. That's why these days I don't care about mixing literary stuff with other things, but at the same time I know distinctions have to be made through the organization of space. All those thematic exhibitions whose approach to art didn't, at first sight, concern me, have been very useful to me in producing all the subsequent shows.

JEAN-FRANÇOIS CHOUGNET, THIERRY PRAT, THIERRY RASPAIL

We won't dwell on the role of hanging, a subject that has been kicked around a lot. But in your comments you went imperceptibly from the "visualization of something that hasn't yet been visualized" to the question of space and architecture. That concerns the exhibition medium as such. Isn't that the living dimension of art, its physical specificity?

HARALD SZEEMANN

No, but the physical aspect of a work demands its own presence, since I consider every artwork an organism. Everyone needs to create an environment for themselves. Some need clarity, light—Mondrian always placed himself with his back to nature. It's the notion of breathing room that is ultimately important.

When it comes to visualizing non-visualized things, *Penchant for a Synthesis of the Arts* [1983] responded to that need. Indeed, architecture was crucial because instead of using a display case or a text on the wall to explain that Kandinsky was influenced by Steiner, the exhibition architecture revealed it. You saw some Steiner in Kandinsky and some

Kandinsky in Steiner without infringing the autonomy of the work of either of them. If I'd had the vast Tony Garnier Hall for *Penchant for a Synthesis of the Arts*, I would have put a hundred yards between the Bauhaus and Speer, but since I had the same distance between Wagner and Ludwig II of Bavaria and between Steiner and Kandinsky, I didn't want to show Speer at the same level. Decisions are always a mixture of intuition and reflection about the works. For *The Bachelor Machines* [1975], it was the opposition between primal obsession and considered obsession.

JEAN-FRANÇOIS CHOUGNET, THIERRY PRAT, THIERRY RASPAIL

Will you talk about that?

HARALD SZEEMANN

I can tell you if it makes you happy. Anarchy is still the greatest utopia, because it accepts every person as he is. Naturally, when you try to forge a society and everyone clings to a very strong ego, it's more difficult. With an exhibition it's a little as though I manage—temporarily, with all these different things—to create a kind of ideal society.

JEAN-FRANÇOIS CHOUGNET, THIERRY PRAT, THIERRY RASPAIL

Babel?

HARALD SZEEMANN

That's it. At the same time, I feel like Ludwig II of Bavaria, who was always building his castle, temporarily. But since I live in a democracy, after three months the castle is always pulled down.

JEAN-FRANÇOIS CHOUGNET, THIERRY PRAT, THIERRY RASPAIL

So we've gone through the exhibition, we've made associations, comparisons, we've detected the *The Bachelor Machines*, we've been over the ideology. But what do we do with all that?

HARALD SZEEMANN

First, it should be fun, right? Then, what everyone does with the fun is their own business.

JEAN-FRANÇOIS CHOUGNET, THIERRY PRAT, THIERRY RASPAIL

So the main feature an art show is a kind of hedonism?

HARALD SZEEMANN

That seems logical from my perspective. I want to create a temporary world that is rich enough for those who come to see it for two or three hours to have the impression of being steeped in another context that seeks to be a world of its own. And when visitors leave, afterward, what they do is their own thing.

JEAN-FRANÇOIS CHOUGNET, THIERRY PRAT, THIERRY RASPAIL

So we never reach the crisis of utopias we mentioned earlier, because with every exhibition you create a new utopia.

HARALD SZEEMANN

That's right. That's what keeps me alive.

JEAN-FRANÇOIS CHOUGNET, THIERRY PRAT, THIERRY RASPAIL

You've also claimed a "unilateral subjectivity." It's hard to see what "unilateral" means, what "unilateral" adds to subjective. Or maybe it's just more subjective.

HARALD SZEEMANN

I don't know. At that time maybe I was in total chaos and thought I had to come up with an adjective—*einseitig* [unilateral]. When I was running the Kunsthalle in Bern I was criticized for being unilateral, because I was turning off a public that had been built up over time. In fact, I was building up a new public, but the old critics always charged me with being unilateral. So since I'd always been called unilateral, I became almost proud of it, and linked it to subjectivity.

JEAN-FRANÇOIS CHOUGNET, THIERRY PRAT, THIERRY RASPAIL

In your poem/charter on curators, you say, "I'm not afraid of concepts." [1]

HARALD SZEEMANN

Yes, that's right.

JEAN-FRANÇOIS CHOUGNET, THIERRY PRAT, THIERRY RASPAIL

Why aren't you afraid of concepts?

HARALD SZEEMANN

I think everything's a process. If you have a concept but the next day you see something surprising, you toss out the concept. That's all.

JEAN-FRANÇOIS CHOUGNET, THIERRY PRAT, THIERRY RASPAIL

You don't respect them.

HARALD SZEEMANN

No, I don't respect them.

JEAN-FRANÇOIS CHOUGNET, THIERRY PRAT, THIERRY RASPAIL

So it's not a concept exhibition.

HARALD SZEEMANN

No, it is an exhibition of conditioned enjoyment.

JEAN-FRANÇOIS CHOUGNET, THIERRY PRAT, THIERRY RASPAIL

Maybe it's a do-it-yourself exhibition within certain constraints.

HARALD SZEEMANN

Yes, indeed. I must say that in organizing the *Epicenter Ljubljana* show in April I learned a lot. I could have presented or imported what I already knew, but I preferred to ask the Slovenians what they wanted. In that way it became a concept held together by the intensity of seven proposals, incorporating the wishes of others right from the start.

[1] Harald Szeemann, "Impulsion-Harmonie (prière)," *Ecrire les expositions*, La Lettre volée, Brussels 1996, p. 13–15.

Interview with Thierry Raspail [1]

16th Session

Lyon, April 17, 2007

16th SESSION

How long had you known Harald Szeemann when you invited him to be the curator for the Lyon Biennial 1997, and how did you meet him?

THIERRY RASPAIL

I've forgotten—maybe ten years ... to tell the truth, I don't remember meeting Harald Szeemann on any particular day. I was always meeting him at openings and exhibitions, and I was informally involved in conversations he had with two or three artists, but I had never visited him.

16th SESSION

Can you tell me about meeting him and the relationship that you subsequently developed?

THIERRY RASPAIL

I had known him for a long time but we had never been close. I was surprised to learn that he took an interest in what we were doing in Lyon. He had come quite often to the museum but never informed us prior to his visits.

16th SESSION

Among his many exhibitions, which one, or ones, did you appreciate the most? Was it the fact of seeing one of them that made you want to invite him?

THIERRY RASPAIL

It wasn't so much his exhibitions ... I was a student in art history. I did my thesis in 1980, about museums and, in particular, the idea that the museum might not be the locus of art history.

I had been going to museums and exhibitions in Germany and Switzerland for ten years, I knew about pretty much everything. It was from the catalogue—Michel Durand-Dessert still had a copy—that I got to know *When Attitudes Become Form*. In the years 1975–1980 I was quite close to Giovanni Anselmo, Mario Merz, Lawrence Weiner, Sol LeWitt ... Harald Szeemann came up quite often in our conversations.

It was of course the strangeness of his exhibitions that struck me. The artists he selected in the 1970s became historic promptly 20 years later; 40% of them were already the most famous. I loved his big, wild but unexpected exhibitions, which were very much linked to his personality.

16th SESSION

Let's talk about the Lyon Biennial. Could you tell us about the process for selecting the curator?

THIERRY RASPAIL

The process was decided on in agreement with the municipality of Lyon and the French Ministry of Culture. When I came to Lyon in 1984, two projects were in gestation: one of them was a contemporary art museum that would be unlike other museums, the other was to regularly put on an exhibition of national or international stature, whether a historical or a contemporary one.

After three or four years of activity, when I tried to show work by artists who were not very well known in France, in 1988 I organized an important exhibition about the history of the monochrome, *La couleur seule, l'expérience du monochrome*. It began with Monet and Malevich and ended in the contemporary period, with John Armleder and Steven Parrino, for example ... The show was a popular success, with 53,000 visitors. The result of the test was positive, so we could now regularly undertake presenting an exhibition with international ambitions. At the beginning, the idea was to do an annual exhibition, but the mayor of Lyon preferred an exhibition every two years for budgetary reasons. The budget could be doubled with no need for extra subsidies.

This was an exhibition that took place every two years, and not a biennial in the current sense of the term. It so happened that the last Paris Biennial had been held in 1985, and managed to mix bad box office with budgetary overshoot. The Ministry dropped the Parisian event. The project of a biennial exhibition in Lyon went down particularly well because it met with a political desire to decentralize national cultural events out into the provinces. The Ministry agreed to stump up half the budget from the first manifestation.

Then the question of the curator arose. The municipality of Lyon asked that the director of the Museum be the artistic director of the biennial. The state suggested that the artistic director choose a curator (so as not to run out of ideas) and be responsible for the artistic budget.

When the first Biennial was put on, in 1991, there hadn't been an exhibition of French art for 20 years (the last one, in Paris in 1969, had ended badly!). We started by using the concept of an anti-biennial: instead of an international selection, we preferred to concentrate on art produced in France. People looked askance: they said that it was a nationalist position. That was unfair (today, a triennial has been created in Paris to support French art ...). France has been extremely receptive to imported artworks in its collections since the beginning of the 1980s, and in my mind, it was necessary to evaluate the current situation of French artistic production. So we did an "abnormal" biennial.

This effort was criticized, but was a big public success. For the second Lyon Biennial in 1993 we again did an "anti-biennial" by proposing a survey of the century: "avant-gardes," "postmodernism," "trans," and "neo"—where exactly did we stand in relation to these movements? My idea was to revisit the century through the influence of Dada and Fluxus, which I believed had been rather overlooked. So it wasn't a real biennial, more a history exhibition.

In 1995 Lyon was ready to lavishly celebrate the centenary of cinema (Lyon, city of the Brothers Lumière). We wanted to follow up the connections between the visual arts, video, and the history of cinema and introduce interactivity, which was then nascent in France. We were able to ask for an extra budget within the framework of that celebration. The Biennial set up the first broadband connection in an artistic projection, carried out with the MIT in Boston. But I remember that the public had trouble understanding that they were in real-time contact with the people they could see on the other side.

Which brings us to Harald Szeemann ... After these three biennials we needed to move on. The Lyon Biennial also needed to be important for professionals, and become an international event. I saw that Szeemann hadn't been contacted either by documenta or by the Venice Biennial, so I called him and asked him if he was interested in the Lyon Biennial for 1997. He accepted my invitation and suggested we meet at his office in Maggia.

16th SESSION

As for the theme, *L'Autre*, we gather from interviews given by Harald Szeemann on the subject of the Lyon Biennial that it had already been chosen.

THIERRY RASPAIL

Yes, that's true. In fact, I told him that and he replied, "No, I never work on a theme." This question of a theme lasts for long time in art history: to limit the artwork to a thematic is obviously a simplification of its polysemy. But I believed that that philosophical issue of the "Other" problematized our epoch quite well. What I said to him was very simple: "Today, in philosophy, in anthropology, with the advent of globalization, people are reflecting on the issue of the Other, of the outside ... You are an 'other' for me." He said, "Yes, I can be interested in it as a Germanist: in German we use three genders: masculine, feminine, and neutral; I am interested in dealing with the 'das,' the neutral, the other." After a quarter of an hour, he accepted. The genesis of this project is quite simple.

16th SESSION

Did this idea come to you because of his exhibitions and projects, notably in connection with the *Museum of Obsessions*?

THIERRY RASPAIL

No. It seemed to me that there is an exteriority to art. As you know, art has dealt with everything: the body, the visible, the invisible, the unspeakable—it has conquered a huge territory, but nevertheless it remains art. In philosophy and more generally in society, we have witnessed a return of the question of *L'Autre*. It's an old question in France, an important one after the Shoah, Adorno, the imprescriptible. The beginning of globalization coincided with a question that is internal to the question of art: "Are there other histories than the art history we built up?" And regarding Harald, the question was: What constitutes art today?

We didn't develop a theory together; we simply talked quite extensively about questions related to autonomy, non-Western culture, and how we could deal with all this. But we didn't try to define an extremely complicated concept. I think what interested him was the fact that he could affirm the presence of a minor biennial like Lyon in the face of the monsters that were *documenta* and the Venice Biennial. He was always doing something different so he perfectly played his role. *L'Autre*—I think he found that funny. It was a very broad question, he could handle it as he saw fit. The availability of the Halle Tony Garnier, a 20,000-square-meter space, 28 meters high without any pillars, a strange space that he took as an Other, enthused him. He totally played the game.

You would of course need to interpret the works he exhibited to know what problematics of *L'Autre* he was working on. Obviously, I didn't need to make any suggestions to Harald Szeemann. We simply agreed on the point that I could pass on to him information about French artists so he would be familiar with them. Don't go thinking that I was taking a nationalist position again! Afterward, my role was that of a censor: "No, that's too expensive! No, we can't produce that!" That was a difficult position to occupy and particularly strange for me in front of Szeemann. But everything went tremendously well, and he gave the Lyon Biennial a tremendous boost.

[1] Thierry Raspail is co-director of the Lyon Biennial, and director of the Musée d'Art Contemporain in Lyon.

Interview with Harald Szeemann

Ninety

This text below is a collage of excerpts from an interview with Harald Szeemann made by the magazine *Ninety*, Paris, n° 25, October–November–December 1997, p. 1–3. All our efforts to identify the author of the interview met with no success.

NINETY

In their introduction to the guidebook to the Lyon Biennial, artistic directors Thierry Raspail and Thierry Prat, who this year have entrusted the curatorship of the event to you, say that they have chosen to exhibit "an art which, given the times we live in, and to state the point explicitly, is neither one of identity, nor naturalist, nor nationalist [...] an art that gets away from art to meet the world." By coming to you they were counting on your great freedom with regard to consensus and the recognized autonomy of your choices. Can you remind us of what makes your career such an original one?

HARALD SZEEMANN

For 40 years now I have been organizing and mounting exhibitions, each time on a different basis—Kunsthalle Bern, or Cologne, *documenta 5*, Venice Biennial, Kunsthaus Zürich, railway stations, stables, warehouses, covered markets ... group exhibitions, retrospectives, themed exhibitions, single artists etc, etc ... Each time, once I have analyzed the place, I do it uncompromisingly. I hate style, I start out from the intensity of the work. When the two Thierrys put my name forward for the Lyon Biennial, they also wanted me to save that institution, they wanted it to carry on and to survive. In short, I must say that it was not the people who tempted me into launching into this: it was the covered market. This biennial is a love story between that grandiose building and myself.

NINETY

The theme of the 1997 biennial is *L'Autre*. Why choose this rather hackneyed title, so just inviting the critics to have a field day?

HARALD SZEEMANN

It is basically pretty stupid to give curators a theme. It is a provincial thing, which is afraid of anything big. Fortunately this idea of *L'Autre*—chosen by the two Thierrys—is so "rubbery" that I felt free enough to do just about what I wanted with it. Sometimes for an exhibition they set a theme for you to illustrate, but this one needed fleshing out. Of course there were different levels on which to tackle it. However I decided to stay pragmatic after studying the content of earlier biennials. For me the "other" was the big marketplace, and the desire to hold a different kind of exhibition there as compared with the past and, why not, as compared with the major events of 1997: *documenta*, Venice, Münster. I interpreted the Lyon Biennial as a factual circuit with the "other" artists and their works. The exhibition would be "other" for Lyon and for the international scene. And I was the "other" for Lyon.

NINETY

The works are presented according to groupings with different readings. Thematic associations (Bacon, Hucleux, Ming, Franz Gertsch ...) or national identities (An Hong, Pu Lie), conventional solo exhibitions and installations and a video show area (Hanne Darboven, Peter Hutchinson, Gary Hill, Jason Rhoades). There are also powerful works that appear as exemplars of one-off approaches (Beuys, Bourgeois, Serra, Nauman). Such variety is rather disconcerting for the visitor. Is it your intention to provoke astonishment and questioning as much about history as about modernity, on the media (from painting to video), on contemporary creative art, and the role of art, on the status and identity of the artist today?

HARALD SZEEMANN

Here you have eye, heart, soul, stomach, body, etc. You just need to mention them and you hope for different readings from the other. I am very proud to have made a success of a museum room on the portrait that is just so unique—and hence other—that nothing like it has ever been seen in a museum; it has very powerful associations, because the works are very powerful and very surprising in the way they are positioned within the whole. The starting point was *Beauty and the Beast*—Bacon and Gertsch of course.

Another example: there have been quite a few exhibitions of Chinese artists lately. But here again, I wanted an "other" look to this one that broke with the received aesthetics of lyrical abstraction in vogue in the countries of Asia. This is the business of the great hurry of the history of the cultural revolution into the new state capitalism and the invention of new iconographical forms (men scratching) plus the ambiguity of the Chinese smile to the iconoclasm of our icons (*The Large Glass*, broken in the end) but also the taboos (Taiwan) which fascinated me. It really is an "other" history, which gives rise to an "other" art. Actually I am going to China soon, it is fascinating what is going on over there in an atmosphere of freedom within the mind and what in reality is still non-freedom. And I especially like the iconographic aesthetic/anti-aesthetic mix aspect. There are no solo exhibitions here. It is always a matter of works that are singular works, which forcefully conjure up a world or a way of thinking visually.

As for Beuys, Bourgeois, Serra, and Nauman, here with "the revolutionaries of May 1968" you have the exemplary presentation of art forms—the energy of unstable equilibrium, the self-destruction of matter in silence, the break with academicism ...

Why should this variety disconcert visitors? They go from one encounter to another, which is the very least they can expect from an exhibition! Or is it that life has become so ideologically, so sensually dull that we cannot bear the ups and downs any more, the variety, "the other"? I am not trying to be provocative, I just want everyone to share my surprise. And then there is one thing that runs through all these choices, and that is the intensity of each work. To find this intensity, the artist himself chooses his medium. If you take the intensity as your starting point, there you have the key to this biennial.

NINETY

How do you view the creative art of today and of the 21st century, in Europe and in the world, especially in countries like China?

HARALD SZEEMANN

I am optimistic. There will be a great blossoming. It was no accident if I placed *The Rat King* by Katharina Fritsch exactly in the middle of the big market like a metaphor for the new strategies for survival together. For art, as I said, I am very optimistic, and if the artists stay that way too, I hope that one day society will follow them as it always has done. I know there are all kinds of academism just now in art, but I hope that in this biennial I have given shape to a factual circuit through the live wires of today and from today not only backward in time but also looking a little into the future as well. In fact, if behind the appearances of what we see in a work there wasn't another dimension to be discovered and felt, I would never exhibit that piece of work.

Interview with Artists: Chris Burden and Franz Gertsch Julija Cistiakova and Yuka Tokuyama

These following interviews were conducted via e-mail and postal correspondence during the month of June 2007.

Interview with Chris Burden:

JULIJA CISTIAKOVA AND YUKA TOKUYAMA

How were you contacted the first time by Harald Szeemann, and invited to participate in the Lyon Biennial?

CHRIS BURDEN

Harald Szeemann saw an exhibition of my works at the MAK [the Museum of Fine Arts] in Vienna (February–August 1996). The exhibit included my sculpture, *The Flying*

Steamroller (1996). In December 1996, Mr Szeemann telephoned me and left a message asking if I would be willing to exhibit *The Flying Steamroller* in the Lyon Biennial in 1997. His phone message was followed by a hand-written fax that reiterated his invitation.

JULIJA CISTIAKOVA AND YUKA TOKUYAMA

Could you tell us about the process of your participation in the biennial? What was the process of selection and installation of your work?

CHRIS BURDEN

I agreed to lend *The Flying Steamroller* to the Lyon Biennial, and in early February 1997 Mr Szeemann came to my studio in Topanga, California, to discuss the details of the exhibition. He showed me the layout of the exhibition space and showed me where he would like to have *The Flying Steamroller* placed. Mr Szeemann and his team arranged the shipment and the installation of the sculpture. I sent my assistant to Lyon to oversee the installation. She was graciously welcomed by Mr Szeemann and his "family."

JULIJA CISTIAKOVA AND YUKA TOKUYAMA

We would like to know the itinerary of the artwork according to the functioning of big art manifestations and the circulation of art information.

CHRIS BURDEN

After the Lyon Biennial, Mr Szeemann had hoped to exhibit *The Flying Steamroller* in the Venice Biennial, but a covered, protected space could not be obtained. After Lyon, *The Flying Steamroller* was exhibited at the Frieze Art Fair in London, in October 2006.

JULIJA CISTIAKOVA AND YUKA TOKUYAMA

Harald Szeemann had an idea of a "machine célibataire"—a belief in eternal energy flow as a way to avoid death, as the erotic of life, the bachelor as a rebel-model, as anti-procreation. You presented a gigantic machine *The Flying Steamroller* at Lyon. Did you see references to the "bachelor machine" in your work?

CHRIS BURDEN

I assume Mr Szeemann was intrigued and finally chose *The Flying Steamroller* for the Lyon Biennial because it referred to a "bachelor machine."

<u>Interview with Franz Gertsch:</u>

JULIJA CISTIAKOVA AND YUKA TOKUYAMA

When and how did you meet Harald Szeemann?

FRANZ GERTSCH

Harry and I both lived in Bern. When we met in the bars we just nodded to each other. Later he was the director of the Kunsthalle, and we got closer. He knew what I was doing but he didn't find my work interesting enough to exhibit. It was only when I started my hyper-realistic paintings in the early 1970s, and he visited me at my gigantic studio in the attic of an old brewery close to the Aare river and he was preparing *documenta 5*, which had as its subject "Questioning Reality," that it became quite self-evident that he wanted to exhibit me, i.e. with the monumental painting *Medici*.

JULIJA CISTIAKOVA AND YUKA TOKUYAMA

You were invited to the Lyon Biennial in 1997. Can you tell us about the selection and installation of your work there?

FRANZ GERTSCH

When Harald Szeemann saw my woodcuts for the first time in 1989 at the Musée Rath and the Cabinet des Estampes in Geneva, he found them "sensational" and he promised to do something with them as soon as they fitted into his concept. This happened only in 1997 for the Lyon Biennial. There he showed nine pieces of the rainbow series of *Natascha*, which was a big commitment in so far as eight of the nine pieces were in different museums and private collections. Thanks to his and my tenacity, we succeeded in showing the complete series.

JULIJA CISTIAKOVA AND YUKA TOKUYAMA

We are interested in the itinerary of the works before and after the Lyon Biennial.

FRANZ GERTSCH

They were exhibited for the first time in 1991 at the Lenbach Haus in Munich in one room, for the second time at the Lyon Biennial, where they were shown in a row for the first time.

JULIJA CISTIAKOVA AND YUKA TOKUYAMA

Can you tell us about the difference in the collaboration between Szeemann and the artists in *documenta 5* in 1972, and the Lyon Biennial in 1997?

FRANZ GERTSCH

I think at least two of us stayed young in our spirit forever. He, with his relationship to artists worldwide, with insatiable curiosity for the new and the timeless old that has to be newly discovered; I, on the other hand, was always a *Einzelgänger* (a solitary outsider) and obsessively concentrated on my work. *documenta 5* was the first time at that I had other contact with participating artists, which was great enrichment for me. When I helped with the installation of the exhibition for two weeks, my relationship with Harald became deeper. It was different at the Lyon Biennial, where I visited with my wife only for the opening and we were together with other participating artists for the dinner.

JULIJA CISTIAKOVA AND YUKA TOKUYAMA

For *documenta 5* Harald Szeemann proposed the theme "Questioning Reality—Image Worlds Today." Your work also considers the questions of "the reality of image" in the frame of political propaganda as well as the "reality of the imaged" as in Photo-Realism. And at the Lyon Biennial there was an appearance of new medias that raised other questions on the reality/virtuality of image. Did you have any discussions with Szeemann on these questions?

FRANZ GERTSCH

It might seem strange, but I can't remember having discussed with him deep art-philosophical questions. However, our conversations when we ate and drunk together were stimulating, inspiring, and encouraging. Finally, I won't forget to add that my encounter with Harald was one of the biggest strokes of luck in my artistic career.

Interview with Josy Kraft [1]

Yuka Tokuyama

Basel, March 30, 2007

YUKA TOKUYAMA

Can you tell me about *L'Autre—4th Lyon Biennial* in 1997? Do you think it was a good exhibition?

JOSY KRAFT

Yes, absolutely. I think it was a good collection as a selection of artists. But the system they work with is a bit strange. Thierry Raspail and Thierry Prat are the two directors, the "directeurs artistiques." What does that mean? Last year there were people from the Palais de Tokyo (Paris), who were chosen by the two "artistic directors;" before that was the team from the Consortium (Dijon). This year there is Hans Ulrich Obrist and many others ... How can you manage with so many different curators? You can never succeed in your concept of the exhibition as a whole, it's impossible!

YUKA TOKUYAMA

There were many French artists participating in the biennial. Was that the choice of Szeemann or Prat-Raspail?

JOSY KRAFT

Harald selected all the artists. It was clear for him that he should also show the French artists. The two Thierrys proposed some artists to him, and maybe they were French, but Harald made the final selection.

YUKA TOKUYAMA

The relation between artworks and the space was particularly visible in the overall view at the 4th Lyon Biennial. There were a lot of partitions for each piece. How did it function with the whole space of the Halle Tony Garnier?

JOSY KRAFT

It was like a city. Once you entered the Halle, you were in a Manhattan. You walked through a city in the Halle, you discovered the artworks ... There was a space between each cabinet, like town squares with sculptures, so it was like a city in the big space.

YUKA TOKUYAMA

When for the first time you saw the Halle Garnier, were there any already existing structures or not?

JOSY KRAFT

No, it was empty. It was amazing to see this great space. We constructed everything. Christoph [Zürcher] drew a rough plan following Harald's idea and then the architect from the biennial, Dominique Hurtebize, made a final plan. There were discussions between Harald and the two Thierrys. Harald would say "I need this wall five meters high," but they would reply "no, because it's too expensive ... we do not have it in the budget." The problem with the Lyon Biennial was that they had a tremendous amount of money for the promotion. Of course PR is needed, but this kind of things made Harald mad, "Why do they spend so much money on such ridiculous things?"

YUKA TOKUYAMA

You were working for several shipping companies and now have your own company. When you worked with Szeemann for the shows in the institutions, did you have to be competitive?

JOSY KRAFT

No. With Harald I had no competition to work; he negotiated with the institutions. But of course, sometimes I also worked with other companies. For example, for a big international show like the biennial I had a general contract to organize all transportation of artworks but I didn't need to take care of shipping, for example from Spain, because there was our colleague, a Spanish shipping company, who could do that. I checked their bills and then the biennial office paid them.

YUKA TOKUYAMA

Compared to Lyon Biennale, in which he showed artists of different origins, at the exhibition *Epicenter Ljubljana* of the same year, most participating artists were from the West. Was there any specific reason for this?

JOSY KRAFT

If you look at art history in Europe between the 1960s and 1980s, there were lots of exhibitions with macho paintings. So Harald made sculpture exhibitions such as *Traces, Sculptures, and Monuments of their Precise Journey* (1985) at the Kunsthaus Zürich or *Zeitlos* (*Timeless*), in Berlin in 1988. In Ljubljana people saw one of these shows and were fascinated by the way Harald treated the classical, modern, and contemporary sculpture. They asked him to show sculpture and installations that they had seen in the West. Harald showed only the contemporary artists. It was also a question of space.

YUKA TOKUYAMA

In Lyon Szeemann showed many Chinese artists, and later for *Blood & Honey—The Future is in the Balkans* in 2003 in Austria, he showed Balkan artists. How did he see the non-Western artists?

JOSY KRAFT

Neither Chinese nor Balkan artists are making copies of Western art. Harald was always looking for fresh and new things. That's why he was fascinated by the Balkans and by China.

YUKA TOKUYAMA

Szeemann first visited China in 1997, after the Kwangju Biennial in Korea. That means he had not been to China to select the artworks.

JOSY KRAFT

Interestingly, since Harald's death, people are saying that Chinese art appeared on the international scene at the Venice Biennial in 1999, but this is wrong. It was in 1997 because of Uli Sigg, the Swiss Ambassador to China, who showed him photographs of some works from his collection. In 1997, after Lyon and Kwangju, Harald went to China at his invitation. Uli Sigg organized a meeting for Szeemann with Chinese artists. I think none of them came from their country to Lyon. It was too difficult to invite them.

YUKA TOKUYAMA

Could you tell us about this Chinese art collector Uli Sigg?

JOSY KRAFT

He has a huge collection of Chinese art. He doesn't really consider it an art collection. He conceives it as an archive of Chinese art from 1975 to the present. Approximately 200 different artists are in his collection. He is a businessman, but has always been interested in art. He always realized that something was different in China: the 25 meter-high porcelain bones, or the column made of human fat. No of Western artist can do such work (money and manpower are missing here). Uli Sigg was buying, and buying, and buying ... Then he made such tremendous collection, which was partly presented at the Kunstmuseum in Bern in 2005.

YUKA TOKUYAMA

How did Szeemann proceed with the selection of artists and artworks?

JOSY KRAFT

He had a perfect eye, like a musician has a perfect ear. He saw a work and chose a work, not an artist. Then he bought the catalogue to keep it as a memory. He never showed the artist but the artwork. First, he saw the work, and then he went to see the artist. He always had time for the artists. He was working with the artist, but for the artwork. For example, he himself partly paid the cost of the shipping of the *Rattenkönig* (*The Rat King*, 1992–1993) by Katharina Fritsch, but he never showed her other works. For him, Katharina's the best work was *The Rat King* and he needed it for his exhibition. There was no budget for transporting *The Rat King* from New York to Europe. The office of the Lyon Biennial didn't have the budget and we were looking for a sponsor but could not find one ... Then we had to decide whether we show it or not. But Harald absolutely wanted to show this work because it was an essential thing for the exhibition. He never made compromise. It was April 30th. We had to decide to ship it from The Dia Foundation in New York or not. We took the risk: Harald paid for it from his own pocket and so did I. But we still didn't have money to ship it back to New York, so it was kept in my storage in Switzerland. Then Szeemann showed it again at the Venice Biennial in 1999. For that, Venice paid a part of the shipment we paid in 1997. In 2001 in Venice, there was a young female artist who was installing her video piece. The work was situated at the entrance, where was too much light. She wanted to have a plasma monitor. But neither the biennial office nor the gallerist had the money to pay 3,000 euros for it. So Harald gave his own money to the young artist. He knew the right place to spend money, and this kind of behavior was very typical of him. For Harald, art had to be perfect. Here is a good example: we were hanging Cy Twombly's huge piece while Harald was working in another place in the space. When Harald came back and saw it, he said, "Can we hang it four centimeters up?" We had to remove the huge canvas, remake a support and hang it again, which was not an easy job. But we knew that it was what he wanted, so we did it. Then he said smiling, "Don't you think it's better?" Another example was really a hard job for us. For *Zeitlos* (*Timeless*) at the Hamburger Bahnhof in Berlin, we installed Richard Long's piece of six tons of stones. When we finished it, he came to see the piece. He looked around the space and said, "This piece should be one and a half meters back." I saw his eyes not smiling but serious. So we reinstalled six tons of material, moving it to make a circle with a sharp edge with three piles of stones!

YUKA TOKUYAMA

But was it apparently better after changing these installations? Were you convinced by the result? Wasn't it hard for you to answer all his demands?

JOSY KRAFT

No, it wasn't hard. We saw that it was better and we were satisfied with his installation, with all the jobs we did. The most important thing for him was an overview, harmony and balance, which are created by distances between pieces and light. You know, people didn't know what he liked but he knew what he didn't like. There is a phrase in H.J. Müller's book, *Exhibition Maker*, which I like and find very apt, "He never saw himself as artist. But he was artist of exhibitions."

[1] Josy Kraft was a member of Harald Szeemann's team from 1972 to 2005.

[Page 191] Invitation letter from Harald Szeemann to Richard Serra

[Page 192] Letter from Richard Serra to Harald Szeemann

FAX-MESSAGE

HARALD SZEEMANN
Tel. 091/753
+ 091/795
Fax 091/796
CH-6652 TEGNA

Agentur für geistige Gastarbeit

...o Richard Serra	DATE 19-11-96
	N° of PAGES 1

...OM: HARALD SZEEMANN CH-6652 TEGNA

...AX: 091-796 (HOME)/091-7531219 (OFFICE)
01-2512464 (KUNSTHAUS ZÜRICH)

...EL: 091-796 (HOME)/091-753 23 37 (OFFICE)
01-2516765 (KUNSTHAUS ZÜRICH)

Dear Richard,

I'm again preparing a show, actually the Lyon Biennale. The given theme is "The Other" and I would like to ask you if your „Hours of the Day" wouldn't be a great sculpture to show in this context. There is enough space to remake the Zurich Kunsthaus dimension (70 × 19 m). The dates: July 4 – Sept 15, 97. What do you think?
Best wishes to you and Clara

Harald

MUSEUM DER OBSESSIONEN
MUSEO DELLE OSSESSIONI
MUSÉE DES OBSESSIONS
MUSEUM OF OBSESSIONS

Dear Harry,

Nice seeing
you in Lyon
In thinking the
space over I've
come to the conclusion
that the work, OWO
would be best
placed diagonally on
center after the
towers at entrance

Richard

Conclusion

Julija Cistiakova and Yuka Tokuyama

Eighty-six artists from different generations and backgrounds, all extremely varied from an artistic standpoint, were included in the 4th Lyon Biennial of Contemporary Art in 1997. The success of this show earned the biennial an indisputable national and international reputation. And it was thanks to Harald Szeemann's contribution that this event henceforth became part of the international art-scene calendar. Thierry Raspail would even declare that, "The biennial was saved by Harald Szeemann." [1] Right from the start, Szeemann was perfectly aware of the stakes behind the invitation to curate it, and he also knew that the offer was motivated by his personality, fame, experience, and relationships with artists and networks (institutions, collectors, sponsors). But one other factor was crucial. *documenta 5* was a breakthrough show through its transformation of the exhibition medium into a spectacle, palpably pushing it toward the culture industry, and ultimately granting considerable scope to the role of curator as sole decision maker. [2] Twenty-five years later, in Lyon, France, Szeemann realized that this biennial had to make the headlines. Although he was given a very limited budget, he had to place the Lyon Biennial on the map of contemporary art, among the ever-growing number of international exhibitions and biennials. Furthermore, the show had to appeal not just to the art scene and a limited circle of connoisseurs, but to the general public.

Szeemann was used to showing certain works repeatedly in different places and exhibitions, and this enabled him to spread transport and installation expenses. When he couldn't manage that arrangement, he wouldn't hesitate to invest his own money. This he did in order to include Katharina Fritsch's monumental work, *The Rat King* in Lyon. So when he was named head curator of the Venice Biennial in 1999, he decided to show the work again, and since the transport was covered by the biennial, he was able to recover some of his outlay. [3] Harald Szeemann was capable of making practical decisions that in no way compromised his artistic decisions. In order to show Louise Bourgeois' *Red Room* (*The Parents*), he sought a private sponsor with whom he shared the installation costs. The work was presented first in Ljubljana as part of his 1997 show *Epicenter Ljubljana*, and then went on to Lyon. Szeemann himself described this as "the fragile balance of curatorship [...] I have to make a big exhibition in Western Europe and get a lot of money and then I come to help you with little money ... So we have equality!" [4] Most of the Chinese works of art shown in Lyon, except for those by artists living in France, arrived thanks to help from Uli Sigg, who was then Switzerland's ambassador to China and a great collector of Chinese art.

Such "recycling" was also favored by the ubiquity of the "Szeemann taste." For example, Wolfgang Laib and Pipilotti Rist were both included in the three large exhibitions he organized in 1997 in Ljubljana, Lyon, and Kwangju. He was also highly open to suggestions from other people, even if the final choice of artists was ultimately his own. In Lyon, the organizers submitted their own ideas to him, admitting concern about the space allocated to French artists—who in the end largely dominated the show. The weight of outside pressure could thus make itself felt. [5] However, Szeemann once again managed to add an entirely personal touch to the show, notably by deciding to include Henry Ughetto, "the 'other' in the region."

L'Autre—4th Lyon Biennial, was conceived from an idea that Szeemann developed for *documenta 5*, one that accompanied him throughout his life: *Individual Mythologies*, described as "everyone's attempt to impose their own order on the grand disorder."[6] The theme of *L'Autre* yielded an anthology of ideas that were not part of a precise concept,[7] as illustrated by one of the methods Szeemann used to develop this show, namely compiling a set of proverbs, which included the tautological expression, "everything is always other."[8] Instead of a specific concept, the exhibition provided a heterogeneous support for the presentation of works and ideas that were occasionally contradictory or conflicting. The interior of the Halle Tony Garnier, fragmented by white partition walls, was conceived as a town or landscape, built in such as way as to allow for the creation of these *Individual Mythologies*.[9] If we wanted to describe Szeemann's curatorial method after 1997, we would certainly refer to "heterogeneous assemblage" within a totally open attitude that tended toward the universal. *L'Autre* was in a certain way a concrete example of his *Museum of Obsessions*, "which can not be done in a museum."[10] Szeemann's interpretation of the theme of *L'Autre* leaned toward universality. The "trans-energetic" idea he developed for *Epicenter Ljubljana* also surfaced in Lyon.[11] For Szeemann, in fact, use of a theme allowed him to pull together works and ideas that would open a show to all possible interpretations. Following the Lyon exhibition, the Venice Biennials of 1999 and 2001 did not refer to a specific concept,[12] but rather to openness and optimism.[13] The titles of these shows perfectly illustrate the curator's determination to free himself from the strict framework of themes, in order to approach the universal: *dApertutto* (*Aperto Over All*) and *Plateau of Humankind*.

[1] Cf. 16th Session, "Interview with Thierry Raspail," p. 183.

[2] "His main contribution to the genre of the exhibition should be seen, rather, in his assertion of the curatorial ego and in the transition he established between the exhibition for art lovers and the exhibition as spectacle, product of the culture industry." Xavier Douroux, Yves Aupetitallot, "A propos de Harald Szeemann: Tentative d'épuisement de l'autre," in *Art Press*, n° 226, 1997, p. 31.

[3] Cf. Yuka Tokuyama, "Interview with Josy Kraft," p. 189–190.

[4] Cecilia Liveriero Lavelli, Franklin Sirmans, "Harald Szeemann, Curator as Author: From Ljubljana to Lyon to Kwangju," in *Flash Art*, issue 30, n° 195, Summer, 1997, p. 89–90.

[5] "He was always somewhat constrained in putting on these big events—by the commissioners, the collectors, the gallery owners, and of course by the costs involved." Cf. François Aubart, Fabien Pinaroli, "Interview with Tobia Bezzola," p. 30.

[6] Harald Szeemann, *Ecrire les expositions*, La Lettre volée, Brussels 1996, p. 33.

[7] Cf. First Exhibition Concept for *L'Autre—4th Lyon Biennial*, p. 151–157.

[8] Cf. First Press Release, p. 158.

[9] " I'm trying to create a landscape, or a small town, in which each home or cabin is one aspect of 'the other.'" Cf. Jean-François Chougnet, Thierry Prat, Thierry Raspail, "Interview with Harald Szeemann," p. 173.

[10] Ibid.

[11] "It is precisely here that this exhibition has an opportunity: it is an epicenter, that is, a new type of group exhibition, trans-age, trans-erotic, trans-energetic." In Harald Szeemann, *Epicenter Ljubljana*, Moderna Galerija, Ljubljana 1997, p. 10.

[12] When asked, "Do you have a theme or an overall idea?" Szeemann replied, "No, there's no theme." See Christian Bernard, "Entretien avec Harald Szeemann," in *Art Press*, n° 247, July, 1999, p. 18–23. See also Harald Szeemann, *49th Venice Biennial—Plateau of Humankind*, Electa, Milan 2001: "The Plateau of Humanity is not a theme as such but rather a declaration of responsibility—history, to the events of the present day."

[13] "I wanted to make an optimistic exhibition. I don't care about style. I don't care about taste." Cf. Liveriero Lavelli, Sirmans, "Harald Szeemann, Curator as Author," p. 89–90.

Part IV: Information

1) Harald Szeemann's Biography (Bern, 1933–Tegna, 2005)

Fabien Pinaroli and Karla G. Roalandini-Beyer

Harald Szeemann finished his art-history thesis on "The Beginnings of Modern Book Illustration (Nabis, *Revue blanche*, Alfred Jarry, *Artwork Theater*, Ambroise Vollard)" in the late 1950s. This study revealed what was already a penchant for cross-disciplinary discussions (literature, theater, film, archaeology, and so on). In using the exhibition as a vector of subjectivity, Szeemann contributed to a reconsideration of this medium that transcended the conventions of art history and its focus on movements and styles. "My life has been in the service of a medium, and this medium is not the image, which is reality in itself, but the exhibition that presents reality," he explained. Subsequently he was to take up very different professional activities, including journalism and graphic design. Several years were devoted to the theater.

Szeemann's interest in contemporary art was sparked by a meeting with Arnold Rüdlinger, director of the Kunsthalle Bern from 1946–1955, one of the first museums in Europe to show the new American artistic developments. Through Rüdlinger, Szeemann met many artists whom he often visited in their studios. Soon Franz Meyer, Rudlinger's successor at the Kunsthalle Bern (1955–1961), recommended Szeemann to curate the contemporary section of the exhibition *Painters-Poets/Poets-Painters* held at the Kunstmuseum St Gallen in 1957. Discovering the opportunities for self-expression in this job, Szeemann decided to make this the basis of his professional development as an *exhibition maker*.

In speaking about his practice, Harald Szeemann referred to two main mentors: Georg Schmidt, the director of the Kunstmuseum Basel at that time, and William Sandberg, the director of the Stedelijk Museum in Amsterdam—both of whom resigned from their positions in 1963. These tutelary figures, in his view, represented diametrical opposites: he admired the former's discernment and sensitivity to artworks and the latter's opting to always give priority to informing visitors, even if this was often at the expense of the presentation of the artworks themselves. Both of these influences can be seen in Szeemann's own practice. Starting very early on he developed a two-fold approach that he called "selective information and/or informative selection."

In 1961, at 28, he was appointed director of the Kunsthalle Bern, which he transformed into an intense experimental laboratory, mounting both monographic and group shows, featuring outsider art as well as avant-garde work, and mixing together fashion, design, cinema, etc. He launched projects that involved working closely with artists and produced events and ephemeral environments that went further in the direction already explored by artists themselves. The

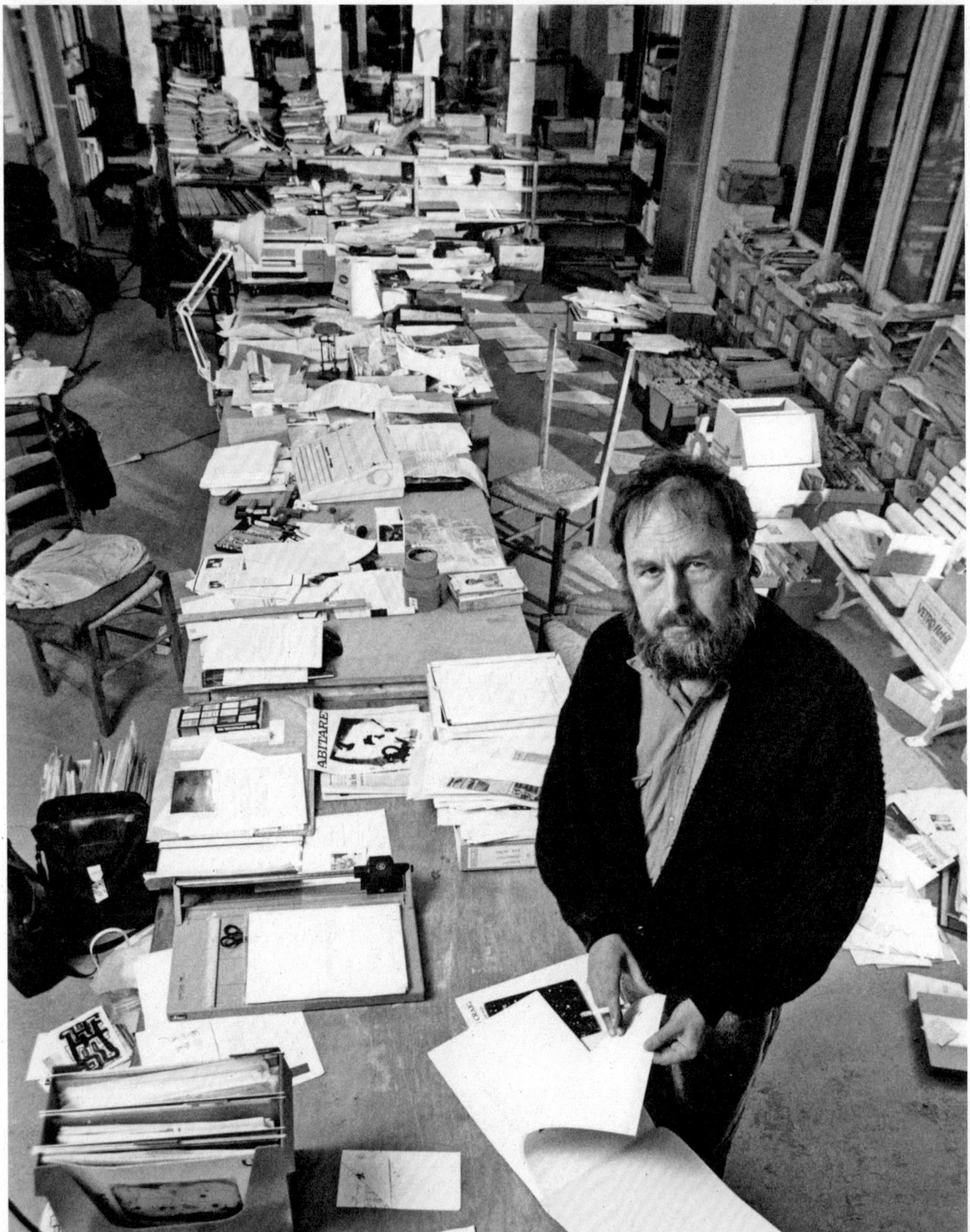

Harald Szeemann in his archive at the Fabbrica rosa, Maggia, 1990

exhibition *When Attitudes Become Form: works, concepts, processes, situations, information*, which he organized in 1969, was the high point of this process. The subtitle he chose was telling in this regard. Szeemann described it as "a structured chaos." A new type of exhibition was launched. Considered a scandal by many people, this show provoked lively polemics. Szeemann was forced to resign from his post in September 1969. On October 1, he created the *Agency for Intellectual Guest Labour*, and officially became an "independent curator."

Szeemann started working on a film entitled *Height x Length x Width* together with Bernhard Luginbühl, Markus Raetz, and Balthasar Burkhard. In 1970, he organized *The Thing as Object* in Nuremberg and, along with Wolf Vostell, *Happening & Fluxus* in Cologne. This same year he was appointed General Secretary of *documenta 5*, which was inaugurated in Kassel in 1972. He conceived it as a 100-day-long event. For this occasion he created a large cabinet of curiosities around the Hegelian question of the relation between the reality of the image and the reality of what is portrayed. At the same time he presented a cutting-edge survey of international avant-garde art in all its diversity. The period following *documenta* was particularly difficult for Szeemann. The members of the committee accused him of responsibility for a dramatic budget overrun, which he was supposed to reimburse personally. He was forced to imagine another way of making exhibitions. From that time on he began spending most of his time in Tegna, in the Ticino region in southern Switzerland, the home of his companion Ingeborg Lüscher.

Starting in 1974 Szeemann carried out his activities under the auspices of what he called the *Museum of Obsessions*. He also turned his curatorial practice toward a search for intensely motivated forms of expression which he defined as *Individual Mythologies*. This led to a radical innovation: the organization in 1974 of a very personal show in his own Bern apartment—which later became the Galerie Toni Gerber—*Grandfather: A Pioneer Like Us*, a collection of various objects that belonged to his grandfather, a professional hairdresser and the secret inventor of the perm. At the same time, with the 1975 exhibition *The Bachelor Machines*, he developed an independent model for curatorial activity by offering museums "turnkey" exhibitions. He launched a complex and forward-looking theoretical endeavor around modern myths such as the refusal to procreate as the driving force in modern artistic creativity. In 1978 he began a series of shows about the utopian political and social projects carried out at Monte Verità in the Ticino, where he started three museums one after another. Later he organized a highly significant thematic exhibition: *Penchant for a Synthesis of the Arts: European Utopias Since 1800* (1983).

In 1980 he founded *Aperto*, intended to give emerging international artists a chance to show their work in conjunction with the Venice Biennale. The following year he jointed the curatorial team at the Kunsthaus Zürich, where the position of "permanent independent curator" was created especially for him. Among the major retrospectives of work by artists he had long championed were Mario Merz, Cy Twombly, Richard Serra, Walter De Maria, and Josef Beuys. He simultaneously pursued his career as an independent curator, developing a stronger interest in sculpture, and more particularly in monumental works. At that time he began to look for very large non-museum spaces, such as the Saint-Louis chapel at the Salpêtrière hospital in Paris, the Deichtorhallen in Hamburg, the Halle Tony Garnier in Lyon, and so on.

At that time, Szeemann's curatorial practice particularly highlighted the existing bonds between the work of a stage director and that of a curator. The space between the works, which allow them to "breath," and the way they are lit, became more and more important. The exhibition space itself was however less a stage than a showcase in which the exhibitions were spread so delicately that they were described by Szeemann himself as "poems in space." They shared the capacity to offer visitors an experience that appeals to the emotions. *Traces, Sculptures, and Monuments of their Precise Journey* in Zurich (1985), *De Sculptura* in Vienna (1986), *Zeitlos* (*Timeless*) in Berlin, *a-Historial Soundings* in Rotterdam (1988), *Illuminate* in Hamburg (1989), *LightSpeed* in Tokyo (1990), and *GAS: Grandiose, Ambitious, Silent* in Bordeaux (1993), for instance, induced an almost spiritual experience.

From the beginning of the 1990s, Szeemann mounted huge thematic exhibitions. His *Visionary Switzerland* in 1991 was the first of a series of "national" shows that would focus on Austria in 1996 and Belgium in 2005. His interest also focused on the East, and manifested itself through the exhibitions *Epicenter Ljubljana* in 1997, and *Blood & Honey—the Future is in the Balkans* in 2003. He was also asked to organize major international shows during this period. Most notably, he served as the artistic director of the Lyon Biennial and Kwangju Biennial in 1997, the Venice Biennial in 1999 and 2001, and the Seville Biennial in 2004. These events presented an overview of contemporary art, emphasizing the work of young artists while also exploring the new possibilities afforded by the fall of the Berlin Wall in Eastern Europe and the changes in Asia, especially in China. Nevertheless, Szeemann's driving impulse remained his *Individual Mythologies*.

Harald Szeemann described himself as "an untamed thinker who nourishes himself with the mythical and utopian nature of human spirit and activity." [1] He passed away in 2005 without having been able to carry out the two exhibitions, *La Mamma* and *Il Sole*, which he had planned since the end of the 1970s to complete the research initiated with *The Bachelor Machines* (1975), and developed with *Monte Verità* (1978), and to thus form a trilogy of fundamental themes (the bachelor, the mother, the sun).

[1] Harald Szeemann, *Museum der Obsessionen*, Merve Verlag, Berlin 1981, p. 20.

2) Illustrated Chronology of Exhibitions

This chronology is based on the information taken from:

- The poster of the exhibition *8 ½: documentation 1961–1969*, Paris, 1970;
- Hans-Joachim Müller, *Harald Szeemann. Exhibition Maker*, Hatje Cantz Verlag, Ostfildern, 2006;
- The list of exhibitions at the Kunsthalle Bern from 1961 to 1969 (provided by the Kunsthalle Bern, 2007);
- Tobia Bezzola and Roman Kurzmeyer (eds.), *Harald Szeemann: with by through because towards despite*, Springer, Vienna/New York; Voldemeer, Zürich 2007, p. 729–735.

The presentation of this chronology emphasizes the interlinked nature of Szeemann's activities. The period of the exhibition is the main entry. It was important to make a distinction between exhibitions Szeemann produced and those he represented that were produced by other institutions. The touring exhibitions are in parenthesis: the first city mentioned indicates the venue where the exhibition was conceived first. The exhibitions installed by Harald Szeemann at other institutions are mentioned by city followed by date. Depending on availability, we have tried to give the most exhaustive information on Szeemann's collaborations with institutions.

Note: The dates in the chronology are grouped by year and follow the format dd/mm.

1957

03.08–20.10

Kunstmuseum, St Gallen

Malende Dichter—Dichtende Maler

24.09–27.09

Kleintheater Kramgasse 6, Bern

Hugo Ball (1886–1927): Manusckripte, Photographien, Bücher

(Bern → Zürich: 4.11.1957)

Club Bel Etage, Zürich

1961

08.07–03.09

Kunsthalle, Bern

Otto Tschumi

(Bern → Glarus)

Kunsthaus, Glarus

02.09–24.09

Städtische Galerie, Biel

Buri, Gürtler, Iseli, Luginbühl, Meister, Spescha, Schaffner

09.09–15.10

Kunsthalle, Bern

Hans Aeschbacher: Skulpturen und Zeichnungen

21.10–26.11

Kunsthalle, Bern

Prähistorische Felsbilder der Sahara: Expedition Henri Lhote im Gebiet Tassili-n-Ajjer

1962

17.02–11.03

Kunsthalle, Bern

Puppen—Marionetten—Schattenspiel: Asiatica und Experimente

17.03–23.04

Kunsthalle, Bern

Charles Lapicque

(Bern → München → Grenoble → Le Havre)

Städtische Galerie im Lenbachhau, München/Musée de Peinture et de Sculpture, Grenoble/Maison de la Culture, Le Havre

28.04–27.05

Kunsthalle, Bern

Lenz Klotz, Friedrich Kuhn, Bruno Müller, Matias Spescha

02.06–01.07

Kunsthalle, Bern

Walter Kurt Wiemken

(Bern → St Gallen)

Kunstmuseum St Gallen

07.07–02.09
Kunsthalle, Bern
Francis Picabia (1879–1953): Werke von 1909 bis 1924
(Marseille → Bern)
4 Amerikaner: Jasper Johns, Alfred Leslie, Robert Rauschenberg, Richard Stankiewicz
(Stockholm → Amsterdam → Bern)
Moderna Museet, Stockholm/Stedelijk Museum, Amsterdam
13.10–25.11
Städtische Galerie, Biel
Harry Kramer: Automobile Skulpturen—Marionetten—Filme
20.10–25.11
Kunsthalle, Bern
Kunst aus Tibet

1963

16.02–24.03
Kunsthalle, Bern
Auguste Herbin (1882–1960)
(Bern → Amsterdam)
Stedelijk Museum, Amsterdam
20.04–19.05
Städtische Galerie, Biel
Englebert van Anderlecht, Bram Bogart
(Bern → Bruxelles)
Palais des Beaux-Arts, Bruxelles
04.05–03.06
Kunsthalle, Bern
Alan Davie
(Baden-Baden → Bern → Darmstadt → London → Amsterdam)
Staatliche Kunsthalle, Baden-Baden
Piotr Kowalski
12.07–18.08
Kunsthalle, Bern
William Scott
(Bern → Belfast)
Ulster Museum, Belfast
Victor Pasmore
18.08–15.09
Städtische Galerie, Biel
Heinz-Peter Kohler, Gregory Masurovsky
24.08–15.09
Kunsthalle, Bern
Bildnerei der Geisteskranken—Art Brut—Insania pingens
21.09–27.10
Kunsthalle, Bern
Louis Moillet

02.11–01.12
Kunsthalle, Bern
Etienne-Martin
(Bern → Amsterdam → Eindhoven)
Stedelijk Museum, Amsterdam/Stedelijk van Abbemuseum, Eindhoven

1964

15.02–22.03
Städtische Galerie, Biel
Varlin

22.02–30.03
Kunsthalle, Bern
Serge Brignoni: Gemälde und Skulpturen von 1924 bis 1963

04.04–10.05
Kunsthalle, Bern
Victor Vasarely: Werke von 1935 bis 1963
(Hannover → Düsseldorf → Bern → Berlin → Den Haag)
Kestner-Gesellschaft, Hannover/Kunstverein für die Rheinlande und Westfalen, Düsseldorf/Haus am Waldsee, Berlin/ Gemeentemuseum's-Gravenhage, Den Haag

17.04–24.05
Städtische Galerie, Biel
Ferdinand Hodler: Landschaften der Reife und Spätzeit
(Zürich → Biel)
Kunsthaus, Zürich

30.04–25.10
Musée cantonal des Beaux-Arts, Palais de Rumine, Lausanne
Art suisse au XXème siècle—Schweizer Kunst im 20. Jahrhundert—Arte svizzera nel XX° secolo
[Prepared in collaboration with A. Rüdlinger, F. Meyer, R. Berger, M. Pianzola, G. Fischer, E. Henry, R. Wehrli]

20.05–21.06
Kunsthalle, Bern
Hundertwasser
(Hannover → Bern → Hagen → Wien → Amsterdam → Stockholm)
Kestner-Gesellschaft, Hannover/Karl-Ernst-Osthaus-Museum, Hagen/ Museum des 20. Jahrhunderts, Wien/Stedelijk Museum, Amsterdam/ Moderna Museet, Stockholm
Louise Nevelson
(Turin → Bern)
Galleria Galatea, Torino
Anselmo Boix-Vives

03.07–06.09
Kunsthalle, Bern
Ex Voto
[Exhibition later touring to 12 cities in the United States]

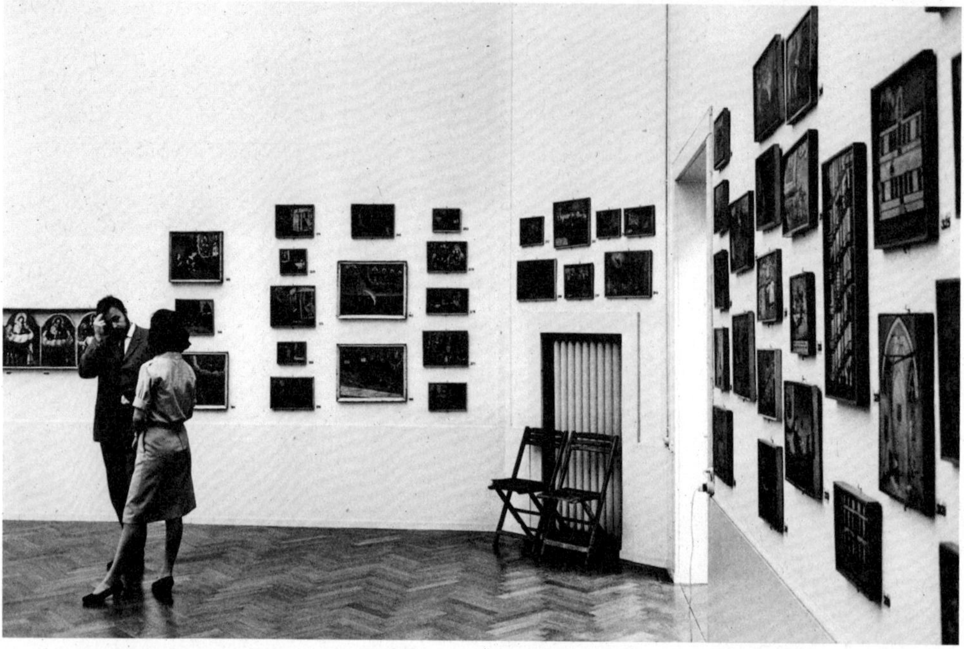

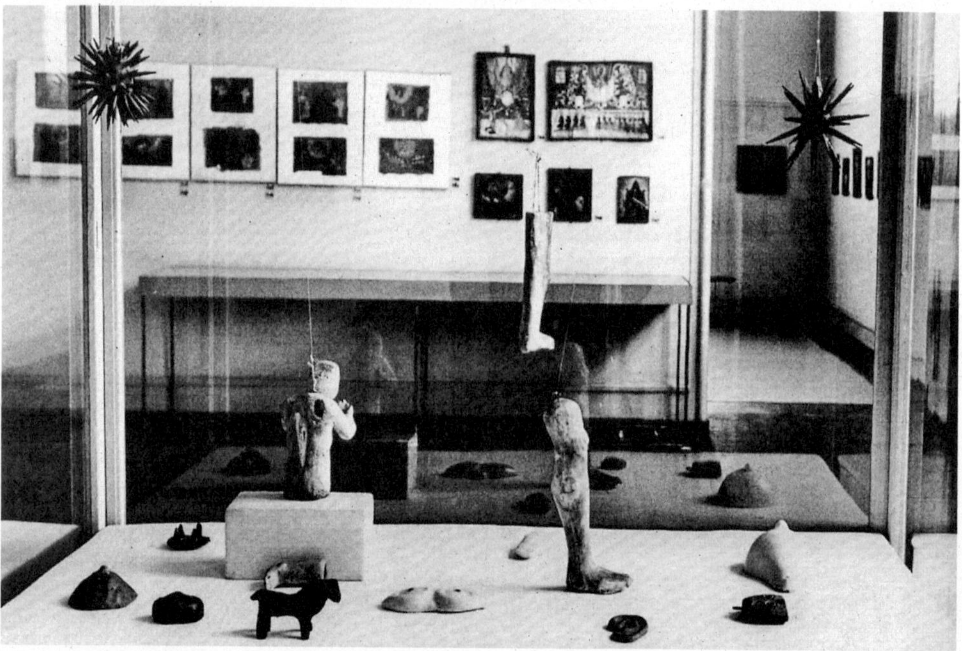

Ex Voto, Kunsthalle Bern, 1964

11.09–11.10
Kunsthalle, Bern
Jean Prouvé: Industrielles Bauen
(Bern → Paris → München → Genève)

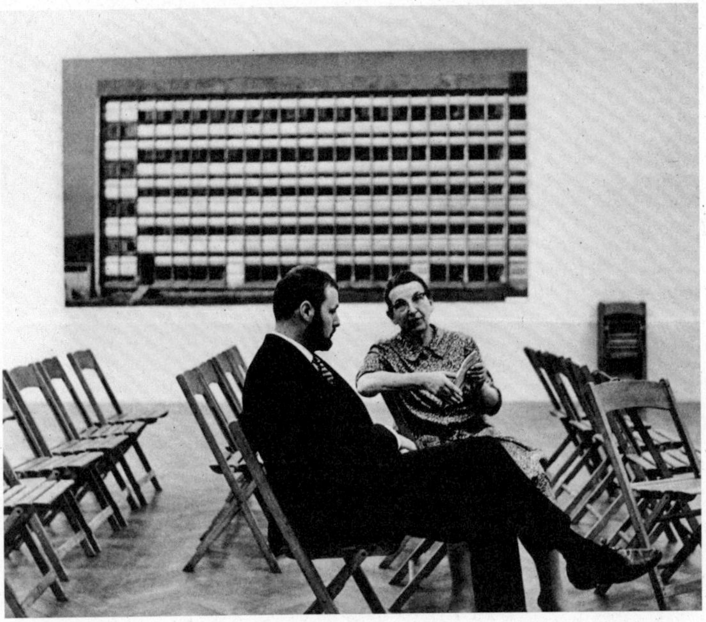

Jean Prouvé, Kunsthalle Bern, 1964

17.10–22.11
Städtische Galerie, Biel
25 Berner und Bieler Künstler

23.10–29.11
Kunsthalle, Bern
Joseph Albers
(Bern → Milano)
Drei Initialgesten: Duchamp, Kandinsky, Malewitsch Tom Doyle

1965

20.02–28.03
Kunsthalle, Bern
Robert Müller: Skulpturen und Zeichnungen
(Amsterdam/Bern → Bruxelles → Düsseldorf → Wien)
Stedelijk Museum, Amsterdam/Palais des Beaux-Arts, Bruxelles/Museum des 20. Jahrhunderts, Wien/Kunstverein für die Rheinlande und Westfalen, Düsseldorf
[Co-production Stedelijk Museum, Amsterdam/Kunsthalle, Bern]

27.02–04.04
Städtische Galerie, Biel
Oscar Wiggli: Skulpturen und Zeichnungen
Charles Jörg

03.04–09.05
Kunsthalle, Bern
Der Mensch: Weltausstellung der Photographie
[Touring to 41 locations in Europe. Exhibition designed and realized by Karl Pawek in Hamburg, and financed by *Stern* magazine]

21.05–22.06
Kunsthalle, Bern
Otto Meyer-Amden (1885–1933)
(Bern → St Gallen → Chur)
Kunstmuseum, St Gallen/Kunsthaus Chur
Lyonel Feininger (1871–1956)
(Biel → Bern)
Städtische Galerie, Biel
[Conceived and realized by MoMA—Museum of Modern Art, New York]

03.07–05.09
Kunsthalle, Bern
Licht und Bewegung: Kinetische Kunst/Lumière et mouvement/Luce e movimento
(Bern → Bruxelles → Baden-Baden → Düsseldorf)
Palais des Beaux-Arts, Bruxelles/Staatliche Kunsthalle, Baden-Baden/
Kunstverein für die Rheinlande und Westfalen, Düsseldorf
Neue Tendenzen der Architektur

11.09–17.10
Kunsthalle, Bern
Walter Linck: Skulpturen—Mobiles—Zeichnungen
(Bern → Dortmund)
Rolf Iseli: Neuere Werke von 1964 bis 1965

23.10–05.12
Kunsthalle, Bern
Giorgio Morandi
(Bern → Biennale di Venezia)

1966

02.04–08.05
Kunsthalle, Bern
Jean Gorin, Jean Dewasne, Constant: drei Ausstellungen

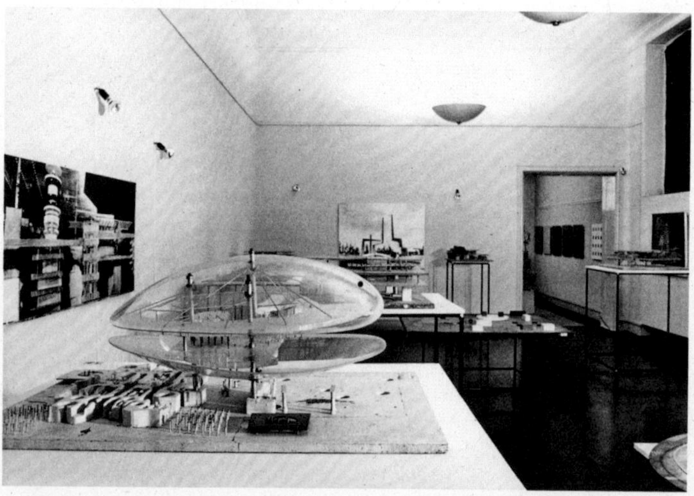

Jean Gorin, Jean Dewasne, Constant: Three Exhibitions, Kunsthalle Bern, 1966

25.05–03.07
Kunsthalle, Bern
Weiss auf Weiss
F-111 von James Rosenquist
11 Pop Artists: The new image (Philipp Morris Edition)

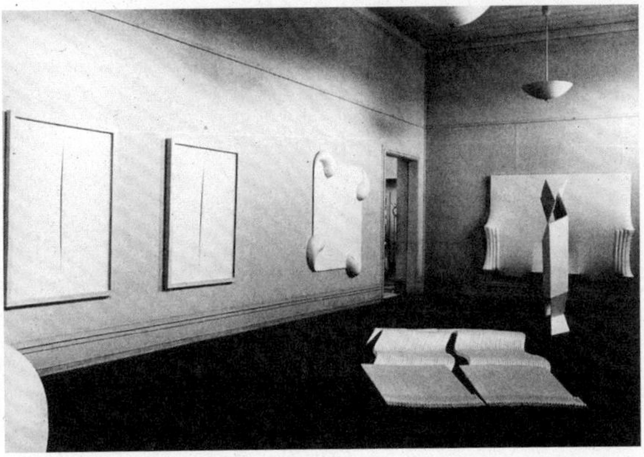

Weiss auf Weiss (*White on White*), Kunsthalle Bern, 1966

09.07–04.09
Kunsthalle, Bern
Mark Tobey: Werke von 1933 bis 1966
(Amsterdam/Bern → Hannover → Düsseldorf)
Stedelijk Museum, Amsterdam/Kestner-Gesellschaft, Hannover/
Kunstverein für die Rheinlande und Westfalen, Düsseldorf
[Co-production Stedelijk Museum, Amsterdam/Kunsthalle, Bern]

21.10–04.12
Phantastische Kunst—Surrealismus
(Bern → Tel-Aviv)
Tel-Aviv Museum of Art

04.11–04.12
Halfmannshof, Gelsenkirchen
Bern 66

<u>1967</u>

04.02–22.02
Kunsthalle, Bern
5 Junge englische Künstler
(Venezia → Mannhein → Bern → Rotterdam)
Art Council of Great Britain, Biennale di Venezia/
Museum Boijmans van Beuningen, Rotterdam

25.02–02.04
Kunsthalle, Bern
Junge englische Bildhauer
(Bern → Amsterdam → Düsseldorf)
Stedelijk Museum, Amsterdam/Kunstverein für die Rheinlande
und Westfalen, Düsseldorf

14.04–21.05

Kunsthalle, Bern

Formen der Farbe/Shapes of Color

(Amsterdam → Stuttgart → Bern)

Stedelijk Museum, Amsterdam/Württembergischer Kunstverein, Stuttgart

08.07–17.09

Kunsthalle, Bern

Science Fiction

(Bern → Paris → Düsseldorf)

Musée des Arts Décoratifs, Paris/Kunstverein für die Rheinlande und Westfalen, Düsseldorf

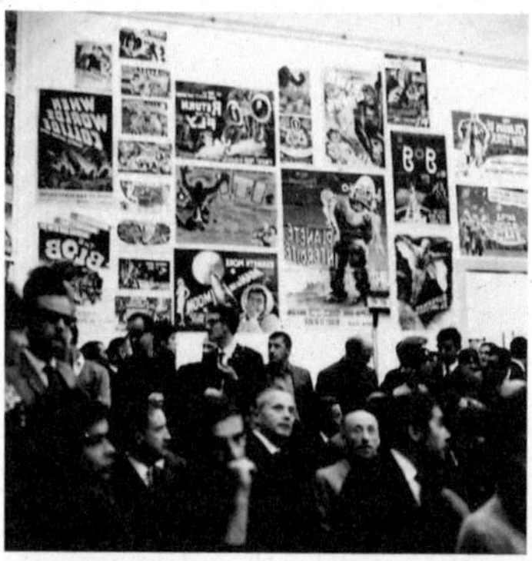

Science Fiction, Kunsthalle Bern, 1967

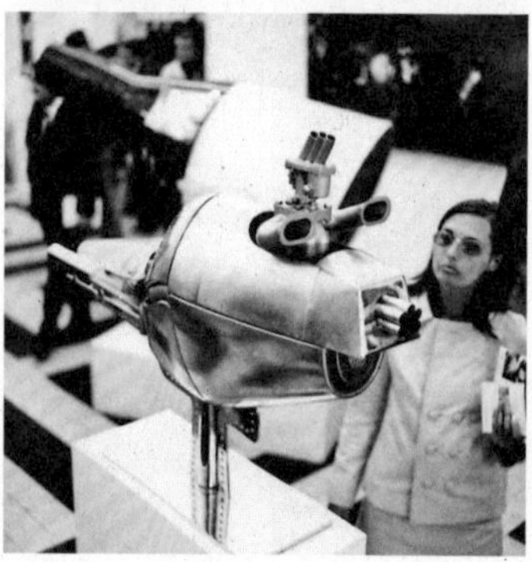

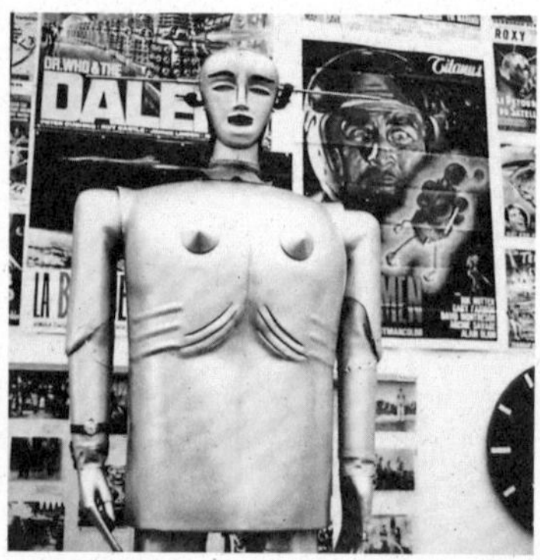

28.10–26.11

Kunsthalle, Bern

Otto Nebel: Werke von 1918 bis 1967

1968

23.02–31.03

Kunsthalle, Bern

Roy Lichtenstein

(Amsterdam → London → Bern → Hannover)

Stedelijk Museum, Amsterdam/Tate Gallery, London/Kestner-Gesellschaft, Hannover

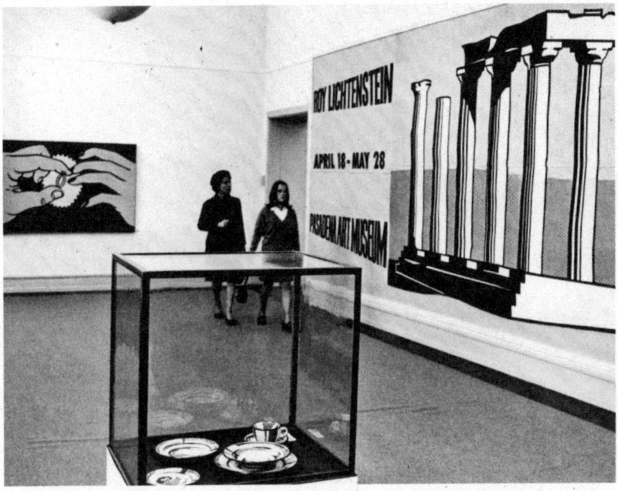

Roy Lichtenstein, Kunsthalle Bern, 1968

06.04–12.05
Kunsthalle, Bern
Max Bill: Malerei und Plastik von 1928 bis 1968
(Bern → Hannover → Düsseldorf → Den Haag → Zürich)
Kestner-Gesellschaft, Hannover/Kunstverein für die Rheinlande und Westfalen, Düsseldorf/Gemeentemuseum s'-Gravenhage, Den Haag

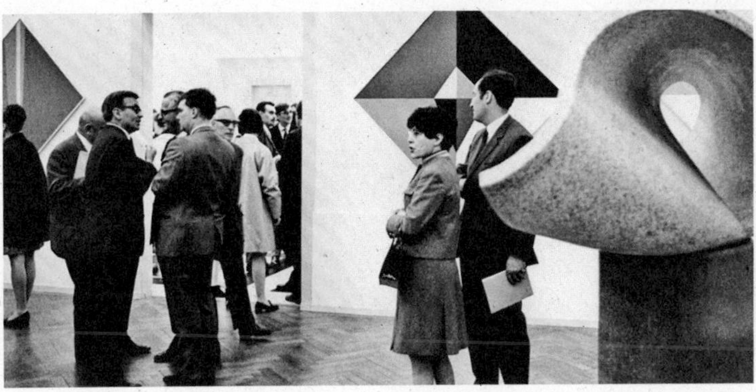

Max Bill, Kunsthalle Bern, 1968

21.05–30.06
Kunsthalle, Bern
Jesús Rafael Soto: Kinetische Werke von 1950 bis 1968
(Bern → Hannover → Düsseldorf → Amsterdam → Bruxelles → Paris → Oslo)
Kestner-Gesellschaft, Hannover/Kunstverein für die Rheinlande und Westfalen, Düsseldorf/Stedelijk Museum, Amsterdam/ Musée d'Art moderne de la Ville de Paris/Palais des Beaux-Arts, Bruxelles/ Stiftung Sonja Henie-Niels Onstad, Oslo

20.07–29.09
Kunsthalle, Bern
12 Environments: 50 Jahre Kunsthalle Bern
(Bern → Utrecht → Recklinghausen)

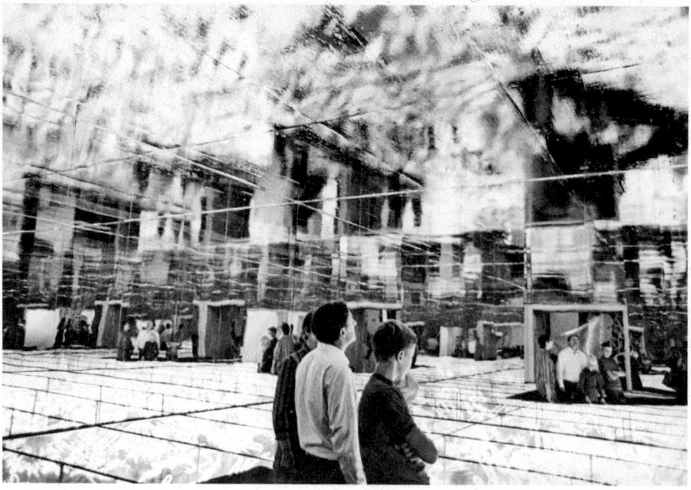

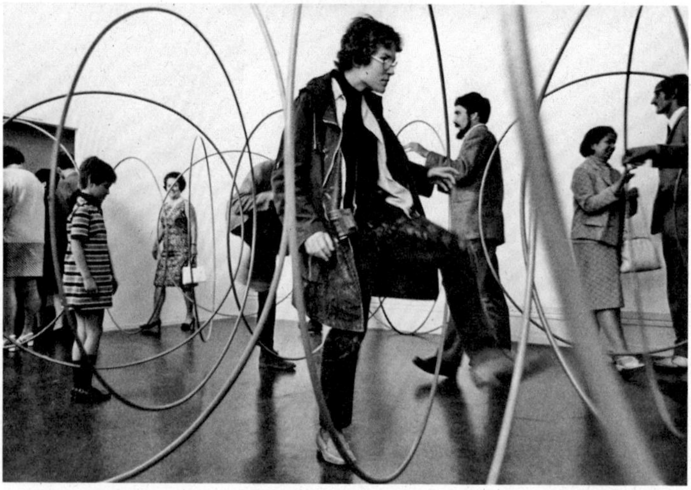

12 Environments, Kunsthalle Bern, 1968

05.10–27.10
Kunsthalle, Bern
20 Jahre Kunstpflege der Stadt Bern: 1947–1968

02.11–01.12
Kunsthalle, Bern
Junge Kunst aus Holland

1969

25.01–09.03
Kunsthalle, Bern
Die Frau: 2. Weltausstellung der Photographie
[Curated by Karl Pawek, the exhibition was organized by *Stern* magazine in collaboration with 261 art institutions in 36 countries]

22.03–27.04
Kunsthalle, Bern
Live in your Head.
When Attitudes Become Form: works, concepts, processes, situations, information/ Wenn Attitüden Form werden: Werke, Konzepte, Vorgänge, Situationen, Information/ Quand les attitudes deviennent forme: œuvres, concepts, processus, situations, information/Quando attituini diventano forma: opere, concetti, processi, situazioni, informazione
(Bern → Krefeld: 09.05–15.06 → London: 28.08–27.09)
Museum Haus Lange, Krefeld/ICA-Institute of Contemporary Arts, London

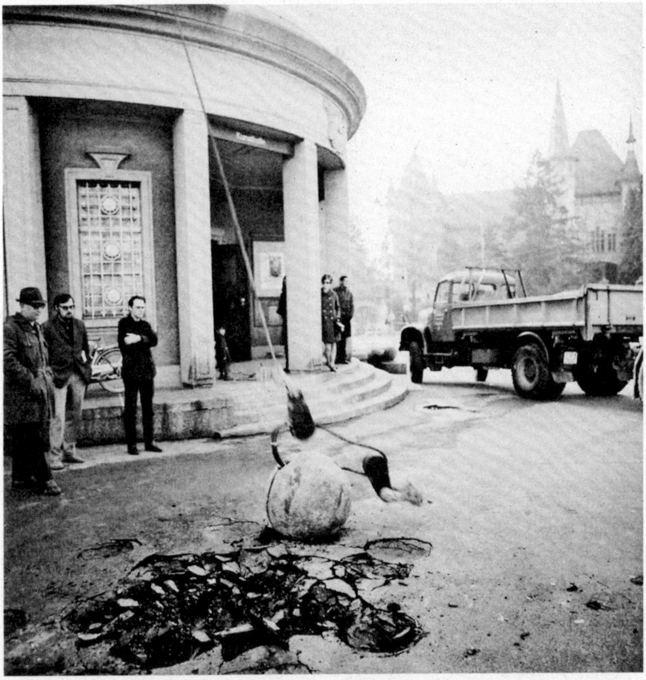

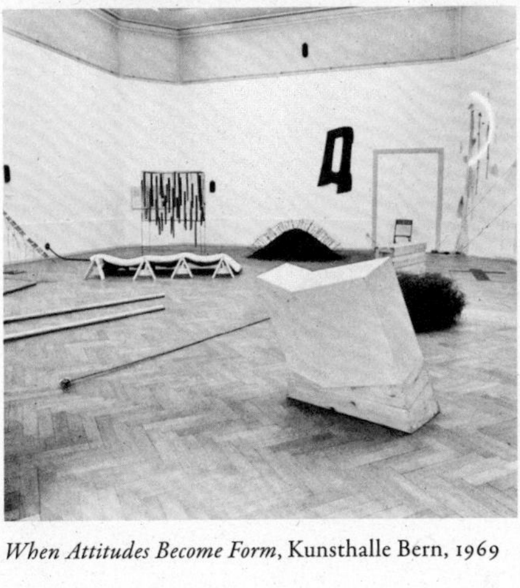

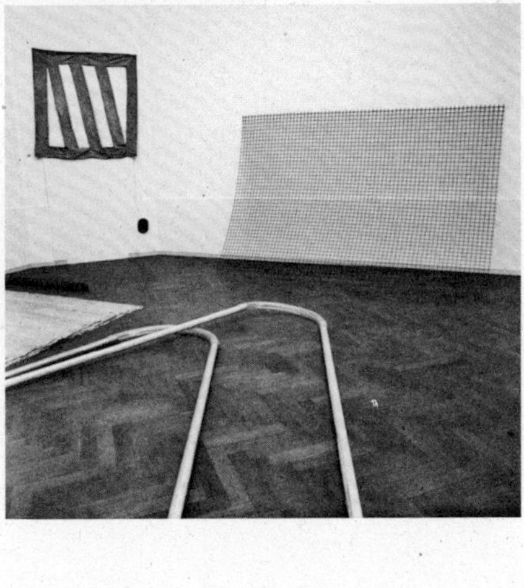

When Attitudes Become Form, Kunsthalle Bern, 1969

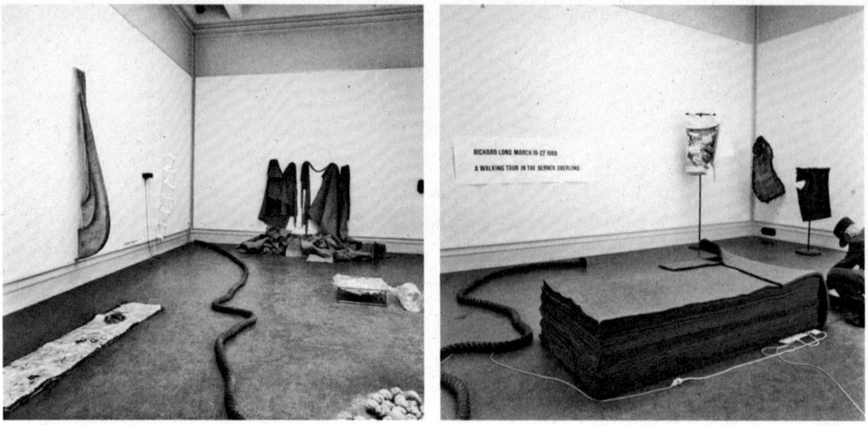

When Attitudes Become Form, Kunsthalle Bern, 1969

[April]
Gebrüder Loeb AG Warenhaus, Bern
Bekannte Berner Künstler haben unsere Schaufenster gestaltet

03.05–01.06
Kunsthalle, Bern
Freunde—Friends—Amis—d'Fründe (Karl Gerstner, Dieter Roth, Daniel Spoerri, André Thomkins und ihre Freunde und Freundesfreunde)
(Bern → Düsseldorf)
Städtische Kunsthalle, Düsseldorf

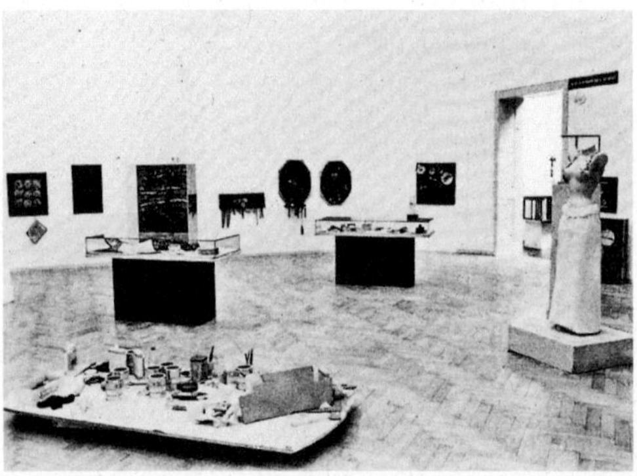

Freunde—Friends—Amis—d'Fründe, Kunsthalle Bern, 1969

07.06–06.07
Kunsthalle, Bern
22 junge Schweizer
(Amsterdam → Bern)
Stedelijk Museum, Amsterdam

12.07–28.09
Kunsthalle, Bern
Sammlung Karl Ströher
Part I: 12.07–17.08
Part II: 23.08–28.09

(München → Bern → Hamburg → Darmstadt → Berlin → Düsseldorf)
Neue Staatsgalerie, München/Kunstverein, Hamburg/Hessisches Landesmuseum, Darmstadt/Nationalgalerie, Berlin/Städtische Kunsthalle, Düsseldorf

08.11–07.12
Kunsthalle, Bern
Pläne und Projekte als Kunst
[The exhibition was planned by Harald Szeemann but realized after his resignation by Felix Zdenek, interim director]

1970

05.02–07.03
Galerie Claude Givaudan, Paris
8½: documentation 1961–1969

10.07–30.08
Kunsthalle, Nürnberg
Das Ding als Objekt: Europäische Objektkunst des 20. Jahrhunderts
(Nürnberg → Oslo)
Sonja Henies og Niels Onstads Stiftelser, Høvikodden/Oslo

06.11.1970–06.01.1971
Kölnischer Kunstverein
Happening & Fluxus
(Köln → Stuttgart → Amsterdam → Berlin)
Württembergischer Kunstverein, Stuttgart

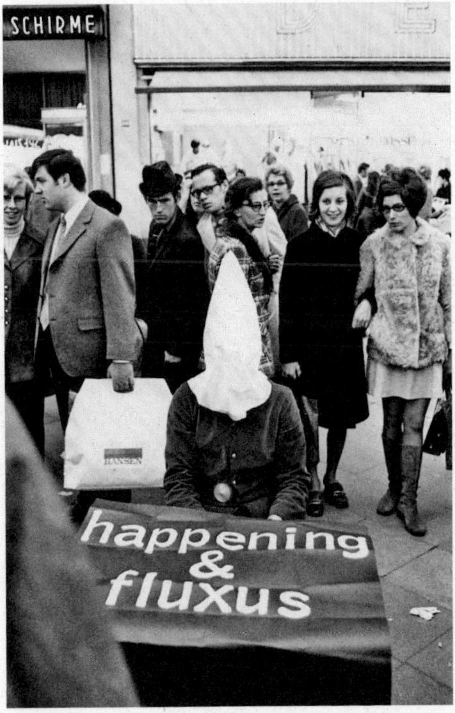

Happening & Fluxus, Kölnischer Kunstverein, Cologne, 1970

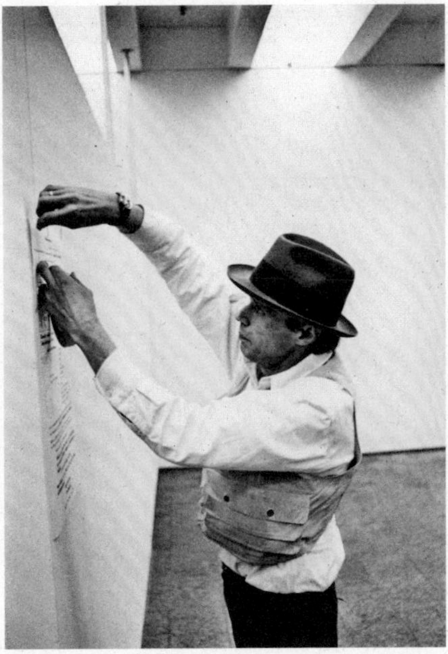

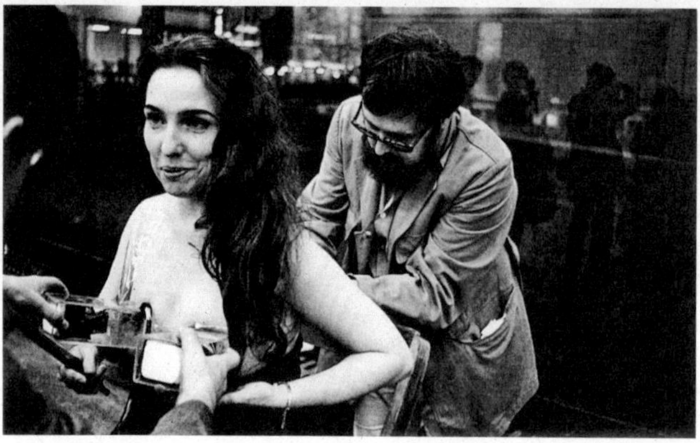

Happening & Fluxus, Kölnischer Kunstverein, Cologne, 1970

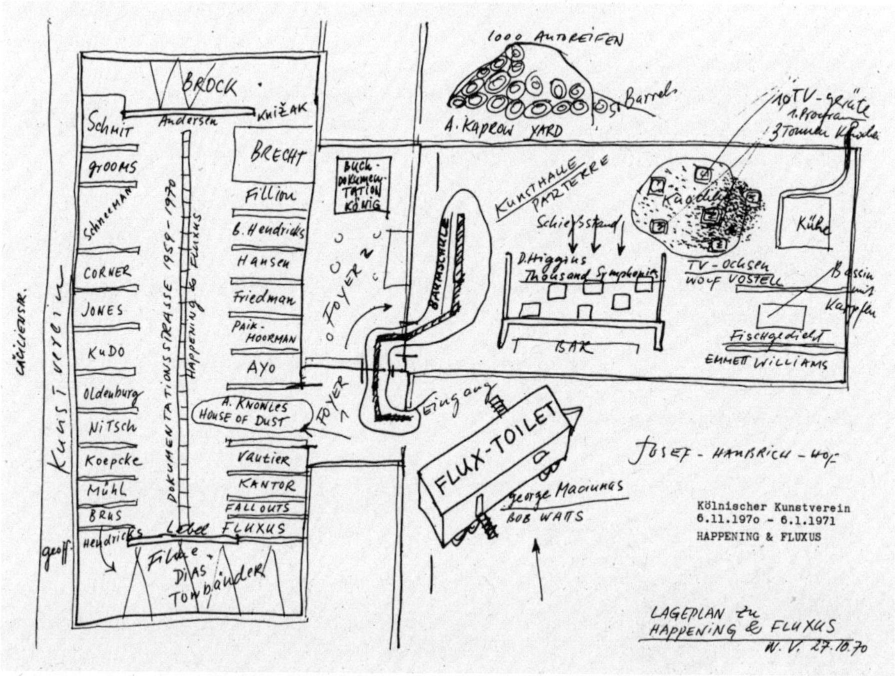

Floor plan of the exhibition *Happening & Fluxus*, 1970. Drawing by Wolf Vostell

<u>1971</u>

29.04–13.05

Bonython Gallery, Sydney

I Want to Leave a Nice Well-Done Child Here: 25 Australian Artists

(Sydney → Melbourne)

National Gallery of Victoria, Melbourne

[May]

Warenhaus Gebrüder Loeb AG, Bern

Die Strasse: Schaufenstrausstellung

[Exhibition realized in several shop-windows of the Loeb department store]

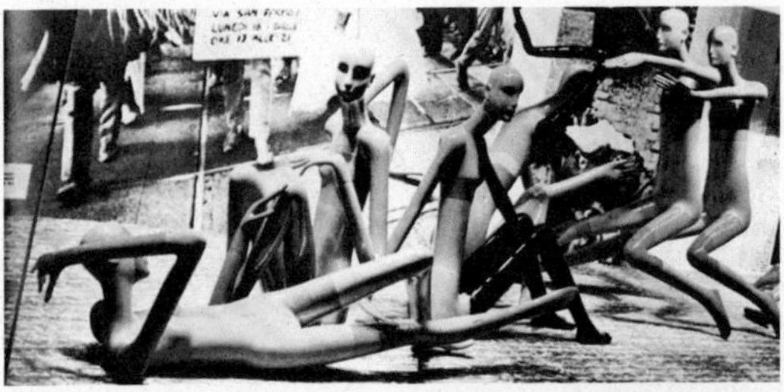

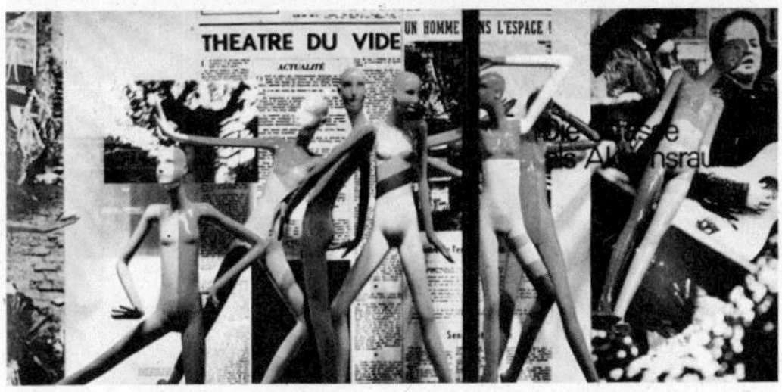

The Street, Loeb, Bern, 1971

1972

20.06–08.10

Neue Galerie and Museum Fridericianum, Kassel
documenta 5: Befragung der Realität, Bildwelten heute/
documenta 5: Questioning Reality—Image World Today

[July]

James Lee Byars in Bern
21.07 (16:30–18:30) *The First International Perfume Exhibition*
22.07 (09:00–12:00) *Zeitglockenturm*

1974

16.02–25.04

Galerie Toni Gerber, Bern
Grossvater: Ein Pionier wie wir

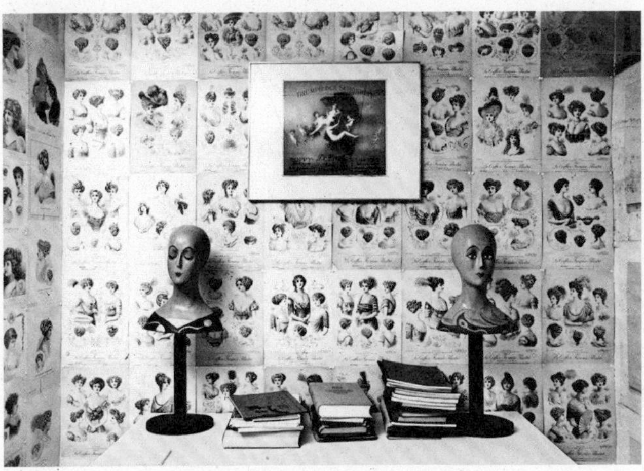

Grandfather: A Pioneer Like Us, Galerie Toni Gerber, Bern, 1974

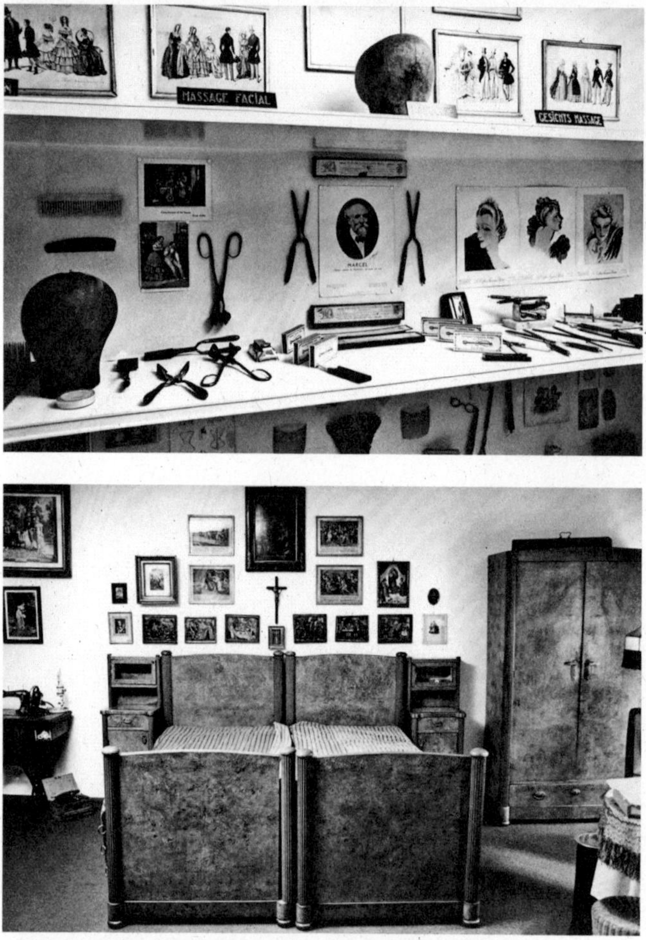

Grandfather: A Pioneer Like Us, Galerie Toni Gerber, Bern, 1974

[April]
Palazzo della Permanente, Milano
Guy Harloff

1975–1977
04.07.1975–17.08.1975
Kunsthalle Bern
Junggesellenmaschinen/Les Machines célibataires/The Bachelor Machines
(Bern → Venezia: 07.09–30.10.1975 → Bruxelles: 17.12.1975–18.01.1976 → Düsseldorf: 17.02–28.03.1976 → Paris: 28.04–05.07.1976 → Malmö: 01.09–17.10.1976 → Amsterdam: 20.11.1976–02.01.1977 → Wien: 02.02–28.02.1977)
Biennale di Venezia: Un laboratorio internazionale/Palais des Beaux-Arts, Bruxelles/Städtische Kunsthalle, Düsseldorf/Musée des Arts Décoratifs, Paris/Malmö Konsthall, Malmö/Stedelijk Museum, Amsterdam/Museum des 20. Jahrhunderts, Wien

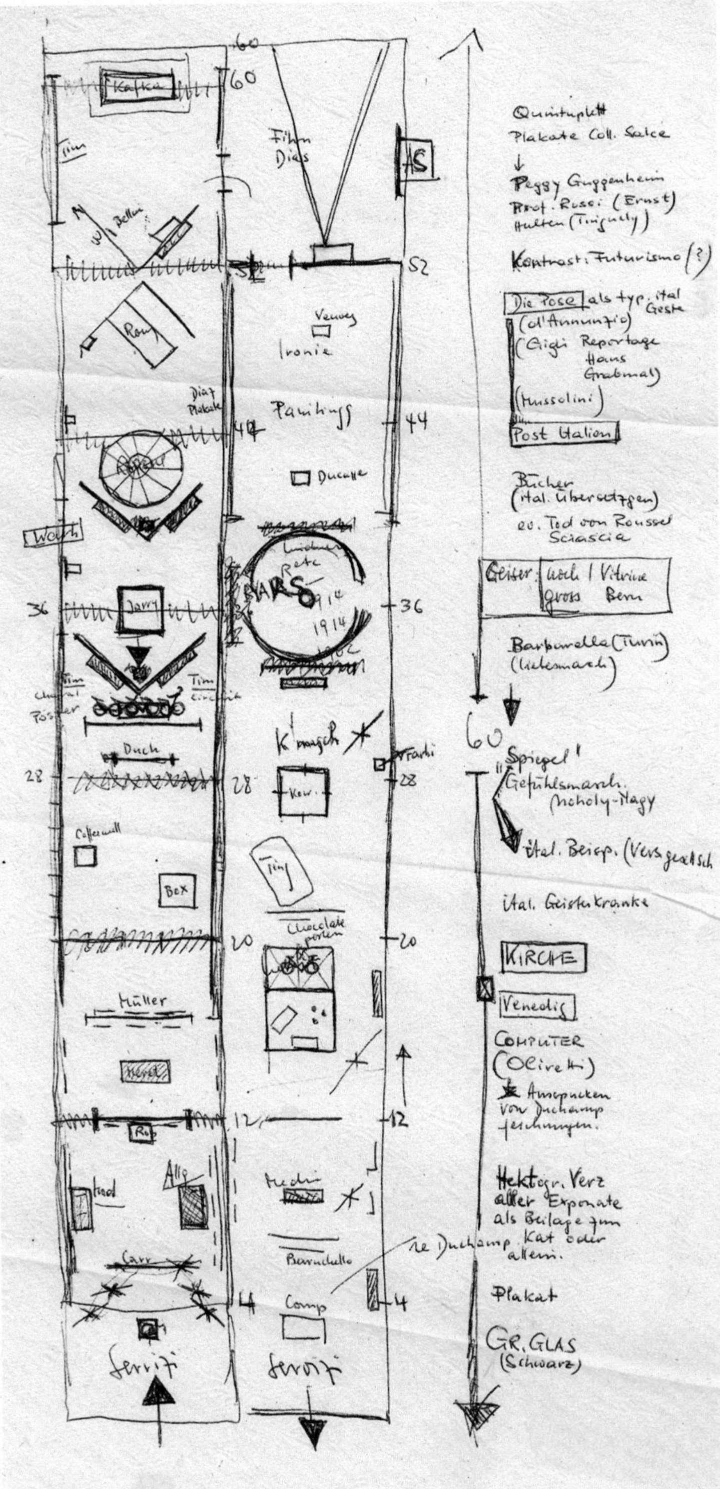

The Bachelor Machines,
Venice Biennial, 1975.
Drawing by Harald Szeemann

The Bachelor Machines, Kunsthalle Bern, 1975

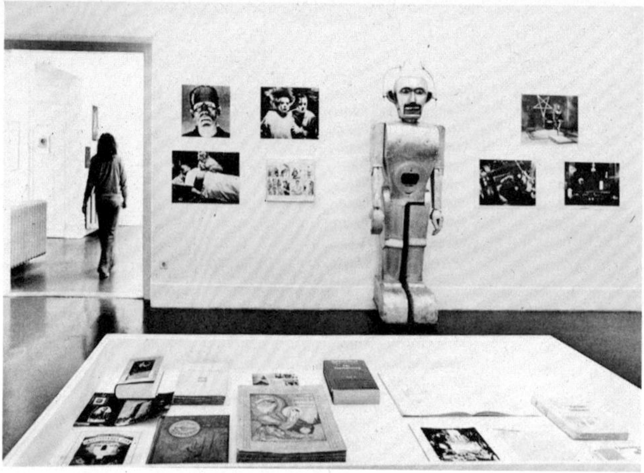

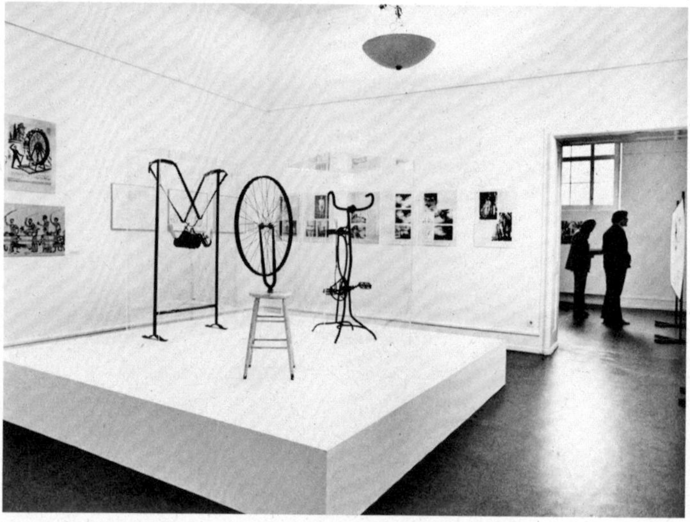

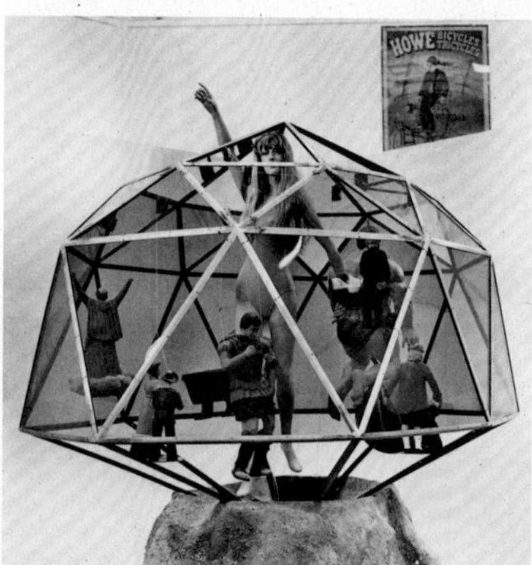

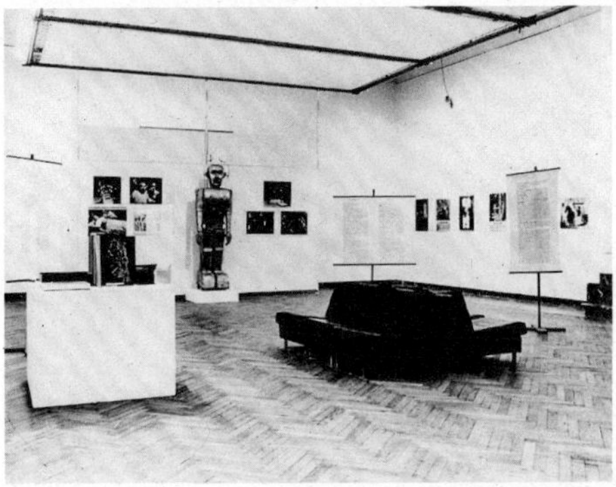

The Bachelor Machines,
Palais des Beaux-Arts, Brussels,
1975–1976

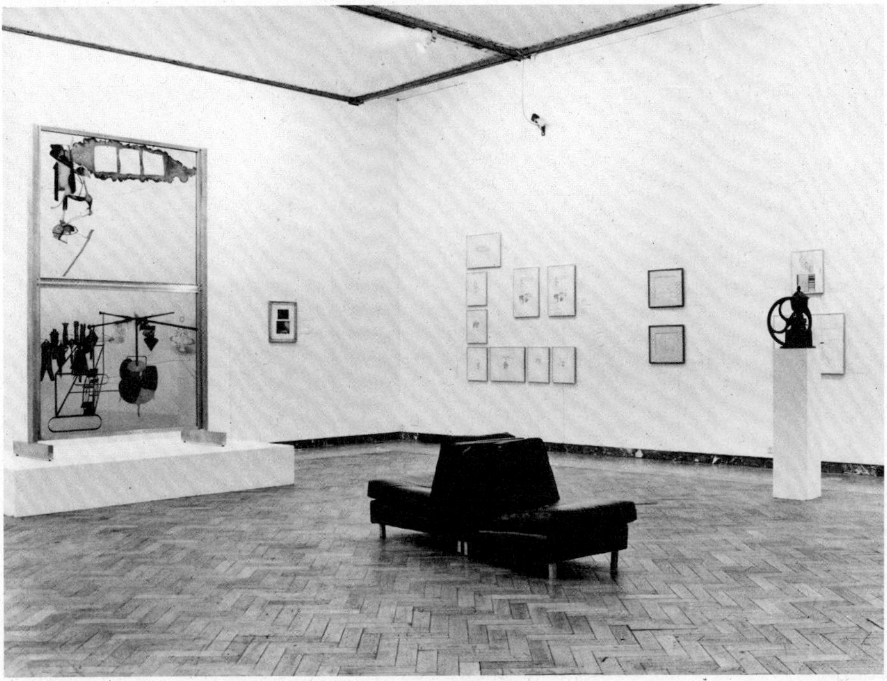

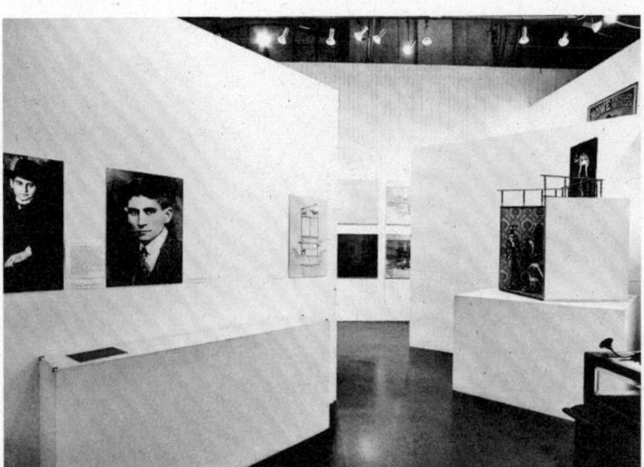

The Bachelor Machines,
Musée des Arts Décoratifs,
Paris, 1976

1978–1980

07.07.1978–30.8.1978

Ascona (Museo Communale/Casa Anatta, Monte Verità/Collegio Papio/Isole di Brissago)

Monte Verità: Berg der Wahrheit/Mountain of Truth

(Ascona → Zürich: 17.11.1978–28.01.1979 → Berlin: 25.03–06.05.1979 → Wien: 13.09–11.11.1979 → München: 23.10–21.12.1980)

Kunsthaus, Zürich/Akademie der Künste, Berlin/Museum des 20. Jahrhunderts, Wien/Museum Villa Stuck, München

[Since 1981, permanently exhibited in the museum Casa Anatta in Ascona]

1980

01.06–28.09

La Biennale di Venezia. Giardini di Castello, Magazzini del Sale alla Zattere, Venezia

Aperto 80. L'arte degli anni Settanta

1981

Inauguration: 18.04

Monte Verità, Ascona

Museo Casa Anatta

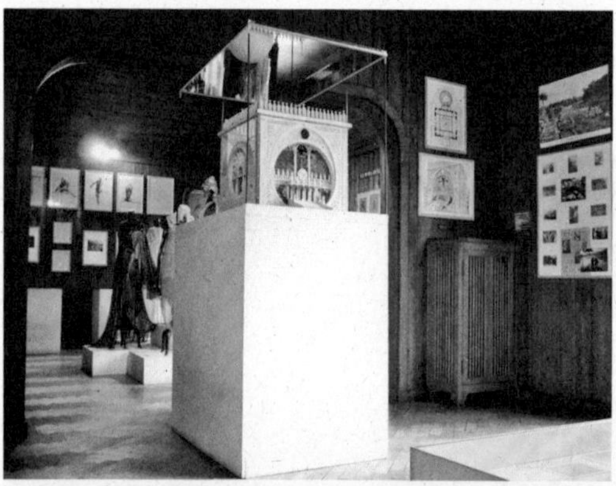

Monte Verità, Museo Casa Anatta, Ascona, 1981

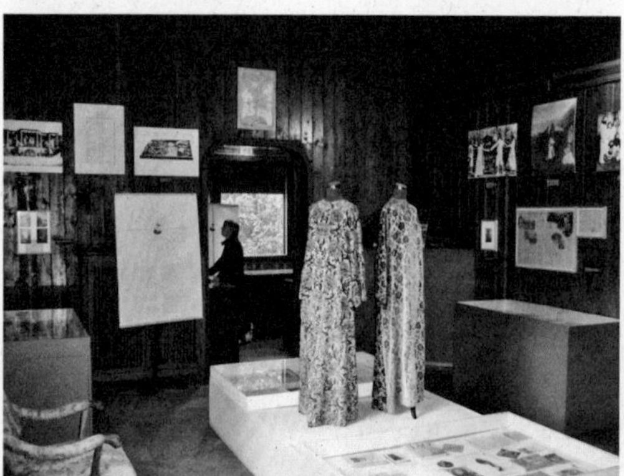

1982

Inauguration: 12.09

Santuario-Convento Madonna del Sasso, Orselina

Museo Madonna del Sasso

1983

11.02–30.04

Kunsthaus, Zürich

Der Hang zum Gesamtkunstwerk: Europäische Utopien seit 1800

(Zürich → Düsseldorf: 28.05–10.07.1983 → Wien: 10.09–13.11.1983 → Berlin: 23.12.1983–19.02.1984)

Städtische Kunsthalle and Kunstverein für die Rheinlande und Westfalen, Düsseldorf/Museum Moderner Kunst/Museum des 20. Jahrhunderts, Wien/Schloss Charlottenburg, Berlin

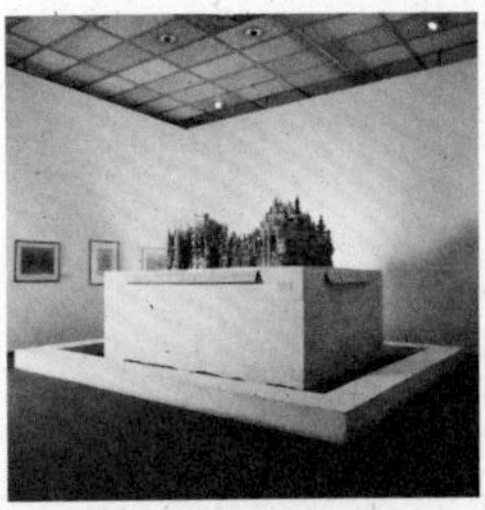
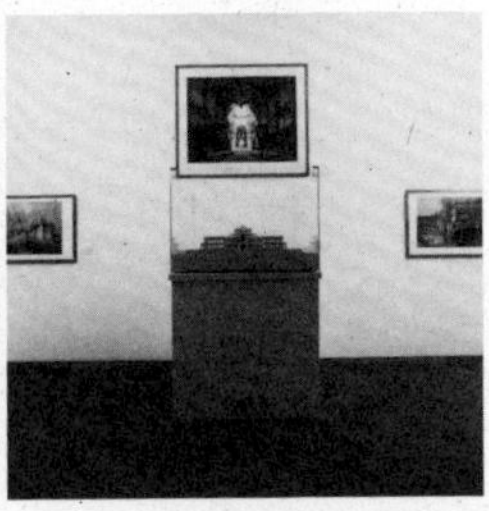

Penchant for a Synthesis of the Arts: European Utopias Since 1800, Kunsthaus Zürich, 1983

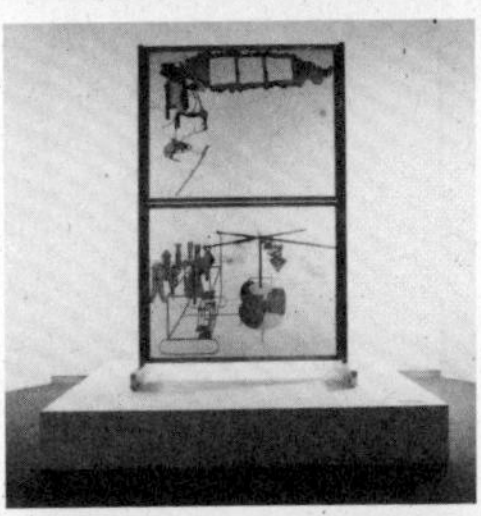
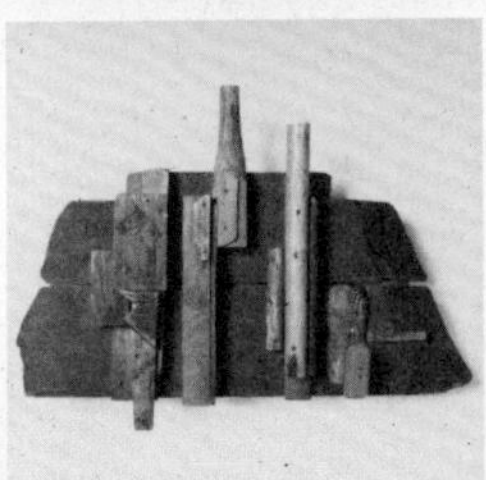
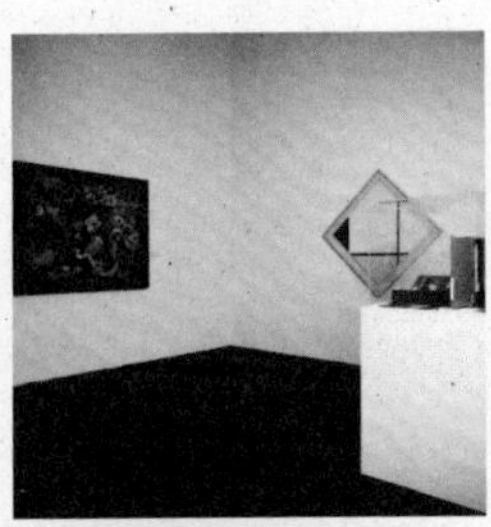
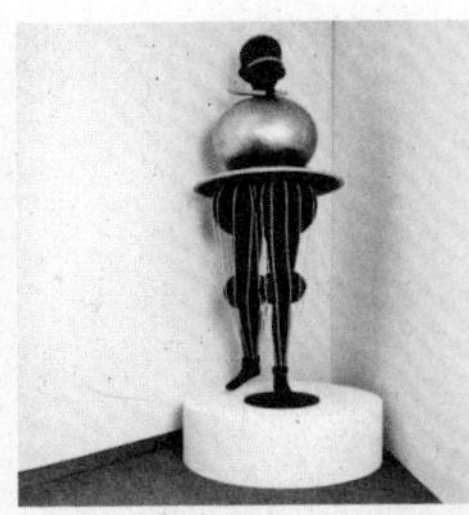
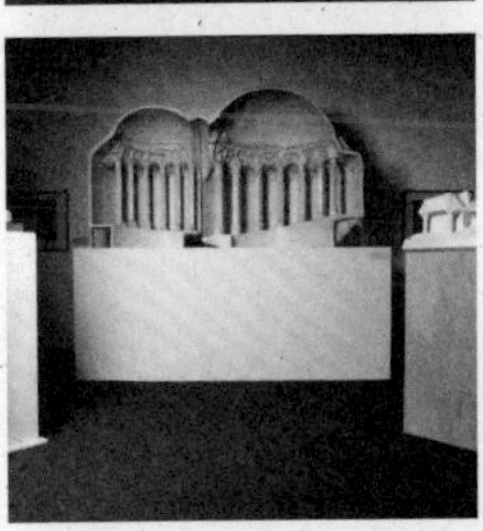
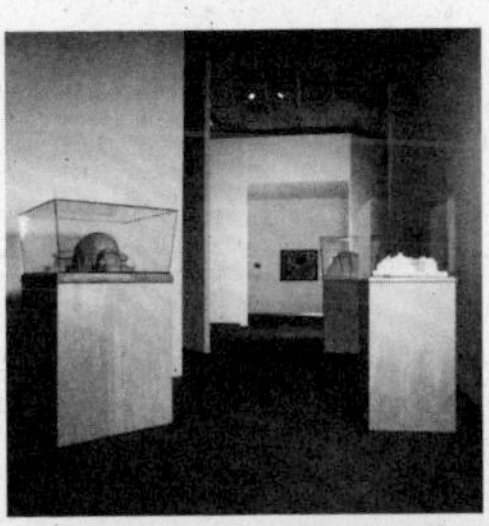
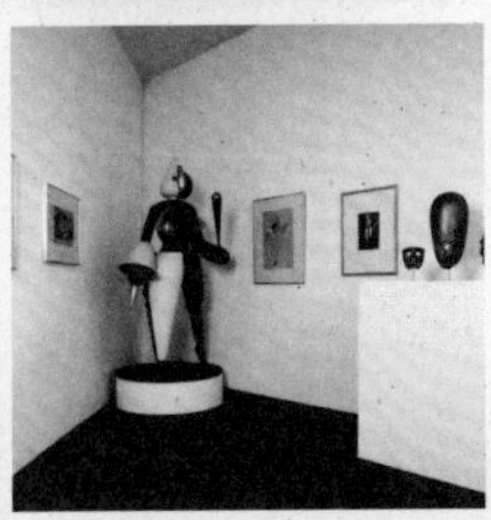
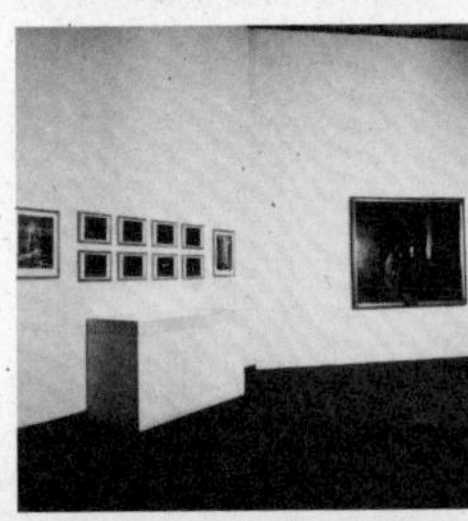
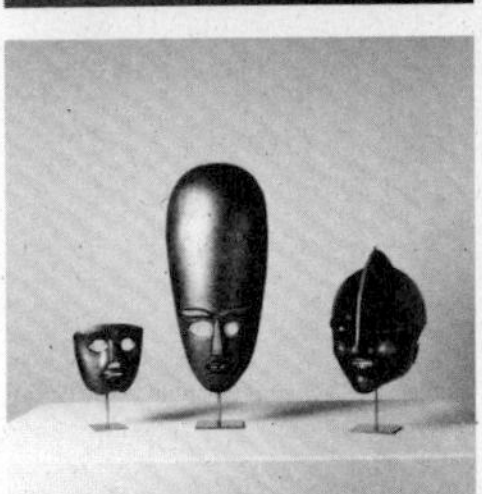
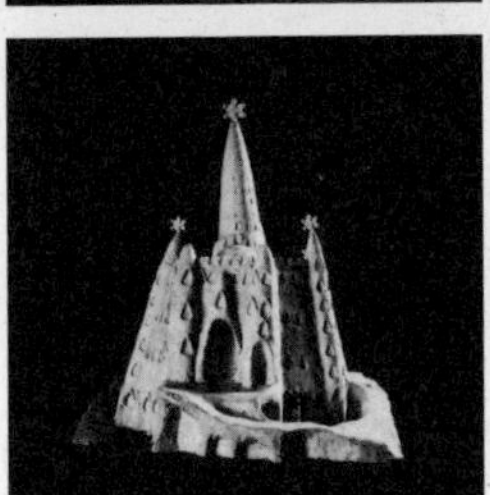
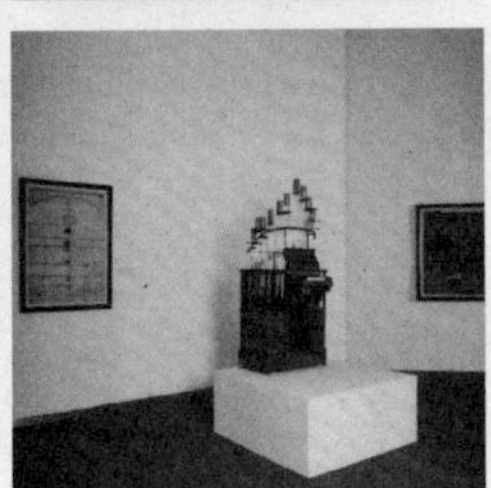
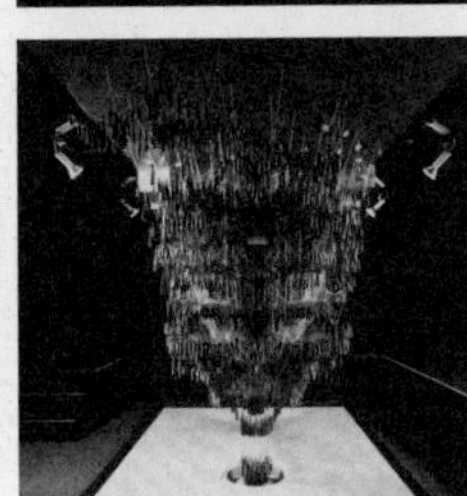

Inauguration: 09.04
Monte Verità, Ascona
Museo Casa Selma
20.05–31.07
Kunsthaus, Zürich
James Ensor
(Zürich → Antwerpen: 20.08–30.10)
Koninklijk Museum voor Schone Kunsten, Antwerpen
19.11.1983–22.01.1984
Kunsthaus, Zürich
Jörg Immendorff

1984

05.04–13.05
Kunsthaus, Zürich
Sigmar Polke
(Zürich → Köln)
Josef-Haubrich-Kunsthalle, Köln
14.12.1984–10.03.1985
Kunsthaus, Zürich
Alfred Jarry (1873–1907)

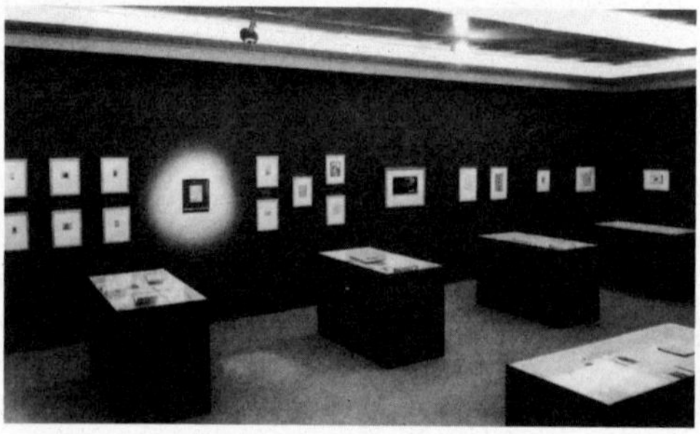

Alfred Jarry, Kunsthaus Zürich, 1984

1985

03.04–27.05
Kunsthaus, Zürich
Mario Merz

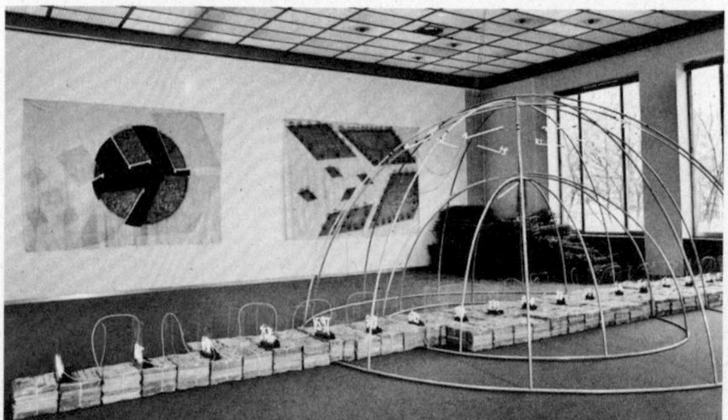

Mario Merz, Kunsthaus Zürich, 1985

29.11.1985–16.02.1986
Kunsthaus, Zürich
Spuren, Skulpturen und Monumente ihrer präzisen Reise

1986

15.03–04.05
Kunsthaus, Zürich
Jean Fautrier: von 1925 bis 1935
(Amsterdam: 11.01–02.03 → Zürich)
Stedelijk Museum, Amsterdam
[Co-production Stedelijk Museum, Amsterdam/Kunsthaus, Zürich]

16.05–20.07
Messepalast Wien (Wiener Festwochen)
De Sculptura

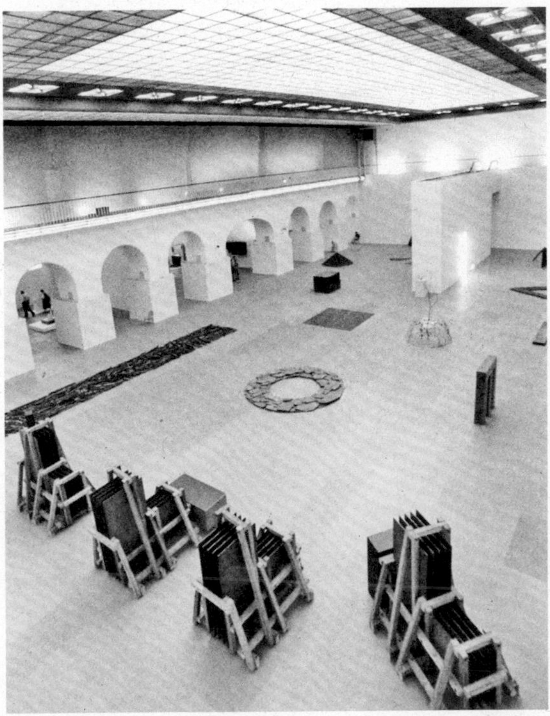

De Sculptura, Messepalast, Vienna, 1986

07.06–17.08
Albergo Monte Verità/Museo Comunale d'Arte Moderna & Centro Culturale Beato Pietro Berno, Ascona
De Marées a Picasso: Capolavori del Museo Von der Heydt di Wuppertal
(Ascona → Bern → Madrid: 17.11.86–25.01.87 → Barcelona: 13.02.87–3.05.87 → Tel Aviv → München → Washington)
Kunstmuseum, Bern/Fundació Juan March, Madrid/Museu Picasso, Barcelona/Tel Aviv Museum of Art, Tel Aviv/Museum Villa Stuck, München

Inauguration: 12.08
Monte Verità, Ascona
Museo Elisarion
[Pavilion for the panoramic painting *Klarwelt der Seligen* by Elisàr von Kupffer (1872–1942)]

13.12.1986–01.02.1987
Städtische Kunsthalle, Düsseldorf
SkulpturSein

1987

18.02–29.03
Kunsthaus, Zürich
Cy Twombly: Bilder, Arbeiten auf Papier, Skulpturen
(Zürich → Madrid: 22.04–30.07.1987 → London: 25.09–15.11.1987 → Düsseldorf: 11.12.1987–31.01.1988 → Paris: 17.02–17.04.1988)
Palacio Velázquez, Madrid/Palacio de Cristal, Madrid/Whitechapel Art Gallery, London/Städtische Kunsthalle, Düsseldorf/MNAM-Centre Georges Pompidou, Paris

05.06–23.08
Kunsthaus, Zürich
Eugène Delacroix
(Zürich → Frankfurt am Main → Madrid: 02.03–20.04.1988)
Städtische Galerie im Städelschen Kunstinstitut, Frankfurt am Main/Museo del Prado, Madrid
Victor Hugo
Charles Baudelaire

17.11.1987–03.01.1988
Festival d'Automne. Chapelle Saint-Louis de la Salpêtrière, Paris
Mario Merz

1988

22.06–25.09
Hamburger Bahnhof, Berlin
Zeitlos

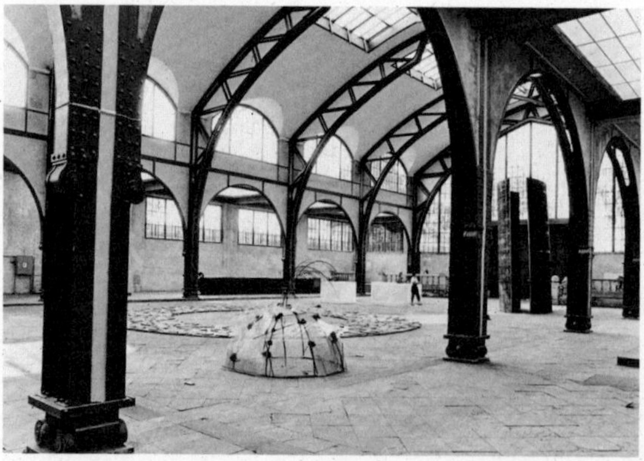

Zeitlos (*Timeless*),
Hamburger Bahnhof, Berlin, 1988

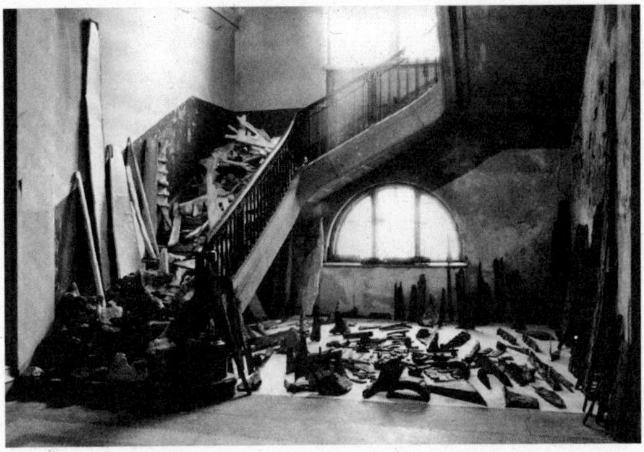

Zeitlos (Timeless),
Hamburger Bahnhof, Berlin, 1988

06.08–23.10

Ascona (Monte Verità/Museo Comunale d'Arte Moderna/Centro Culturale Beato Berno)
Marianne Werefkin
(Ascona → München → Hannover)
Villa Stuck, München/Kunstverein, Hannover

28.08–02.10

Museum Boijmans van Beuningen, Rotterdam
a-Historische klanken/a-Historical Soundings
[Harald Szeemann's selection from the collection of the Museum Boijmans van Beuningen]

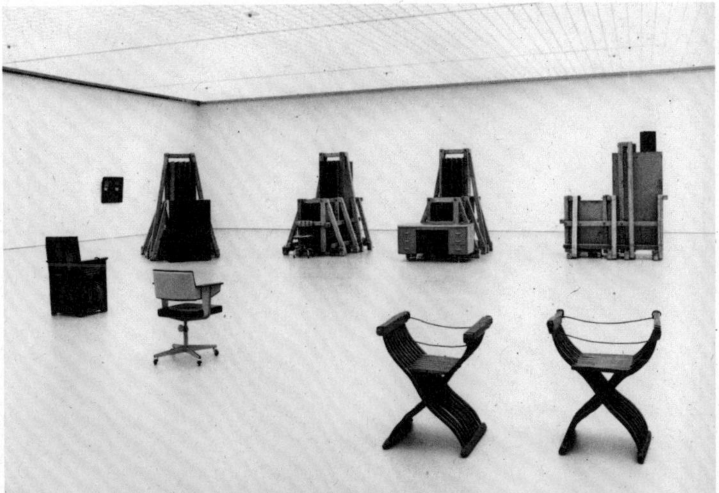

a-Historical Soundings, Museum Boijmans van Beuningen, Rotterdam, 1988

07.10–15.11

Festival d'Automne. Chapelle Saint-Louis de la Salpêtrière, Paris
Etienne-Martin

25.11.1988–19.02.1989

Kunsthaus Zürich

Egon Schiele und seine Zeit: Österreichische Malerei und Zeichnung von 1900 bis 1930 aus der Sammlung Leopold

(Zürich → Wien → München → Wuppertal)

Kunstforum Länderbank, Wien/Kunsthalle der Hypo-Kulturstiftung, München/Von-der-Heydt-Museum, Wuppertal

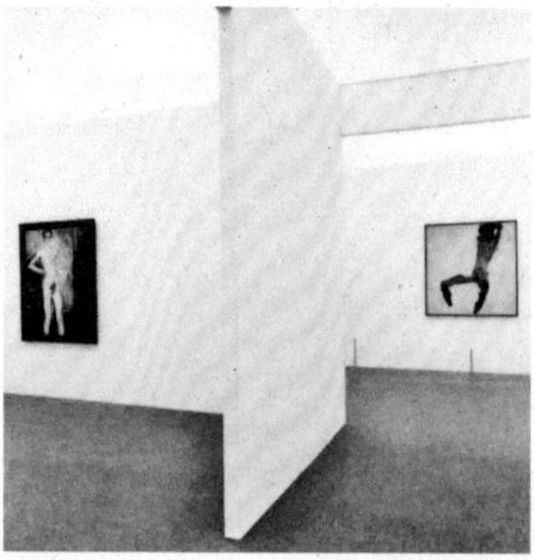

Egon Schiele and his Time, Kunsthaus Zürich, 1988

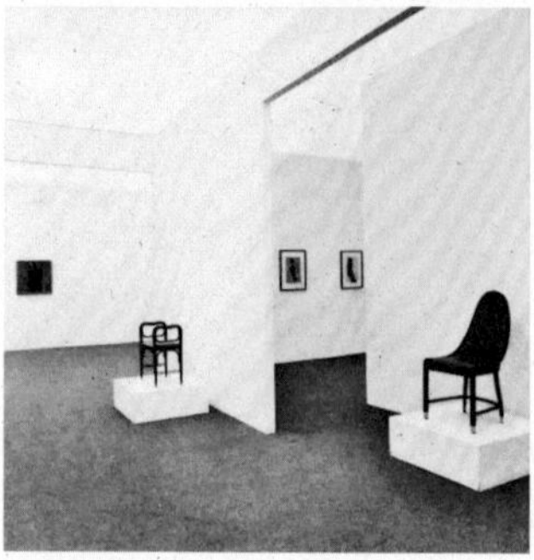

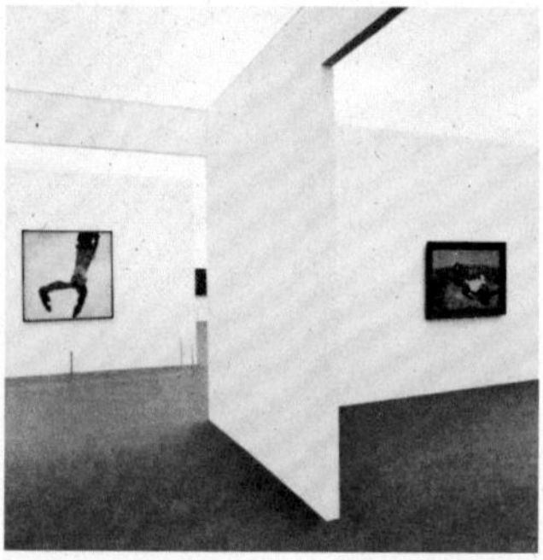

1989

05.04–28.05

Ascona (Monte Verità/Museo Comunale d'Arte Moderna/ Centro Culturale Beato Berno)

Piet Mondrian (1872–1944)

11.11.1989–18.02.1990

Deichtorhallen, Hamburg

Einleuchten: Will, Vorstel und Simul in HH

01.12.1989–11.02.1990

Kunsthaus, Zürich

Zum freien Tanz, zu reiner Kunst: Suzanne Perrottet (1889–1983) und Mary Wigman (1886–1973)/De la danse libre vers l'art pur

(Zürich → Ascona: 15.04–10.06.1990 → Marseille: 19.04–09.06.1991 → Bonn: 26.06–15.09.1991)

Museo Comunale d'Arte Moderna, Ascona/Centre de la Vielle Charité, Marseille/Stiftung Hans Arp und Sophie Taeuber-Arp, Bahnhof Rolandseck, Bonn

1990

09.03–29.04
Kunsthaus, Zürich
Richard Serra: The Hours of the Day

23.05–08.07
Kunsthaus, Zürich
Georg Baselitz
(Zürich → Düsseldorf: 28.07–09.09)
Städtische Kunsthalle, Düsseldorf

18.08–29.09
Kunsthalle, Luzern
Niele Toroni

30.09–16.12
Museo Communale d'Arte Moderna, Ascona
Mario Merz

01.12.1990–24.02.1991
Watari Museum of Contemporary Art, Tokyo
LightSeed

1991

02.03–20.05
Museo Communale d'Arte Moderna, Ascona
Ettore Jelmorini

08.05–20.07
Galleria del Credito Valtellinese "Refettorio delle Stelline", Milano
Georg Baselitz: Werke aus der Sammlung Ackermeier Berlin

06.09–27.10
Museo Communale d'Arte Moderna, Ascona
Niele Toroni: Impronte di pennello N.50 ripetute a intervalli regolari (30 cm)

01.11.1991–26.01.1992
Kunsthaus, Zürich
Visionäre Schweiz
(Zürich → Madrid: 10.03–18.05.1992 → Düsseldorf: 26.06–30.08.1992)
Museo Nacional Reina Sofía, Madrid/Städtische Kunsthalle und Kunstverein für die Rheinlande und Westfalen, Düsseldorf

1992

20.02–20.04
Kunsthaus, Zürich
Walter De Maria: The 2000 Sculpture

11.04–31.05
Museo Communale d'Arte Moderna, Ascona
Wolfgang Laib

20.04–12.10
Expo '92, World Exhibition. Pabellón de Suiza/Swiss Pavilion/Pavillon Suisse, Sevilla
Unexpected Switzerland

1993

19.03–23.05

capcMusée d'art contemporain, Bordeaux

GAS: Grandiose Ambitieux Silencieux

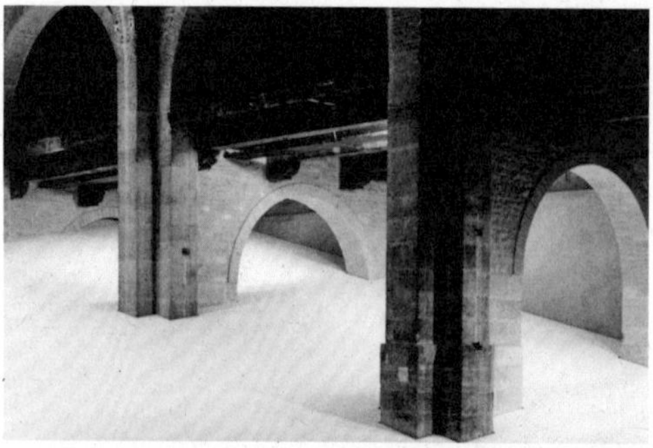

GAS: Grandiose, Ambitious, Silent,
capcMusée d'art contemporain, Bordeaux, 1993

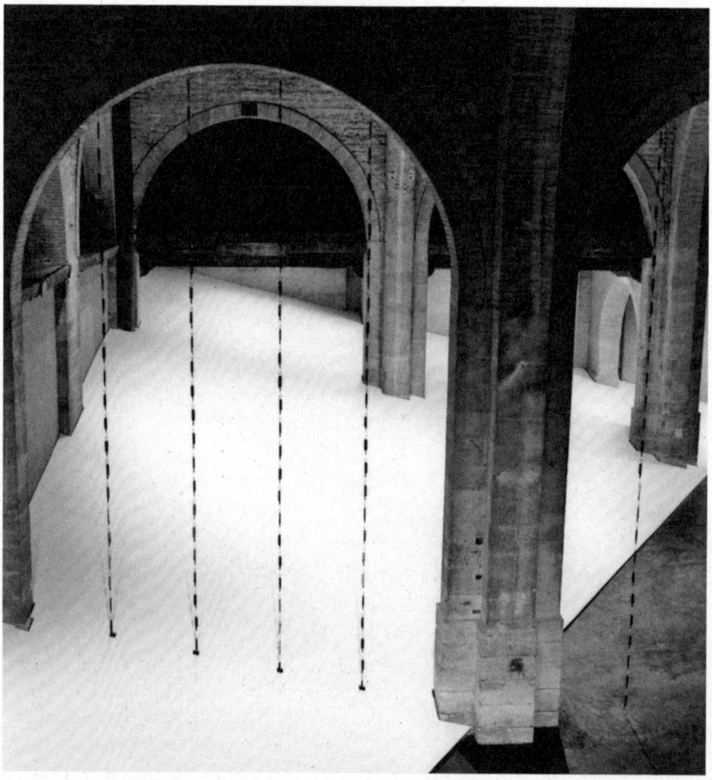

26.11.1993–20.02.1994

Kunsthaus, Zürich

Joseph Beuys

(Zürich → Madrid: 15.03–06.06.1994 → Paris: 30.06–03.10.1994)
Museo Nacional Reina Sofía, Madrid/MNAM-Centre Georges Pompidou, Paris

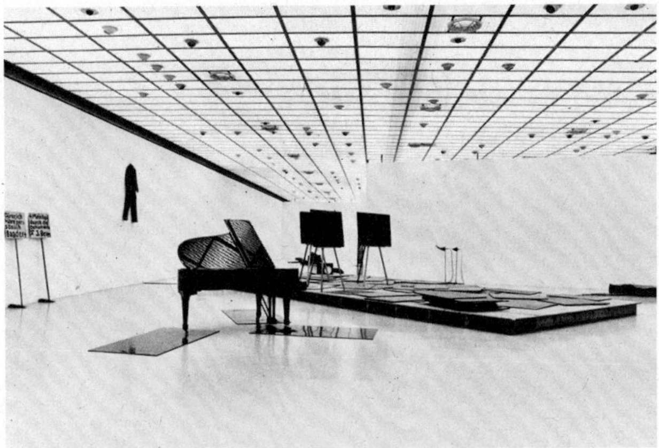

Joseph Beuys, Kunsthaus Zürich, 1993

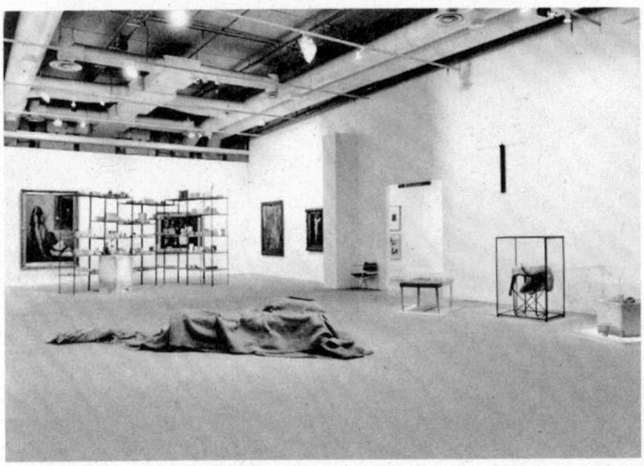

Joseph Beuys, MNAM-Centre Georges Pompidou, Paris, 1994

1994

[November]

Creativity in Switzerland

[An exhibition in the form of a contribution to the magazine *Swissair Gazette*]

14.07–08.10

Kunsthaus, Zürich

Bruce Nauman

(Minneapolis → Madrid → Zürich → Los Angeles → Washington D.C. → New York)

Walker Art Center, Minneapolis/Museo Nacional de Arte Reina Sofia, Madrid/Museum of Contemporary Art, Los Angeles/Hirshhorn Museum and Sculpture Garden, Smithsonian Institution, Washington D.C./Museum of Modern Art, New York

1995

09.11.1995–25.02.1996

Kunsthaus, Zürich

100 Jahre Kino: Illusion—Emotion—Realität: Die 7. Kunst auf der Suche nach den 6 Andern

(Zürich → Wien: 29.08–17.11.1996)

Kunsthalle Wien am Karlsplatz und Semper-Depot, Wien

1996

10.09–10.11

MAK—Österreichisches Museum für Angewandte Kunst, Wien

Austria im Rosennetz

(Wien → Zürich: 06.12.1996–23.02.1997)

Kunsthaus Zürich "Wunderkammer Österreich"

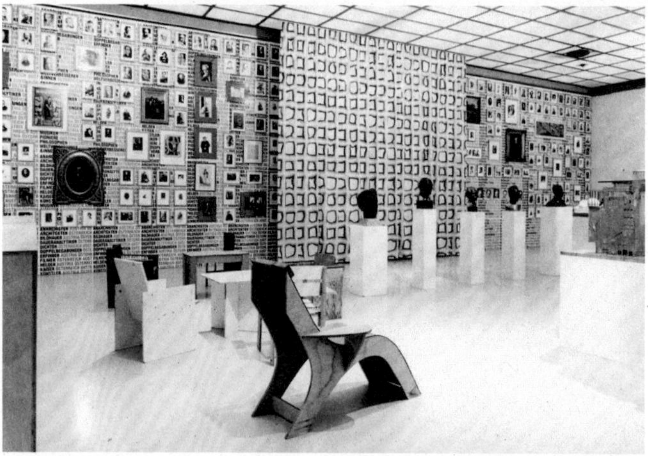

Austria in a Net of Roses, MAK, Vienna, 1996

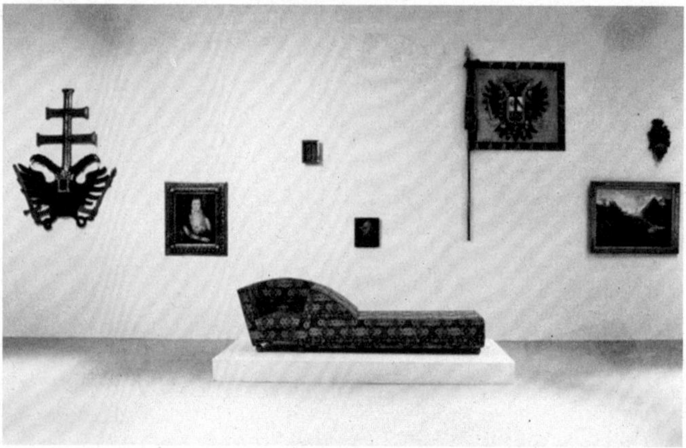

1997

08.04–31.05

Moderna galerija Ljubljana

Epicenter Ljubljana

09.07–24.09

4ème Biennale d'art contemporain de Lyon. Halle Tony Garnier, Lyon

L'Autre

01.09–27.11

2nd Kwangju Biennial

Speed & Water

1998

24.06–03.07

Atelierhaus der Akademie der bildenden Künste, Wien

Diversities, Spices & Academies: Ausgewählte Studentenarbeiten

15.08–18.10

Appenzell

Wahlverwandtschaften: Jason Rhoades

16.10–29.11

Ferdinand Boberg's Power Station, Skansen

Thousand Islands (Reality Models): Serge Spitzer

16.10–29.11

Hallwylska Museet, Stockholm

Close Encounters: Torbjørn Rødland

1999

13.06–07.11

48ª Biennale di Venezia, Esposizione internazionale d'arte. Arsenale/Corderie/Giardini di Castello, Venezia

dAPERTutto/APERTO overALL/APERTO parTOUT/APERTO überALL

27.08–07.11

Kunsthaus, Zürich

Weltuntergang & Prinzip Hoffnung

26.11.1999–01.01.2000

Kunsthaus, Zürich

Walter De Maria: The 2000 Sculpture

(Zürich → Berlin: 03.03–27.08)

Nationalgalerie im Hamburger Bahnhof/Staatliche Museen zu Berlin

01.12.1999–09.04.2000

Museum Jean Tinguely, Basel

Tinguely's Favorites: Yves Klein

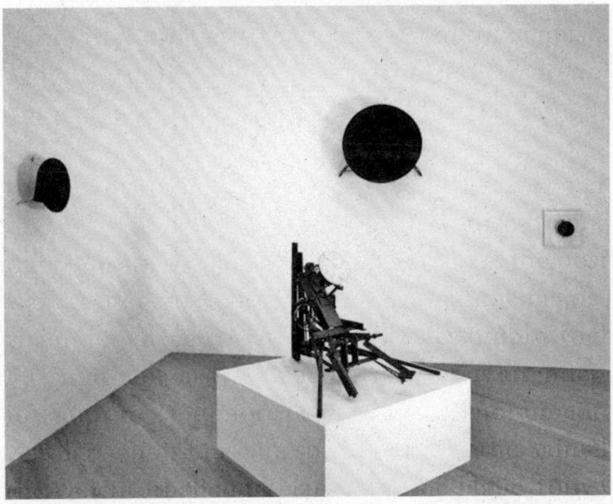

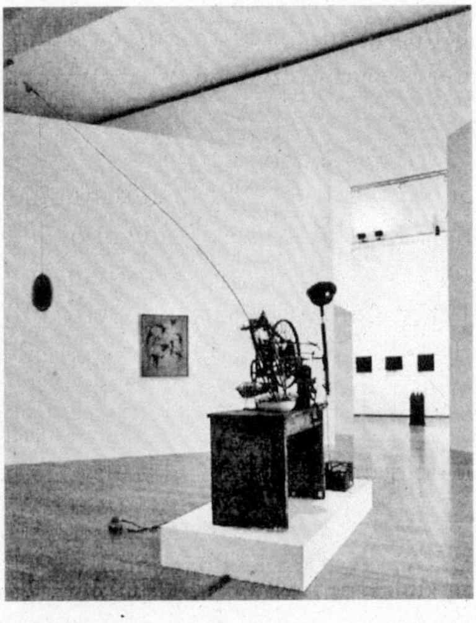

Tinguely's Favorites: Yves Klein, Museum Jean Tinguely, Basel, 1999

2000

05.04–14.05

Espace BBL—Banque Bruxelles Lambert, Bruxelles

ForwArt: Georges Adéagbo

26.05–30.07

Sydney Biennial

Agents of Change

15.07–27.08

Kunsthaus Zürich

Bruce Nauman, sein eigener Nachbar: Carte de Visite 5

Inauguration: 05.08

Verscio, Ticino

Museo Comico nel Teatro Dimitri: The collection of Dimitri Clown

15.12.2000–28.01.2001

Zachęta Narodowa Galeria Sztuki, Warszawa

Beware of Exiting Your Dreams: You May Find Yourself in Somebody Else's

2001

10.06–04.11

49ª Biennale di Venezia, Esposizione internazionale d'arte. Arsenale/Corderie/ Giardini di Castello, Venezia

Platea dell'umanità/Plateau of humankind/Plateau der Menschheit/ Plateau de l'humanité

2002

20.03–30.06

Museum Jean Tinguely, Basel

Tinguely's Favourites: Marcel Duchamp

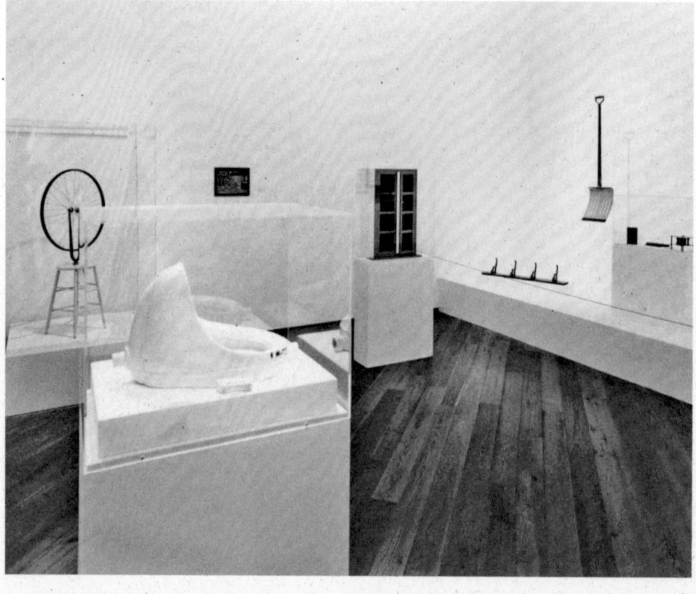

Tinguely's Favorites: Marcel Duchamp, Museum Jean Tinguely, Basel, 2002

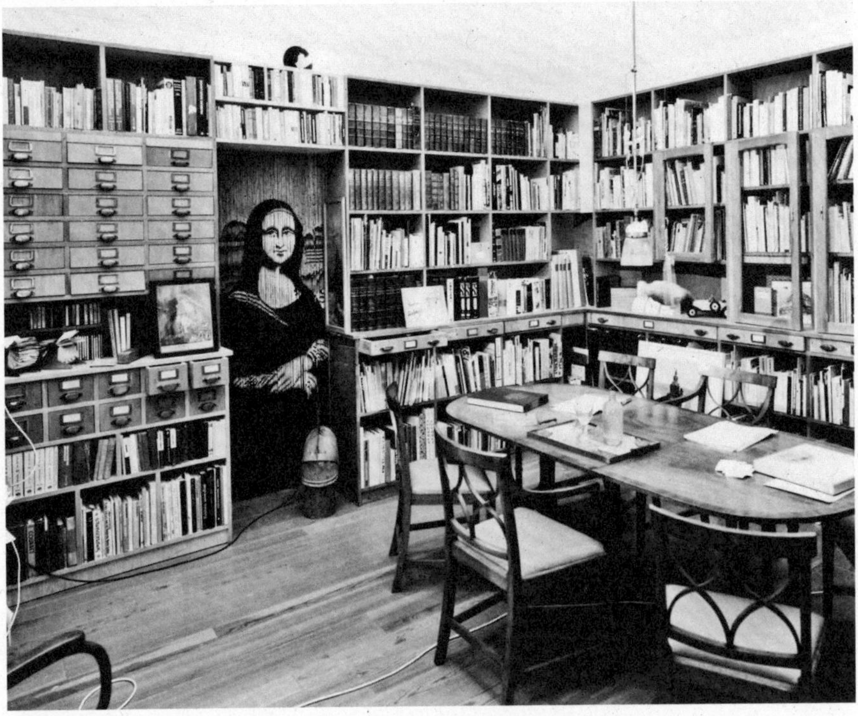

Tinguely's Favorites: Marcel Duchamp, Museum Jean Tinguely, Basel, 2002

15.05–20.10

Expo 02. Pavillion of the Swiss National Bank, Arteplage, Biel
Geld und Wert. Das letzte Tabu/Money and Value. The Last Taboo

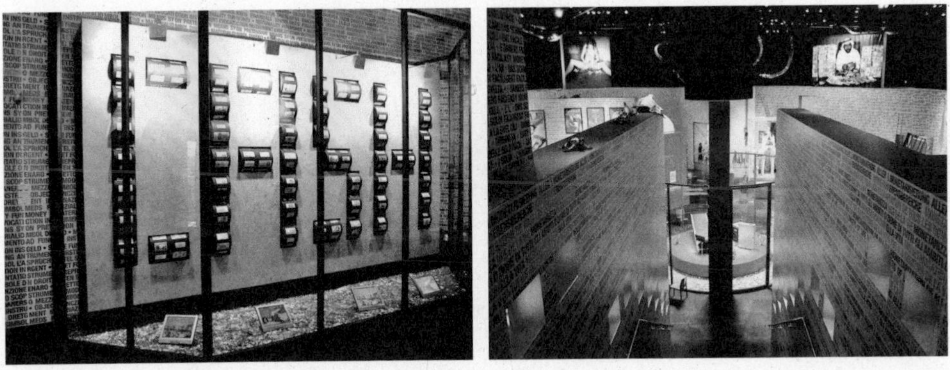

Money and Value—The Last Taboo, Expo 02, Biel, 2002

01.08–11.08

$55^{\text{ème}}$ Festival Internationale du Film, Locarno
In Progress

11.10.2002–19.01.2003

Maison Victor Hugo, Paris
Aubes: Rêveries au bord de Victor Hugo

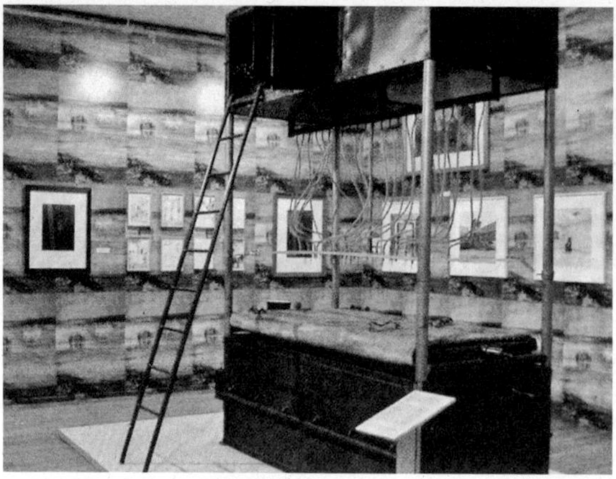

Aubes: Rêveries au bord de Victor Hugo,
Maison Victor Hugo, Paris, 2002

2003

16.05–28.09

Sammlung Essl, Klosterneuburg, Wien
Blut & Honig: Zukunft ist am Balkan

20.07–31.12

Mostra internazionale d'Arte all'Aperto. Vira Gambarogno e Ascona
G2003

2004

12.10.2003–5.01.2004

P.S.1 Contemporay Art Center, New York
The Real Royal Trip/El Real Viaje Real
(New-York → Valladolid: 10.02–02.05.2004)
Museo Patio Herreriano de Arte Contemporáneo Español, Valladolid
El real viaje Real: El Retorno/The Real Royal Trip: The Return to Homeland

18.03.2004–16.01.2005

Swarovski Kristallwelten, Watten, Austria
Verzauberung auf Zeit: Fliehpunkte

28.05–24.10

Fundació Joan Miró, Barcelona
La bellesa del fracàs—El fracàs de la bellesa/La belleza del fracaso—El fracaso de la belleza/The Beauty of Failure—The Failure of Beauty

03.10–05.12

First International Biennial for Contemporary Art. Monasterio de la Cartuja de Santa María de las Cuevas, Sevilla
La alegría de mis sueños/The Joy of my Dreams

2005

04.03–15.05

Palais des Beaux-Arts, Bruxelles
La Belgique visionnaire: C'est arrivé près de chez vous

Selected Bibliography

References

Books

- Bruce Altshuler, *The Avant-Garde in Exhibitions. New Art in the 20th Century*, University of California Press, Berkeley 1994.
- Roland Barthes, *Mythologies*, Hill and Wang, New York 1975.
- Beatrice von Bismarck et al. (eds.), *Interarchive*, Verlag der Buchhandlung Walther König, Cologne 2002.
- Luc Boltanski, Eve Chiapello, *The New Spirit of Capitalism*, Verso, London 2005.
- Sonia Combe, *Archives interdites*, Albin Michel, Paris 1994.
- Jacques Derrida, *Archive Fever: A Freudian Impression*, University of Chicago Press, Chicago 1995.
- Jacques Derrida, *Mal d'archive*, Galilée, Paris 2003.
- Jacques Derrida, *Geneses, Genealogies, Genres, and Genius. The Secrets of the Archive*, Columbia University Press, New York 2006.
- Patricia Falguières, *Les chambres des merveilles*, Bayard, Paris 2003.
- Arlette Farge, *Le goût de l'archive*, Seuil, Paris 1989.
- Bruce Ferguson, Reesa Greenberg, Sandy Nairne (eds.), *Thinking About Exhibitions*, Routledge, London/New York 1996.
- Jean-Marc Poinsot, *L'atelier sans mur*, Art Edition, Villeurbanne 1991.
- Paul Ricœur, *Temps et récit "Tome 3: le temps raconté"*, Seuil, Paris 1985.
- Gerhard Theewen, *Obsession Collection*, Salon Verlag, Cologne 1996.
- Frances A. Yates, *The Art of Memory*, Routledge and Kegan Paul, London 1966.

Articles

- Nathalie Heinich, Michaël Pollak, "Du conservateur de musée à l'auteur d'exposition: l'invention d'une position singulière," *Sociologie du travail*, CNRS-Dunod, XXXI, n° 1, 1989.

On Harald Szeemann

Books

- Tobia Bezzola, Roman Kurzmeyer (eds.), *Harald Szeemann: with by through because towards despite*, Springer, Vienna/New York; Voldemeer, Zurich 2007.
- Lucrezia De Domizio Durini, *Harald Szeemann: il pensatore selvaggio*, Silvana Editoriale, Milan 2005.
- Nathalie Heinich, *Harald Szeemann, un cas singulier: entretien*, L'Echoppe, Paris 1995.
- Hans-Joachim Müller, *Harald Szeemann: Exhibition Maker*, Hatje Cantz, Ostfildern 2006.

Articles

- "Entretien avec Harald Szeemann," in *ArTitudes*, n° 21/23, p. 22–23.
- Yves Aupetitallot, Xavier Douroux, "A propos de Harald Szeemann, Tentative d'épuisement de l'autre," in *Art Press*, n° 226, July 1997.
- Christian Bernard, "Ouvrir Venise," in *Art Press*, n° 247, June 1999, p. 18–23
- Tobia Bezzola, "Natürliches pathos/Natural pathos: Harald Szeemann (1993–2005)," in *Parkett*, n° 73, May 2005.
- Jean-Pierre Bordaz, "Entretien avec Harald Szeemann," Jean de Loisy (ed.), *Hors limites. L'art et la vie 1952–1994*, Centre Georges Pompidou, Paris 1994, p. 259–267.
- Jean-Pierre Bordaz, "La mise en forme de l'art. A propos de *When Attitudes Become Form* et *Happening & Fluxus*," Jean de Loisy (ed.), *Hors limites. L'art et la vie 1952–1994*, Centre Georges Pompidou, Paris 1994.
- Anne Dagbert, "Quand les attitudes deviennent forme," in *Art Press*, n° 121, January 1988, p. 36–39.
- Anaïd Demir, "Harald The Man," in *Technikart*, n° 35, September 1999.
- Urs & Rös Graf, "Agentur für geistige Gastarbeit, Dr. Szeemann, Münstergasse 48," in *werk, bauen + wohnen*, n° 4, 1971, p. 261.
- Jean-Yves Jouannais, "Harald Szeemann. Des expositions faites d'amour et d'obsession," in *Art Press*, hors série "66/96, Avant-gardes et fin de siècle," n° 17, 1996, p. 100–108.
- Catherine Millet, "*Zeitlos*, un poème dans l'espace," in *Art Press*, n° 126, June 1998.
- Hans Ulrich Obrist, "Mind Over Matter: Interview with Harald Szeemann," in *Artforum*, November 1996.

- Jean-Marc Poinsot, "Harald Szeemann. Quand les attitudes deviennent forme et quelques problèmes du musée d'art contemporain," *Collection*, capcMusée d'art contemporain, Bordeaux 1990, p. 25–33.
- Karen Rudolph, "L'Autriche sur le divan de Szeemann", in *Beaux-Arts Magazine*, n° 148, September 1996.
- Didier Semin, Isabelle Ewig, "Comment se fait une exposition? A propos de *When Attitudes Become Form*," in *Les Cahiers du Musée national d'art moderne*, n° 73, October 2000, p. 5–7.
- Carolee Thea, "Harald Szeemann," in *Foci: Interviews with 10 International Curators*, Apex Art Curatorial Program, New York 2001.

Filmography

- Marlène Belilos, *Quand les attitudes deviennent forme*, 30 min., color, sound, 1969.
- Hans-Joachim Müller, Gaudenz Meili, *Verzauberung Auf Zeit, Harald Szeemann*, 76 min., color, sound, 1992.
- Chika Schultze-Rhonhof, *Visionär oder Manager? Ausstellungsmacher*, 44 min., color, sound, 1987.
- Jacques Senger, *Les grands entretiens: Harald Szeemann*, TSR, 1998.
- David Wittenberg, *Harald Szeemann und die Kunst der Ausstellung "Das Weite suchen"*, 55 min., color, sound, 2005.

By Harald Szeemann

Books

- Harald Szeemann, Jean-Christophe Ammann, *Von Hodler zur Antiform*, Benteli Verlag, Bern 1970.
- Harald Szeemann, Georg Jappe, Aurel Schmidt, *Dokumente zur aktuellen Kunst 1967–1970. Material aus dem Archiv Szeemann*, Kunstkreis Luzern 1972.
- Harald Szeemann, *Beuysnobiscum Eine kleine Enzyklopädie*, Philo&philo fine arts, Berlin 1997.
- Harald Szeemann, *Ecrire les expositions*, La Lettre volée, Brussels 1996.
- Harald Szeemann, *Individuelle Mythologien*, Merve, Berlin 1985.
- Harald Szeemann, *Museum der Obsessionen; von/über/zu/mit*, Merve Verlag, Berlin 1981.
- Harald Szeemann, *Zeitlos auf Zeit: das Museum der Obsessionen*, Lindinger und Schmid, Regensburg 1994.

Articles

- Harald Szeemann, "Ecce museum: Much chaff, little grain," Mack Gerhard (ed.), *Art Museums into the 21st Century*, Birkhauser/Basel 1999.
- Harald Szeemann, "Journal et carnets de voyage touchant aux préparatifs et aux retombées de l'exposition *When Attitudes Become Form: works, concepts, processes, situations, information* et à rien d'autre," in *Les Cahiers du Musée national d'art moderne*, n° 73, October 2000, p. 8–35.
- Harald Szeemann (ed.), "Echanges de vues d'un groupe d'experts," in *Museum*, vol.XXIV, n° 1, 1972, p. 4–32.
- Harald Szeemann, "Sur la colline des utopies: de Hesse à Kandinski en passant par Rudolf Laban," Claire Rousier (ed.), *Etre ensemble. Figure de la communauté en danse depuis le XXe siècle*, Centre national de la danse, Paris 2003, p.16–40.
- Harald Szeemann, "*When Attitudes Become Form* (*Quand les attitudes deviennent forme*), Bern 1969," Katharina Hegewisch, Bernard Klüser (eds.), *L'art de l'exposition, une documentation sur trente expositions exemplaires du XXe siècle*, Editions du Regard, Paris 1998, p. 369–382.

Exhibition catalogues

- *Science Fiction*, Musée des Arts décoratifs, Paris 1967.
- *Live in Your Head. When Attitudes Become Form: works, concepts, processes, situations, information*, Kunsthalle Bern, Bern 1969.
- *Happening & Fluxus*, Kölnischer Kunstverein, Cologne 1970.

- *documenta 5. Befragung der Realitat, Bildwelten heute*, C. Bertelsmann Verlag, Munich 1972.
- *Junggesellenmaschinen/Les Machines célibataires*, Musée des Arts décoratifs, Paris 1976
- *a-Historische klanken: De keuze van Harald Szeemann*, Museum Boijmans van Beuningen, Rotterdam 1988.
- *Zeitlos: Kunst von heute im Hamburger Bahnhof*, Prestel Verlag, Berlin 1988.
- *Visionäre Schweiz*, Kunsthaus Zürich, Zurich 1991.
- *Joseph Beuys*, Centre Georges Pompidou, Paris 1994.
- *Austria im Rosennetz*, Kunsthaus Zürich and MAK, Vienna 1996.
- *Epicenter Ljubljana*, Moderna Galerija Ljubljana, Ljubljana 1997.
- *Biennale di Venezia: 48ª esposizione internazionale d'arte, dApertutto*, Marsilio, Venice 1999.
- *12th Biennale of Sydney 2000*, Sydney 2000.
- *Biennale di Venezia: 49ª esposizione internazionale d'arte, Platea dell'Umanità*, Electa, Venice 2001.
- *El real viaje real*, P.S.1 Contemporary Art Center, Long Island City, New York 2003.
- *Blut und Honig: Zukunft ist am Balkan*, Sammlung Essl, Klosterneuburg 2003.
- *Money and Value*, Expo '02, Biel 2003.
- *La alegria de mis sueños: 1ª Bienal internacional de arte contemporàneo de Sevilla*, Sevilla 2004.
- *La bellesa del fracàs. El fracàs de la bellesa*, Fundació Joan Miró, Barcelona 2004.

On *documenta 5*

Catalogues

- *documenta 5*, C. Bertelsmann Verlag, Munich 1972.
- *Skandal und Mythos. Eine Befragung des Archivs zur documenta 5*, Kunsthalle Wien, Vienna 2002.
- Gabriele Mackert, "Sich einrichten im Widerspruch, Harald Szeemanns *documenta*," *50 Jahre/Years documenta 1955–2005. Archive in Motion*, Steidl, Göttingen 2005, p. 253–262.

Articles

- "Complaint dept," in *The Feminist Art Journal*, May 1972.
- *Informationen. Kultur für alle*, n° 7, 8, 9, 11 May–June 1970/July–August 1972.
- *Kunst Nachrichten*, Stuttgart, n° 3, November 1972.
- Eric Banks, "Reality: Ideology at *d5*," in *Artforum*, October 1972.
- Claude Bouyeure, "*documenta 5* ou l'Homme," in *Le Monde*, 1972.
- Guy Brett, "An ambiguous Approach to Reality," in *The Times*, 5 July 1972.
- Jean Clair, "Du musée imaginaire à l'imaginaire muséal," in *Chroniques de l'Art Vivant*, n° 32, August–September 1972, p. 2–6.
- Christiane Duparc, "Paris, désert culturel," in *Le journal de Paris*, 8 April 1970, p. 31–32.
- Nigel Gosling, "Crystal Balls in Kassel," in *The Guardian*, 10 September 1972.
- Walter Grasskamp, "For exemple, *documenta*, or how is art history produced?," Bruce Ferguson, Reesa Greenberg, Sandy Nairne (eds.), *Thinking About Exhibitions*, Routledge, London/New York, 1996, p. 67–78.
- Axel Hecht, "Geschrumpfte Superschau," in *Argus*, 15 May 1972.
- Arnold Kohler, "L'Art est-il superflu?," in *La Tribune de Genève*, Tuesday July 25, 1972.
- Hilton Kramer, "Exhibition Is a Melange That Assumes Culture Is an Outworn Fiction," in *The New York Times*, March 1972.
- Irmeline Lebeer, "Une école de la Vision?," in *Chroniques de l'Art Vivant*, n° 32, August–September 1972, p. 6–8.
- Catharina Manchanda, "Reconsidering the Object of Photography: German Artists, Curators and Critics in Light of *documenta 5*," a dissertation submitted to the Graduate Faculty in Art History, New York, 2005.
- Jacques Michel, "L'Art en quête de la réalité," in *Le Monde*, 5 July 1972.
- Lothar Orzechowski, "*documenta*, was nun?," in *Argus*, 12 October 1972.
- Yann Pavie, "Vers le musée du futur. Entretien avec Harald Szeemann," in *Opus International*, n° 36, June 1972, p. 39–44.

- Francois Pluchart, "Documentalement réussi!," in *ArTitudes*, n° 8/9, July/August/September 1972.
- Harold Rosenberg, "The Art World: Inquiry'72: On The Edge," in *The New Yorker*, September 9, 1972.
- John Russel, "Expand Your Notions," in *The Sunday Times*, July 16, 1972.
- Caroline Tisdall, "Document of a Dead End," in *Arts Guardian*, July 10, 1972
- Engel William, "Die Planer haben den Kitsch nicht vergessen," in *Argus*, June 30, 1972.

Filmography

- Jef Cornelis, *documenta 5*, 42 min., color, sound, 1972.
- Johannes Freisel, *Dokumente zur documenta 5 in Kassel*, 44 min., color, sound, 1972.

On *L'Autre—4th Lyon Biennial*

Catalogue

- *L'Autre, 4th Lyon Contemporary Art Biennial*, Réunion des Musées Nationaux, Paris 1997.

Articles

- "*L'Autre*. Entretien avec Harald Szeemann, commissaire de la 4ème Biennale de Lyon," in *Ninety*, n° 25, October–November–December 1997, p. 1–3.
- Valère Bertrand, "Harald Szeemann: the Other or Reign Without Dividing," in *Cimaise*, vol. 44, n° 247, 1997, p. 5–14.
- Christoph Blase, "L'Autre: 4th Biennale d'Art Contemporain de Lyon," in *Artforum*, October 1997.
- Jean-François Chougnet, Thierry Prat, Thierry Raspail, *A propos de la Biennale d'art contemporain de Lyon 1997. Entretien avec Harald Szeemann*, La conscience du vilebrequin, Lyon 1997.
- Amanda Crabtree, "4th Lyon Biennale," in *Art Monthly*, September 1997.
- Xavier Douroux, Yves Aupetitallot, "A propos de Harald Szeemann. Tentative d'épuisement de l'autre," in *Art Press*, n° 226, July 1997, p. 26–31.
- Catherine Hémery, "Biennale de Lyon: the Others," in *Espace*, n° 42, 1997–1998, p. 10–20.
- Martin J. Hill, "Art and the Other," in *Art Net*, September 1997, texte disponible *via* http://www.artnet.com/magazine_pre2000/reviews/hill/hill9-08-97.asp
- Jean-Yves Jouannais, "La biennale d'art contemporain," in *Art Press*, n° 227, October 1997.
- Cecilia Lavelli, Franklin Sirmans, "Harald Szeemann: Curator as Author—From Ljubljana to Lyon to Kwangju," in *Flash Art*, vol. 30, n° 195, 1997, p. 89–90.
- Sarah McFadden, "The Other Biennial," in *Art in America*, vol. 85, n° 11, 1997, p. 84–91.
- Philippe Piguet, "Entretien avec Harald Szeemann et Catherine David: à quoi servent les grandes messes de l'art contemporain?," in *L'Œil*, n° 487, 1997, p. 32–34.
- Yvonne Resseller, "Sous le signe de L'Autre. Biennale de Lyon," in *Flux News*, n° 13, July 1997.
- Rachel Sukman, "Curators Talk," in *Terminal 5*, n° 5, October 1997.

Guest Authors' Biographies

<u>Hal Foster</u>

Townsend Martin '17 Professor and Chair in the department of Art and Archaeology at Princeton University. A co-editor of *October*, he also writes regularly for *Artforum* and the *London Review of Books*. He has written and edited numerous influential books on postmodernism, art, and culture: *The Anti-Aesthetic: Essays on Postmodern Culture* (Bay Press, 1983), *The Return of the Real: The Avant-Garde at the End of the Century* (MIT Press, 1996), *Design and Crime: and Other Diatribes* (Verso, 2002), and *Prosthetic Gods* (MIT Press, 2004). He also co-authored *Art Since 1900: Modernism, Antimodernism, Postmodernism* with Rosalind E. Krauss, Yve-Alain Bois, and Benjamin H. D. Buchloh (Thames & Hudson, 2004), and *Pop* with Marc Francis (Phaidon, 2005).

<u>Jean-Marc Poinsot</u>

Professor of History of Contemporary Art at Université Rennes 2. He is one of the founders of the *Archives de la critique d'art*, and was until 2001 the director of this archive and of the magazine *Critique d'art*. From 2001 to 2007 he was Head of the Department of Research and Studies at the Institut National d'Histoire de l'Art (INHA) in Paris. A major aspect of his work concerns the history and aesthetics of exhibitions as well as contemporary artists' relation to language. In 2001 he edited the writings of Daniel Buren for the capcMusée d'art contemporain in Bordeaux (*Les Ecrits: 1965–1990*). He is also the author of *L'atelier sans mur* (Art Edition, 1991) and *Quand l'œuvre a lieu* (MAMCO, 1999).

<u>Tobia Bezzola</u>

Worked as an assistant to Harald Szeemann from 1992 to 1996. He is a curator at the Kunsthaus Zürich, where he has realized many exhibitions and publications on modern and contemporary art and on photography: *Max Beckmann and Paris* (1998), *Alberto Giacometti 1901–2001* (2001), *SADE/SURREAL* (2001), *Ferdinand Hodler. Landscape* (2004), *The Decision of the Eye: Henri Cartier-Bresson and Alberto Giacometti* (2005), *The Art of the Archive* (2005), *Miroslav Tichý* (2005), *André Breton—Dossier Dada* (2005), *Feast of Color* (2006). He co-authored, with Roman Kurzmeyer, the catalogue raisonné of Harald Szeemann's exhibitions: *Harald Szeemann: with by through because towards despite* (2007).

<u>Balthasar Burkhard</u>

Upon completing his training in photography, Balthasar Burkhard (born 1944 in Bern) was hired by Kurt Blum who was then working for the Kunsthalle Bern. When Harald Szeemann was appointed director in 1961, Burkhard took over from Blum and became the institution's official photographer until Szeemann's resignation in 1969. Burkhard documented the exhibitions and participated in the realization of the catalogues and communication items. Burkhard's work, which was then rooted in "straight photography," evolved greatly in contact with the artists he worked with at the Kunsthalle, and the confrontation with new artistic practices. Balthasar Burkhard's œuvre has been exhibited in prestigious exhibitions and institutions worldwide since 1970. His first retrospective was organized by the Musée Rath in Geneva in 1997.

Imprint

Harald Szeemann: Individual Methodology is a research project developed under the tutorship of Florence Derieux by the 16th Session of the Ecole du Magasin—Centre National d'Art Contemporain de Grenoble: François Aubart, Julija Cistiakova, Haeju Kim, Lucia Pesapane, Fabien Pinaroli, Karla G. Roalandini-Beyer, Yuka Tokuyama, Sadie Woods. www.ecoledumagasin.com/session16

Editorial Direction

Florence Derieux

Editors

François Aubart, Julija Cistiakova, Haeju Kim, Lucia Pesapane, Fabien Pinaroli, Karla G. Roalandini-Beyer, Yuka Tokuyama, Sadie Woods.

Coordination of the 16th Session

Alice Vergara-Bastiand

Translations

French-English:

Deke Dusinberre, Linda Gardiner, Charles Penwarden (Jean-Marc Poinsot), Susan Pickford, Louise Read (Foreword, Preface, Introduction, Balthasar Burkhard's Biography), Leo Stephen Torgoff

Editing and Correction

Clare Manchester

Design

Corinne Zellweger

Typeface

Garamond

Acknowledgements

The editors would like to acknowledge the generosity of Harald Szeemann's family—Ingeborg Lüscher, Una Szeemann, Jérôme Szeemann—who allowed and helped the research.

The editors feel endebted to Tobia Bezzola for his assistance and support.

Special thanks to
Jean-Christophe Ammann, Yves Aupetitallot, Colette Barbier, Lionel Bovier, Bazon Brock, Sébastien Brun, Chris Burden, Bureau de la Biennale de Lyon, Balthasar Burkhard, François Burkhardt, Giovanni Carmine, Johannes Cladders, Jef Cornelis, Juliette Duca, Jana Intihar Ferjan, Hal Foster, Gilles Gavillet, Franz Gertsch, Urs and Rös Graf, Pieter Glatzel, Clara Heyworth, Thomas Hirschhorn, Moritz Hoesch, Kasper König, Josy Kraft, Irmeline Lebeer, Rainer M. Mason, Claes Oldenburg, Luca Peverini, Philippe Pirotte, Jean-Marc Poinsot, Thierry Prat, Karin Prätorius, Thierry Raspail, Gianna Ruepp, Marc Sautereau, Giada Sottomano, Virginie Theviot, Lawrence Weiner, Christoph Zürcher

Thanks to the publishers
Bookstorming, Edition Voldemeer Zürich, La conscience du vilebrequin, Verlag der Buchhandlung Walther König, Verso Books, werk, bauen + wohnen

Cover Images

Archive Harald Szeemann

Photography Credits

Blaise Adilon, Christian Baur, Leonardo Bezzola, Walter Binder, Kurt Blum, Simon Chaput, Balthasar Burkhard, Frédéric Delpech, Walter Dräyer, Carl Heinz Eberth, Verena Eggmann, Erró, Gaechter + Clahsen, Maria Gilissen, Philippe de Gobert, Guy Harlott, Brigitte Hellgoth, Vera Isler, Monique Jacot, Jannes Linders, F. Meyer-Henn, Margaret Nissen, Ad Petersen, Violette Pini, Martha Rocher, Didi Sattmann, Harry Shunk, Hans-Peter Siffert, Niklaus Stauss, Harald Szeemann, Erhard Wehrmann, Albert Winckler, Gilberto Zorio, 16th Session

Printing and Binding

Che Huber/noir sur noir, Geneva for JRP|Ringier

Le Magasin—Centre National d'Art Contemporain de Grenoble

Direction:
Yves Aupetitallot

Exhibitions Coordinator:
Inge Linder-Gaillard, assisted by Anaëlle Pirat

Administration:
Thomas Vasseur, Head Administrator; assisted by Jacqueline Dervaux, Director's Administrative Assistant; Katia Ecrement, Accountant; Denis Bastien, Technician; and Lassad Chaouachi, Maintenance

Press:
Anne Morel, Press Officer; assisted by Frédéric Besson, Webmaster; and Catherine Giraud, Assistant; with the support of Claudine Colin Communication, Paris

Public Programs:
Anne Langlais-Devanne, Coordinator of Public Programs; assisted by Laure Heinen, Associated Teacher; Roxane Leroux, Assistant; Aurélie Bouzom, Chloé Chassany, Christelle Colborati, Pierric Favret, Guillaume Le Moine, Roman Scrittori, Karine Trabucco, Agnès Vidal, Public Service Team, Mylène Duaut; and Marie Herny, Interns

Ecole du Magasin—Curatorial Training Program:
Alice Vergara-Bastiand, Coordinator
Catherine Quéloz, Liliane Schneiter, Pedagogical Team
Florence Derieux, Tutor for the 16th Session

Bookshop:
Alice Vergara-Bastiand, Manager
Fadma Kaddouri, Bookseller

Published by

JRP|Ringier Kunstverlag AG
Letzigraben 134
CH–8047 Zurich
T +41 (0) 43 311 27 50
F +41 (0) 43 311 27 51
info@jrp-ringier.com
www.jrp-ringier.com

Co-published by

Le Magasin—Centre National d'Art Contemporain
155 Cours Berriat
F–38028 Grenoble Cedex 1
T +33 (0)4 76 21 95 84
F +33 (0)4 76 21 24 22
communication@magasin-cnac.org
www.magasin-cnac.org

Le Magasin—Centre National d'Art Contemporain de Grenoble is a non-profit organization presided by M. Daniel Janicot and supported by the Ministère de la Culture et de la Communication—Direction Régionale des Affaires Culturelles Rhône-Alpes, Région Rhône Alpes, Département de l'Isère, Ville de Grenoble.

In collaboration with

Royal College of Art
Department of Curating Contemporary Art
Kensington Gore
GB–London SW7 2EU
T +44 (0)20 7590 4493
www.cca.rca.ac.uk

ISBN 978-3-905829-09-9

© 2007, the authors, the photographers, Le Magasin—Centre National d'Art Contemporain de Grenoble, and JRP|Ringier Kunstverlag AG.

MAGASIN

prohelvetia

FONDATION D'ENTREPRISE RICARD

Royal College of Art
Postgraduate Art and Design

Repubblica e Cantone Ticino
DECS
SWISSLOS

JRP|Ringier publications are available internationally at selected bookstores and from the following distribution partners:

Switzerland

Buch 2000
AVA Verlagsauslieferung AG
Centralweg 16
CH–8910 Affoltern a.A.
buch2000@ava.ch
www.ava.ch

Germany and Austria

Vice Versa Vertieb
Immanuelkirchstrasse 12
D–10405 Berlin
info@vice-versa-vertrieb.de
www.vice-versa-vertrieb.de

France

Les presses du réel
16 rue Duentin
F–21000 Dijon
info@lespressesdureel.com
www.lespressesdureel.com

UK

Cornerhouse Publications
70 Oxford Street
UK–Manchester M1 5NH
publications@cornerhouse.org
www.cornerhouse.org/books

USA

D.A.P./Distribution Art Publishers
155 Sixth Avenue, 2nd Floor
USA–New York, NY 10013
dap@dapinc.com
www.artbook.com

Other countries

IDEA Books
Nieuwe Herengracht 11
NL–1011 RK Amsterdam
idea@ideabooks.nl
www.ideabooks.nl

For a list of our partner bookshops or for any general questions, please contact JRP|Ringier directly at info@jrp-ringier.com, or visit our homepage www.jrp-ringier.com for further information about our program.